Political Competition and Economic Regulation

Although there is much literature on tax competition, very little research has been devoted to the effects of interjurisdictional competition on economic regulation. This is the first book of its kind to provide comprehensive historical evidence on how competition among states – or lack of it – affects regulation, especially labour market regulation. Bernholz and Vaubel have gathered together case studies from the United States, Canada, Germany and Switzerland as well as the European Union and the global economy.

The contributors take a 'public choice' perspective, assuming self-interested policy makers who operate under institutional and market constraints. The case studies in this volume go some way in demonstrating how in a decentralized but interdependent system, policy makers learn from the regulatory experience of other states and how a low level of regulation requires not only political fragmentation but also considerable mobility of resources among states. However, they also show that if market integration is followed by political centralization, examples of regulatory collusion and attempts to raise rivals' costs are likely to abound.

This book reveals important implications as to whether European political integration leads to more regulation and whether 'globalization' restrains regulation. It will be of great interest to both economists and students engaged with political economy, public choice and regulation.

Peter Bernholz is Professor of Economics, Emeritus, at the University of Basel, Switzerland. **Roland Vaubel** is Professor of Economics at the University of Mannheim, Germany.

Routledge explorations in economic history

1 **Economic Ideas and Government Policy**
Contributions to contemporary economic history
Sir Alec Cairncross

2 **The Organization of Labour Markets**
Modernity, culture and governance in Germany, Sweden, Britain and Japan
Bo Stråth

3 **Currency Convertibility**
The gold standard and beyond
Edited by Jorge Braga de Macedo, Barry Eichengreen and Jaime Reis

4 **Britain's Place in the World**
A historical enquiry into import controls 1945–1960
Alan S. Milward and George Brennan

5 **France and the International Economy**
From Vichy to the Treaty of Rome
Frances M.B. Lynch

6 **Monetary Standards and Exchange Rates**
M.C. Marcuzzo, L. Officer and A. Rosselli

7 **Production Efficiency in Domesday England, 1086**
John McDonald

8 **Free Trade and its Reception 1815–1960**
Freedom and trade: volume I
Edited by Andrew Marrison

9 **Conceiving Companies**
Joint-stock politics in Victorian England
Timothy L. Alborn

10 **The British Industrial Decline Reconsidered**
Edited by Jean-Pierre Dormois and Michael Dintenfass

11 **The Conservatives and Industrial Efficiency, 1951–1964**
Thirteen wasted years?
Nick Tiratsoo and Jim Tomlinson

12 **Pacific Centuries**
Pacific and Pacific Rim economic history since the 16th century
Edited by Dennis O. Flynn, Lionel Frost and A.J.H. Latham

13 **The Premodern Chinese Economy**
Structural equilibrium and capitalist sterility
Gang Deng

14 **The Role of Banks in Monitoring Firms**
The case of the Crédit Mobilier
Elisabeth Paulet

15 **Management of the National Debt in the United Kingdom, 1900–1932**
Jeremy Wormell

16 **An Economic History of Sweden**
Lars Magnusson

17 **Freedom and Growth**
The rise of states and markets in Europe, 1300–1750
S.R. Epstein

18 **The Mediterranean Response to Globalization Before 1950**
Sevket Pamuk and Jeffrey G. Williamson

19 **Production and Consumption in English Households 1600–1750**
Mark Overton, Jane Whittle, Darron Dean and Andrew Hann

20 **Governance, the State, Regulation and Industrial Relations**
Ian Clark

21 **Early Modern Capitalism**
Economic and social change in Europe 1400–1800
Edited by Maarten Prak

22 **An Economic History of London, 1800–1914**
Michael Ball and David Sunderland

23 **The Origins of National Financial Systems**
Alexander Gerschenkron reconsidered
Edited by Douglas J. Forsyth and Daniel Verdier

24 **The Russian Revolutionary Economy, 1890–1940**
Ideas, debates and alternatives
Vincent Barnett

25 **Land Rights, Ethno Nationality and Sovereignty in History**
Edited by Stanley L. Engerman and Jacob Metzer

26 **An Economic History of Film**
Edited by John Sedgwick and Mike Pokorny

27 **The Foreign Exchange Market of London**
Development since 1900
John Atkin

28 **Rethinking Economic Change in India**
Labour and livelihood
Tirthankar Roy

29 **The Mechanics of Modernity in Europe and East Asia**
The institutional origins of social change and stagnation
Erik Ringmar

30 **International Economic**
    Integration in Historical
    Perspective
    Dennis M.P. McCarthy

31 **Theories of International Trade**
    Adam Klug
    Edited by Warren Young and
    Michael Bordo

32 **Classical Trade Protectionism**
    1815–1914
    Edited by Jean Pierre Dormois
    and Pedro Lains

33 **Economy and Economics of**
    Ancient Greece
    Takeshi Amemiya

34 **Social Capital, Trust and the**
    Industrial Revolution,
    1780–1880
    David Sunderland

35 **Pricing Theory, Financing of**
    International Organisations and
    Monetary History
    Lawrence H. Officer

36 **Political Competition and**
    Economic Regulation
    Edited by Peter Bernholz and
    Roland Vaubel

Political Competition and Economic Regulation

Edited by Peter Bernholz and Roland Vaubel

For the Egon Sohmen Foundation

Routledge
Taylor & Francis Group

LONDON AND NEW YORK

First published 2007
by Routledge
2 Park Square, Milton Park, Abingdon, Oxon OX14 4RN

Simultaneously published in the USA and Canada
by Routledge
270 Madison Ave, New York, NY 10016

Routledge is an imprint of the Taylor & Francis Group, an informa business

© 2007 Selection and editorial matter, Peter Bernholz and Roland Vaubel; individual chapters, the contributors

Typeset in Times by Wearset Ltd, Boldon, Tyne and Wear
Printed and bound in Great Britain by TJI Digital, Padstow, Cornwall

British Library Cataloguing in Publication Data
A catalogue record for this book is available from the British Library

Library of Congress Cataloging in Publication Data
A catalog record for this book has been requested

ISBN10: 0-415-42985-4 (hbk)
ISBN10: 0-203-94687-1 (ebk)

ISBN13: 978-0-415-42985-6 (hbk)
ISBN13: 978-0-203-94687-9 (ebk)

Contents

Notes on contributors   ix

1   The effect of interjurisdictional competition on regulation:
    theory and overview   1
    PETER BERNHOLZ AND ROLAND VAUBEL

2   Politico-economic causes of labour regulation in the United
    States: rent seeking, alliances, raising rivals' costs (even
    lowering one's own?) and interjurisdictional competition   19
    JOHN T. ADDISON

    *Comment: Interjurisdictional competition and labour market
    regulation*   43
    DENNIS C. MUELLER

    Comment: Foreign policy and regulation   49
    GORDON TULLOCK

3   Interjurisdictional competition in regulation: evidence for
    Canada at the provincial level   53
    FRANÇOIS VAILLANCOURT

    *Comment: How can a country like Canada be inhospitable to an
    influence of yardstick competition on regulation?*   103
    PIERRE SALMON

4   Labour market regulation in the EU-15: causes and
    consequences   113
    W. STANLEY SIEBERT

    *Comment: Labour market regulation: interindividual and
    interjurisdictional competition*   137
    JEAN-MICHEL JOSSELIN

Comment: Interjurisdictional collusion and the strategy of raising rivals' costs in EU labour market regulation 148
ROLAND VAUBEL

5   **Political competition and economic regulation in German history**
Was there regulatory competition in early modern Germany? 152
OLIVER VOLCKART

Regulatory competition and regulatory harmonization in the nineteenth century: the example of food protection and labour protection 175
GEROLD AMBROSIUS

Comment: The strategy of raising rivals' costs by federal regulation under Bismarck 194
ROLAND VAUBEL

6   **Regulatory competition and federalism in Switzerland: diffusion by horizontal and vertical interaction** 200
LARS P. FELD

Comment: Yardstick competition among cantonal fiscal rules 241
CHRISTOPH A. SCHALTEGGER

7   **The drivers of deregulation in the era of globalization** 245
FRIEDRICH HEINEMANN

Comment: The uneasy trend to greater economic freedom 267
DAVID HENDERSON

Index 276

Contributors

John T. Addison is Hugh C. Lane Professor of Economic Theory at the University of South Carolina and Research Professor at GEMF/University of Coimbra, Portugal. Since 1 May 2007 he has chair in economics at Queen's University, Belfast. He was appointed research fellow of the Institute for Employment Research of the German Federal Employment Service in 2005, and in the summer of 2006 was Commerzbank Chaired Visiting Professor of Economics at the Technical University of Chemnitz. Addison has published widely in the major economics and specialty labour economics journals, including the *Review of Economics & Statistics*, *Journal of Labor Economics*, *Journal of Business* and the *American Economic Review*. He is the author/editor of a number of labour economics texts, most recently the *International Handbook of Trade Unions* (Edward Elgar 2003). For Elgar he is currently editing *Recent Developments in Labour Economics*.

Gerold Ambrosius is Professor in Economic and Social History at Universität Siegen, Germany. He has studied economics and political science. His main fields of research are the history of the public economy, European economic history and European economic integration, economic history and institutional economics, in particular institutional competition. His main publications on interjurisdictional competition include the book *Regulativer Wettbewerb und koordinative Standardisierung zwischen Staaten: Theoretische Annahmen und historische Beispiele*, Stuttgart 2005, as well as the articles *Globalisierung und multilaterale Konvergenz nationaler Regulierungen vor dem Ersten Weltkrieg* (Jahrbuch für Wirtschaftsgeschichte 2003) and *Regulierungswettbewerb im Deutschen Reich (1871–1914). Welche Erfahrungen sind für die Europäische Union relevant?* (Perspektiven der Wirtschaftspolitik).

Peter Bernholz is Professor of Economics, Emeritus, at Universität Basel, Switzerland. He is Research Fellow of the Center of Public Choice, George Mason University, and a corresponding member of the Bavarian Academy of Sciences. He has been President of the European Public Choice Society. He is author of *The International Game of Power* (1985) as well as co-editor of *Political Competition, Innovation and Growth: A Historical Analysis* (1998) and *Political Competition, Innovation and Growth in the History of Asian Civilizations* (2004).

Lars P. Feld is Professor of Economics at Universität Heidelberg, Germany. He is a member of the Council of Academic Advisors to the German Federal Ministry of Finance and Managing Editor of *Perspektiven der Wirtschaftspolitik*. He received his habilitation degree from Hochschule St. Gallen, Switzerland and was Visiting Fellow at the University of Southern California and Université de Rennes, France. He has published, for example, in the *Journal of Public Economics*, *The Scandinavian Journal of Economics*, *Public Choice*, *Kyklos*, *Economic Policy* and *The European Journal of Political Economy*.

Friedrich Heinemann is head of the research department Corporate Taxation and Public Finance of the Zentrum für Europäische Wirtschaftsforschung (Centre for European Economic Research) in Mannheim, Germany. He studied economics and history, inter alia at the London School of Economics. He is a member of the Academic Board of Institut für Europäische Politik (Institute for European Policy), Berlin. His main research interests include the monetary and fiscal policy of institutions in the European Union and determinants of structural reform and economic growth. He has published inter alia in *Public Choice* and the *European Journal of Political Economy*.

David Henderson is currently Visiting Professor at the Westminster Business School, London. In 1984–92, he was Head of the Economics and Statistics Department at the Organization for Economic Cooperation and Development (OECD) in Paris. Before this, he had worked as an academic economist in Britain, as a British civil servant and with the World Bank. Since leaving the OECD he has been an independent author and consultant working in Britain, France, Belgium, Australia and New Zealand. His 1985 BBC Reith Lectures were published in a book entitled *Innocence and Design: The Influence of Economic Ideas on Policy* (Blackwell 1986). His recent publications include *The Changing Fortunes of Economic Liberalism* (Institute of Economic Affairs, 2nd edition, 2001) and *The Role of Business in the Modern World: Progress, Pressures, and Prospects for the Market Economy* (2004, same publisher).

Jean-Michel Josselin is professor at Université de Rennes, France, where he teaches public economics and public finance. He is also invited professor at the Ecole Spéciale Militaire (Saint-Cyr Coëtquidan, France), teaching applied game theory, and a member of Centre National de la Recherche Scientifique. His main fields of interest are public finance and public choice, constitutional political economy, local public economics and the political economy of multi-level government. With regard to interjurisdictional competition, he is co-author of *Federalism and Subsidiarity in National and International Contexts* (*Handbook of Public Finance*, Kluwer 2004) and *Federalism and Conflict over Principalship* (*Constitutional Political Economy*, 2004) as well as co-editor of *Law and the State: A Political Economy Approach* (Elgar 2005).

Dennis C. Mueller is Professor of Economics at Universität Wien, Austria. He is a past president of the Public Choice Society, the Southern Economic Association, the Industrial Organization Society and the European Public Choice Society. His main research interests are in public choice, industrial economics and constitutional political economy. He is author of *Public Choice III* (Cambridge University Press 2003), *The Corporation* (Routledge 2003) and *Constitutional Democracy* (Oxford University Press 1996).

Pierre Salmon is Professor of Economics, Emeritus, at Université de Bourgogne, Dijon, France. For a few years, he has also been professor of economics at the European University Institute in Florence, Italy, and he has spent some time in the French central administration in Paris. He is a past president of the European Public Choice Society. His two main research interests are methodology and the economic approach to politics. He is the co-author of a book on economic methodology and the co-editor of several books in the second area. Several of his articles and chapters concern yardstick competition among governments, most notably *Decentralisation as an Incentive Scheme* (*Oxford Review of Economic Policy*, 1987).

Christoph A. Schaltegger is economic adviser at the Swiss Federal Department of Finance, a lecturer and research associate of economics at Hochschule St. Gallen, Switzerland, and a research fellow of the Centre for Research in Economics, Management and the Arts (CREMA) in Switzerland. He received his doctorate in economics from Universität Basel, Switzerland. His primary research interests are in the areas of public finance, political economy and institutional economics.

W. Stanley Siebert is Professor of Labour Economics at the University of Birmingham, UK, where he has worked since 1980. He gained his degrees at the University of Cape Town and the London School of Economics. His current research interests centre on policy regulating working conditions and wages. He is co-author of *The Economics of Earnings* (Cambridge University Press 1993), *The Market for Labor* (Goodyear/Scott-Foresman 1979) and *Labour Markets in Europe* (Harcourt-Brace 1997).

Gordon Tullock is currently University Professor of Law and Economics and Distinguished Research Fellow in the James M. Buchanan Center for Political Economy at George Mason University, Fairfax. He holds a joint teaching position in the Department of Economics and the School of Law. He received a J.D. from the University of Chicago in 1947. In 1966, he became Founding Editor of the *Journal of Non-Market Decision Making* (later renamed *Public Choice*) and remained Senior Editor until 1990. He has served as president of the Public Choice Society, the European Public Choice Society, the Southern Economic Association and the Western Economic Association. In 1998 he was honoured as Distinguished Fellow of the American Economic Association. He has published 23 books and several hundred articles, inter alia on federalism and interjurisdictional competition as well as rent-seeking by regulation.

François Vaillancourt is Professor of Economics at Université de Montréal where he has taught since 1976. He has acted as a consultant for various bodies, including the Auditor General of Canada, the OECD, the UNDP and the World Bank. He has published mainly on fiscal federalism and taxation. He is co-author of *Fiscal Decentralization in Developing Countries* (Cambridge University Press 1998).

Roland Vaubel is Professor of Economics at Universität Mannheim, Germany. He received a BA in Philosophy, Politics and Economics from the University of Oxford and an MA in Economics from Columbia University, New York. He has been Visiting Professor in International Economics at the Graduate School of Business, University of Chicago. He is author of *The Centralisation of Western Europe* (Institute of Economic Affairs, London 1995) and co-editor of *The Political Economy of International Organization* (Westview Press 1991) and *Political Competition, Innovation and Growth in the History of Asian Civilizations* (Elgar 2004). He is associate editor of the new journal *Review of International Organizations* (Springer).

Oliver Volckart is a lecturer in economic history at Humboldt-Universität Berlin, Germany. He gained a doctorate in history from Freie Universität Berlin and a habilitation degree in economics from Friedrich-Schiller-Universität Jena, Germany. In 2003–4, he spent a year teaching at the London School of Economics. His research focuses on the period from the fourteenth to the eighteenth centuries, analysing processes of competition and restrictions on competition in both economic and political markets. He is author, inter alia, of *Wettbewerb und Wettbewerbsbeschränkungen im vormodernen Deutschland, 1000 bis 1800* (Mohr Siebeck 2002).

1 The effect of interjurisdictional competition on regulation

Theory and overview

Peter Bernholz and Roland Vaubel

The hypothesis that interjurisdictional competition affects regulation can be traced back to Immanuel Kant's 'Idea of a Universal History from a Cosmopolitan Point of View' (1784):

> The states are already in the present day involved in such close relations with each other that none of them can pause or slacken in its internal civilization without losing power and influence to the rest ... Civil liberty cannot now be easily assailed without inflicting such damage as will be felt in all trades and industries, and especially in commerce; and this would entail a diminution of the powers of the state in external relations ... If the citizen is hindered in seeking his prosperity in any way suitable to himself that is consistent with the liberty of others, the activity of business is checked generally; and thereby the powers of the whole state are again weakened.
>
> (p. 31)

In modern language, market interdependence and political competition among states constrain regulation because each government which interferes with the freedom of contract impairs the economic competitiveness of its country and weakens its own power including its military potential and its strength in international relations. Conversely, regulatory collusion among states would raise the level of regulation. If all governments regulate, no government has to fear a loss of economic competitiveness and of political power.

In Kant's analysis, economic interdependence ('close relations') among the states is mainly due to interstate commerce. Max Weber (1923), with the benefit of hindsight at the industrial revolution, focused on the mobility of capital: 'The separate states had to compete for mobile capital, which dictated to them the conditions under which it would assist them to power' (p. 249).

Jacques Tiebout (1956), after the exodus from Europe in the 1930s and 1940s, stressed the mobility of labour (voting with the feet). All three forms of interdependence through the market have been subsumed under the term 'exit' by Albert Hirschman (1970).

However, governments do not only compete through the market, through political promises, threats and military measures. They also interact by generating (non-excludable) knowledge about efficient policy performance. This is especially important in democracies. The idea goes back to Lord Acton's 'History of Freedom in Antiquity' (1877):

> The distribution of power among several states is the best check on democracy. By multiplying centres of government and discussion it promotes the diffusion of political knowledge and the maintenance of healthy and independent opinion. It is the protectorate of minorities, and the consecration of self-government.
>
> (p. 261)

This non-market interaction among governments has become known as 'voice' (Hirschman 1970) or 'yardstick competition' (Salmon 1987; Besley and Case 1995).[1]

As Pierre Salmon explains in his contribution to this volume, political yardstick competition has to be distinguished from three other mechanisms which also involve interjurisdictional comparisons and are also not based on exit but which do not presuppose interjurisdictional comparisons by the voters:

1   emulation among office-holders aiming at the approval of their peers,
2   interjurisdictional comparisons not by voters but by governments trying to copy the successful innovations of other governments,
3   competition across jurisdictions among office-holders for the purpose not of re-election but of promotion to a position at a higher governmental tier.

Thus, the two necessary characteristics of political yardstick competition as understood here are, first, that the agents who make the interjurisdictional comparisons are the voters or, more generally, the providers of political support and, second, that office-holders are influenced by the comparisons because they seek electoral or political support to improve their chance of remaining in power.

Both types of interjurisdictional competition operate in the age of globalization and both are at the same time threatened by the increasing harmonization and centralization of regulatory policies in federal states and international organizations. If the adoption of common regulations does not require unanimity but merely a (qualified) majority, as is the case in federal states and some international organizations, notably the European Union, regulatory collusion is replaced by the 'strategy of raising rivals' costs'.[2]

George Stigler (1970) was probably the first to point out that the majority of highly regulated states are interested and able to impose their high level(s) of regulation on the minority in order to weaken the latter's competitiveness. Since, by doing so, the majority reduces regulatory competition from the minority, the majority can afford to raise its own level of regulation as well. A formal analysis shows that the resulting common level of regulation may easily be higher than the collusive (unanimous) level.[3] The available evidence (for the EU and ILO) indicates that the highly regulated member states are more likely to vote for such common regulations and that the prevailing common level or regulation tends to exceed the average of the pre-existing national regulations.[4]

As George Stigler (1971) has emphasized, regulation tends to be demanded by well-organized interest groups, which want to be protected against market competition. This raises two important questions, first, how interjurisdictional competition or attempts to restrain it affect the political influence of interest groups and, second, whether these groups are themselves influencing the degree of interjurisdictional competition. The answer is controversial.

According to a famous argument that goes back to James Madison,[5] political centralization by federation reduces the power of 'factions' or interest groups because the various regional interests tend to block each other. Such blocking is likely to occur but it is not the whole story. Well-organized groups pursuing diverse and partly contrary interests – say, unions and employers' associations – may agree on government regulations – say, barriers to entering the goods market – at the expense of poorly organized third parties – say, consumers (Bernholz 1973). Moreover, similar interests represented in a majority of regions will be more influential at the federal or international level because, as we have seen, centralization reduces the scope for comparison (yardstick competition) and raises the cost of 'exit' for those who suffer from the regulation.

Madison's conclusion has been supported by Mancur Olson (1966), but for a different reason. As Olson points out, political centralization weakens the incentive to organize an interest group because it reduces the share of the collective benefit which each member of the group can internalize. It also raises the cost of organizing the relevant interest group (because the group has more members) and the cost of lobbying (because the federal parliament has more members). Finally, centralization limits the lobbyists' access to the political executive because there is only one instead of several (Bernholz and Breyer 1984: 364–7; Mueller in this volume).

However, there are also additional arguments to the effect that centralization raises the power of interest groups and the level of regulation demanded by them:[6]

1 Centralization weakens the individual voter's incentive to acquire and use political information because the weight of the individual vote declines ('rational ignorance').
2 Centralization raises the voter's cost of information because federal or international regulation is farther removed from his attention and less intelligible (especially if foreign languages are involved).
3 In federal or international negotiations among jurisdictions, interest group collusion seems less suspect or improper to the voters (Salmon 1987).
4 Centralization reduces the cost of lobbying for regionally homogeneous

interests because they have to address only one regulator (Laffont and Martimort 1998).

5   Centralization forces the elected politicians to delegate more regulatory power to bureaucrats who are more responsive to the demands of interest groups because they do not need to be re-elected (Crain and McCormick 1984).

6   Centralization increases the bureaucracy's need for information supplied by interest groups (Nollert 1996).

Quite apart from interest group pressure, centralization, by reducing openness and exposure to external shocks, may weaken the voters' demand for protection by internal regulation. Or, conversely, globalization and interjurisdictional competition among countries may increase the demand for protective state regulation and insurance for the same reason (Rodrik 1998; Heinemann in this volume).

Thus, from a theoretical point of view, we cannot determine whether interjurisdictional competition or, quite the contrary, political centralization favours deregulation. The answer is theoretically ambiguous, and it has been hotly contested for centuries. It is a question which has to be answered empirically.

This led us to assemble a number of case studies, both verbal and econometric, which analyse the historical evidence. Has federation in the United States, Canada, Switzerland, Germany and the European Union led to regulatory collusion and attempts to raise rivals' costs? Has globalization lowered the level of regulation and, if so, in which fields? There is an extensive literature showing that tax competition tends to lower the level of taxation and government spending. Since government transfers and regulations are substitutes in catering for interest groups and protecting the median voter against risk, we might expect similar results for regulation. Is the case of regulation really analogous? If not, why not?

In the first case study John Addison reviews the political economy of federal, state and local labour regulation in the United States. The number of *federal* regulatory programmes covering labour standards, civil rights, occupational health and safety, labour relations and hiring and separation decisions has dramatically increased from 18 at the time of the New Deal to 40 in 1960 and some 180 by the mid-1990s. Before the New Deal legislation, from the 1860s onwards, there had been important state-level regulations of worker safety and compensation for injury in mining and manufacturing. However, after the New Deal, Addison detects a liberalization of superannuated legislation at the state level. For example, quite a few states repealed their prevailing wage laws, prevented their cities from establishing local minimum wages and, under the Taft–Hartly Act (1947), used their right to prohibit union shops by so-called right-to-work laws. As Norton (1986) shows, right-to-work laws are found in a large minority of states, and every one of them lies outside the Manufacturing Belt. At times, however, depending on the party in power at the federal level, labour unions find it easier to obtain regulation at the state or local level. In the field of wrongful dismissal legislation, the probability of state-level regulation has been shown to depend positively on the fraction of neighbouring states that have already adopted the regulation (Dertouzos and Karoly 1992, 1993). This is consistent with yardstick competition (but also with exit or common-cause interdependence).

Federal regulation provides several examples of the strategy of raising rivals' costs. It has been conventional to attribute national legislation on minimum wages to the congressional majority of northern states wherein the envisaged minima were generally exceeded and which coalesced to suppress low-wage competition from the smaller number of southern states paying lower wages and which in turn voted against the Federal Fair Labor Standards Act (1938). Addison suggests that the raising rivals' costs argument is yet more transparent in the case of the Davis–Bacon Act (1931) which imposed the prevailing local wage on workers from other states, notably on black construction workers from the South. Another example of raising rivals' costs by federal labour regulation is the Occupational Safety and Health Act (1970). Addison discusses the economic evidence of Bartel and Thomas (1985, 1987) which shows that smaller firms and older plants experienced a significantly larger unit-cost effect. He also notes Pashigian's analogous results for the Environmental Protection Act (1970). Finally, the strategy of raising rivals' costs has also been detected in state-level regulation of workers' safety and compensation before the New Deal (Fishback 2005). However, Addison concludes that we have far less information on the politico-economic causes of labour mandates than on their effects, and even the involvement of the various labour market actors has largely been adduced from the legislation's pay-offs to them.

Dennis Mueller in his comment raises the question whether the US economy would be more efficient today if the power to regulate labour markets would have been reserved for the states or the federal government. He assumes that it is cheaper for an interest group to buy legislation from a state legislature than from Congress. However, as labour unions can be expected to be eventually powerful enough to get legislation through Congress, having the states be responsible for most regulation in labour markets may be a way to avoid some of the inefficiencies of labour market regulations.

Mueller's reason for favouring state-level to federal regulation is not that he trusts yardstick competition (as opposed to interjurisdictional competition by exit) in this field. In a world in which democratic decisions are made using simple majority rule and well-organized interest groups can use the political process to advance the interests of their members over other members in the community, yardstick competition need not be welfare enhancing. Once one group of workers convinces its legislature that it should introduce some sort of labour regulation to protect them against 'unfair competition', the stage is set for the spread of this redistribution policy with its attendant inefficiencies to other communities. Winning votes in this way may be easier than trying to increase governmental efficiency and cut taxes.

Why is labour market regulation less restrictive in the United States than it is in Europe? In Mueller's view this is due to the separation of powers between the President and two houses of Congress, the weakness of the parties, the absence of coalition governments, the single-member-district representation and the high mobility of labour (and capital?).

Gordon Tullock looks at various US regulations designed to protect domestic labour against foreign competition – including product regulations. He argues that such rent-seeking involves an error because it is inefficient, but that it is probably unavoidable because there are natural limits to the diligence and intelligence of the political decision makers. However, he sees ways of reducing such rent-seeking. He calls upon all economists to turn their minds to that modest but achievable goal.

Interjurisdictional competition in Canada is analysed in the second case study. François Vaillancourt suggests that the strategy of raising rivals' costs has not been pursued among the Canadian provinces because there is no geographically based decision-making body at the federal level. Moreover, framework laws are not generally used in Canada. In the House of Commons, party discipline is notably strong so that majority coalitions along provincial lines are not possible across parties. (This leaves the possibility that a regionally based majority of the deputies of the ruling party might impose their will on the minority by way of the strong party discipline.)

Vaillancourt shows that interjurisdictional competition among the Canadian provinces has been favoured by their autonomy to adopt diverse and innovative solutions due to the insistence of Quebec and largely by their strong reliance on own revenue sources (from about 60 to about 90 per cent). But he is not sure whether the number of provinces (ten plus three territories) has been large enough for effective interjurisdictional competition. Regulation is a provincial responsibility in the field of wholesale and retail trade, utilities, construction, mining as well as forestry and to some extent in transportation, financial institutions and labour law. There are large differences among the provinces but interjurisdictional competition has not prevented them from adopting labour market regulations which are stricter and much more pro-union than in the United States.

As for incorporation regulation, an econometric study by Cumming and MacIntosh (2000) reveals that the costs of incorporation have a significant impact on the number of incorporations in five of the ten provinces, but the provinces cannot be shown to react competitively to such interjurisdictional arbitrage by firms. The deregulation of Sunday shopping made possible by a Supreme Court decision in 1985 started in the West and with Eastern politicians pointing to the example of the more Western provinces (yardstick competition). A quantitative analysis of provincial minimum wages by Green and Harrison (2005) shows that the changes are strongly correlated among the provinces but converge to the mean ('race to the middle'). Some provinces prevent employers from requiring their workers to retire at a certain age. The first province to do so was Quebec (1982), and to some extent it was used as a model by others. Vaillancourt does not find much evidence of interjurisdictional interaction in provincial anti-smoking regulation but he presents several examples in the field of taxation, government expenditure and social insurance (tax credits to Labour-Sponsored Venture Capital Funds, childcare, university fees, balanced-budget legislation and medical care). There is more interjurisdictional yardstick competition in taxation and government spending than in regulation. Quebec is often the initiator of new provincial policies in Canada. But yardstick competition does not necessarily yield good economic policies. Provincial autonomy and therefore interjurisdictional competition has been weakened by the strings attached to categorical grants from the federal government which harmonize social policies at the highest level of intervention observed. However, some Canadian regulations are strongly affected by those of the United States (notably in electricity).

Vaillancourt's panel data analysis for the number of provincial regulations and their number of pages in 1975 to 1999 reveals that regulation depends positively and mostly significantly on (lagged) regulation in neighbouring provinces and is also affected by various control variables.

Pierre Salmon in his comment emphasizes that Vaillancourt's contribution is limited to the Canadian provincial level, that is, it ignores yardstick competition among the municipalities, between Canadian provinces and US states and vertical yardstick competition between the federal, the provincial and the municipal level. Even though the powers of the Canadian municipalities are not constitutionally entrenched as for instance in Switzerland, competition among them seems to be a significant phenomenon. Salmon presents an example where the citizens of a city in Quebec obtained from their municipal government a by-law banning the use of pesticides for non-essential purposes and where this regulation was copied by other municipalities in Quebec, upheld by the Constitutional Court, imitated by cities outside Quebec and finally even taken up by federal legislation.

Salmon does not agree with Vaillancourt that the fairly small number of provinces weakens interjurisdictional competition in Canada. Small numbers, it is true, increase the danger of collusion, but he does not see much evidence of regulatory collusion among Canadian provincial governments. Yardstick competition is a robust mechanism which can work well both when the number of jurisdictions is large and when it is small. Indeed, most of the theoretical literature discusses interjurisdictional competition as a strategic interaction between two jurisdictions, and the empirical tests assume the mechanism to work only between contiguous jurisdictions.

Salmon notes a number of difficulties in testing for yardstick competition. Mechanisms of yardstick competition are difficult to disentangle from other mechanisms leading to the same observable outcomes. They may alternatively be due to a similar way of responding to an exogenous shock affecting all jurisdictions or to mobility-based competition. Moreover, if the incumbents expect their voters to compare among governments, this by itself will affect their regulatory decisions even if the voters do not actually make such comparisons. Thus, yardstick competition may manifest itself only in the mind of the incumbents. Finally, many regulations are too technical to benefit from the attention of a sufficient number of voters. Frequently, it is yardstick competition over much more visible macroeconomic variables (economic growth, the unemployment rate) which may induce governments to reconsider inconspicuous regulations. For all these reasons, it is important that Vaillancourt actually looks into the minutes of parliamentary debates.

In the next chapter Stanley Siebert presents a public choice analysis of labour market regulation in the European Union. The EU's stance is grounded in the denial of the benefits of interjurisdictional competition. The Charter of Fundamental Social Rights of Workers (1989), the Social Chapter of Maastricht (ratified in 1993 and incorporated in the Treaty of Amsterdam in 1997) and the Charter of Fundamental Rights (adopted in 1999 and incorporated in the ill-fated constitutional draft of 2004) are all in the direction of compressing regulatory differences. The expansion of EU labour regulation was born out of a concern that the increased competition resulting from completion of the single market by 1992 (as envisaged by the Single European Act of 1986) would trigger a race to the bottom in labour standards. However, in Siebert's view, the finding of Koeniger *et al.* (2004) that, generally, trade widens wage differentials goes against the popular view that openness increases people's demand for labour regulation.

So far interjurisdictional competition in the EU has mainly been between the UK and the rest. With regard to employment protection, France is most protective and the UK is least protective (Botero *et al.* 2004). The UK falling into line by establishing a minimum wage in 1999 may have been an attempt to pre-empt an EU directive. However, British wages are still relatively flexible. Paradoxically, this is likely to reduce UK opposition to further EU regulation of working conditions: hikes in job conditions have less effect on employment since wages simply fall in response to the better conditions.

Since labour market regulation has been shown to drive up long-term unemployment and youth unemployment in particular (Bertola *et al.* 2004; Botero *et al.* 2004), it seems to be inefficient and has to be explained by public choice theory. Siebert's explanation is that the median voter, who is employed, promotes employment protection to raise his wages and to improve his working conditions. But why then is there such a large difference between the UK and, say, France? Siebert argues that employment protection is closely associated with legal formalism. While the English common law tradition conferred more power on the judiciary, on the continent centuries of absolute government have given rise to a tradition of powerful administrative authority (Hayek 1960), culminating in the Napoleonic code and manifested today in France's 2,000-page Code du Travail. Given a predisposition to intervene, these countries began with some degree of labour market regulation, which then created its own constituency of rent protectors and affected the preferences of the median voter. Thus, regulatory competition in the European Union is essentially a competition among different traditions of legal origin.

Jean-Michel Josselin in his comment emphasizes the scope for legal competition in French civil law. Neither Parliament's alleged monopoly in the provision of legal rules nor the alleged overwhelming power of public judges do exist in reality. The Civil Code, it is true, rests on the Roman codification of contract law, but in the field of property rights it is based on the Germanic tribal customs. Thus, Josselin attributes the French penchant for regulation more to a deeply engrained quest for equality and to rent seeking by well-organized interest groups.

Josselin argues that the merger of unitary states in a federal system can raise the level of regulation because the majority may raise the minority's cost. Regulatory competition is probably better promoted in a confederate framework or by devolution to lower levels of government. But this would have to include the downwards transfer of the juridical capacity of regulation. It might be easier to base interjurisdictional competition on function rather than territory. Such functional competition would require an organized market for different forms of labour contract provided by competing suppliers. It would be a way of testing the efficiency of alternative labour regulations.

Roland Vaubel's comment focuses on interjurisdictional collusion and the strategy of raising rivals' cost in the European Union's policy of labour market regulation. The introduction of qualified majority voting has enabled the majority of regulation-prone member states to impose their high level of regulation on the rest. Several examples are provided. The voting record of the Council shows that the southern member states tend to support more EU regulation than the northern member states do. The ability to raise the minority's cost leads the majority to favour more restrictive regulations also in their own countries. The earliest example of raising rivals' cost by EU labour market regulation was the British policy of not vetoing the Social Agreement of Maastricht in 1991 but of opting out.

Chapter 5 contains three case studies on the history of regulatory competition in Germany: one on early modern Germany up to the end of the Holy Roman Empire by Oliver Volckart, one on nineteenth-century Germany (and Europe) by Gerold Ambrosius and one on Bismarck's strategy of raising rivals' costs by Roland Vaubel.

Oliver Volckart argues that in pre-modern Germany two essential conditions for regulatory competition failed to exist. First, political authorities were not necessarily interested in attracting mobile factors of production because their revenues did not, or did only insignificantly, depend on taxation. Second, they faced resistance from well-organized interest groups which regarded foreign immigrant workers and investors as intruders and were powerful enough to shape and enforce their own regulations and anti-competitive institutions. A large number of authorities able to regulate production and services existed side by side within the same territory. Craft-guilds and peasant communities restricted immigration. The East German nobility did not have any interest in the arrival of non-servile peasants from the West. Nor did it give their peasants the slightest chance to leave their manor. Towns demanded fines from emigrating citizens.

This changed when monopolistic territorial states began to emerge in the late seventeenth and eighteenth centuries. In the Religious Peace Agreement concluded at the Augsburg Imperial Diet (1555) and the Peace Treaty of West-phalia (1648), the princes agreed to grant their subjects the right to emigrate because denominational heterogeneity within their principalities would have undermined the legitimacy of their rule. With the advent of the modern monopolistic state, local interest groups lost the power to adopt and enforce regulations on their own. While under modern conditions a centralization of regulatory power would certainly not be expected to lead to an easing of regulation, in the transformation of the pre-modern German economy full state control over regulation was a necessary prerequisite for regulatory competition among jurisdictions. Another necessary condition was that the rise of the monopolistic territorial state did not lead to a centralized all-German empire: at the end of the eighteenth century more than 300 states existed within the borders of the Holy Roman Empire.

However, there are no instances where a pre-modern government tried to increase the attraction of its territory by abolishing the privileges of the traditional corporations and creating a level playing field. The governments competed by granting subsidies and other privileges to investors and immigrants from other jurisdictions, for example, by exempting them from the regulations and charges of the local guilds. This weakened the established artisans' incentive to maintain their guild regulations. Few regulations were formally repealed; most of them simply dropped out of existence because they ceased to be enforced.

Gerold Ambrosius, drawing on his recent German book (Ambrosius 2005), tries to explain German and European regulation of food and labour markets in the nineteenth century, especially the second half, up to the First World War. In the German Reich, that is, from 1870 onwards, food and labour regulations were gradually harmonized in an upward direction. The food law of 1879 created the framework for numerous special statutes. Food regulations were demanded by consumers for the entire Reich in order to create legal certainty at a time of increasing adulteration of foodstuffs. Trade and industry also pressed for uniform regulations applicable to the entire Reich because, in their opinion, differences in regulations among the member states led to unfair competition and were bothersome. Harmonization would enable them to reap economies of scale and save transaction costs. The argument was repeatedly brought forward during the negotiations in the Reichstag that Germany was lagging behind other countries such as France, England or Switzerland.

At the international level, from the 1880s onwards, the European states went over from the origin principle (mutual recognition) to the destination principle, but not to harmonization. Thus, the degree of regulatory competition remained higher at the international level than within Germany. Producers tended to reject the origin principle if foreign producers enjoyed competitive advantages because of lower standards of regulation. Moreover, owing to the larger internal market, they increasingly tried to use product regulations as non-tariff barriers to imports from abroad. Consumers, on the one hand, favoured institutional competition because they hoped that competing regulations would improve the quality of domestic products and protect consumer sovereignty. On the other hand, they sometimes supported the transition to the destination principle because they distrusted foreign regulations. Parliaments and governments of the European states kept a close eye on one another in the matter of food regulation.

Labour market regulation in the German Reich was agreed by parties and governments because it was a salient issue and of relevance to electoral tactics. It was demanded by an ever-increasing proportion of the citizens, and it was to contribute to the cultural identity of the united Germany. Entrepreneurs were, of course, generally in favour of low standards. When, however, they had to accept a higher standard of regulation in their own state, they were in favour of raising standards in other states, too. Politicians who sided with the employers supported institutional competition because they expected it to lead to deregulation or at least not to rising standards of regulation. The subsidiarity principle, enshrined in the spirit of the constitution but not clearly stated in the constitutional law, was interpreted one-sidedly by the Reichstag and the central government to mean that the only tasks to be left to the member states were those they themselves did not want to deal with or which were explicitly excluded by the constitution.

At the European level, a number of international labour standards were adopted and ratified in 1904 and 1906. But even in fields in which no international agreements were concluded, national labour legislation moved into the same direction, and regulatory convergence occurred. The various states were affected by more or less the same factors, faced similar problems with regard to working conditions and naturally reacted with very similar measures. However, parliaments and governments were well informed about the laws and bills in other states and reacted to them. Until well into the second half of the nineteenth century, Great Britain was the model for continental European countries – for the Prussian factory law of 1839 just as for the French law of 1841, for the Swiss initiatives just as for the Belgian bills. Conversely, the British parliament and government took careful note of foreign labour protection laws as in the Redgrave Report of 1853. The successful conclusion of international agreements was facilitated by the fact that the number of cooperating states – 15 at the Berne Convention of 1906 – was relatively small. The representatives of those countries that had more advanced labour protection laws tried to extend their own higher standards to the other countries, while the representatives of the other countries sought to maintain their lower standards as exceptions. Countries like Belgium which were suspected of aiming to improve their competitive position through low standards were not only subject to moral but also to political or economic pressure, for example, threats of trade sanctions.

Roland Vaubel's case study analyses Bismarck's strategy of raising rivals' costs by federal regulation. The analysis is based on the voting record of the Bundesrath, the second chamber of parliament in which the governments of the member states were represented. Since this voting record was usually not published and, from 1880 onwards, could even be declared secret, it has been reconstructed from the handwritten notes of the delegates of Baden and Württemberg and the comments of contemporaries. But in many cases, Bismarck, who as Prime Minister of Prussia presided over the Bundesrath, did not even bother to take votes. Together with its East German allies, Prussia raised the level of regulation, taxation and tariff protection and imposed it on the more liberal minority of states in the Northwest (Hamburg, Bremen, Lübeck, Oldenburg) and Southwest (Baden, Hesse, Württemberg).

The suppression of the Northwestern states had already began in the Norddeutscher Bund (North German Federation) in 1867–71 with the Notgewerbegesetz (Emergency Trade Law) of 1868, the Gewerbeordnung (Trade Regulation) of 1869 and the Gesetz über Aktiengesellschaften (Law concerning Joint-Stock Companies) of 1870. After 1870–1, when the South German states were added and the 'Empire' was founded, the Prussian-led majority coalition in the Bundesrath imposed at least five federal regulations on the less restrictive minority in the West: the Seemannsordnung (Sailors' Regulation) of 1872, the Gewerbeordnung (Trade Regulation) of 1884, the Bäckereiverordnung (Bakeries Regulation) of 1896, the Innungsgesetz (Guilds Law) of 1897 and the Gewerbeordnung (Trade Regulation) of 1908. Bismarck, who was dismissed in 1890, also imposed the Schutzzollgesetz (Tariff Law) of 1879 and the Stempelsteuergesetz (Stamp Duty Law) of 1884 on a recalcitrant liberal minority and deprived Hamburg of its free harbour in Altona, Wandsbek and Unterelbe in 1881 (Zollanschluss). The history books of the time and still today convey the impression of federal harmony and Prussian tolerance and liberalism. However, scholarly work by some South German authors, who are extensively quoted by Vaubel, reveals that this image is misleading.

In Chapter 6 Lars Feld analyses regulatory competition and collusion in Switzerland. He starts by reviewing the theoretical literature on interjurisdictional competition. In his view, the theoretical literature criticizing regulatory competition tends to ignore three crucial facts:

1   governments do not systematically do what they ought to do,
2   it is not reasonable to assume that markets are hardly informed about regulatory standards (as in the lemons case),
3   competitive processes are crucial for innovation.

He then surveys the empirical evidence on interjurisdictional competition in the field of taxation, public spending, tort law, incorporation law (in the US) and administrative law (in Switzerland).

In nineteenth-century Switzerland regulations of commerce, labour and trade originated mainly from the powerful guilds. Liberalization started mostly in the Swiss border cantons of Thurgau and St. Gall (both created during the Napoleonic years) as well as in Basle-Country, Ticino and Aargau where the guilds were not very strong. The Swiss Federation founded in 1848 and dominated by the liberal, mostly protestant cantons initially did not favour regulatory collusion. On the contrary, by imposing mutual recognition of cantonal regulations, it established a system of regulatory competition which kept the cantonal ability to regulate in check. The driving force behind regulatory competition was mobility among the cantons. However, the existence of an arena and incentives for lobbying at the federal level soon induced interest groups to seek protection from the federal government. Many exceptions from the freedom of commerce were granted, thus reducing the scope for regulatory competition. The federal government provided opportunities for the conservative, more strictly regulated cantons to raise their rivals' costs – especially during the interwar period. In the last 25 years, the federal government has tried to get rid of cantonal regulations and facilitate trade in services across cantons. These attempts culminated in the Swiss Common Market Law of 1995 and an extension which is underway.

Feld ends with a cross-section analysis regressing the number of regulations around the year 2000 on regulations in neighbouring cantons, an index of direct democracy, the share of Catholics, income per capita, population and population density. The OLS estimates reveal significant positive neighbourhood effects and negative direct democracy effects. Separate regressions are estimated for examination requirements and additional quality requirements as well as for commerce, services, the legal profession and all sectors. Similar but weaker results are obtained from a two-stage least squares estimate using a dummy for German-speaking cantons as the instrument. Feld concludes that mimicking behaviour appears to be important in cantonal regulation while direct democracy restricts the ability of cantons to introduce additional regulations.

Christoph Schaltegger complements Feld's study with an analysis of inter-cantonal yardstick competition in fiscal regulation. He shows that balanced budget requirements are spreading among the Swiss cantons and that one canton explicitly studies and imitates the regulation of the others. Deficits, debt, spending and revenue per capita tend to be lower in cantons which have enacted balanced budget requirements. In a panel data analysis, balanced budget requirements have a significantly negative effect on deficit spending. Thus, yardstick competition among fiscal rules seems to favour fiscal discipline.

The last chapter is devoted to the question of whether globalization, by increasing interjurisdictional competition among countries, has favoured deregulation at the national level. An early example of such an outcome was the financial deregulation (with regard to interest rate ceilings, term limits and minimum reserve requirements) due to the rise of the euro–dollar market. A recent panel analysis by Abiad and Mody (2003) also shows that trade openness reduces financial regulation.

Friedrich Heinemann in his contribution to this volume presents panel data analyses for four separate markets: the financial market, the labour market, the product market and international trade. The data set covers 21 OECD countries in 1975 to 1998, 2001 or 2002.

The index of financial deregulation takes account of credit and interest controls as well as restrictions on international transactions. It indicates a massive dismantling of controls from the beginning. Financial globalization as proxied by gross private capital flows and direct investment from abroad relative to GDP has dramatically increased since the mid-1990s. The two series bear a significantly positive correlation. In a multivariate dynamic specification, financial deregulation depends positively and significantly on foreign direct investment, deregulation elsewhere and internal political decentralization. It is also spurred by low economic growth.

Heinemann's labour market indicator measures employment protection and unemployment benefits. It shows a rising trend. In the multivariate analysis, labour market deregulation and benefit cuts are hampered by trade openness but facilitated by internal political decentralization. Both left and right wing governments are significantly more willing to deregulate and cut benefits than those associated with the political centre.

The index of product market deregulation reflects barriers to entry, public ownership, market structure, vertical integration of networks and final consumer services as well as price controls outside manufacturing. It indicates a strong trend towards deregulation and depends positively and significantly on deregulation in other countries.

Finally, the trade-related indicator is constructed on the basis of effective tariffs relating revenues from customs and import duties to the value of imports. It reveals a sustained liberalizing tendency. In the multivariate analysis, the liberalization of international trade turns out to be significantly stronger in the European Union countries, and it is positively affected by a deregulated labour market.

Heinemann concludes that, while globalization as measured by trade openness and capital mobility has a rather limited impact on regulation and, therefore, leaves much leeway for national regulatory policies, yardstick competition has been quite effective in bringing about deregulation – at least in the financial and product markets.

David Henderson takes a more philosophical perspective of deregulation in the age of globalization. Using a different database, the Economic Freedom in the World index, he confirms that, among the largest countries, all except one (Venezuela) have become less regulated, with the late 1970s marking a watershed. The developing and former communist countries have liberalized more than the advanced countries. Deregulation has been most extensive in financial markets and network industries like transport and power generation. When it comes to labour markets, however, the evidence suggests that in many if not most of the 50 countries, the overall balance has shifted towards more regulation, not only in the OECD but also in a number of developing countries, especially in Latin America.

Though emulation has played a part, governments remain almost as free to determine their choice of policies as they were 30 years ago. Systems competition has not been a strong influence, except in a few areas of policy such as corporate taxation.

Crises do not necessarily trigger deregulation; in the 1970s they led to all sorts of interventionist measures. Deregulation in the 1980s and 1990s was not so much due to sudden negative shocks as to chronic and growing concerns about economic performance. Governments that were less subject to these pressures to act were influenced both by these experiences and by a concomitant shift in the general climate of opinion. Deregulation had little to do with the role of interest groups. It was less opportunist and more directed towards general welfare. Today it is less opposed by producer groups than by so-called 'public interest' non-governmental organizations which rely on pre-economic ideas or 'do-it-yourself economics'. The main and growing interventionist challenge is the quest for 'corporate social responsibility' and common international norms and standards which restrict employment opportunities.

Summing up, we have found much evidence of exit and yardstick competition in our case studies. However, the effects of political fragmentation or centralization on regulation seem to be less uniform than their effects on taxation. The main reason is that regulation, unlike taxation, is very often sought by powerful interest groups or even by electoral majorities – also at the lower levels of government. In these circumstances, yardstick competition is an unreliable tool. Interest groups or electoral majorities in one jurisdiction may imitate the regulations introduced in another jurisdiction.[7] Thus, in the case of regulation, interjurisdictional competition by exit and entry is likely to be more beneficial than yardstick competition. However, interest groups and electoral majorities may also use regulation to restrict exit and entry. Political fragmentation is not identical with interjurisdictional competition.[8] If political fragmentation is to increase interjurisdictional competition and reduce internal regulation, it has to give more freedom of choice to the victims of regulation.

Clearly, this volume is no more than a beginning. It is an attempt to open up a new field of research, regulatory competition, side by side with the existing literature on tax competition.

Most of the chapters and comments included in the volume have been presented at a conference held in Heidelberg in June 2005. We gratefully acknowledge financial support from the Egon Sohmen Foundation. Egon Sohmen was an Austrian economist who received his PhD from the Massachusetts Institute of Technology and who taught at Yale University, the University of the Saar and the University of Heidelberg. He was one of the leading architects of Germany's transition to flexible exchange rates, that is, interjurisdictional competition in the field of money.

Notes

1 The term 'yardstick competition' had previously been used in the theory of industrial organization (e.g. Shleifer 1985).
2 For a survey of the theoretical and empirical literature see Boockmann and Vaubel (2005). The term has also been used in the industrial organization literature.
3 See the graphical analysis in Boockmann and Vaubel (2005).
4 Ibid.
5 Federalist Paper No. 10 (1787/1995: 64f.).
6 See also Vaubel (1986, 1994). The view that political centralization increases the power of organized interest groups has been taken, for example, by Lee (1985), Aranson (1990) as well as Andersen and Eliasson (1991). The last two authors

conclude from their study of European lobbying: 'The EC system is now more lobby-ing-oriented than any national European system' (p. 178).
7 For example, Gray (1994: 237f.) shows how the regulation of railroads, occupational health, minimum wages and child labour spread among the US states during the 'Pro-gressive Era'. See also Bernholz *et al.* (1998).
8 We have drawn the same lesson from our analysis of interjurisdictional fragmentation in the history of Asian civilizations, especially with regard to India (Bernholz and Vaubel 2004: 14).

References

Abiad, Abdul and Mody, Ashoka (2003) 'Financial Reform: What shakes it? What shapes it?' *IMF Working Paper*, WP/03/70, Washington, DC: International Monetary Fund.

Acton, Lord (1877/1967) 'The history of freedom in antiquity', in William H. McNeill (ed.) *Lord Acton: Essays in the Liberal Interpretation of History*, Chicago: The University of Chicago Press, pp. 243–70.

Ambrosius, Gerold (2005) *Regulativer Wettbewerb und koordinative Standardisierung zwischen Staaten: Theoretische Annahmen und historische Beispiele*, Stuttgart.

Andersen, S.A. and Eliasson, K.A. (1991) 'European Community lobbying', *European Journal of Political Research*, 20, 173–87.

Aranson, Peter E. (1990) 'The European Economic Community: Lessons From America', *Journal des Economistes et des Etudes Humaines*, 1, 473–96.

Bartel, Ann P. and Thomas, Lacy Glenn (1985) 'Direct and indirect effects of regulation: A new look at OSHA's impact', *Journal of Law and Economics*, 28, 1–25.

—— (1987) 'Predation through regulation', *Journal of Law and Economics*, 30, 239–64.

Bernholz, Peter (1973) 'Die Machtkonkurrenz der Verbände im Rahmen des politischen Entscheidungssystems', in Hans-Karl Schneider and Christian Watrin (eds) 'Macht und ökonomisches Gesetz', *Schriften des Vereins für Socialpolitik*, 74/II, Berlin: Duncker & Humblot, pp. 859–81.

Bernholz, Peter and Breyer, Friedrich (1984) *Grundlagen der Politischen Ökonomie*, Tübingen: J.C.B. Mohr.

Bernholz, Peter, and Vaubel, Roland (eds) (2004) *Political Competition, Innovation and Growth in the History of Asian Civilizations*, Cheltenham: Elgar.

Bernholz, Peter, Streit, Manfred E. and Vaubel, Roland (eds) (1998) *Political Competition, Innovation and Growth: A Historical Analysis*, Berlin: Springer.

Bertola, G., Blau, F. and Kahn, L. (2004) 'Labour market institutions and demographic employment patterns', IZA Workshop on Wage Inequality, Technology and Institutions.

Besley, Timothy and Case, Anne (1995) 'Incumbent behaviour: vote seeking, tax setting, and yardstick competition', *American Economic Review*, 85, 25–45.

Boockmann, Bernhard and Vaubel, Roland (2005) The Theory of Raising Rivals' Costs and Evidence from the International Labour Organization, University of Mannheim, mimeo.

Botero, Juan C., Djankov, S., La Porta, R., Lopez-de-Silanes, F. and Shleifer, A. (2004) 'The regulation of labour', *Quarterly Journal of Economics*, 118, 1339–82.

Crain, W. Mark and McCormick, Robert E. (1984) 'Regulators as interest groups', in James M. Buchanan and Gordon Tullock (eds) *The Theory of Public Choice-II*, Ann Arbor: The University of Michigan Press, pp. 287–304.

Cumming, Douglas J. and MacIntosh, Jeffrey G. (2000) 'The role of interjurisdictional competition in shaping Canadian corporate law', *International Review of Law and Economics*, 20, 141–86.

Dertouzos, James N. and Karoly, Lynn A. (1992) *Labor-Market Responses to Employer Liability*, Santa Monica, CA: The Rand Corporation.

—— (1993) 'Employment effects of worker protection: evidence from the United States', in Christoph F. Buechtemann (ed.) *Employment Security and Labor Market Behavior – Interdisciplinary Approaches and International Evidence*, Ithaca, NY: ILR Press, pp. 215–27.

Federalist Papers (1787/1987) edited by I. Kramnick, Middlesex: Penguin.

Fishback, Price V. (2005) 'The Irony of Reform: Did large employers subvert workplace safety reform, 1869 to 1930?' *NBER Working Paper*, 11058, Cambridge, MA: National Bureau of Economic Research.

Gray, Virginia (1994) 'Competition, emulation and policy innovation', in Lawrence C. Dodd and Calvin Jillson (eds) *New Perspectives on American Politics*, Washington, DC: Congressional Quarterly Inc.

Green, David A. and Harrison, Kathryn (2005) *Racing to the Middle: Minimum Wage Setting and Standards of Fairness*, University of British Columbia, mimeo.

Hayek, Friedrich A. von (1960) *The Constitution of Liberty*, London: Routledge and Kegan Paul.

Hirschman, Albert O. (1970) *Exit, Voice and Loyalty*, Cambridge, MA: Harvard University Press.

Kant, Immanuel (1981) 'Idea of a universal history from a cosmopolitan point of view', in Patrick Gardiner (ed.) *Theories of History*, New York: Free Press, pp. 22–34.

Koeniger, W., Leonardi, M. and Nunziata, L. (2004) 'Labour market institutions and wage inequality', Discussion paper, 1295, Institute for Labour Research (IZA): Bonn.

Laffont, Jean-Jacques and Martimort, David (1998) 'Transaction costs, institutional design and the separation of powers', *European Economic Review*, 42, 673–84.

Lee, Dwight R. (1985) 'Reverse revenue sharing: a modest proposal', *Public Choice*, 45: 279–89.

Nollert, Michael (1996) 'Verbandliche Interessenvertretung in der Europäischen Union: Einflussressourcen und faktische Einflussnahme', *Zeitschrift für Politikwissenschaft*, 6, 647–67.

Norton, R.D. (1986) 'Industrial policy and American renewal', *Journal of Economic Literature*, 24, 1–40.

Olson, Mancur (1966) *The Logic of Collective Action*, Cambridge, Mass.: Harvard University Press.

Rodrik, Dani (1998) 'Why do more open economies have bigger governments?' *Journal of Political Economy*, 106, 997–1032.

Salmon, Pierre (1987) 'Decentralisation as an incentive scheme', *Oxford Review of Economic Policy*, 3, 24–43.

Shleifer, Andrei (1985) 'A theory of yardstick competition', *Rand Journal of Economics*, 16, 319–27.

Stigler, George J. (1970) 'Director's law of public income redistribution', *Journal of Law and Economics*, 13, 1–10.

—— (1971) 'The theory of economic regulation', *Bell Journal of Economics and Management Science*, 2, 3–21.

Tiebout, Charles M. (1956) 'A pure theory of local expenditures', *Journal of Political Economy*, 64, 416–24.

Vaubel, Roland (1986) 'A public choice approach to international organization', *Public Choice*, 51, 39–58.

—— (1994) 'The political economy of centralization and the European Community', *Public Choice*, 81, 151–90.

Weber, Max (1923/1961) *General Economic History*, New York: Collier.

2 Politico-economic causes of labour regulation in the United States

Rent seeking, alliances, raising rivals' costs (even lowering one's own?) and interjurisdictional competition

John T. Addison

A common error in popular expressions of political economy is the presumption that all firms oppose . . . regulations because these edicts raise costs. The flaw in this presumption arises from an exclusive focus . . . on the 'direct effects' of regulation . . . (T)he often pronounced heterogeneity among firms [also] gives rise to . . . 'indirect effects' – the competitive advantages that arise from asymmetrical distributions of regulatory effect among different groups of firms and workers. It is extremely important to recognize that for many firms and workers the indirect effects of regulation can outweigh . . . the direct effects.

(Bartel and Thomas 1987: 239–40)

Our own research and experience with the issue of unjust dismissal indicate that employers and employer organizations have almost always opposed unjust-dismissal legislation. Except for the state of Montana, we know of no instances in which employers have taken the initiative to propose legislation in response to judicial decisions modifying the employment-at-will doctrine.

(Stieber and Block 1992: 792)

No other kind of labor legislation [as workers' compensation] gained such general acceptance in so brief a period in this country.

(Weiss 1935: 575)

Historically, supporters of unions . . . have favored the primacy of federal law and regulations over state and local laws or regulations. The success of the living wage movement in galvanizing local sentiment suggests that groups favorable to labor might do well to rethink their preferences for national politics . . . and consider the benefits of devolution of labor regulations to states and localities.

(Freeman 2005: 28)

Does anyone seriously believe that an efficient balance can be achieved through a political process? The flexibility to respond to the demands of market competition yields enormous benefits, but such benefits, because they tend to be diffused and delayed, have no organized constituency. So policies that restrict labor market flexibility create costs that are largely ignored politically. But these restrictions typically concentrate the benefits of security (protection from competition) on politically organized groups that will notice them and lobby hard for them, always in the name of fairness.

(Lee 1996: 103)

Introduction

In this chapter we discuss the political economy of labour regulation in the United States. As a practical matter, the subject has been neglected by labour economists who have almost exclusively focused on the *effects* of legislation. The determinants of regulation have tended only to be investigated in the context of potential omitted variables and simultaneous equations bias. The role of rent seeking in the political market place has rarely been carefully analysed in the area of labour regulation. Rather, the tendency has been to assert and at best to infer such influence. In the cases of unemployment insurance and workers' compensation, for example, the cross-subsidization involved – respectively, from low- to high-unemployment industries and from low- to high-accident industries – has been argued to create incentives for those so subsidized to engage the polity, underscored by the phenomenon of rational ignorance. Similarly, it has been conventional to attribute national legislation on minimum wages to the congressional majority of northern states which coalesced to suppress competition from the smaller number of southern states paying lower wages and which in turn voted against the Fair Labor Standards Act. This strategy of *raising rivals' costs* has of course almost invariably been laid at the door of organized labour for virtually all labour regulation. That is, organized labour has always and everywhere been credited with supporting labour legislation as a means of raising the costs of non-union labour and hence shifting demand in its favour (that is reducing competition for its jobs).

The US situation is necessarily complicated by the fact that much labour legislation is state-originated or -financed and administered. One of the strengths of federalism is said to be the opportunity it presents for the development of intergovernmental competition. The models of Tiebout (1956) and Oates and Schwab (1988) demonstrate the efficiency features of interjurisdictional competition, and a number of observers otherwise hostile to labour mandates see potential benefit in some such programmes, most notably workers' compensation (from a transaction costs perspective). The argument is that the absence of federal influence admits of substantial variation across states that can permit experimentation that over time reveals desirable and undesirable features, allowing the gradual evolution of the system (Bellante and Porter 1990: 673). By the same token, there are undoubtedly negative effects (spillovers) that need to be addressed and a potential role for government in holding the ring and monitoring competition among states and local governments. These issues have been well rehearsed in the taxation literature (see for example Altemeyer-Bartscher and Kuhn 2005; Wildasin 1989, 2004; Wilson 1986, 1999; Wilson and Wildasin 2004), but to my knowledge have largely escaped serious consideration in the labour regulation literature.

A further issue in labour regulation is the role of the common law. We will examine the view that legislation is a potential antidote in a federal system to the inefficiencies introduced by activist judiciaries. The issue here is the attenuation of a specific common law doctrine, but absent this there is also the basic issue of the costs of using the court system that we will address in the particular context of workers' compensation. But the idea that the courts have been more susceptible to capture than the legislature and that the switch to the latter at the beginning of the last century in the United States was an efficient response is left to others (see in particular Glaeser and Shleifer 2003), even if the notion of *differential subversion* is encountered in addressing the efficacy of state versus federal legislation. Nor for that matter do we elaborate on the role of the courts as a vehicle for restraining overarching legislation at state (and federal) level.[1]

At this stage it seems premature to seek a unified framework for evaluating labour regulation in the United States (but for a general approach, see Amable and Gatti 2004). Rather, we elect to provide information on several types of labour regulation at federal state and local level, each of which offers a different spin on regulatory behaviour. We first examine the political economy of the Occupational Safety Act and Health to show the scope that exists for raising the costs of rivals by engaging the polity. We then turn to the case of unjust dismissals to show how regulation might be a corrective to the actions of interventionist judiciaries. Next, we tackle right-to-work legislation as an example of a partial political escape route affixed to national legislation. Only then do we consider state-level safety regulation and workers' compensation, which arena offers the richest literature on the political economy of regulation and formal evidence on the use of regulation to raise rivals' costs. Finally, we take a look at living wage ordinances and prevailing wages to update the minimum wage argument and identify the union 'interest'. In a concluding section, we draw together the threads of the preceding arguments.

Themes in labour regulation

The scope for raising rivals' costs: the case of OSHA

Perhaps the best estimates of the net benefits to (some) firms and workers[2] of labour regulation are provided by Bartel and Thomas (1985, 1987) in the context of Occupational Safety and Health Administration (OSHA) regulations. The authors use the term 'predation' to describe the actions of these interest groups. We focus here on the authors' analysis of the direct and indirect effects of complying with OSHA regulations, as well as Environmental Protection Agency

(EPA) pollution abatement determinations.[3] Recalling the first of our opening quotations, the direct effects of regulation are the partial equilibrium effects of workplace safety laws on individual firms and persons. The indirect effects stem from compliance asymmetries and enforcement asymmetries. Compliance asymmetries stem from economies of scale (smaller firms experience a larger unit-cost effect) and plant age, while enforcement asymmetries refer to regulations that are 'systematically skewed' against particular groups of firms or workers. In each case, the authors have strong priors. The authors contend that there are strong economies of scale for compliance with OSHA regulations, and also that plants located in northern and midwestern states by virtue of their age would have higher compliance costs were the regulations evenly enforced (their own research pointing to regional enforcement asymmetries favouring these Frost-Belt firms, as well as more intensive enforcement against small and non-union firms).

Bartel and Thomas (1987) evaluate the effects of regulation on total industry rents, namely, workers' wages and the price cost margin. The authors approximate the compliance costs of OSHA by the dollar value of penalties assessed for violations of safety standards (some 90 per cent of the total) in 22 states, 1974–8.[4] For the wage equation, these compliance costs are divided by the number of workers, for the price–cost margin they are divided by the value of shipments. The other key independent variables are plant size (percentage of workers in plants with 250 or more employees), the percentage of industry employment that is in the Frost Belt, and the percentage of workers in the industry covered by a collective bargaining agreement. Each is interacted with the regulation variable(s). For the wage equation, the controls include several characteristics of the workforce, average establishment size, overtime hours, research and development expenditures and advertising expenditure per employee, the four-firm concentration ratio, the annual growth in shipments, and year dummies. The union variable is interacted with the regulation argument and with the two intangible capital measures to detect evidence of differential rent seeking. The price–cost margin equation additionally includes various proxies for expenses, the value of assets again in relation to sales, and the annual growth in materials cost. Here the large firm and Frost-Belt variables are interacted with the regulation variable (and unionism).

The direct effects of OSHA regulations are obtained simply by suppressing the interaction terms. For the price–cost margin (wages) these direct effects are sizeable and negative (positive). Allowing for indirect effects based on the heterogeneity of regulatory cost burdens, the interaction terms between the regulation variable and the large firm proxy and a Frost-Belt location are both positive and well determined, reflecting compliance and enforcement asymmetries. Also as expected, the advantage of larger firms and a Frost-Belt location is attenuated in the presence of unionism: estimated at mean coverage, unions gobble up almost one-half of these regulation-induced rents. Turning to the wage equation, the interaction terms are again as expected: the coefficients for the firm size and regional interaction terms are positive and statistically significant. The direct effects of regulation on wages are now negative and well determined, but there is no indication of successful union dissipation of advertising rents (as was indicated in the price–cost margin equation).

To determine whether predators gain on net, the authors estimate the relative importance of the direct effects and indirect effect of the regulations at their mean values (and mean values of the dependent variables). Estimates are provided for minimum, mean and maximum values of the large firm and Frost-Belt arguments.[5] For an industry with the maximum share of workers in establishments with at least 250 workers, the reported net gain in profits is 2.9 per cent; for an industry with the largest percentage of its workers in the Frost Belt the profits gain is 9.1 per cent. The wage gains for unionized workers in these two settings are 3.2 and 3.8 per cent, respectively.

The bottom line from this study of federal legislation is that three distinct groups gain from federal regulation. The logical inference is that they may be expected to support OSHA or EPA legislation actively and that the indirect effects of regulation are indicative of predation rather than innocuous by-products of the public pursuit of workplace safety (Bartel and Thomas 1987: 241).

Legislation as a corrective: the political compromise hypothesis

In an interesting discussion of unjust dismissal legislation in the United States at state level, Krueger (1991) argues that legislation is an antidote to the if not casuistic rulings of the American courts then certainly to the manner in which they have attenuated the common law (hire and fire) at-will principle. He seemingly accepts that the at-will doctrine would otherwise permit efficient transacting. Given the judicial innovations, however, there is scope for unjust dismissal legislation to clarify property rights to jobs and to reduce uncertainty or limit employer liability. He thus offers a second-best rationale for legislation.

His analysis proceeds at two levels. The first is a discussion of the origins of legislation in the one US state – Montana – to have adopted an unjust dismissal statute; the other is an analysis of legislative proposals in all state legislatures linked to the degree of attenuation of the at-will principle. The former treatment identifies inter alia the large awards given to those adjudged to have been wrongfully dismissed in Montana, as well as other states (see also Dertouzos *et al.* 1988). Attention shifts in the *ceteris paribus* analysis to broader developments and in particular the (up to) three types of exceptions to at-will recognized in 41 state courts – the public policy, implied contract and good faith exceptions – and the ten pieces of legislation that have been introduced in nine states, including Montana. The maintained hypothesis is that legislation can be expected to receive support from both sides of industry because the attenuation of at-will has produced uncertain and incomplete property rights to jobs and large transaction costs or highly variable awards in disputes over improper dismissals. Enter the *political compromise hypothesis*: unjust dismissal laws may be 'an acceptable compromise between limited employer liability and assumption of fault' (Krueger 1991: 653). The prediction is that legislation is more likely in states where exceptions have already been recognized by the courts.

Krueger provides logit regression estimates of the determinants of proposed legislation, 1981–8. In substitution for each (lagged) exception entered individually, in a final set of specifications he includes the total number of exceptions. Controls include the proportion of workers in a state who are union members, the proportion of Democrats in the state legislature, the proportion of state employment in manufacturing and the state unemployment rate. On average, recognition of the public policy exception in a given year increases the probability that a state legislature will propose an unjust dismissal statute in the following by 8.5 percentage points, while a good faith exception increases it by 6.7 percentage points and an implied contract exception by 2 percentage points (although the coefficient estimate on which this last estimate is based is poorly determined). For their part, the specifications using the total number of exceptions recognized in a state in a given year imply that each additional exception raises the probability of legislative innovation in the following year by approximately 5 percentage points. The coefficient estimates of all the other arguments are statistically insignificant. While arguing that laws may be an efficient alternative to an attenuated at-will doctrine, Krueger has to conclude that the threat to employers is not yet great enough to provoke sufficient support for proposed legislation to enter the statute books. One reason of course may be the heightened use of temporary or atypical workers not subject to the predations of the courts (see below).

Krueger's view has attracted controversy, most obviously because there is no attempt to model employer support. Another issue is whether the bills introduced into the nine state legislatures accurately portray employer support for legislation. Thus, for example, Stieber and Block (1992) argue that employers may have been reacting to other legislation that they had no hand in shaping and which arguably was more coercive. Krueger (1992: 797) counters that employers will be 'less resistant to' – or even reluctantly favour – legislation if the common law has been modified. In turn, this comment reveals the lingering imprecision of the argument. Why for example should the public policy exception be the seemingly most important exception? How costly has it proven in practice? And what were the differences between the four states in the sample recognizing all three exceptions – California, Connecticut, Montana and Nevada – that led just one of them to enact the proposed legislation?

The most interesting conclusion of Krueger's (1991: 659) political compromise model is that the 'threat to employers under the common law is not yet great enough in most states to provoke sufficient support for legislation'. As was hinted at earlier, one reason for this may be the growth in employment forms not subject in practice to judicial review, most notably temporary agency employment which has grown much faster than open-ended employment in the last three decades. Autor (2003) has recently examined the growth of the temporary help service (THS) industry between 1979 and 1995 and linked this to the erosion of the common law at-will principle. Using data the Census Bureau's County Business Patterns files and the ORG files of the Current Population Survey, he finds that THS employment is positively associated with the implied contract exception, but not to the other exceptions in his favoured fixed effects specification that also contains a set of state-specific time trends. This result, which is consistent with his priors,[6] is robust to additional controls such as labour force demographics and the percentage of the state workforce that is unionized. (Interestingly, the latter coefficient estimate is negative and highly significant, indicating that temporary employment grew less rapidly in states where unions declined less – given the decline in union density of more than one-third over the sample period – which is of course consistent with union opposition to THS employment.) The bottom line is the finding that the implied contract exception contributed about 500,000 additional jobs (or some 20 per cent) to the growth of THS employment. Independently, slower rates of union decline added to this total.

In Krueger (1991) the exceptions to at-will are taken to be exogenous. In a subsequent study of the state employment effects of these legal incursions, 1980–7, Dertouzos and Karoly (1992, 1993) argue that the probability of having one of the wrongful dismissal doctrines is strongly related with a number of state characteristics. Their instruments are whether a state had a right-to-work (RTW) law (see below), whether it had a Republican governor, the level and change in union density, the change in unemployment, the percentage of neighbouring states recognizing a similar exception, the percentage change in lawyers per capita, and year dummies. They find that right-to-work states and those with a Republican governor (indicative of a conservative attitude toward labour) are less likely to have either a tort-based or contract-based exception, while the converse is true for the degree of unionization variable. There is also some evidence of spillover or *yardstick competition*: the higher the fraction of neighbouring states that have recognized the respective doctrine, the more likely is the state to have the doctrine. The effect of the other instruments is either mixed or statistically insignificant.

Dertouzos and Karoly model the determinants of the exceptions to at-will in an attempt to provide unbiased estimates of their employment effects, since they argue there is simultaneous determination of the employment and the legal environment. Having instrumented the doctrine/remedy, the authors use the predicted values in place of the actual doctrines/remedy in the employment equation. Their principal finding is that aggregate employment is on average 2.9 (1.8) per cent lower following a state's recognition of tort (contractual) damages for wrongful termination in a fixed effect model in which the regressors include gross state product and the growth in gross state product. The crucial issues here as elsewhere are that the instrument should have a direct causal impact on the exception to at-will and no effect on the outcome indicator other than through its influence on the at-will exception. As noted by Autor *et al.* (2001: 33–5), two of the variables selected as instruments (court activities in neighbouring states and the presence of a right to work law) have a substantial regional component relating to the south (the former negatively and the latter positively). Since the south has grown persistently faster than other US regions since 1930, there is a correlation between the two instruments and pre-existing growth rates which has the effect of biasing the results toward finding that wrongful discharge laws lower employment. Accordingly, the appropriate estimation strategy is to give each state its own time trend. In their replication of the Dertouzos and Karoly model including a linear state trend, Autor *et al.* (2001, Table 18) fail to obtain statistically significant coefficient estimates for the instrumented wrongful-termination doctrines.

Nevertheless, the bottom line is that there is evidence of an employment cost to this form of employment protection, even if on the basis of Autor *et al.*'s study this is less than suggested by Dertouzos and Karoly and applicable to an exception found to be statistically insignificant in Krueger's logit analysis of statutory innovations.[7] Accordingly, the political compromise model might still have legs in the context of the attenuation of employment at will, and the absence of actual legislation reflects the level-of-costs argument advanced by its proponent.

Right-to-work legislation

The 1935 National Labor Relations Act (NLRA) required employers to bargain in good faith with unions that represented a majority of their employees, and made it illegal for employers to impede their employees' right to organize. Further, section 8(c) of the NLRA allowed employer–union agreements requiring union membership as a condition of employment. The 1947 Labor–Management Relations Act (Taft–Hartley), which restricted some aspects of union activity (by identifying unfair labour practices on the part of unions), still permitted union (if not closed) shops but unequivocally authorized states to adopt right-to-work laws prohibiting these arrangements under section 14(b). As a matter of fact, 12 states had statutes prohibiting at least some forms of compulsory unionism prior to Taft–Hartley, so that the main technical legal effect of this section was to remove the possibility for unions to challenge right-to-work laws in court on grounds of federal supremacy.

Atypically, the determinants of right-to-work laws have been somewhat studied in the labour economics literature. But the purpose is again indirect: to obtain unbiased estimates of the effects of the law on several outcome indicators. Chief among these has been union membership, hypothesized to be reduced in the presence of right-to-work laws either by reason of increased union organizing and maintenance costs (as union shops cannot be used to curb free riding), or because of reduced bargaining power (stemming from the lack of universal membership within the bargaining unit) leading to reduced benefits from unionism and a long-run decline in membership. To the extent that right-to-work laws mirror existing but unobserved tastes for unionism and the extent of unionism, there is both an omitted variables problem and a simultaneous equations bias. The effects literature has therefore sought in often ingenious ways to control for the non-random presence of right-to-work laws (for surveys, see Moore and Newman 1985; Moore 1998).

Variables in the right-to-work equation have tended to reflect the simple view that employers favour and unions oppose such legislation. Union density is found to have a strongly negative impact on the likelihood that a state has a right-to-work law, although distinct employer arguments do not seem to have been deployed. Other variables have included economic development (poor states tend to adopt RTW laws to promote growth), degree of urbanization or population density (higher values for both of which are presumed to indicate 'collectivist views' facilitating the passage of legislation), and the proportion of the workforce that is female (higher shares are supposed for various reasons – tastes, labour force attachment and job composition grounds – to favour right-to-work laws).

After taking the taste effects into account or treating the right-to-work status of states as endogenous, the point effects of the laws are often poorly determined. The same appears to be true of fixed-effect and disequilibrium models as well. One exception is Ellwood and Fine's (1987) fixed effect stock-adjustment model which suggests that right-to-work laws have a sizeable initial effect on organizing success that decays through time. And in several more recent studies this support for the notion that right-to-work laws may have real and not simply symbolic effects has gained ground somewhat (see below).

Interestingly, Ellwood and Fine also report that in the period before passage of a right-to-work law, union organizing activity is not depressed but is rather somewhat above average. They speculate that such laws may even be passed when unions are becoming stronger. Not dissimilar reasoning can be deployed to explain Taft–Hartley at the national level. That is, the unprecedented wave of strikes in the winter of 1945 and the first half of 1946, coupled with evidence of widespread union racketeering, may have brought about a consensus that the 1935 Act had been too one sided. On this view, Taft–Hartley went some way to even the scales (Baird 1998: 482).

A similar line of reasoning also surfaces in an interesting case study of right-to-work campaigns in Louisiana in the 1940s, 1950s and 1970s by Canak and Miller (1990), who focus on the involvement of business. The authors frame their study as a test of whether the two sides of industry are always in opposition or whether there is evidence of an historical accord between big business and labour. They conclude that typically both large and small businesses oppose unions, but that some companies, again from both segments, mute their opposition when they perceive that unions are capable of effective retaliation. The link with the previous argument resides in Canak and Miller's contention that union organizing drives mobilized anti-labour organizations in each of the three decades examined. In the 1940s and 1970s larger companies in Louisiana played a public role in organizing and financing right-to-work campaigns. Their opposition became sotto voce in the 1950s, which new-found reticence the authors ascribe to pragmatic necessity: 'The dominant [postwar] position of American business ... made it possible to enjoy fast growth and high profits. They feared business interruptions more than high wages and, therefore, avoided public support for RTW so as not to foster conflict with their unionized workers' (Canak and Miller, 1990: 264). What made the actions of business successful were inter-union divisions and, ultimately, international competition *and* redistricting. The actions in question are, sequentially, the passage of laws restricting union strikes activity, the passage of right-to-work legislation in 1954 and its repeal in 1956, and a new-right-to-work law in 1976.

We noted earlier that the modern literature points to there being some independent impact of right-to-work laws after all – although this is true for some measured outcomes (namely, union membership and union organizing) and not others (wages). The large sums spent by business interests in seeking such legislation, or resisting its repeal, would seem to indicate that rolling back union security has positive financial implications. A recent events study of shareholder wealth in response to the passage of the 1976 Louisiana law and a right-to-work law passed in Idaho in 1985 finds that the cumulative effect of enacting these laws was to increase the stock value of (the sample of 23) Louisiana firms by 2.2 to 9.5 per cent and that of (12) leading Idaho firms by 2.4 to 2.9 per cent (Abraham and Voos 2000).[8] This study offers support for the view that right-to-work laws do matter, although it remains possible in both cases that the political debate helped shape public opinion against unions if not simply reflecting public opinion.

Currently, with the passage of Oklahoma's law in 2001, some 22 states have right-to-work laws. Two-thirds of the laws were passed in the 1940s and 1950s in the immediate wake of Taft–Hartley. Equally, a large number of states had restrictions on union security prior to the Act, under state rules and judge-made law, so the early adoption of legislation was less of a sea change than might appear. Although sentiment in Congress now probably favours legislation, practicalities rule this out. Accordingly, the innovations at state level will have to substitute for national right-to-work legislation. To quote Baird (1998: 491): 'The right-to-work battle will continue to be fought in the states, one state at a time, again and again'.

The case of workplace safety reform and workers' compensation

Some of the most interesting work on the political economy of regulation has documented the course of state-level safety regulation in mining and manufacturing, and the related reform of workers' compensation, introduced well in advance of the New Deal legislation.[9] This literature identifies the circumstances where employers favoured legislation to raise rivals' costs, but more generally pays close attention to the bargaining process between employers and workers.[10] We examine safety regulation and workers' compensation in turn.

Workplace safety legislation

The pioneering study is Fishback's (2005) analysis of the role of large firms in influencing safety regulations in coal mines and factories, 1869–1930. He characterizes their strategies as either defensive (either opposing regulation outright or limiting the breadth of regulation), or predatory or subversive (raising rivals' costs). His focus is primarily on safety regulations rather than workers' compensation per se. (Fishback and Kantor 1995, 1996, 1998 and 2000 focus exclusively on workers' compensation which, as we shall see, is depicted as a 'win-win' situation for large firms, unions and political reform groups, if not the insurance industry.) The strategies of large employers (establishments with 500 or more employees) are inferred to differ as between branches. It is expected that a strategy of raising rivals' costs will be associated with earlier adoption of state laws, wider regulation and with more resources devoted to policing the regulations; and conversely for defensive strategies.

For manufacturing, he considers the determinants of the introduction of labour administrations (with and without coercive power) and factory inspectorates (to enforce the regulations). For coal mining, he considers the determinants of the introduction of coal mine safety laws, a regulation index based on a count of the number of mine regulations introduced, and the inspection budget.

The methodology for *manufacturing* is a Weibull hazard specification with time-varying regressors. The goal is therefore to address the timing of labour administration and factory inspectorate innovations. Apart from the proxy for large firms (average employment size), the regressors are manufacturing employment, either a union index (measuring the share of workers in manufacturing relative to the national average) or the number of union chapters, and a dummy for southern states. It is found that the hazard ratios are greater than unity for larger firms, consistent with earlier adoption. Specifically, a one standard deviation increase in firm size is associated with a 31 (28) per cent increase in the conditional probability of adopting some form of labour administration (factory inspectorate). Fishback argues that this finding is *inconsistent* with the view that large firms sought to obstruct legislation. The union hazard ratios are both mixed and poorly determined, so that it is difficult to conclude that they either contributed to or were opposed to legislation. One interpretation, and that favoured by Fishback, is that unions were probably more interested in building up their organizational strength to obtain influence than to engage the polity.

Opposite results are obtained for *coal mining* in regressions estimated over a reduced number of states (with bituminous coal production). That is, larger mines are not associated with earlier adoption of coal safety legislation. This time, however, the union 'effect' exceeds unity and is statistically significant at conventional levels. Since the former result might indicate that '... larger mines were indifferent to coal regulations or that they were unsuccessful in staving off the efforts of reformers' (p. 19), Fishback also estimates OLS and state and year fixed effect models of the determinants of the size of the inspection budget per coal worker and a coal mining law index capturing the reach of legislation. The size of mine argument is negatively associated with each outcome indicator. Union effects are measured by the share of the workforce in the United Mineworkers and are weak throughout, a result that might hint at inadequate inspections and (as before) induced self-reliance to effect change. Fishback concludes that taken in the round his results for mining indicate that larger employers were successful in limiting the reach of legislation and in reducing inspection budgets.

At issue of course is why employers adopted a defensive strategy in one sector but not in the other. Fishback's answer exploits the disparate nature of manufacturing vis-à-vis mining (such that a common set of laws may have left many parts of the manufacturing sector unaffected); the more adversarial nature of industrial relations in coal mining, coupled with the fact that the reform proposals emanated largely from organized labour; and the virtual absence of women in coal mining (it being easier to 'sell' regulation for women and harder to obstruct regulation).

Workers' compensation

State workers' compensation plans provide for employer-mandated no-fault insurance covering workplace injuries, coupled with limits on liability from lawsuits. The passage of workers' compensation laws in several states during the 1910s constituted one of the earliest and most important government interventions in the workplace. Currently, workers' compensation is compulsory in all but three states (New Jersey, South Carolina and Texas).[11] Workers are eligible for medical and partial indemnity (lost wage) benefits when disabled by job-related injury or illness. Employers are liable regardless of fault but may dispute the severity of an injury or illness or challenge whether it is work related. Workers' compensation costs are nominally paid through employer payroll taxes (but see below). A few states require that employers insure through a state-operated insurance system. Many states operate a state system but permit insurance through private insurance companies or self-insurance. (The system exhibits close to full experience rating in the case of larger firms.)

Prior to workers' compensation a system of common law negligence liability obtained. Employers were obligated to exercise 'due care' in protecting their workers against hazards at the workplace. Employees bore the burden of proof, however, and had to demonstrate that the employer's negligence was the cause of the injury. A negligent employer might nevertheless rely on one of three legal escape routes, including contributory negligence.

The change from negligence liability to a no-fault system is well described by Fishback and Kantor (2000). They give chapter and verse on the high transactions costs (in money and uncertainty) to employers of using the courts and describe how 25–40 per cent of any compensation awarded to employees might be swallowed up in legal fees. Accordingly, they identify a broad consensus favouring reform and describe the outcome as a win-win situation – for all but trial lawyers. Disputation was over the details: state-run versus private insurance and the level of indemnity benefits. In the former area, organized labour lined up against the insurance companies (employers offered mixed support for a state-run insurance fund); in the latter organized labour and large employers were in obvious contention (but see immediately below). The outcomes were determined by variations in the political strength of these groups (see also Fishback and Kantor 1996).

Additional insight into employer support for workers' compensation (and the speed with which the laws were enacted across most states) can be gleaned from an analysis of wages. Fishback and Kantor (1995) contend that although expected injury compensation rose considerably with the passage of the state laws – both as a result of more individuals receiving compensation and compensation levels that were considerably higher than under negligence liability – much or all of the employers' costs were shifted back onto employees. The authors construct three panels for relatively dangerous industries – coal mining (1911–22), lumber (1910–13, 1915, 1921 and 1923), and union contracts in the building trades (1907–13) – in each case regressing hourly earnings in a state on an index of expected injury benefits (computed both prior to and after the introduction of workers' compensation) and a fairly wide set of controls (product prices or demand index, output per man, unionization, strike activity and occupation dummies, etc). For coal mining the authors' fixed effect estimates suggest that workers not only paid for the sharply stepped increase in their expected benefits, but may also have fully paid the employers' costs of purchasing insurance to provide those benefits. In the lumber industry, there appears to have been a full wage offset. But in unionized business construction (and indeed unionized coal mining) the coefficient estimate for the expected benefits variable was statistically insignificant, indicating an absence of any downward adjustment. These results were broadly robust to specification and to sample (restricting the sample to states and years when workers' compensation was in effect). Fishback and Kantor (1995: 737) conclude: 'The presence of wage offsets for nonunion workers also helps solve one of the major puzzles in political economy of the passage of workers compensation [viz. the leadership taken by employer groups] ... Many employers may have supported the legislation in anticipation of passing a substantial portion of the costs onto their workers in the form of lower wages'.

Nevertheless, Fishback and Kantor (1998) also report that employers (while favouring workers' compensation) and unions feuded over the issue of benefit levels, noting that where they were unable to reach a compromise the introduction of workers' compensation was delayed for up to 15 years! One reason for this is the failure to observe wage offsets in union settings, noted earlier. Employers of unionized labour may then have had a strong incentive to minimize the size of injury benefits that they paid. Further, we have seen that the cost of insurance was not fully shifted back on to (non-union) workers outside of coal mining. Nor was this pass back instantaneous. In this later study, therefore, Fishback and Kantor focus attention on the determinants of their index of expected injury benefits, 1910–30. The key regressors are an index of the risk of accidents in manufacturing, an index of unionization in manufacturing, measures of the strength of farm and manufacturing interests, the proportions of large and small firms, and manufacturing value added per worker. In addition, as indicators of the 'political climate' the authors identify power shifts in the legislature, percentage of the presidential vote for a republican candidate and for a socialist candidate, and the presence of a workers' compensation bureaucracy (instrumented). One of the most important findings is that states with higher manufacturing risk had lower benefit levels. In turn, this suggests that employers in the most dangerous industries had considerable strength in state legislatures, and used this influence to keep their overall accident costs down. That said, greater union density in a state and the presence of a bureaucratic agency to administer the law (the alternative was through the court system) were each associated with higher expected benefits, *ceteris paribus*. There is also some indication in the authors' data that political party shifts in either one or both legislative chambers at state level were associated with higher benefit levels. But political attitudes as indexed through votes in national elections were unimportant in explaining benefits, which result the authors interpret as suggesting that the views of state-level political parties did not necessarily match those of their national-level parents. Fishback and Kantor supplement this analysis with case studies of the political battle over benefits in the states of Ohio, Minnesota and Missouri. These case studies offer a much more detailed investigation of the role of interest groups in shaping the final content of workers' compensation laws and the timing of those laws (see in particular the case of Missouri).

The bottom line with respect to both safety regulation and workers' compensation is that the bills that entered into law were 'more evolutionary than revolutionary' and the result of compromises (Fishback 1998: 760). The employer side had political clout and in order to secure legislation labour had in many instances to work with them or a subset of them. There was clearly no large-scale redistribution of income involved and even for unionized workers, where there is little evidence of wage offsets, employers may have made adjustments along other margins of the employment relationship. Efficiency may also have been served by workers' compensation. Risk-averse workers may have gained because of the difficulty of obtaining insurance privately under the prior system of negligence liability, while for the employer side savings in transaction costs were supplemented by the wage offsets. That said, we know of no study examining whether the variation in programmes across states has promoted an efficient evolution of the system. We do know that more recent changes in employers' costs of workers' compensation in the 1970s and 1980s have continued to be largely shifted to employees in lower wages (Gruber and Krueger 1990).

The surprising case of living wage ordinances

Living wage laws have been in operation in the United States since they were first introduced in Baltimore in 1994. Today around 100 cities, counties and school districts have such ordinances. They resemble minimum wage laws but differ in setting a higher wage (ranging from $8.25 to $13 per hour, compared with the national minimum wage of $5.15) that is most often fixed with reference to the poverty line ($8.70 for a family of four with a single full-time earner). That said, they are much more highly restricted, usually covering city contractors and, at one-quarter the frequency, companies receiving business assistance from the city.

Just as with minimum wages, most of the literature covers the *effects* of such regulation on the wage or poverty outcome, although Neumark (2001) explores the notion that municipal unions organize to pass living wage laws as a form of rent seeking. Focusing on the narrow coverage of the laws, Neumark argues that these 'other interests' (the municipal unions) raise the wages that contractors must pay and thereby reduce the incentives for cities to contract out work ordinarily done by municipal employees. (His maintained hypothesis is that if the goal of ordinances is poverty reduction, they should be more general wage floors; on which more below.) Neumark examines the wage and employment consequences of living wage laws in 19 cities. But first he seeks some prima facie evidence of union involvement. To this end, he first conducts a simple Internet search, looking for joint mention of living wages and the cities concerned (that is those with the ordinances) and next adds a union descriptor (beginning with the AFL-CIO). A large share of the former number of hits included the AFL-CIO, or a specific union; most were for two unions that play a prominent role in organizing local government workers: the American Federation of State, County and Municipal employees (AFSCME) and the Service Employees International Union (SEIU). In a final step, he looks for evidence of union advocacy for living wages in the material, and cites some such instances of involvement.

Neumark's *ceteris paribus* analysis uses quarterly data from the CPS ORG files from January 1996 through to December 2000. The match is Standard Metropolitan Statistical Area (SMSA) for cities, an imperfect fit since suburban residents may work in the city; it is local government employees for municipal workers, which is again an imperfect match as some individuals may work for units of government below state level. The sample is restricted to SMSA individuals aged 16–17 years. The dependent variables are (i) the share of unionized municipal workers in the city's labour force, and (ii) the wages of unionized municipal workers. It is expected that living wage laws reduce the incentive to contract out, thereby raising the city-level employment share of unionized municipal workers. This is dubbed a 'strong test' because the more obvious result may simply be an increase in union bargaining power, rather than in contracting behaviour. This leads to the second and weaker test, which is that this enhanced bargaining power only impacts wages. It is anticipated that markets for low-wage unionized workers – specifically, those earning less than the median wage – will be most impacted. The methodology is difference-in-differences. Formally, the right-hand-side variables are the higher of the federal or state minimum wage, and the city living wage, as well as the city and year (and quarter) dummies. All wage variables are in logs and are converted to hourly equivalents.

There is no evidence that the share of the workforce made up of unionized municipal workers – the strong test – is affected by the living wage, irrespective of whether or not a distinction is drawn between low-wage (that is below-median) unionized municipal workers and independent of the lags on the living wage and minimum wage arguments. However, for the weaker test, namely, that living wages will boost the wages of unionized municipal workers, there is evidence that living wages ordinances boost union pay both contemporaneously and with a four-quarter lag. For below-median unionized municipal workers, living wages exceeding the minimum wage by 30 per cent – which apparently is not uncommon (see also Adams and Neumark 2005a, Table 1) – would have the effect of raising the wages of union workers by around 4.5 per cent. It is reported that living wages do not influence the earnings of 'municipal worker groups' for whom they are not expected to apply (for example teachers and police), which gives us some confidence in the prior results, and also that the positive earnings effect on union wages holds for the centre of the wage distribution but not the extremes (substituting percentiles from the 30th to the 90th for the median), suggesting some fragility of the wage result.[12]

Further, case studies of living wage ordinances in Los Angeles, San Jose, Oakland and San Diego by Zabin and Martin (1999) call into question the test used by Neumark (2001), while offering some political insights. In the first place, the authors see the narrow scope of living wage ordinances as strategic – helping guarantee success – and as providing a basis for expansion from service contractors through to recipients of direct subsidies, loans and or tax breaks through to holders of public leases and different agencies (port authorities, airports, redevelopment agencies and other local government bodies), and product suppliers. The inevitability of gradualness – a phased extension of coverage – is necessitated by the 'fragmentation of local government and the sheer number of public funding streams in an urban economy' (p. 31). The union role is also perceived very differently from Neumark: unions are directly tied to the effectiveness of the ordinances. Living wage laws are either targeted to cover groups that are likely to be organized or have recently been organized. Ordinances are also linked to related laws that help the climate for unionism such as labour peace laws. So the regulations are seen as structured to support union organizing. Next, the case studies link the success of living wage campaigns to inclusive coalitions of unions and community organizations (after admittedly fractious relationships in the 1960s and 1970s). Low-income peoples' organizations and unions are said to be now organizing the same communities, and labour-community coalitions are portrayed as instrumental to the formulation and passage of living wage ordinances. Links to national associations on each side of the coalition and integration of platforms, preferably in hybrid organizations, are also identified as important ingredients of success. Finally, living wage ordinances have to be rooted in a broader 'growth with equity' agenda, encompassing economic justice, high road competition and redevelopment or industry clusters.

Subsequent analysis has focused a little more on the political dimension. We noted earlier the importance of the involvement of a variety of organizations or coalition building to the passage of living wage laws. Luce (2005) reports that the involvement of the parties also carries over to the enforcement of the ordinances: implementation is weaker (less worker monitoring and more firm waivers) when left solely to city administrators. Stronger enforcement is duly reflected in stronger wage effects (see below). Interestingly, although seven states have acted to prevent cities from establishing their own minimum wages, there are no signs that the living wage movement is in retreat and the number of cities with living wage laws has continued to grow in the present decade at the same pace as in the 1990s. Freeman (2005: 17) links this success to non-worker organizations, arguing that '[living wage] campaigns succeed in part because citizens find it easier to engage about local economic issues than about abstract national economic issues, and in part because the campaigns can produce fine-tuned and economically efficient pay increases'. By the latter remark, he is refer-ring to the fact that most studies (at establishment level)[13] have found that living wages occasion little loss of employment despite the pay increases, so he regards them as efficient tools for redistribution. By the same token, he is con-cerned by the relatively small numbers of workers affected by living wages, and advocates that living wage campaigns 'scale up'. Interestingly, Freeman sees greater potential for reforms at local level than at the national level. The vehicle is to be 'creative use' of procurement policies (see next subsection), their poten-tial popularity being flagged by the success of living wage policies.

Finally, evidence with a bearing on some of the above arguments and inferen-tially on yardstick competition in living wages is contained in recent analysis of CPS data.[14] In a paper stimulated by the odd finding that living wage laws apply-ing to city contractors do not raise wages but that ordinances applying also to employers receiving business assistance (financial assistance, tax abatements, low interest loans and so on) from the city do have this effect,[15] Adams and Neumark (2005b) examine the contribution of their differential enforcement and geographical concentration to the wage (and employment) outcomes of living wage ordinances. The authors deploy monthly CPS data (for 1996 to 2002) to estimate wage and employment regressions for low-wage (bottom decile) workers across cities and over time, using a difference-in-differences methodol-ogy. Consistent with their earlier research (Neumark and Adams 2003a, 2003b), it is reported that the hourly wages (employment) of those in the bottom decile are positively (negatively) related to living wages where the ordinance *also* covers businesses receiving business assistance (i.e. does not just apply to city contractors). Furthermore, irrespective of coverage, the wage and employment differences between cities are increased when ordinances are accompanied by living wages in nearby cities and where living wages are more broadly enforced. But the stronger effects for business assistance ordinances than for contractor-only ordinances are not produced by differences in enforcement; rather, for wages at least, it is whether or not nearby cities have living wage laws that seemingly accounts for the result that business assistance ordinances have stronger effects than contractor-only ordinances. For employment, negative effects are amplified for both types of ordinance and they are substantial.

A postscript on prevailing wage laws

Prevailing wage laws at state level requiring construction workers on state-funded works projects be paid at levels prevailing for similar work in the geo-graphic area of the project largely postdate federal legislation in the form of the

1931 Davis–Bacon Act[16] (although eight states enacted wage laws between 1891 and 1923). As of 1969, 40 states had prevailing wage laws on the books.

Analysis of the effects of federal regulation on wages and construction costs confronts an identification problem – average wages in a location are themselves a function of the prevailing wage – so that research has shifted to exploit differences in state prevailing wage regulations (Thieblot 1986). The most recent research focuses on the nine states that *repealed* their prevailing wage laws between 1969 and 1993. Kessler and Katz (1999) compare wage outcomes in repeal and non-repeal states (excluding Minnesota which passed prevailing wage legislation in 1973) using a difference-in-differences methodology and individual data from the Census and the CPS. So the test is essentially the difference between the change over time in the relative blue-collar construction or non-construction wage in the two sets of states. It is reported that repeal is associated with a decline in the relative wages of construction workers of between 2.3 and 3.9 per cent. For union members, however, the relative wage premium on construction work is reduced by 5.9 percentage points, which effect increases to 11.2 percentage points after five years. Even if the immediate outcome gives the better estimate of the equilibrium effect of repeal, the outcome is still major, the union premium being in the order of 20 per cent.

This careful study provides insights into the opposition of unions to repeal of state prevailing laws and an indication of the rent seeking that is involved in their passage. What is lacking is an equally careful analysis of the political economy of repeal.

Conclusions

Many of the labour laws that we now have on the books were adopted prior to the New Deal: limits on child labour, limits on working time, safety legislation and workers' compensation laws. As we have seen, the causes of some of these early pieces of legislation at state level have been analysed and with them the bargaining process between employers and workers as filtered through state-level politics. Interestingly, we have far less information on the political economy of national labour mandates, since the modern preoccupation has been to analyse the *effects* of legislation. Viewed from this imperative, the causes of mandates have only been examined in the interests of obtaining unbiased estimates of their consequences. Auxiliary equations apart, the political involvement of the labour and product market actors have been adduced from the payoffs to them of legislation. Another line of inquiry has been opened up by the actions of the courts. At the broadest level, legislation has been seen as a broad antidote to the 'subversion' of the courts. Less dramatically, individual pieces of legislation have been sponsored because of the high transactions costs of using the courts. On the other hand, recourse to the law has also been seen as a remedy for overarching state and local legislation.

In reviewing the effects of US labour legislation, Addison and Hirsch (1997: 166) conclude that workplace mandates may have rather muted benefits and costs, noting that the effects of mandates are mitigated in part through market escape routes, the shifting of costs and the mobility of resources, and in part via a political process that shows some sensitivity to both benefits and costs. Our discussion of rent seeking, codification, coalitions, judicial review and interjurisdictional competition gives some credence to this position, without of course claiming that the regulations generally work well or consistently for employers and employees (or even regulators). As a case in point, yardstick competition may have very different welfare implications in the area of labour regulation than it does for product market regulation.

Lest our limited discussion of national mandates still convey the impression that the US labour market is unregulated at the federal level, however, let us dispel that notion by observing that by the mid-1990s the US Department of Labor was administering some 180 regulatory programmes covering labour standards, civil rights, occupational health and safety, labour relations, and hiring and separation decisions (see Commission on the Future of Worker–Management Relations 1994a, b). At the time of the New Deal experiment the corresponding frequency was 18 and it was still only 40 as late as 1960.

Thus, it is no exaggeration to say that there has been a rapidly expanding role of government and the courts in providing workers with rights and protections in the workplace. This development has moreover coincided with a marked *decline* in unionism. The feedback from laws to reduced unionism is difficult to pin down, but it seems inevitable that protection against various forms of discrimination, and legislation on worker safety, advance notice of plant closings, and mandated family leave have contributed to the reduced demand for unionism. In much of our discussion the maintained hypothesis has been that high union density strengthens the political influence of unions on legislation. Now the argument is the other side of the coin: further reductions in unionism are likely to yield increased reliance on government to define rights at the workplace.

These prospects engender little enthusiasm because it is widely accepted that the system of employment protection is costly, intrusive and overly litigious. Reform proposals are in the wing, centring on notions of conditional deregulation and so-called market-based systems of enterprise rights (see, respectively, Levine 1997 and Edwards 1997). Since these proposals seek to deliver a balance between flexibility or productivity and fairness, they inevitably return us to Dwight Lee's (1996: 103) admonition: 'Does anyone seriously believe that an efficient balance can be achieved through a political process?' But we are not speaking of the first best and arguably heightened globalization will play an important role in the process.

By the same token, it may now be easier or cheaper for unions and their supporters to engage state legislatures than Congress. We saw some indication of this in our discussion of living wage laws. Indeed, Richard Freeman (2005: 28) exhorts unions to 'rethink their preference for national politics and regulation' and 'consider the benefits of devolution of labour regulations to states and localities' and, more concretely, to scale up living wage campaigns. Any such redirection may be expected to threaten or reverse the liberalization of superannuated legislation that we have detected at state level, beginning of course with prevailing wage legislation in construction.

Notes

1 Although it is as well to point out that the plethora of state bills seeking to restrict outsourcing (usually by banning the state from contracting with companies planning to employ offshore workers) would, if passed, likely succumb to legal challenge under the US constitution on the grounds that they violate the Foreign Commerce Clause (Art. 1, §8, cl. 3). This clause restricts the states' power to interfere with inter-state or foreign commerce. By the same token, even if never enacted into law, such bills may already have had a chilling effect on the growth of information technology outsourcing by local and state governments.
2 On the magnitude of *worker* rents in the regulated trucking and airline industries, see Hirsch and Macpherson (1998, 2000).
3 On the competing interests involved in environmental protection per se and the effects of EPA regulation on factor shares and the size distribution of firms, see Pashigian (1984, 1985).
4 As a practical matter, the authors restrict the effects of OSHA and EPA regulation to have the same proportional relationship within each equation. For the price–cost margin (wages), the former effect is roughly 9 (31) per cent of the latter.
5 To simplify the discussion, I have neglected the issue of import competition. This study does include a measure of import penetration and finds that firms facing strong competitive pressures from imports are badly hurt by regulation. Specifically, where the value of industry net imports to shipments is at its maximum value (40 per cent), the effect of regulation is to reduce profits by almost one-half (49 per cent).
6 Violations of the public policy and good faith doctrines are actionable irrespective of the identity of the employer, while staffing arrangements (such as temporary help) cannot be used to shield firms from civil rights compliance. So there are no advantages to temporary employment here. Only the implied contract exception offers relief in so far as THS employment is ipso facto temporary (other than for the line staff of the temporary employment agency itself).
7 The main part of Autor *et al.*'s (2001) study is devoted to the effect of the public policy, implied contract and good faith exceptions upon state employment and wages, using data from the CPS monthly files, 1978–99. Inconsistent with Krueger (1991), the authors find a statistically significant negative effect of the public policy exception on wages, suggesting that workers pay for the attenuation of at-will in one of the two categories deemed important by Krueger in generating proposals for an unjust dismissal statute. Consistent with Autor (2003), the authors find no reduction in wages associated with the implied contract exception and a small negative effect on employment (which adverse effect is strongest for less-educated males and younger workers).
8 For a review of studies examining the role of right-to-work laws in state industrial development, see Moore (1998: 460–3).
9 In addition to safety regulation and workers' compensation, states also successfully introduced legislation limiting the hours of children and women. The laws seemingly had little independent impact, the main influence behind observed reductions in hours being technology (for example Goldin 1990). In reviewing this literature, Fishback (1998) speculates that among the prime movers were those firms who had earlier most reduced their child labour and male-intensive industries respectively.
10 Progressive era reformers also figure in Fishback's model, and are depicted as seeking to impose reforms on larger employers.
11 Observe that even in these states most employers choose voluntary coverage so as to limit their liability.

12 Why the very lowest paid union workers are unaffected by the ordinances is something of a puzzle.
13 See the summary contained in Fairris and Reich (2005).
14 There is controversy over the use of CPS to measure living wage outcomes largely because it does not identify the actual beneficiaries of living wage campaigns (see Freeman 2005, fn. 15).
15 And also result in reduced employment and lower poverty (see Neumark and Adams 2003a, 2003b).
16 Stigler (1970) and Heller (1986) contend – but do not test the argument – that federal minimum wages introduced under the Federal Fair Labor Standards Act in 1938 were passed by the Congressional majority of northern states, wherein the envisaged minima were generally exceeded, so as to extinguish low-wage competition from the southern states who voted against the legislation. The raising rivals' costs argument is yet more transparent in the case of prevailing wage legislation. In justifying the first draft of the bill in 1927, Congressman Bacon stated:

> The Government is engaged in building in my district a Veteran's Bureau hospital ... Several New York contractors bid, and in their bids, of course, they had to take into consideration the high labor standards prevailing in the State of New York ... The bid, however, was let to a firm from Alabama who had brought several thousand non-union laborers from Alabama into Long Island, NY, into my district. They were herded onto this job, they were housed in shacks, they were paid a very low wage, and the work proceeded ... It seemed to me that the federal Government should not engage in construction work in any state and undermine the labor conditions and the labor wages in that State ... The least the federal government can do is comply with the local standards of wages and labor prevailing in the locality where the building construction is to take place.
>
> (US Congress 1927)

Bacon's proposal was eventually enacted into law in 1931, and it took another four years before the definition of the prevailing wage was determined. While we know of no formal analysis of the political economy of Davis-Bacon, the facts are that the regulations, and the manner of their enforcement, meant that wages were often set according to the union scale and that a 1935 amendment of the Act reduced the minimum contract amount covered to $2,000 (as sought by the union movement). More recent criticism of Davis–Bacon has centred on its purported discriminatory intent: on the facts that the Alabama construction workers in question were black (contested) and most major construction worker unions at that time excluded blacks (uncontested) (cf. Bernstein 1993 and Philips *et al.* 1995; see also Kessler and Katz 1999).

References

Abraham, Stephen E. and Voos, Paula B. (2000) 'Right-to-work laws: new evidence from the stock market', *Southern Economic Journal*, 67, 345–62.

Addison, John T. and Hirsch, Barry T. (1997) 'The economic effects of employment regulation: what are the limits?' in Bruce E. Kaufman (ed.) *Government Regulation of the Employment Relationship*, Madison, WI: Industrial Relations Research Association, pp. 125–78.

Adams, Scott and David Neumark (2005a) 'The effects of living wage laws: evidence from failed and derailed living wage campaigns', IZA Discussion Paper No. 1566, Bonn.

—— (2005b) 'When do living wages bite?' *Industrial Relations*, 44, 164–92.

Altemeyer-Bartscher, Martin and Kuhn, Thomas (2005) 'Incentive-compatible grants-in-aid mechanisms for federations with local tax competition and asymmetric information', unpublished paper, Chemnitz University of Technology.

Amable, Bruno and Gatti, Donatella (2004) 'The political economy of job protection and income distribution', IZA Discussion Paper No. 1404, Bonn.

Autor, David H. (2003) 'Outsourcing at will: the contribution of unjust dismisssal legislation to the growth of employment outsourcing', *Journal of Labor Economics*, 21, 1–42.

Autor, David H., Donahue III, John J. and Schwab, Stewart J. (2001) 'The costs of wrongful discharge laws', unpublished paper, Massachusetts Institute of Technology.

Baird, Charles W. (1998) 'Right to work before and after 14(b)', *Journal of Labor Research*, 19, 471–93.

Bartel, Ann P. and Thomas, Lacy Glenn (1985) 'Direct and indirect effects of regulation: a new look at OSHA's impact', *Journal of Law and Economics*, 1, 1–25.

—— (1987) 'Predation through regulation: the wage and profit effects of the Occupational Health Administration and the Environmental Protection Agency', *Journal of Law and Economics*, 30, 239–64.

Bellante, Don and Porter, Philip K. (1990) 'A subjectivist economic analysis of government-mandated employee benefits', *Harvard Journal of Law and Public Policy*, 13, 657–87.

Bernstein, David (1993) 'The Davis Bacon Act: let's bring Jim Crow to an end', Cato Briefing Paper No. 17, 18 January.

Canak, William and Miller, Berkeley (1990) 'Gumbo politics: unions, business and Louisiana Right-to-Work legislation', *Industrial and Labor Relations Review*, 43, 258–71.

Commission on the Future of Worker-Management Relations (1994a) *Fact Finding Report*, Washington, DC: US Department of Labor and US Department of Commerce.

—— (1994b) *Report and Recommendations*, Washington, DC: US Department of Labor and US Department of Commerce.

Dertouzos, James N. and Karoly, Lynn A. (1992) *Labor-Market Responses to Employer Liability*, Santa Monica, CA: The Rand Corporation.

—— (1993) 'Employment effects of worker protection: evidence from the United States', in Christoph F. Buechtemann (ed.) *Employment Security and Labor Market Behavior – Interdisciplinary Approaches and International Evidence*, Ithaca, NY: ILR Press, pp. 215–27.

Dertouzos, James N., Holland, Elaine and Ebener, Patricia (1998) 'The legal and economic consequences of wrongful termination', Rand Corporation document R-3602-ICJ, Santa Monica, CA: The Rand Corporation.

Edwards, Richard (1997) 'Alternative regulatory approaches to protecting employees' workplace rights', in Bruce E. Kaufman (ed.) *Government Regulation of the Employment Relationship*, Madison, WI: Industrial Relations Research Association, pp. 403–27.

Ellwood, David T. and Fine, Glenn (1987) 'The impact of Right-to-Work laws on union organizing', *Journal of Political Economy*, 95, 250–73.

Fairris, David and Reich, Michael (2005) 'The impacts of living wage policies: introduction to the special issue', *Industrial Relations*, 44, 1–13.

Fishback, Price V. (1998) 'Operations of "unfettered" labor markets: exit and voice in American labor markets at the turn of the century', *Journal of Economic Literature*, 36, 722–65.

—— (2005) 'The irony of reform: did large employers subvert workplace safety reform, 1869 to 1930?' NBER Working Paper No. 11058, Cambridge, MA: National Bureau of Economic Research.

Fishback, Price V. and Kantor, Shawn Everett (1995) 'Did workers pay for the passage of Workers' Compensation laws?' *Quarterly Journal of Economics*, 110, 713–42.

—— (1996) 'A prelude to the welfare state: compulsory state insurance and workers' Compensation in Minnesota, Ohio, and Washington, 1911–1919', *Journal of Economic History*, 56, 809–36.

—— (1998) 'The political economy of Workers' Compensation benefit levels, 1910–1930', *Explorations in Economic History*, 35, 109–39.

—— (2000) *A Prelude to the Welfare State: The Origins of Workers' Compensation*, Chicago, IL: University of Chicago Press.

Freeman, Richard B. (2005) 'Fighting for other folks' wages: the logic and illogic of living wage campaigns', *Industrial Relations*, 44, 14–31.

Glaeser, Edward L. and Shleifer, Andrei (2003) 'The rise of the regulatory state', *Journal of Economic Literature*, 41, 401–25.

Goldin, Claudia (1990) *Understanding the Gender Gap: An Economic History of Women*, New York: Oxford University Press.

Gruber, Jonathan and Krueger, Alan B. (1900) 'The incidence of mandated employer-provided insurance: lessons from workers' compensation insurance', NBER Working Paper No. 3557, Cambridge, MA: National Bureau of Economic Research.

Heller, Thomas (1986) 'Legal theory and the political economy of American federalism', in M. Caepelletti, M. Seccombe and J. Weiler (eds), *Integration through Law. Europe and the American Experience*, Berlin: Walter de Gruyter, pp. 254–317.

Hirsch, Barry T. and Macpherson, David A. (1998) 'Earnings and employment in trucking: deregulating a naturally competitive industry', in James Peoples (ed.) *Regulatory Reform and Labor Markets*, Norwell, MA: Kluwer Academic Publishing, pp. 61–112.

—— (2000) 'Earnings, rents, and compensation in the airline labor market', *Journal of Labor Economics*, 18, 125–55.

Kessler, Daniel P. and Katz, Lawrence F. (1999) 'Prevailing wage laws and construction labor markets', NBER Working Paper No. 7574, Cambridge, MA: National Bureau of Economic Research.

Krueger, Alan B. (1991) 'The evolution of unjust-dismissal legislation in the United States', *Industrial and Labor Relations Review*, 44, 644–60.

—— (1992) 'Reply by Alan B. Krueger', *Industrial and Labor Relations Review*, 45, 796–9.

Lee, Dwight (1996) 'European links and other odd connections – comment on Addison', *Journal of Labor Research*, 17, 101–3.

Levine, David I. (1997) 'They should solve their own problems: reinventing workplace regulation', in Bruce E. Kaufman (ed.) *Government Regulation of the Employment Relationship*, Madison, WI: Industrial Relations Research Association, pp. 475–97.

Luce, Stephanie (2005) 'The role of community involvement in implementing living wage ordinances', *Industrial Relations*, 44, 32–58.

Moore, William J. (1998) 'The determinants and effects of Right-to-Work laws: a review of the recent literature', *Journal of Labor Research*, 19, 445–69.

Moore, William J. and Newman, Robert J. (1985) 'The effects of Right-to-Work laws: a review of the literature', *Industrial and Labor Relations Review*, 38, 577–85.

Neumark, David (2001) 'Living wages: protection for or protection from low-wage workers?' NBER Working Paper No. 8393, Cambridge, MA: National Bureau of Economic Research.

Neumark, David and Adams, Scott (2003a) 'Detecting effects of living wage laws', *Industrial Relations*, 42, 531–64.

—— (2003b) 'Do living wages reduce urban poverty?' *Journal of Human Resources*, 38, 490–521.

Oates, Wallace E. and Schwab, Robert M. (1988) 'Economic competition among jurisdictions: efficiency enhancing or distortion inducing?' *Journal of Public Economics*, 35, 333–54.

Pashigian, B. Peter (1984) 'The effect of environmental regulation on optimal plant size and factors shares', *Journal of Law and Economics*, 27, 1–28.

—— (1985) 'Environmental protection: whose self-interests are being protected?' *Economic Inquiry*, 23, 551–84.

Philips, P., Mangum, G., Waitzman, N. and Yeagle, A. (1995) 'Losing ground: lessons from the repeal of nine 'little Davis–Bacon' Acts', unpublished paper, Department of Economics, University of Utah.

Stieber, Jack and Block, Richard N. (1992) 'Comment on Alan B. Krueger. The evolution of unjust-dismissal legislation in the United States', *Industrial and Labor Relations Review*, 45, 792–96.

Stigler, George J. (1970) 'Director's law of public income distribution', *Journal of Law and Economics*, 13, 1–10.

Thieblot, Armand J. (1986) *Prevailing Wage Legislation: The Davis–Bacon Act, State 'Little–Davis–Bacon' Acts, the Walsh–Healey Act, and the Service Contract Act*, Philadelphia, PA: University of Pennsylvania Research Unit.

Tiebout, Charles M. (1956) 'A pure theory of local expenditure', *Journal of Political Economy*, 64, 416–24.

Weiss, Harry (1935) 'Employers' liability and workmen's compensation', in John R. Commons (ed.) *History of Labor in the United States, 1896–1932*, New York: Augustus M. Kelley.

Wildasin, David E. (1989) 'Interjurisdictional capital mobility: fiscal externality and a corrective subsidy', *Journal of Urban Economics*, 25, 192–212.

—— (2004) 'Competitive fiscal structures', unpublished paper, University of Kentucky.

Wilson, John D. (1986) 'A theory of interregional tax competition', *Journal of Urban Economics*, 19, 296–315.

—— (1999) 'Theories of tax competition', *National Tax Journal*, 52, 269–304.

Wilson, John D. and Wildasin, David E. (2004) 'Capital tax competition: bane or boon', *Journal of Public Economics*, 88, 1065–91.

Zabin, Carol and Martin, Isaac (1999) 'Living wage campaigns in the economic policy arena: four case studies from California', unpublished paper, Center for Labor Research and Education, Institute of Industrial Relations, University of California, Berkeley.

COMMENT: INTERJURISDICTIONAL COMPETITION AND LABOUR MARKET REGULATION

Dennis C. Mueller

John Addison's interesting chapter describes the political origins of several types of labour market regulations in the United States. His account of the origins of these regulations and the differences across states, based on a thorough review of the existing literature, shows very clearly how effective interest groups in the United States have been in introducing legislation at the state level, or in some cases, blocking legislation. These findings are quite consistent with what we know from the public choice literature and particularly from the literature on rent seeking. Well-organized interest groups like labour unions are typically very effective at advancing the interests of their members.

The aim of the conference that led to this volume was to explore 'the effect of interjurisdictional competition on regulation.' Early on in his chapter, Addison gives the reader the impression that his chapter will shed light on this question when he states, 'One of the strengths of federalism is the opportunity it presents for the development of intergovernmental competition . . . issues have been well rehearsed in the taxation literature . . . but to my knowledge have largely escaped serious consideration in the labour regulation literature'. This reader interpreted this statement to imply that the chapter would fill this gap, but it did not. This is, I suspect, not so much a failure of the author as a lacuna in the literature. Those studying labour market regulations at the state level have simply not been interested in the question of whether interjurisdictional competition on regulation of labour markets has improved efficiency in the United States.

One result from the literature on labour market regulation that does suggest interjurisdictional competition exists pertains to the evidence of spillovers across states. 'The higher the fraction of neighbouring states that have recognized the respective doctrine [in this case an exception to at-will employment relations], the more likely is the state to have the doctrine'. Here we would appear to have a good example of the effects of 'yardstick competition' (Besley and Case 1995). Much of the discussion of yardstick competition has assumed that it is welfare enhancing. This is probably a reasonable assumption when the competition is over tax rates, as in the article by Besley and Case. Unfortunately, the assumption that yardstick competition enhances welfare is less tenable when it comes to labour market regulations. Many of these *reduce* the efficiency of the labour markets and are arguably welfare reducing. This observation leads to a more general point about the beneficial effects of interjurisdictional competition to which I now turn.

All collective decisions can be divided into two broad categories – those that affect allocative efficiency and those that bring about redistributions of income and wealth. The normative rational for the state is that it can increase the welfare of all of its citizens by improving the allocation of resources (providing public goods, correcting for externalities and so on), and by providing certain forms of redistribution in the form of social insurance programmes and rich-to-poor redistribution (Mueller 2003, Chapters 2, 3). The literature that assumes that interjurisdictional competition has positive effects on social welfare implicitly assumes that government activity is confined to these socially beneficial state activities. It typically begins by citing Tiebout (1956), Oates and Schwab (1988), as well as Besley and Case (1995), and several of the chapters in this volume begin in the same way. In the Tiebout model, local communities compete for highly mobile citizens by providing different bundles of public goods at different tax prices. This competition for citizens constrains each community to undertaking only those activities that can make everyone better off, like improvements in allocative efficiency. If redistribution takes place it must be of the 'Pareto optimal' type, where both the givers and the recipients are made better off from the redistribution (Hochman and Rodgers 1969). In equilibrium, each community contains people with identical preferences for public goods. Although the Tiebout model assumes that preferences are revealed by 'voting with the feet', rather than through a voice process, if a voice vote were taken once all communities are in equilibrium, the bundle of public goods quantities and taxes would receive unanimous support in each community. Oates and Schwab allow for both mobile firms and mobile citizens, but again obtain an equilibrium similar to that of Tiebout. In particular, firms are provided with public goods also, but have no incentive to move since they only pay taxes for the public services that they consume, that is, each community is constrained to using *benefit taxes*.

States and local communities in the United States use the simple majority rule, however, not the unanimity rule. Under the simple majority rule, collective choices can be expected to combine improvement in allocative efficiency with redistribution, or to involve pure redistribution (Mueller 2003, Ch. 5). Successful majorities will enrich themselves at the expense of minorities. Members of well-organized interest groups will enrich themselves at the expense of poorly organized interest groups or at the expense of those who are not organized at all.

These predictions are well supported in Addison's chapter. Labour market regulations redistribute the flow of income to union workers and in some cases to their employers.[1] The losers from labour market regulations vary depending on the form of regulation – consumers, tax payers, non-union workers, the unemployed. In none of the cases discussed can one claim that the regulations have clearly led to a more equitable distribution of wealth.

Once one recognizes that government actions can be both efficiency reducing and efficiency enhancing, the effects of interjurisdictional competition become more complicated. The predictions for Tiebout competition remain unchanged. No one will migrate to another community if the other community has policies like labour market regulations that will make her worse off. At the same time, some people might flee from communities that adopt such policies if they are not the beneficiaries from them. Thus, in a mobile world, states and local communities will be somewhat constrained in their choice of regulations to bring about redistributions of income and wealth.

The recognition that government actions can be both efficiency reducing and efficiency enhancing does have important implications, however, when it comes to interpreting the effects of yardstick competition. If one state introduces a labour market regulation, which benefits union workers but harms non-union workers and consumers, union leaders in a neighbouring state may be moved to demand similar legislation in their state. The beneficiaries of such regulations do not emphasize the fact that the regulation will redistribute income to themselves, of course, but claim that the regulation will eliminate some sort of market failure or correct some social injustice. The union leaders in the neighbouring state can observe what arguments were effective in the nearby state where the regulation was introduced, and advance the same arguments in their state *citing their neighbour as showing the way*. Thus, in a world in which democratic decisions are made using the simple majority rule, and well-organized interest groups can use the political process to advance the interests of their members over other members of the community, yardstick competition need not be welfare enhancing. Once one group of government workers convinces its legislature that it should introduce a 'living wage ordinance' to protect the government workers from 'unfair competition' from firms that *pay less than a living wage*, the stage is set for the spread of this pure redistribution policy with its attendant inefficiencies into other communities.

Here it is perhaps important to note a very significant difference between political competition and market competition. We expect inefficient firms to disappear in a healthy market economy and thus for competition to increase efficiency. Similarly, the yardstick competition story, as a predictor of increased *governmental* efficiency, assumes that voters recognize differences in efficiency across local communities and hold their elected officials responsible should their community be lagging its neighbours in terms of efficiency. But politicians can win votes not only by cutting taxes and providing public goods more efficiently, they can also win votes – and campaign contributions to buy votes – by redistributing income and wealth from some groups to others. Winning votes in this way may be easier than trying to increase governmental efficiency and cut taxes. If redistribution schemes are better vote getters than improvements in allocative efficiency, yardstick competition might simply take the form of having more and more policies, like labour market regulations, that are redistributive.

Returning to the question of interjurisdictional competition and labour market regulation, the key question we would like to ask is whether the United States' economy would be more efficient today if the states had been denied the power to regulate labour markets, and all labour market regulation had to be at the federal level? If we assume that it is 'cheaper' for an interest group to buy legislation from a state legislature than from the US Congress, then the first state-level regulations of labour markets would have been introduced before the beneficiaries of these regulations could have induced the US Congress to introduce them. The cumulative effect of all state-level regulations might then be worse for the efficiency of the US economy than it would have been had these regulations been confined to the federal level.

On the other hand, once the US Congress introduces a labour market regulation – like say the minimum wage – it exists everywhere. States which had not bowed to union pressure for a minimum wage would find that they now had to comply with the federal law. To the extent that labour unions and supportive interest groups can be expected to be eventually powerful enough to get legislation through Congress, having the states be responsible for most regulation in labour markets may be a way to avoid some of the inefficiencies of labour market regulations, at least in some parts of the United States. The work of Mancur Olson (1965) on interest groups suggests that it takes time for them to reach their full political power. One might thus expect that by now unions would have obtained their full strength at the national level, and some statistics that Addison presents toward the end of his chapter suggests this is so. He claims that the number of regulatory programmes administered by the US Labor Department has grown from 18, at the time of the New Deal, to 40 in 1960 to 180 by the mid-1990s. Unions and their affiliated interest groups appear to have done quite well at the federal level.

What are the implications for Europe of the US experience? Addison's chapter clearly demonstrates that interest groups have played a significant role in determining the amount and form of labour market regulation at the state level in the United States. Presumably, they have also influenced the amount of regulatory activity at the federal level. In a previous paper I have argued that interest groups are politically more powerful in Europe than they are in the United States, and that this helps to explain why the state sectors are so much larger in most European countries than in the United States, and in particular why the amount of redistributive transfers is so much larger in Europe (Mueller 2002). My reasoning went as follows. If an interest group wants to 'buy' some redistributive legislation in the United States, it must buy the votes of at least 218 members of the House, 51 Senators and, if it does not want the bill vetoed, it would be prudent to contribute something to the president. In Austria an interest group need only buy the votes of two parties to obtain legislation. Although it is reasonable to assume that a single Congressman's vote costs less than all of the votes of a party in one of Europe's governments, it is also reasonable to assume that a party's votes can be bought for less than the sum over all Congressmen and Senators needed to pass legislation in the United States.

When a member of Congress retires, or dies, or is defeated in an election, an interest group's investments in her are wiped out, and it must begin anew to invest in someone else. European parties seldom die and are rarely defeated in the sense that they win *no* seats in an election. Thus, once an interest group in Europe has established a clientele relationship with a party, it can probably maintain this relationship over time with fairly modest additional investments.

A third reason to expect interest groups to have more political influence in Europe stems from the multiparty nature of most European parliamentary systems. With parties strung out along a broader ideological spectrum in Europe than in the United States, it is easier for an interest group to find a party with an ideology coming fairly close to its own.

Finally, in corporatist countries like Austria, interest groups can be directly integrated into the process of drafting and passing legislation. In Austria some union leaders hold seats in the parliament purely because of their positions in the unions.

An implication of this argument is that labour interest groups should be more effective at gaining favourable regulations in Europe than they are in the United States, and this appears to be the case. The general consensus among labour market experts appears to be that labour markets are more regulated and inflexible in Europe than in the United States. An interesting exception here is the United Kingdom with a fairly unregulated and flexible labour market. The fact that the United Kingdom employs a similar kind of single-member-district representation to that of the United States lends further credence to the arguments given above about the relative strengths of interest groups in the United States and, multiparty, continental Europe.

Most regulations governing labour markets in the European Union exist at the member state level. Thus, the European Union would appear to be well-suited to achieving the beneficial effects of interjurisdictional competition in the area of labour market regulations. Europeans are far less mobile than Americans, however, in part no doubt because of the barriers to mobility caused by language differences. Thus, the voting-with-the-feet mechanism for bringing about interjurisdictional competition has not until now and is not very likely in the future to be important in preventing governments from introducing efficiency-destroying labour market regulations. The main burden for achieving interjurisdictional competition in Europe must be born by yardstick competition. Here again there is little evidence to date that it has been very effective. Both Ireland and the United Kingdom have less labour market regulation and more flexible labour markets than France, Germany, Spain and several other continental European countries. Both Ireland and the United Kingdom have grown faster and have substantially lower levels of unemployment in recent years than their continental European neighbours. Yet there is little evidence that these continental European countries are prepared to liberalize their labour markets, even though the bulk of their citizens would benefit from labour market deregulation. Any effort in the French, German and Spanish parliaments to introduce such liberalizing legislation would result in paralysing strikes by the leading labour unions. Large majorities of citizens who would benefit from labour market liberalization in their countries are held in hostage by a minority of well-organized labour unions willing to sacrifice the welfare of the larger community for their own interests.

Thus, as is the case in the United States, yardstick competition does not increase economic efficiency in areas where the actions of government are targeted on redistribution policies that benefit narrow, but politically powerful interests. Leaders of the Left in France urged their supporters to vote against the draft constitution on 29 May 2005 because, they claimed incorrectly, it would force France to accept some of the liberal economic policies that have been adopted in the United Kingdom. These opinion leaders do not appear to be looking sideways across the English Channel and seeing how much better the

Irish and British economies are performing than are those of France and its neighbours. Instead, they are looking backward toward the 1960s, when economic growth was brisk in continental Europe and it was possible to have both low unemployment and rigid labour markets. Alas, those days are gone.

Note

1 See, also the chapter by Siebert in this volume.

References

Besley, Timothy and Case, Anne (1995) 'Incumbent behavior: vote-seeking, tax-setting, and yardstick competition', *American Economic Review*, 85(1), 25–45.

Hochman, Harold M. and Rodgers, James D. (1969) 'Pareto optimal redistribution', *American Economic Review*, 59, 542–57.

Mueller, Dennis C. (2002) 'Interest groups, redistribution and the size of government', in Stanley L. Winer and Hirofumi Shibata (eds) *Political Economy and Public Finance*, Cheltenham, UK: Edward Elgar, pp. 123–44.

—— (2003) *Public Choice III*, Cambridge: Cambridge University Press.

Oates, Wallace E. and Schwab, Robert M. (1988) 'Economic competition among jurisdictions: efficiency enhancing or distortion inducing?' *Journal of Public Economics*, 35(3), 333–54.

Olson, Mancur Jr. (1965) *The Logic of Collective Action*, Cambridge, Mass.: Harvard University Press.

Tiebout, Charles M. (1956) 'A pure theory of local expenditures', *Journal of Political Economics*, 64, 416–24.

COMMENT: FOREIGN POLICY AND REGULATION

Gordon Tullock

It would be nice if countries could impose any regulation on their own trade and internal affairs without affecting foreigners. Unfortunately this is not true. Let me begin with a particularly clear example, which is also comic. In the United States we have laws prohibiting the import of things made by slave labour. In the 1920s some Russian refugees pointed out that the Soviet Union maintained a massive set of slave labour camps and that many of their products were sent to the United States. They then raised the problem of why we were permitting those imports.

It is not obvious why the American government found this a difficult programme, but they did. After some thought a customs inspector was formally commissioned to go to the Soviet Union and investigate whether they had slave labour. They could, of course, have saved a great deal of trouble by simply looking at the books in the average public library written by former inhabitants of the slave labour camps. I remember that somewhat later when I looked in a Rockford public library there was a full shelf of such books. I presume that some were fiction, but surely not all of them.

In any event, an official was appointed and applied for a visa in order to visit the Soviet Union and look at their production establishment in Siberia. The Soviet Union refused to issue the visa. The response of the American government was to decide that since they could not directly investigate they assumed the report as false and we did not refuse to accept importation of things produced by slave labour in the Soviet Union. So far as I know this was the only effort to ban the import of these slave labour products, and it failed completely.

I think in a way this is a good example of domestic regulations on foreign trade. We rarely in fact refuse to accept the import of things which have been produced under conditions which violate our regulations. Sometimes if our regulations have created monopolistic conditions in the United States the pressure groups which caused the regulations will also take action to prevent the import of things which violate those regulations.

Normally, of course, what the pressure group objects to are low prices on the imports, not the failure of the exporting country to enforce American laws. To take one example, sugar is very expensive in the United States. This is a result of a very successful pressure group composed of a very small group of producers of sugarcane in the United States. Sugarcane does not grow well in the United States, and it is possible to make sugar from other sources, but it is still true that we have a small very successful pressure group, located just across the straight from Cuba, which prevents imports. I should point out that although it is a massive inconvenience for Castro, the restrictions were in place long before his successful overthrow of the previous government.

Recently this slave labour prohibition has actually had some application. It has been alleged that the diamonds produced in Sierra Leone are produced by unfree labour. We have therefore refused to accept them as imports, although it is not obvious that the customs inspector looking at a diamond can tell whether it has or has not come from Sierra Leone. Perhaps De Beers assists us in enforcing this rule because it does have some monopoly benefits for them.

There are, however, some cases where regulations do in fact affect international trade. The US for example has a set of safety requirements for aircraft, and these would apply even if the aircraft was imported. I imagine Airbus pays careful attention to these rules. If different nations had not only different safety rules for aircraft, but ones that actually conflicted, it would indeed make international trade in aircraft more difficult. So far as I know this is a merely theoretical possibility rather than a real one. In the modern world, however, governments are accustomed to making very detailed regulations on things which are manufactured in their country or imported. I know of no careful study of the effect of these but I would think that the sum total would be quite sizeable. At the moment I am concerned with regulations which have what I would call respectable motives. They are genuine efforts to improve the quality of some products or services and not an effort to obtain monopoly gains.

There are, of course, cases where a monopolistically motivated regulation is disguised as a safety regulation. The ingenuity of pressure groups and rent seekers is almost infinite. We can feel confident that at least some regulations imposed allegedly for safety reasons actually protect a domestic industry. I know of no formal studies of this phenomenon but it is almost certainly true even if I cannot produce an example.

There is, however, one area where domestic regulations have a great effect on foreign countries. This is the restriction on banking and other forms of investment. In most countries banking is subject to very strict regulation as are other forms of capital investments and transfers. In general these regulations are an effort to avoid clever investors from saving money by not paying the full tax. But although this is the motive, in practice the regulations go much further.

There is also the desire to make use of such regulations to handicap or make impossible the type of trade which is objected to by a certain government. The United States, for example, as part of its effort to reduce the production and sale in the United States of certain drugs, attempts to prevent payment for such drugs going through the regular banking system. I have no idea how effective this is, but it surely leads to some annoying regulations. There are also rather extensive regulations intended to prevent evasion. These are designed pretty much for domestic reasons, but they clearly can cause difficulties for international trade.

There are also a large number of rather detailed regulations with respect to given products which are intended to promote their safety. I know of no specific examples, but I feel sure that many of these regulations have at least as large an effect on imports as they do on safety. Presumably the regulations are carefully surveyed by the rent-seeking organizations in Washington and also by the commercial attachés of various foreign countries in Washington. I do not actually know of any empirical evidence on this, but I suspect the net effect on trade is annoying but not major.

But let me consider the general problem of rent seeking. Suppose we have a King who is firmly secure on his throne. His sole objective in ruling is to maximize his income. The efficient way of doing this is high taxation, taxes so high that the population barely stays alive. He should not do anything which interferes with the efficiency of production which almost any rent-seeking regulation will do. It is not normally noticed but rent-seeking activities reduce the total taxpaying capacity of a nation. Thus our unscrupulous, selfish and intelligent King will not only not engage in rent seeking himself, he will also prevent all others from doing so. The King could have higher taxes and more expensive mistresses if he only wiped out the rent seeking.

Note that it is not only a King, a democracy in which all of the voters are perfectly intelligent would also prevent rent seeking. It might have a very severely discriminatory tax against the highly productive, but not enough to make them less productive. Rent seeking then, involves an error. A higher income could be gained by maximizing the efficiency of the economy and taxing it heavily. That is true whether we think of my tyrannical King or the efficient democracy which aims at maximizing individual incomes.

We would be better off if we could prevent rent seeking unless it happened that we personally gain more from any particular inefficient operation than the cost inflicted on us as part of the general society. This is an unlikely condition. It is not only unlikely for you and me, it would be unlikely for a perfect King.

Why then do we see rent seeking? The answer has to be some kind of inefficiency. The people who are in control of the society, if there are such people, would gain more by ideally efficient production and taxes designed to transfer wealth to them.

Since neither kingdoms nor democracies are perfectly intelligent, the existence of mistakes is not surprising. It should be kept in mind that not only perfect intelligence but a great diligence is necessary to prevent rent seeking from occurring in the government. The King would not have the time to look at every single piece of his government. But even if we assume that he is able to create an ideally efficient bureaucracy, it could not survey every single thing in the economy. The prospect that some people, including of course some real bureaucrats, look at their own benefit rather than at the benefit of the entire nation or the divine King is a necessary condition for large-scale rent seeking. It is not only necessary, it is very common, and it is difficult, if not impossible, to think of any way to change that.

We are then confronted with the situation in which the government will not be perfectly efficient not because the people involved in it are less than perfectly intelligent, although that is also true, but because their motives are not those which would lead them to attempt to produce perfect efficiency. Consider a perfect bureaucracy in which the only source of revenue for the bureaucrats was in their particular share of the total GNP. They would be motivated to maximize GNP, but it is very hard to think of any way one could organize this type of pay off.

To make it even more difficult, assume we have a democracy and inquire whether it can be so organized that no one could obtain revenue from any activity that reduced the total national product. Take the case of someone who competed with me, the above condition would be impossible unless it were true that the taxes derived more than is paid for the direct efficiency cost. This will be just as true if I were a courtier in Versailles as if I were merely a peasant somewhere.

We thus find that rent seeking is inefficient, but also that it is probably unavoidable. We can think of ways of making it less common. If the only taxes were non-graduated income taxes, if the only payments were always made to people who submitted competitive bids, per capita income would surely be higher than it is now. We will not be able truthfully to maximize our incomes by abolishing rent seeking. But there may be ways of reducing it and I hope that all economists will turn their minds to that modest but achievable goal.

3 Interjurisdictional competition in regulation

Evidence for Canada at the provincial level

François Vaillancourt

The purpose of this chapter is to present some evidence on the existence and effect of interjurisdictional competition on regulation at the provincial level for Canada. Given the pioneering nature of this work, we limit ourselves to evidence at the provincial level. The topic is of interest since Canada is one of the oldest federations and is located next to the United States where this issue has been widely studied. Yet in Canada, little work appears to have been done on this issue. The chapter is divided in two parts. First, we examine the institutional framework of the Canadian federation to establish where and how competition may manifest itself. Then we present some empirical evidence on interjurisdictional competition in Canada.

The Canadian federation: how competitive can it be in terms of regulations?

Research on interjurisdictional competition must be informed by the institutional arrangements in place in the country studied. Hence in this section, we present information on the responsibilities of the various levels of government in Canada.[1] We first discuss the general framework of governance and then turn to a sectoral analysis.

General framework of governance

Constitutional/legal setting

The Canadian Constitution (the British North America Act – BNA Act – of 1867) created a strong central government. It was given sole possession of the key revenue source at that time, customs duties, and made responsible for economic development (banking, railways, tariffs and so on), while the provinces were left to handle such local matters as health and social services, which were not very important in the nineteenth century. To reinforce central power further, the federal government was also permitted, in certain circumstances, to disallow provincial legislation and to declare certain 'local works' of national interest – an example is uranium mining which was taken over by the federal government during the Second World War for national security reasons and remains under its jurisdiction 60 years later.[2]

The pre-eminence of the federal government remained essentially unchallenged until the end of the First World War. During the 1920s and 1930s, however, matters began to change when a series of decisions by the Judicial Committee of the Privy Council in London (which remained Canada's final court of appeal until 1949) reserved the field of transfers to individuals (workers' compensation, welfare, unemployment insurance, old age pensions) for the provinces. As a result of these decisions, explicit constitutional amendments were required to allow for the creation of federal programmes of unemployment insurance (in 1940) and old age pensions (in 1951).

The Constitution contains a list of exclusive federal powers, a list of exclusive provincial powers, and a list of concurrent powers (agriculture and immigration with federal paramountcy, and pensions with provincial paramountcy). Federal powers include, amongst others, defence, foreign affairs, money and banking, transportation and communications. Provincial powers include education (subject to linguistic or religious safeguards of a constitutional nature for minorities), health, municipal and local affairs, roads and so on. There is no constitutional provision for intergovernmental interaction; some provinces purchase policing services from the federal government, some educational services from one another. There is an implicit federal spending power that gives it the right to offer provinces grants to alter their behaviour in areas of provincial jurisdictions.

There are no provincial constitutions. Moreover, since municipal governments have no constitutional status in the BNA Act, they are entirely the creatures of provincial law and hence completely subject to provincial choices. Provinces thus can at will modify the number, boundaries and powers of their local governments, and they have done so in the past.

In addition to the Constitution, various agreements in areas such as immigration help define the roles and responsibilities of the provincial and federal governments, but such agreements play only a minor role. Of greater relevance are the legal documents linked to federal transfers (laws, regulations and so on) and judicial decisions of the Supreme Court in areas such as telecommunications (cable television was deemed to be a federal and not a provincial jurisdiction in the 1960s) and environmental issues, which have, according to more recent judgements, been determined to be both a federal and a provincial responsibility. Such judgements are important because the list of powers drafted in 1867 does not always deal clearly with more recent developments and concerns.

One intriguing aspect of the legal system is its bilingual nature: all federal laws are proclaimed in both English and French. In court proceedings, lawyers can use the most favourable interpretation to their client if there are differences between the two texts; this is the case amongst others in tax cases.

Provinces in Canada are constitutionally able to tax anything they want to tax (except international and inter-provincial trade), setting their own rates, using their own definition of tax bases and collecting taxes themselves. In fact, they raise most of their resources from the same sources as the federal government – taxes on income and sales. The provincial personal income tax is collected on behalf of all provinces except Quebec by the federal government; this requires these provinces to use the federal definition of taxable income while Quebec is free to use its own definition. It has done so to offer a more favourable treatment of children than at the federal level and, mainly in the late 1970s to early 1980s, to create financial instruments used to encourage the purchase of various types of financial investments such as shares in Quebec firms and labour-sponsored investment funds. This was rendered possible by its control of not only its personal income taxes but also of its own Securities and Exchange Commission. Hence, the civil law province (see below) was more innovative than the common law provinces in the field of financial instrument in the 1970s and 1980s.

One important aspect of the Constitution is that it enshrines one (federal) criminal code, but two property law systems: civil law based on the Napoleonic code in Quebec and common law in the rest of Canada. In the case of criminal law, it is administered by the provinces, which means that the Attorney General of each province decides what offences to prosecute. This can lead to de facto differences in criminal law. The best known case is the decision taken by the Quebec provincial government not to prosecute, as of 10 December 1976, Henry Morgentaler a medical doctor, founder of abortion clinics. This decision was taken after several acquittals by Quebec juries based on their acceptance of the defence of necessity to justify performing an illegal act. Notwithstanding this Quebec decision, Dr Morgentaler was prosecuted in Manitoba and Ontario in 1983; on 28 January 1988, the Supreme Court of Canada struck down Canada's abortion law. Hence from 1976 to 1988, one had de facto two abortion regimes in Canada.[3]

The main distinction between contract law in civil law and common law settings is that the latter is not formally codified. Civil law contract law is easily accessible since it is codified in a way that follows didactic logic and all the most usual contracts (sales, donations, gaming, transactions and so on) are subject to a codified set of rules. Both the civil law and the common law put emphasis on public order. In common law all contracts that go against social and economic interests are forbidden as a result of public order and public morality clauses. Thus the interpretation of contract law under common law can evolve more quickly through judgements; this creates both flexibility and uncertainty, while civil law which has been codified by the legislator is both more stable and less flexible. Another distinction is that under common law, contracts have to be negotiated in good faith, while under civil law the obligation of good faith is codified and extends to the execution of contractual obligations. Overall, though there are differences in the elaboration and enunciation of contract law and in its procedure under common law and civil law, the resolution of a contractual problem of the same nature under identical circumstances would be very similar (Bélanger and Grenon 1997).

However, interesting distinctions remain between Quebec and common law environments. For example, Quebec has become a 'class action haven' (Kugler and Kugler 2004). One factor explaining this is that Quebec has the most complete consumer protection legislation in Canada. This is significant since a conviction for violation of the Consumer Protection Act may entail punitive damages even without the evidence of fraud, bad faith or even fault. A second factor is that in Quebec the costs of initiating a class action are small, while they can be very high in other jurisdictions when certification is denied. In Quebec, if certification is denied the class representative only has to pay $50 in court costs. In addition no expertise is allowed prior to an authorization hearing. Cost is not a deterrent in Quebec to the decision to launch a class action law suit, the government even has a fund for financial assistance of class actions when it feels that authorization is likely and the consumer can't finance his or her claim. Because the legislature wants to provide quick and inexpensive access to justice in class action cases, the entire process, from the filing to the trial, takes about a year.

Can these differences in legal systems matter from an economic perspective? There is recent literature on the topic of the impact of the legal system on economic performance.[4] Starting with a paper by La Porta *et al.* (1998), scholars have been trying to identify the impact of the common law system on the development of financial markets and consequently on long-term economic growth of a country. In their paper 'Law and finance', La Porta *et al.* ran regressions on a panel of 49 countries and found that former English colonies were doing much better economically than countries historically under French influence. By controlling for important judicial, political and historical variables, the authors concluded that common law offered a better environment for financial markets to emerge and develop, by favouring investors' rights more efficiently than in civil law countries.[5] Their methodology, as much as their conclusions, has been debated since with research spurred by their initial work.

It would seem straightforward to apply the same methodology to Canada, that is to try to isolate the influence of the civil law in Quebec on its financial, regulatory and economic development. However, there are important limitations to the application of regression analysis, as used in the cross-country studies. Quebec distinguishes itself from the rest of Canada not only by a different legal code, but also by its linguistic (81 per cent francophone with French as the sole official language) and religious (83 per cent Catholic) make-up. Religion is a factor that needs to be considered in any study of economic growth and regulatory development. In fact, it has also been addressed in a subsequent La Porta *et al.* paper where the authors did indeed find a significant impact of religion on the efficiency of government.[6] Studies have investigated the role of the Catholic Church in Quebec's economic development to assess the relevance of Weber's thesis on Protestantism and capitalism, but were inconclusive.[7] Also, the secessionist movement in the province, active politically since the 1960s, is an important factor affecting not only the political environment of the province, but also its economic activity. The Parti Québécois, the secessionist party, has been in power for 18 years of the 1975–2005 period and this has certainly influenced the economic climate of the province. Hence, a regression analysis where a dummy variable would be used to capture the effect of the civil law regime on the growth of Canadian provinces would not only capture the intended underlying judicial institution, but it would also capture the effect of all the characteristics enumerated above. Therefore, it does not seem to be possible in the case of Canada and the province of Quebec to isolate the effect the Napoleonic code had on the development of the province's financial and regulatory institution and its economic development.

Political setting

Canada is a monarchy with the monarch (of Canada, as per his or her status as monarch of the United Kingdom), the formal Head of State, being represented by a Governor-General, who is appointed on the advice of the Prime Minister and who has a purely ceremonial role. Parliament has two chambers, the House of Commons and the Senate. Although the older eastern provinces have a disproportionate share of Senate seats relative to their population, this does not matter much since the appointed Senate is ineffectual.[8] Members are elected to the House of Commons in British parliamentary fashion, that is, by a plurality of votes in a single round election in a territorially based constituency. The combination of a 1915 requirement that no province can have a number of members of the House of Commons less than its number of senators and a 1985 requirement that no province can suffer a drop in its absolute number of members in the House means that some provinces have smaller constituencies than others. To adjust for population increases in some provinces, the number of members of parliament has to be increased – from 301 to 308 following the 2001 census, for example.

Canada has generally had a government with a majority (50 out of 60 years, usually Liberal since 1945) in the House of Commons. Majority governments have similarly also governed in the unicameral systems of the provinces for most of the time. Coalitions, formal or implicit, between parties thus play a role in policy decisions only very rarely. Party discipline is notably strong in Canada at both the federal and provincial levels. Members rarely defy party leaders or formally change parties. In two cases of minority government, implicit (1972 to 1974) and explicit (2004 to 2005) support was offered by the New Democratic Party to the Liberals.[9]

As a result of these arrangements, it is not possible to have coalitions of provinces acting to raise the costs of other provinces by imposing on them behaviour they do not subscribe to such as uniform labour legislation and so on. Hence we do not have the impact of qualified majority voting documented by Vaubel (2004) for the European Union and the United States of America, where a geographical majority uses majority decision-making to increase the costs of their rival. We do not have this since there is no geographically based decision-making body and since framework laws are not generally used in Canada.

Before moving to a more detailed sectoral review, let us see how the three conditions promoting interjurisdictional competition listed below apply to Canada using information from Table 3.1:[10]

*   a fragmented structure containing a sufficiently important number of authorities;
*   a high level of local autonomy in order to encourage innovation and diversity;
*   a strong reliance of the subnational governments on own revenue sources.

One notes that:

*   A fragmented structure containing a sufficiently important number of authorities. The number of provinces is ten; in addition, there are three territories that are large in size but very small in population and remote from the rest of Canada. Is this a sufficiently important number? Especially as five of the provinces have a population of less than a million. The answer is certainly not a clear-cut yes.
*   A high level of local autonomy in order to encourage innovation and diversity. In this case, the answer is a clear-cut yes. One must note in particular the long tradition of Quebec acting as an initiator of provincial demands for more autonomy. This is explained by the fact that the majority of the population is not only French speaking but unilingual French speaking and thus both incapable of living outside Quebec (and northern new Brunswick and Ontario but these are poorer parts of Canada) and wanting to have the provincial government, which they control, deliver the largest possible amount of public services in their language.[11]
*   A strong reliance of the subnational governments on own revenue sources. In this case, the answer is a qualified yes. Provinces in Canada vary greatly in terms of their reliance on own revenues from about 60 to about 90 per cent.

The sectoral frameworks of governance

We now examine the regulatory framework by broad sector of the economy.

Agriculture

Agriculture is a joint area of responsibility with federal paramountcy. Issues such as the use of genetically modified food or meat inspection (mad cow) are federal. There is no major regulatory domain at the provincial level.

Fisheries

Fisheries is a federal responsibility. Coastal provinces will argue that federal policies are insensitive to their specific needs but can do nothing about it. An

Table 3.1 Key demographic, economic and geographic features of Canada's provinces, 2003

	NFD	PEI	NS	NB	QUE	ONT	MAN	SASK	ALTA	BC
Area (km^2)	405,212	660	5,284	72,908	1,542,056	1,076,395	647,797	651,036	661,848	944,735
Population ('000)	520	138	936	751	7,487	12,238	1,163	995	3,154	4,147
Density – population	1.3	24.4	16.9	10.3	4.9	11.4	1.8	1.5	4.8	4.4
% population Catholic 2001	36.9	47.4	36.6	53.6	83.4	34.7	29.3	31.7	26.7	17.5
% population francophone 2001	0.4	4.3	3.8	32.9	81.2	4.4	4.1	1.9	2	1.5
GDP ($000,000)	18,015	3,883	28,813	22,358	254,263	493,416	38,078	36,778	170,631	142,418
GDP per capita	34,644	28,138	30,783	29,771	33,961	40,318	32,741	36,963	54,100	34,342
Total revenues ($000,000)	4,761	1,129	7,531	6,236	66,702	81,154	9,681	8,533	28,402	30,999
% revenues from own sources	62.19	64.48	69.83	67.96	83.71	85.73	71.99	82.61	88.31	86.49
% transfers	37.8	35.5	30.2	32.0	16.3	14.3	28.0	17.4	11.7	13.5

Sources: Author using Statistics Canada data (Cansim II 384 0013) and (Cansim II 385 0001) Census 2001, Statistics Canada, 'Mother Tongue and Religion'. Area is from www.statcan.ca/english/Pgdb/phys01.htm.

Notes

NFD: Newfoundland; PEI: Prince Edward Island; NS: Nova Scotia; QUE: Quebec; ONT: Ontario; MAN: Manitoba; SASK: Saskatchewan; ALTA: Alberta; BC: British Columbia.

emerging issue is the conciliation of native fishing rights, conferred by treaties, and modern commercial fisheries. Since native affairs are a federal responsibility, this issue remains within the realm of that government.

Forestry

Forestry is a provincial responsibility. Provinces set the ownership regime, cutting rights and so on. Natural differences in the type of forest and location with respect to major US markets have somewhat isolated each provincial market from one another. Since the 1980s, repeated trade disputes with the US over softwood lumber have probably contributed more to creating a common policy than any domestic initiative. We have evidence on regulations for four provinces: Quebec, Ontario, Alberta and British Columbia.

- Forestry in riparian zones, especially those with salmon stocks, is subject to government regulation. The most restrictive requirements (those requiring the widest mandatory no-harvest buffer zones) are found in Quebec provincial salmon streams and British Columbia provincial fish and domestic water channels.
- From the numbers of Table 3.2 it is obvious that the rules concerning clear cutting in Quebec private forest lands are the least stringent since there is no size limit.
- Concerning roads' culvert at stream crossing and abandonment, Quebec private lands are also the ones subjected to the most lenient requirements. Concerning culvert size in provincial lands, Ontario has the most flexible rules, since it does not have a required size, but instead mandatory fish passage.

Table 3.2 Some aspects of forestry policies, four Canadian provinces

	British Columbia	*Alberta*	*Ontario*	*Quebec*
Forest cover (million ha.)	60.6	38.2	58.0	83.9
Riparian Protection (width of buffer)	Varies with width of channel; max: 100 m	Varies by type of tree: max 60 m	Increases With steepness of slope; max 90 m	Stronger for salmon in public forest; max: 60 m
Clear-cut size limit (hectares)	60 (N and S interior) 40 (Coastal and S interior)	Spruce 32	260	Private: none Public: 50 (South) 100 (Central) 150 (North)

Source: 'Global Environment Forest Policies: Canada as a Constant Case Comparison of Select Forest Practice Regulations', Chapter 3, Forest Policies in the United States and Canada, www.ifor.ca/docs/Ch3USCAN716.pdf.

- Concerning road abandonment Quebec and Ontario have more flexible requirements than Alberta and British Columbia.
- Concerning reforestation on provincial lands, the requirements are similar, however on Quebec private lands the requirements are only voluntary.

Mining

Mining, including oil and gas but excluding uranium, is a provincial responsibility. Provinces set the exploration rules, ownership regimes and royalties. There does not appear to be competition between provinces to attract mines, particularly by varying environmental standards. In recent years, tougher environmental regulations in British Columbia were seen as favouring exploration in Chile, not Ontario. A key issue was the inter-temporal irreversibility of decisions.

Manufacturing

Manufacturing is an area of provincial responsibility in that capital markets and labour issues are provincial. However, both levels of governments intervene through subsidies to maintain or attract employment. The federal government intervenes through subsidies mainly in sectors where international competition is important such as aircraft manufacturers (Bombardier versus Embraer), aircraft engines (Canadian versus US plants of United Aircrafts/Pratt and Whitney) or clothing and textiles (impact of foreign imports on domestic employment). It also enacts regulation on food safety or clothing flammability. Provincial governments have different policies with the Quebec government most active in offering subsidies, directly and through investments by provincially owned firms in projects. On the other hand, the Alberta and Ontario governments prefer a policy of lower taxes, although since 2003, this has been found wanting in the automotive sector in the face of subsidies to new plants by US states and is thus now changed in Ontario.[12]

Construction

Construction is an area of provincial responsibility. Provinces differ in the degree of regulation they impose on the sector; Quebec has a wide-ranging provincial government decree that sets wages rates, creates barriers to mobility for workers from other provinces and promotes the use of unionized employees. Alberta on the other hand has much looser regulations. This is in agreement with the overall regulation of labour markets described in Table 3.3 below.

Transportation

Transportation is both a federal responsibility – air, rail and water – and a provincial one – road. There is no national highway programme in Canada

(Vaillancourt and Turgeon 2002) and thus the federal government has little leverage in this area.[13] While it is constitutionally responsible for inter-provincial and international trucking, it has delegated its powers to the provinces, who first occupied the field in 1927 (Ontario), through the Motor Vehicle Transport Act of 1954. This is quite different from the case in the US. Economic deregulation was implemented in 1987. One interesting point is that NAFTA has increased the impact of US truckers' regulations (drugs, hours) in Canada.[14] For example, the 2004 change in the hours of services regulation in the US is affecting the debate in Canada on the hours of service allowed here: in general, there appears to be a preference for harmonization.[15]

Communications

Communications is a federal responsibility; regulations are applied by the Canadian Radio and Television Commission (CRTC) to radio, TV, telephone and cable companies in the area of programming (Canadian content), pricing, industry structure and so on; this is the most heavily regulated sector of the Canadian economy.

Utilities

Electricity, gas (intra-provincial) and water distribution are under provincial regulation. Inter-provincial and international oil and gas pipelines are under federal jurisdiction. The interesting sector is electricity; prices reflect differences in average cost of production, that is lowest in provinces with a high hydro component, that is Quebec (164/171 TWh), Manitoba (33/33.5) and British Columbia (43/45.8).[16] There is no national electricity market in Canada. Until the mid-1990s, each[17] provincial electricity market was served by a natural monopoly responsible for generation, transmission and distribution. But in the late 1980s and early 1990s, technological changes made the use of small gas turbines economical, while American regulators moved to ensure access to all producers to the transmission and distribution networks. In 1996, the American Federal Energy Regulatory Commission (FERC) issued Order 888; it requires the formation of Regional Transmission Authorities (RTO). From Canada's perspective, the key requirement is that of reciprocity; Canadian transmission companies must provide access to American companies that wish to sell electricity to Canada to maintain their access to the American market. Hence, this required breaking up the provincial monopolies to the satisfaction of the FERC. Thus, the requirements from US agencies to maintain access to the US market have done more to open up the Canadian market to private producers than Canadian initiated policies.[18] Saunders (2003: 2) for example notes that this 'was influential in accelerating the pace of electricity sector restructuring in Canada'. He proposes as a policy response the creation of a Canadian national body gathering together the provincial utilities when facing off with the FERC.

Wholesale and retail trade

Wholesale and retail trades are under provincial jurisdiction. One key regulatory aspect has been store opening hours which vary across provinces and in some cases within provinces across municipalities. This is examined later in the chapter.

Financial institutions

Financial institutions are regulated by both the federal and provincial governments as follows:

- Banks are federally chartered and large (by US standards) in terms of domestic market shares, with the top five serving the national market.
- Credit unions are provincially regulated and dominant in the domestic Quebec market.
- Trusts can be federal or provincial but in practice large trusts are owned by large banks and thus under federal supervision.
- Securities markets are provincially regulated; Canada is the only OECD country without a national SEC although attempts to create one have been ongoing, particularly since 2002. Stock exchanges and stockbrokers, although mainly owned by large banks, are provincially regulated.
- Real estate brokers are provincially regulated.
- Incorporation can be provincial or federal.
- Insurance companies can be federally or provincially chartered with little if any movement between the two types.

Services

Services, be they of a personal or professional nature, are provincially regulated. Hotels or restaurants are provincially or locally regulated and inspected. Lawyers, medicinal doctors and other professionals are provincially regulated, with reasonable but not automatic pan-Canadian mobility.

Labour

Labour laws are both a federal and provincial jurisdiction with most workers subject to provincial laws. These laws set items such as normal work week, entitlement to holidays and so on. In particular, they set the rule as to the use of replacement workers in case of strikes. The use of such workers is banned in British Columbia and Quebec. In a comparative study on labour standards in the United States and Canada, the provinces of British Columbia and Quebec were ranked highest (10/10) in North America in terms of collective bargaining provisions for employees[19] as shown in Table 3.3. Using measures on seven legal aspects that relate to employee's rights to unionize, the authors find for these

Table 3.3 Collective bargaining legal context, 1998 and strike replacement legislation in Canada, 2004

Legislation	Composite index, collective bargaining,	Certification vote not required if other indicators indicate willingness to unionize	Ban on replacement workers
	(1)	(2)	(3)
Newfoundland	9	No	No
PEI	9	No	No
New Brunswick	8	No	No
Nova Scotia	6	Yes	No
Quebec	10	No	1978–
Ontario	9	No	1993–5
Manitoba	9	No	No
Saskatchewan	9	No	No
Alberta	6	Yes	No
British Columbia	10	No	1993–
Federal	6	No	No

Source: Columns 1 and 2: Block *et al.* (2003: 124); Column 3: Singh and Jain (2002), updated by author.

provinces the most pro-employee legislation with legal provisions such as the absence of limits on the scope of bargaining, therefore allowing unions to be involved in a wide range of employer decisions, and the absence of required votes for union certification. Other regulations found in Quebec are procedures under which any one of the parties involved can require conciliation, making it harder for employers to use negotiations to eliminate the union. In comparison, Alberta and Nova Scotia rank last in Canada in terms of the collective bargaining index. But their value of 6 is four times higher than the value for the United States as a whole (1.5).[20]

General regulations

A commonly used measure of regulatory burden is the number of regulations or number of pages. In this respect, Quebec distinguishes itself by its number of pages which is substantially higher than for other provinces as reported in Table 3.4.

The Canadian federation: some evidence of interjurisdictional competition?

One way to evaluate the level and intensity of interjurisdictional competition is to measure the rate of innovation by governments. Based on the theories of Schumpeter, this approach considers that competition in a market can be

Table 3.4 Number of regulations and pages of provincial governments for selected years 1975–99

Newfoundland				Prince Edward Island			
Year	Party	Number	Pages	Year	Party	Number	Pages
1975	PC	207	495	1975	Liberal	121	360
1980	PC	353	868	1980	PC	117	285
1985	PC	315	650	1985	PC	143	438
1990	Liberal	290	684	1990	Liberal	132	397
1995	Liberal	162	439	1995	Liberal	122	450
1999	Liberal	110	588	1999	PC	51	177

Nova Scotia				New Brunswick			
Year	Party	Number	Pages	Year	Party	Number	Pages
1975	Liberal	166	463	1975	PC	133	344
1980	PC	193	619	1980	PC	204	571
1985	PC	247	941	1985	PC	514	1,199
1990	PC	346	1,120	1990	Liberal	180	763
1995	Liberal	192	866	1995	Liberal	171	1,192
1999	Liberal	144	714	1999	Liberal	71	814

Quebec				Ontario			
Year	Party	Number	Pages	Year	Party	Number	Pages
1975	Liberal	691	6,357	1975	PC	1,049	2,457
1980	PQ	347	7,288	1980	PC	1,141	2,132
1985	Liberal	445	4,395	1985	PC	703	1,726
1990	Liberal	336	3,160	1990	Liberal	702	2,374
1995	PQ	345	3,644	1995	NDP	549	1,055
1999	PQ	331	5,408	1999	PC	637	1,490

Manitoba				Saskatchewan			
Year	Party	Number	Pages	Year	Party	Number	Pages
1975	NDP	264	658	1975	NDP	296	491
1980	PC	262	791	1980	NDP	297	534
1985	NDP	270	1,421	1985	PC	188	1,098
1990	PC	276	1,467	1990	PC	157	834
1995	PC	199	1,515	1995	NDP	118	756
1999	NDP	183	1,825	1999	NDP	155	897

Alberta				British Columbia			
Year	Party	Number	Pages	Year	Party	Number	Pages
1975	PC	358	1,246	1975	NDP	804	1,008
1980	PC	375	1,251	1980	Social Credit	596	1,048
1985	PC	409	2,758	1985	Social Credit	424	542
1990	PC	398	1,695	1990	Social Credit	494	1,041
1995	PC	302	1,613	1995	NDP	561	1,219
1999	PC	291	1,153	1999	NDP	471	987

Source: *Canada's Regulatory Burden*, Vancouver BC, The Fraser Institute. See: www.fraserinstitute.ca/admin/books/files/aug-forum.pdf3.

Note
NDP: New Democratic Party; PC: Progressive Conservative; PQ: Parti Québécois.

observed directly by the number of innovations by firms.[21] A similar indicator has been used to measure the level of competition among American states with the number of policies adopted between 1976 and 1986 imposing fiscal discipline on governments, policies which were considered innovative at the time. That study compiled data on different laws limiting growth of expenditures and revenues, income tax indexation, laws that enforced programme evaluation, sunset clauses, tax expenditure reports and so on.[22] Similar evidence has not been compiled as systematically for Canada. In this section, we present some evidence on interjurisdictional competition. We will examine regulations in three specific areas:

- Economic activity: Labour-sponsored venture capital funds (LSVCFs), firm incorporation and retail shopping regulations.
- Labour market: use of striking labour replacement, minimum wages and mandatory retirement.
- Education, health and social policy: university fees, Medicare, smoking regulation and childcare.

We will also examine the general regulatory framework and budget-balancing requirements. In all cases, we use both existing evidence and empirical work carried out for this chapter. We examined the journal of the relevant Legislative Assembly (Hansard) at the time of the debate, focusing in particular on speeches by the relevant minister.

Economic activity

Labour-sponsored venture capital funds in Canada

Labour-sponsored venture capital funds (LSVCFs) are one mechanism to increase financial participation by unions in the ownership of capital (Vaillancourt 1997). These funds are mainly meant to help the community save jobs in existing businesses and to encourage the creation of new jobs by the creation of new businesses.

LSVCFs receive a maximum federal tax credit of 15 per cent and minimum of 10 per cent, while the provinces provide additional tax credits whose value varies by provinces. If there is no matching provincial tax credit, the federal minimum of 10 per cent applies. The federal government places a cap on annual individual contributions at $3,500 and requires an eight-year holding period. These requirements vary by provinces.

The first LSVCF in Canada, le Fond de solidarité des travailleurs du Québec (FSTQ), was created in Quebec in 1983. In 1988, the Working Venture Canadian Fund (WVCF) was established by the Canadian Federation of Labour. In 1992, the Crocus Investment fund was established in Manitoba, and the Working Opportunity Fund in British Columbia. New Brunswick's Workers Investment Fund was launched in 1994. In Ontario, several LSVCFs were created in 1994 and 1995. Finally, more recently, in 2002, Saskatchewan's government launched two LSVCFs: Golden Opportunities and Crown Ventures. It is only in Newfoundland, PEI and Alberta that LSVCFs are less present.

The idea of the WVCF was clearly inspired by the Quebec experience. Both the government and the opposition referred to the FSTQ success in Commons Debates at the time the WVCF was debated. On 11 February 1987, Mr Cadieux said:

> Because of the success of the Quebec fund, the Government introduced in yesterday's Budget tax incentives for investment in national venture capital funds sponsored by labour organizations.... The enthusiasm that the Quebec workers have shown for such funds is evidence of the willingness of workers to co-operate in strengthening and developing the economy. I am confident that this success in Quebec will be repeated across the country as the labour movement plays an even larger role as an essential partner in Canada's economy development.[23]

Mr Cassidy of the opposition added: 'In that context, it is my belief that we must welcome the announcement in the Budget of economic incentives to co-operation, that are similar to the support now given to the Quebec Solidarity Fund. This is one of the few positive measures in the Budget tabled by the Minister of Finance'.[24]

In Manitoba and British Columbia's legislative assemblies, references to the Quebec experience were made in order to promote their own LSVCFs. For instance, in Manitoba: '... this is the kind of co-operative approach that has been tried in other provinces, in Quebec, for example. The fund in Quebec, the solidarity fund, has been in existence for many years. It is not a new concept'.[25] In British Columbia: 'By way of comparison, the Quebec Solidarity Fund raised $500,000 during its initial offering in 1984 and $8 million in its second year'.[26]

In Ontario, the situation is different. The government does not seem to need to make any reference to the other LSVCF experience in order to promote their own funds, but the opposition does use the WVCF to discourage the Ontario government from creating new LSVCFs. On 18 November 1993, Mr Kwinter said:

> 'Let me tell you another thing. If you take a look at the WVCF, a fund that has been around for five years and gets heavily tax supported by the provincial government, they had a fund of $146 million, and they have only been able to invest $6 million of that $146 million. That is a combination of the environment that has been created by this government; it is a combination of a lack of confidence that people have in participating.[27]

References to other LSVCF experience are not made in the New Brunswick and Saskatchewan legislative assemblies.

Table 3.5 presents data for LSVCFs in Canada, in 1997. In that year,

Table 3.5 Importance of LSVCF by region, Canada, 1997

Region	LSVCF Investments (millions)	LSVCF % of total regional venture capital
Quebec	2,224	55
Ontario	1,519	48
Prairies	201	39
British Columbia	184	34
Atlantic Canada	79	61

Source: July 2000, Fraser Forum: 'Venture Capital: High-risk, High-return Financing', Fraser Institute, oldfraser.lexi.net/publications/forum/2000/07/section_04.html.

LSVCFs accounted for nearly half of the total amount of venture capital invested (Macdonald and Associates 1998). Vaillancourt (1997) could not find evidence that requiring venture capital to be channelled through LSVCFs is the best way to increase its supply or to allocate its efficiency.

One of the main goals of LSVCFs is employment. Vaillancourt (1997) examined the impact of the FSTQ on employment from 1986 to 1993. He found that the FSTQ had no significant impact on employment creation in the sectors studied, but this finding does not mean that it may not have been helpful in maintaining employment at the firm level.

Firm incorporation

A study by Cumming and MacIntosh (2000) was carried out on the decision of Canadian firms to incorporate in one of the ten provinces or with the federal government. After the adoption of the Canada Business Corporations Act (CBCA) in 1975 by the federal government, the provinces reacted by initiating reforms of their incorporation laws. The authors wanted to test the hypothesis that provinces reacted in a strategic way to maintain or to increase the number of corporations within their jurisdiction, given the revenues associated with the process. Through regression analysis, they tested whether the provincial offer of incorporation regulation, as captured by the different reforms adopted by the provinces, responded to the initiative of the federal government. This was done by regressing the delay between the federal and the provincial government's reforms on the revenues associated with incorporation for each of the provinces and the number of legislators in each jurisdiction. Their results seem to indicate that firms' incorporation revenues do not explain the delay between the provincial reforms and the CBCA, meaning that the provinces with higher revenues did not react faster by reforming the incorporation laws than did lower revenue-yielding provinces.[28] The authors conclude that Canadian provinces did not act strategically to maximize their revenues, but were motivated by the desire to render uniform the incorporation laws in Canada, therefore indicating absence of interjurisdictional competition.

The second part of their study consisted in measuring a demand for 'efficient' incorporation laws by Canadian firms. They wanted to find out if Canadian firms took into account the stringency of incorporation regulation in their choice of the jurisdiction. The stringency of regulation was measured by the administrative costs of legal incorporation. To that end, they regressed the number of incorporations in province *i* on the costs of legal incorporation in that province, the costs of incorporation by the federal government, those of the other provinces and on other control variables such as provincial GDP. They found that costs of incorporation of different jurisdictions have a significant impact on the number of incorporations in five of the ten provinces. The authors conclude that Canadian firms do engage in jurisdictional 'shopping' when they need to incorporate, thereby creating an environment favourable to intergovernmental competition. However, they find that the level of economic activity, as captured by the provincial GDP, is significantly more important in determining the number of incorporations in a given province.[29]

Sunday shopping deregulation across Canada

The Canadian process of Sunday shopping deregulation across Canada started in 1985, after the Supreme Court found the Federal Lord's Day Act inconsistent with the protection of religious freedom enshrined by the 1982 Charter of Rights amendment to the Canadian Constitution. Provinces thus became responsible for this aspect of regulating economic activity. This deregulation occurred from West to East, starting in 1980 with British Columbia's 'Holiday Shopping Regulation Act'. We will review what was said about the deregulation of Sunday shopping in the other provinces in the Legislative Assemblies' debates of each province.

First, we looked at the House of Commons' Hansard to find if there were any references to British Columbia's experience. We could not find any reference to this first Sunday shopping experience before and after the Supreme Court's decision.

In Alberta, there is also no reference to the British Columbia's experience, except in May 1985: 'My question to the minister is whether he's yet had the opportunity to undertake any review of the experience in British Columbia, where municipality-by-municipality shopping hours are in effect and have resulted in quite a lot of commercial chaos in some areas of the province'.[30] Moreover, the government and the opposition often refer to the Supreme Court's judgement on the Lord's Day Act when debating whether Sunday shopping should be regulated by the municipalities or at a provincial level. On the same matter, Ontario's 'Retail Business Act' of 1980 is also cited a few times in the debates.

In the case of Saskatchewan, the government often uses British Columbia and Alberta's experience to influence the Assembly: 'Our legislation, Mr Speaker, is similar to that of Alberta and British Columbia, and certainly, it hasn't destroyed their rural business' or 'There is no domino effect in Alberta, who has similar legislation and has had for seven or eight years; there is no domino effect in British Columbia, where they have similar legislation'.[31]

The Manitoba's government also makes reference to the experience in other provinces. In December 1992, when the 'Retail Businesses Sunday Shopping (Temporary Amendments) Act' was debated, references to past experiences in other provinces were often made. For instance, on 9 December: 'Right now the province of British Columbia, Alberta, Saskatchewan – in fact, all of the other western provinces – as well as Ontario, New Brunswick, Prince Edward Island and, most recently, Quebec, permit Sunday shopping on an expanded basis'.[32]

In the Ontario debates, there is no reference made to the other provinces' legislative experience.

In Quebec, there are many references to the other provinces' experience. For example, on 7 December 1992, Réjean Doyon said:

> Si on regarde l'ensemble des marchés qui nous entourent, des marchés commerciaux qui nous entourent, que nous regardions vers l'Est, avec le Nouveau Brunswick, que nous regardions vers le Sud, avec les États-Unis, que nous regardions vers l'Ouest, avec l'Ontario, partout nous sommes encerclés de marchés commerciaux qui ont décidés de permettre l'ouverture des établissement commerciaux le dimanche.

Moreover, the government bring into play a lot of statistics from other provinces, especially Ontario and Manitoba.[33]

In the Maritimes, New Brunswick's Legislative Assembly members did not seem to make any reference to other provinces' experience. In Nova Scotia, many pilot programmes were instituted from 1990 to 1994; however it was hard to find references to the other provinces in the Debates of the Legislative Assembly. Finally, in Prince Edward Island, the Journal of Legislative Assembly reported an allusion to Nova Scotia, when debating about the 'Rest Day Act'.

To sum up, the members of the Legislative Assemblies of Quebec, Manitoba and Saskatchewan bring up more frequently the experience of the other provinces to prove their point than those of Ontario, Alberta and the Maritimes.

In 2005, the situation in Canada is varied: provinces have adopted different legislation concerning Sunday shopping: providing municipal autonomy (British Columbia, Alberta and Saskatchewan), permitting wide-open Sunday shopping (Manitoba, Ontario, Quebec and Newfoundland), restricting it partially (New Brunswick, Prince Edward Island) or totally (Nova Scotia).

As shown in Table 3.6, there was west to east spread of liberalization of Sunday shopping across Canada.

Labour markets

Strike replacement law

As noted above, union regulation is mainly a provincial responsibility in Canada; federal labour law applies to only a few sectors such as banking,

Table 3.6 Overview of the deregulation of retail business hours for each of the provinces of Canada

Province	Legislations and legal changes	Beginning date
British Columbia	'Holiday Shopping Regulation Act' (1980) passed providing municipal autonomy	1980
	Deregulated shopping hours in Vancouver	14 December 1982
Alberta	'Wide-spread Sunday' shopping began in Calgary and Edmonton	November 1984
	'Municipal Government Amendment Act' (1985) passed officially providing municipal autonomy	1985
Saskatchewan	Provincial legislation providing municipal autonomy	Spring 1988
	Regina chooses to deregulate Sunday shopping	June 1989
	Saskatoon chooses to deregulate Sunday shopping	October 1991
Manitoba	10-month experiment with Sunday shopping	29 November 1992
	Municipal autonomy; Winnipeg allows Sunday shopping	October 1993
Ontario	'Legislation amended to permit Sunday shopping in the month of December'	December 1991
	Wide-open Sunday shopping	3 June 1992
Quebec	Stores in some cities in the Outaouais region (neighbour of Ontario obtains the authorization to open on Sunday)	16 June 1992
	Wide-open Sunday shopping	1 January 1993
New Brunswick	'Temporary amendment to permit shopping in most retail establishments'	November 1991 to January 1992
	'Sunday shopping from the first day following Labour Day to the Sunday immediately preceding Christmas'	September 1992
	'Sunday shopping from first Sunday in August to the second Sunday after Christmas'	August 1996
	Moncton and Dieppe are declared tourist areas and can open commercial establishments on Sunday year-round	3 March 2002
Nova Scotia	'Temporary experiment which allowed every store less than 40,000 sq. feet to open on Sundays'	March 1990 to February 1991
	Temporary experiment with deregulation	October 1993 to January 1994
Prince Edward Island	Open on Sundays from the last Sunday in November to the Sunday preceding Christmas	November 1992
Newfoundland	'Wide-open Sunday shopping throughout the province'	1 January 1998

Source: 'The impact of Sunday shopping deregulation concerning the retail industry for the provinces of Canada' by Jean-François Bélisle, mimeo, 2005.

transportation and communications (telephone and so on). The evolution of these regulations in recent years has been summarized by Singh and Jain with respect to one key provision, the replacement of strikers. Table 3.3 presented earlier summarizes the situation as of 2004.

What one observes is that Quebec first introduced this ban in 1978, in the first mandate of the Parti Québécois government, a left-leaning sovereignist party (trying to maximize the vote for sovereignty to be held in 1980). Ontario followed suit in 1993 during the first and sole mandate of the New Democratic Party (NDP), a left-leaning party, but this was repealed as soon as the right-leaning Conservative party gained power in 1995. Finally, in British Columbia, this was introduced by the NDP government when it took power in 1993 and not repealed by the centrist Liberal government elected in 2003. Hence in this case, it is not interjurisdictional competition that explains provincial behaviour but plain ideological beliefs, along with a desire to reward one's political base.

Minimum wages

A paper by Green and Harrison (2005) examines how provincial minimum wages were set in Canada over the 1969–2000 period. They carry out both a qualitative and quantitative analysis to explain the following trends in the minimum wages:

- an increase in the real minimum wage over the 1969–80 period, a decrease over the 1980–90 period and then stagnation except in Quebec, Ontario and British Columbia;
- the similarity in movement among the provinces, particularly in Atlantic Canada and the tendency for disparities between provinces to go down over time;
- the higher minimum wages associated with left-wing governments and the lower minimum wages associated with poorer provinces.

Their qualitative analysis, which uses both textual analysis and interviews with policymakers, indicates that inter-provincial mobility is not an issue when setting the minimum wage. What matters is comparability with other provinces and thus being both fair and economically reasonable. Hence, there is in general desire to be somewhere in the middle of one's peer group such as all Atlantic provinces for those four provinces or Prairie provinces. Exceptions tend to be ideologically motivated such as the choice by the NDP (left) government of British Columbia in the early 1990s to aim for the highest minimum wage in Canada. Or they can be ideologically motivated but cloaked in economic arguments as when the Conservative (right) government of Ontario froze the minimum wage in 1995 after the NDP (1990–5) had made it the highest in Canada.

Their quantitative analysis uses the ratio *ln* (*minimum wage/median unskilled wage*) as their dependent variable; the minimum wage is the main one, not the age- or sector-specific ones, and when applicable the one for men (some provinces in early years). Various independent variables are included in a total of 18 estimations carried out using either OLS or tobit with 330 observations in a provincial panel. Common variables include GDP growth rate, political orientation of government, average of other provinces' minimum wage and regional dichotomous variables. Various variables include the proportion of the work force in retail, pre-election year and relationship to other minimum wages (below/above average, lowest/highest). Their key findings can be summarized as follows:

- there is no evidence that provinces above or below the overall average are more sensitive to movements in minimum wages in other provinces (p. 42);
- there is no evidence that provinces react more to downward than upward movement of the minimum wage;
- provinces react less strongly to movements in the extremes than movements in the middle of the minimum wage distribution (p. 43);
- the farther away a province was away from the mean in the previous period, the larger the change in the minima wage it institutes ... the change is in the direction of a movement toward the mean (p. 44).

Thus, the authors conclude that there is a race to the middle in the case of the provincial minimum wages in Canada.

Mandatory retirement

Under Canada's Charter of Rights and Freedoms (1982), mandatory retirement at a specified age does not constitute a discriminatory practice.[34] Provincial employment standards legislation determines if it is allowable or not for a private company to implement such a policy, perhaps as part of a collective agreement. In 2005, the Ontario government announced it will ban mandatory retirement by 2006, joining the provinces of Quebec (1982), Manitoba (1983), Alberta (1985), Prince Edward Island (2004) and New Brunswick (2004). Quebec at the same time as it banned this practice allowed access to pensions paid by the social security system in place in that province (Quebec Pension Plan – QPP) from age 60 rather than 65, but with a reduction of 0.5 per cent per month of anticipation (30 per cent at 60). Hence we can examine the official documents to see if reference was made to the Quebec experience when other provinces changed or abolished their mandatory retirement age.

The debates of the Legislative Assembly of Manitoba do not mention the Quebec experience. Likewise, the debates of the Legislative Assembly of Alberta did not cite past experiences from other Canadian provinces as an example. Only in Prince Edward Island is such a mention found, with Mr McAleer (Conservative – Charlottetown Spring Park) making reference to the features of the Quebec *Loi sur l'abolition de la retraite obligatoire* in his speech at the Legislative Assembly on 23 November 2004.[35]

However the removal of the cap does not mean that older workers in these jurisdictions have normal protection against age discrimination. . . . Quebec in 1982 . . . effectively banned mandatory retirement under any circumstances. Quebec does so under its employment standards legislation although a court decision allowed a collective agreement to terminate people at 65 on the ground that it was a fair policy in the face of layoffs.

In 1986, the federal government modified the Canadian Pension Plan (CPP) by allowing for pensions at age 60 on the same actuarial parameters as the QPP. On the matter of flexibility of the retirement age, Mr Malépart (Liberal – Montreal Saint Mary), in his speech at the House of Commons on 26 June 1986, used the example of Quebec's pension plan as a framework to illustrate the potential consequences of implementing such reforms.[36]

Mr Speaker, I want to give figures and illustrate the consequences which ordinary Canadians will face if they decide or are forced to retire at age 60 under the Quebec Pension Plan. . . . Right now the maximum Quebec Pension Plan benefit paid to a person aged 65 is $486.11. Should somebody in Quebec opt for retirement at age 60 he or she gets $340.28 in Quebec Pension Plan benefits . . .[37]

In our opinion, this is the one change in this area that is most directly influenced by the policies implemented in Quebec.

Did the ban of mandatory retirement have an effect on the employment rate of workers most directly affected by this measure, that is those aged 60–64, in Quebec and Ontario? Figure 3.1 shows the two employment rates and the difference between them.[38] The rate is lower in Quebec and the difference between Quebec and Ontario greater since 1982 with the average difference at 8.7 in 1980–2 and 10.6 afterwards (11.3 in the 1983–7 period).

Education, health and social policy

University fees

In Canada, each province can set its own university tuition fees. However, the mobility of students across Canada makes it possible for them to study in provinces other than their province of residence, changing the size and the quality of student enrolment body in each province.[39] Provinces might consider mobility of students in order to retain their own students within their jurisdiction and/or to attract students from other provinces.

In nominal terms, average tuition fees weighted by full-time equivalent students (FTE) for the school year of 1972–3 were $534. By the end of the 1970s, tuition fees had increased slightly but regular increases began in the early 1980s. From 1981–2 to 1982–3, there was a 13 per cent increase in tuition fees. During the following years, increases were smaller, until two major increases occurred

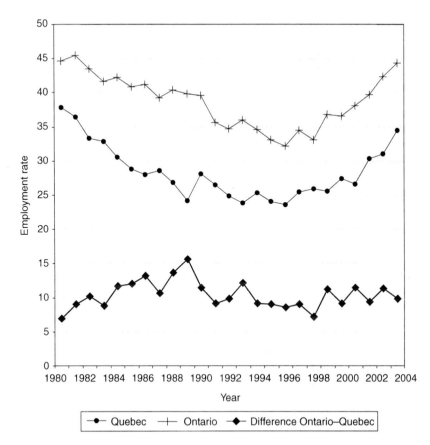

Figure 3.1 Employment rate in Quebec and Ontario for workers aged 60–64: 1980–2004 (source: Author using data from Statistics Canada).

in 1990–1 and 1991–2. During these two years, tuition fees increased by 15 and 17 per cent, respectively, compared with the previous year as shown in Figures 3.2–3.4.

In Quebec, tuition fees had been frozen from the late 1960s until the end of the 1980s, when they were hiked up from $519 per year in 1989–90 to $904 in 1990–1 and then to $1,311 in 1991–2. Tuition fees then were again frozen by the provincial government in 1996.[40] This freeze is still in effect in 2005.

Ontario experienced regular increases of tuition fees from the beginning of the 1980s. These increases were at a higher annual rate in the 1990s. During that decade, universities increased their tuition fees, and they did so more substantially for specific programmes like medicine, law and dentistry.

In British Columbia, tuition fees were stable during the 1970s and increased from the beginning of the 1980s. A tuition freeze was adopted in 1992–3; it lasted two years. Afterwards, another tuition freeze policy was implemented; it

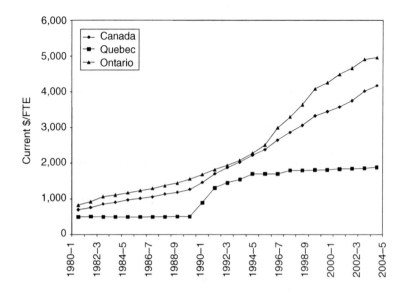

Figure 3.2 Tuition fees, Quebec and Ontario, 1980–1 to 2004–5, current $/FTE (source: Author using data from Statistics Canada.

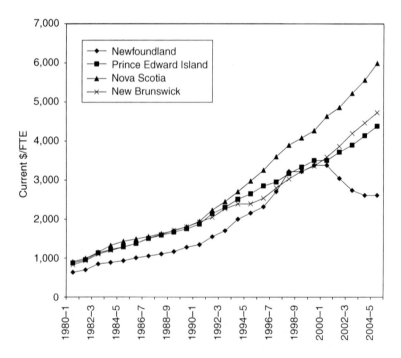

Figure 3.3 Tuition fees in Canada, Atlantic, 1980–1 to 2004–5, current $/FTE (source: Author using data from Statistics Canada.

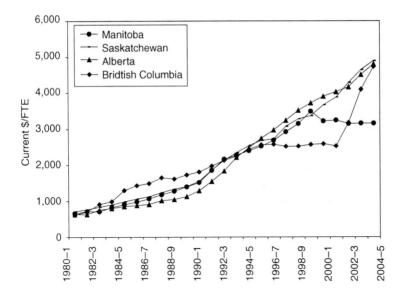

Figure 3.4 Tuition fees in Canada, Western Provinces, 1980–1 to 2004–5, current $/FTE (source: Author using data from Statistics Canada).

held until 2001–2, when tuition fees declined by 5 per cent. Tuition fees started increasing again in 2001–2: they grew by 87 per cent between 2001–2 and 2004–5.

Tuition fees in Manitoba were stable in the 1970s, and then increased regularly from the beginning of the 1980s until the end of the 1990s. Following students' protests, the government reduced tuition fees by 10 per cent in 2000–1. Tuition fees have remained frozen since then.

Newfoundland experienced regular increases of its tuition fees until a political party was elected that promised to reduce tuition fees by 25 per cent over three years. The first 10 per cent decrease was declared in 2001–2, followed by another 10 per cent decrease the following year.

The five other provinces (Saskatchewan, Alberta, New Brunswick, Nova Scotia and Prince Edward Island) all experienced relatively smooth increases of their university tuition fees and never experienced any decrease.

In 1996, in the Legislative Assembly of Manitoba, there were concerns about the decline of enrolment in universities and colleges in that province. In a question addressed to the Minister of Education, a member of the Assembly noted:

In 1995, Manitoba registered the largest drop of any province except Prince Edward Island in both full-time and part-time university enrolment. Enrolments dropped again this year and have remained stagnant in community colleges. Will the minister tell the House what steps she has taken to reverse this trend which seriously undermines the economic future of Manitoba?[41]

Instead of referring to other jurisdictions in her reply, the Minister of Education used a national measure of the decline in enrolment: 'The trend for reduced enrolments in university is nationwide, and the member should know as well that the trend in college enrolment is up'.[42]

We found some quotes in the Hansard of the National Assembly of Quebec where a member compared the finances of universities in Quebec to the finances of universities in Ontario. Thus, the link between the tuition fees policies of the two provinces is implicitly included in the comparison of the broader policies of funding of universities rather than stated explicitly.[43]

Nova Scotia is the province where tuition fees are the highest in Canada. This point has been made by the Canadian Federation of Students in front of the Nova Scotia House of Assembly Committee on Human Resources:

> Nova Scotia is currently an anomaly when it comes to post-secondary education policy. Currently provinces such as Ontario, Manitoba, Quebec and Newfoundland all have freezes or reductions in their tuition fees. It is crucial that the Nova Scotia Government legislate a tuition fee freeze and increases post-secondary education funding, so as to not compromise quality.[44]

It is worth noting that there seems to be an international influence in the tuition fees policy setting. While Quebec compares the finances of its universities with the finances of universities in Ontario, Ontario compares its policies of financing universities with policies of jurisdictions located abroad. In 2005, replying to the opposition concerning the budget of the government, a member of the government of Ontario said:

> If you look at the United States, the number one state in terms of per capita income is not Texas or Alabama, it's Massachusetts. What do you have in Massachusetts? You've got centres of excellence for learning and for health care. You've got MIT. You've got Harvard. That's what we have to emulate. We can't keep harping back on things that happened 40 or 50 years ago. We've got to go ahead, and this budget goes ahead with a $6.2-billion investment in our universities and colleges – unprecedented.[45]

There are also some quotes referring to tuition fees policies in Europe. In Manitoba, such reference have been made in the political debates: 'At the end of the twentieth century in Manitoba, enrolments are falling in universities, enrolments in community colleges of high school students have not increased, and at the end of the twentieth century, while European societies are expanding the number of students in post-secondary education to 50 per cent or even 60 per cent and 70 per cent.'[46] In British Columbia, there have also been some references to European jurisdictions: 'If you look at the European jurisdictions, where in some cases there is no tuition applicable for post-secondary education, we absolutely have seen an increase in terms of access, particularly for people who are low-income and who are faced with financial challenges and the like.'[47]

The impact of interjurisdictional influences concerning tuition fees policies is difficult to detect by looking at the political debates. In Manitoba, where there has been a decline in tuition fees, we can find in the Hansard of this province many quotes noting the alleged negative impact of tuition fees on accessibility and comparison with European jurisdictions. In the case of Quebec, if there are some comparisons with Ontario (where tuition fees are higher), tuition fees have remained frozen since 1996. In the case of Ontario, we found a quote pleading for Ontario to 'emulate' some American states' model of financing universities. Tuition fees in Ontario have increased, most importantly in some specific fields of study. Is international influence more important in Ontario than is inter-provincial influence? It appears so. In British Columbia, we do not see interjuris-dictional influence coming from Europe, as the quote would suggest. Indeed, tuition fees have increased significantly since 2000.

It is not clear what the role of interjurisdictional influence is on the provincial tuition fees policies in Canada. If we can state that provinces do use other juris-dictions for pleading for a specific tuition fees policy, we cannot state what is the role of such influence in the adoption of the provincial policies. What is more important are the political leanings of provincial governments and the fact that incoming governments have made or not made an explicit promise to freeze or reduce fees; no party ever promises to raise them (until 2007 in Quebec)!

Medicare

In various fields of endeavour, one observes differences in provincial behaviour that often become generalized to the rest of the provinces not through yardstick competition but through federal action, usually through a financial bribing of the provinces. For example, the Medicare programme introduced in Saskatchewan in 1962 was not adopted by other provinces until the federal government announced in 1965 a 50–50 cost-sharing Medicare programme implemented in 1968.

The national Medical Care Act, introduced in 1968 and its predecessor, the 1957 Hospital Insurance and Diagnostic Services Act, are interesting examples of yardstick competition *à la Canadienne*. Even though medical insurance had been the subject of public and government attention since the late 1920s, with the Great Depression and the Second World War bringing the government's important social role to the forefront, only a small western province had actually taken steps in providing its citizens with public and universal medical insurance.[48] Saskatchewan's Co-operative Commonwealth Federation (CCF; predecessor of NDP) government elected in 1944 went on in 1947 to introduce the first universal hospital insurance plan. A few other provinces responded to the initiative by offering similar plans to their populations, but the policy innovation was not emulated by all Canadian provinces until 1961, four years after the introduction of the federal plan.[49] Interestingly, not only did the federal government plan follow provincial initiative, its reaction was also the result of pressure by provincial governments. The enactment of the Hospital Insurance Act was forced upon the federal government by a proposal of Ontario's Prime Minister at the 1955 Conference on Tax Agreements.[50] It seems Canadian provinces, although constitutionally mandated, did not exercise full sovereignty over this important field of social policy. To be eligible to funds under the federal plan, provincial governments had indeed to comply with several conditions imposed by Ottawa.

Although its 1947 hospital care plan was an important step in protecting Saskatchewan citizens against the risk of sudden illness or accident and the concurring heavy medical and hospital bills, the CCF government was still seeking to fulfil its 1944 election promise of a universal, public and complete medical care programme. In a 1959 public address, T.C. Douglas,[51] then Saskatchewan's Premier, announcing its government plan finally to introduce public medical insurance went on to add: '*I would like to prophecy that before 1970 almost every other province in Canada will have followed the lead of Saskatchewan and that we shall have a national health insurance program from the Atlantic to the Pacific*'.[52] Building on existing municipal, not-for-profit doctor-sponsored and private insurance plans and taking advantage of the newly introduced Hospital Insurance and Diagnostic Services Act and the federal funds attached to it, it was able in 1962 to impose the first universal, compulsory and tax-supported medical insurance plan by a government in North America.[53] This province, which in the late 1930s had fewer doctors in proportion to the population than anywhere else in Canada,[54] became over the next 30 years the leader of publicly provided medical care.

In 1968, six years after the introduction of Medicare in Saskatchewan, the federal government introduced its national Medical Care Act, laying the foundation of Canada's modern health care system. To receive the important federal funds, every other province in Canada introduced their own provincial Medicare programmes. Those programmes had to meet certain conditions like universality, uniformity, complete coverage for all Canadians with the right to transfer from one province to the other, and a non-profit and publicly administered and operated authority and so on.[55] By 1970, all provinces had such a plan.

Tobacco regulation

In 1997, the Canadian federal government adopted the Tobacco Act, aimed at preventing people from smoking and modifying the habits of smokers. The Tobacco Act replaced the Tobacco Products Control Act (TPCA) and the Tobacco Sales to Young Persons Act (TSYPA). Provinces also adopted anti-smoking laws during the 1990s. Table 3.7 presents the date of adoption of the various laws. Some provinces adopted laws that aimed specifically at banning smoking while others adopted laws regulating smoking bans and other issues related to tobacco use. We can find such laws since 1985, when the federal government adopted the Non-smokers' Health Act, which regulated smoking in

Table 3.7 Laws regulating tobacco use, Canada, 1990–2005

Federal	*Tobacco Act*	*1997*
BC	Occupational Health and Safety Regulation	2002
AB	Protection from Second-Hand Smoke in Public Buildings Act	1999
SK	Tobacco Control Act	2001
MB	The Non-Smokers Health Protection Act	1990
ON	Smoking in the Workplace Act	1990
ON	Tobacco Control Act	1994
QC	Tobacco Act	1998
NB	Smoke-Free Places Act	2004
NS	Smoke-Free Places Act	2002
PEI	Smoke-Free Places Act	2002
NF	Smoke-Free Environment Act	1993

Source: National Clearinghouse on Tobacco and Health Programs. Online at www.ncthp.ca.

federal workplaces. All provinces have laws aiming at managing use of tobacco, except British Columbia. In British Columbia, use of tobacco in the workplace is controlled by the Workers' Compensation Board, a regulatory agency that administers the Workers' Compensation Act. As we can see in Table 3.7, most provinces adopted anti-smoking regulations after the federal Tobacco Act of 1997.

Where have there been inter-provincial influences in the adoption of anti-smoking laws? We found very few quotes revealing inter-provincial influences. One exception is that during the study of the Tobacco Act in Quebec, a member of the National Assembly mentioned approvingly that some provinces had adopted regulations on cigarette packages: Ontario, British Colombia and Manitoba.[56] In Saskatchewan, the Special Committee on Tobacco Control discussed the economic impact of a total ban on the economy. Larry Bird, president the Hotels Association of Saskatchewan, testified in front of that committee and made reference to Ontario. Much more common were references to the well-established health dangers of smoking and to the need to stop the young from becoming smokers. At the beginning of the Second Reading of Bill 47 (Protection from Second-hand Smoke in Public Buildings Amendment Act), the member of the Legislative Assembly of Calgary-Cross declared: 'research has confirmed what many physicians have long suspected, that years of exposure to second-hand smoke puts non-smokers at increased risk of developing disease'.[57]

Such fears were also raised in Ontario in the debate on the Tobacco Control Act in 1994. The Legislative Assembly member of Etobicoke-Humber declared: 'I want to note that one in five preventable deaths among adults in Ontario can be attributed to smoking.... More than 13,000 Ontarians die each year from tobacco use, almost five times as many die from traffic accidents, suicide and AIDS all combined. One Ontarian dies from tobacco use every 40 minutes in Ontario.'[58] Political debates in Nova Scotia also pointed out concerns about the death toll of smoking in the province. 'We have a significant number of deaths as a result of exposure to second-hand smoke. The costs to our health care system are significant. Smoking and the diseases of smoking are preventable'.[59]

Thus, we do not see much inter-provincial influence in the adoption of anti-smoking laws. Provinces seem mainly motivated to adopt such laws because of the effect of smoking on the health of their citizens. It seems likely that these concerns about the health of citizen are partly motivated by the cost of health care and the burden that smoking may cause to governments' finances.

Childcare

Since 1997, Quebec has taken innovative steps towards improving its child welfare policy. Already the most active government in Canada in regards to support for families,[60] the 1997 Early Childhood Education and Care policy brought a new focus in the government's underlying goals by gradually replacing monetary and fiscal assistance with in-kind assistance for parents, the direct supply of childcare services with the introduction of a province-wide, universal, fixed-rate, day care programme set in 1997 at $5 a day (adjusted in 2004 to $7 by the Liberals). A 2004 OECD study noted *'the extraordinary advance made in Quebec, which has launched one of the most ambitious and interesting early education and care policies in North America.'*[61] Other provincial governments have since been under pressure from different interest groups and citizen associations to replace direct monetary assistance to parents (demand-side subsidy) with a supply-side policy. While provincial governments have the constitutional mandate to administer welfare programmes, they have not responded to voters' requests for reform in the child policy area. The reasons may be numerous; one that seems to explain this state of affairs is simply budgetary considerations. Quebec's new, fixed-rate, day-care programme may be popular; it has also proved to be very expensive. From $209 million in 1995, Quebec's direct subsidies to childcare services were up to $1,326 million in 2004.[62] Faced with such a response by provincial governments, it seems that different lobbies and interest groups have turned around and been very active in promoting reforms at the federal level instead.

More generally, after more than 20 years of budgetary deficits, Ottawa's new-found surpluses (1997+) have been targeted by different interest groups in Canadian civil society. Pressure by parents' associations, think tanks and lobbyists has been directed towards the central government, the only one in Canada's present budgetary situation with the resources necessary to implement a global and comprehensive social policy reform. In the February 2005 federal budget, funds were committed to this programme. As of 16 October 2005, seven provinces have signed agreements with the federal government to receive federal funds for early learning and childcare.[63] This follows the federal government's introduction of the National Children Benefit initiative (NCB) in 1998 which was a 'comprehensive strategy to improve the well-being of Canada's children'. In March 2003, it also agreed with all the provincial governments (except Quebec's) on a Multilateral Framework on Early Learning and Care to provide national standards and uniformity in the funding, regulation and administration of child welfare policies across Canada.[64]

Thus, spending power has contributed in Canada to the weakening of provincial autonomy and therefore interjurisdictional competition. By being the only government with the necessary resources for such an important policy reform, the federal government has stepped into provincial areas of responsibility and undermined the potential benefits of intergovernmental competition in the area of social welfare. If we have been witnessing yardstick competition in Canada in child welfare policy, it ironically has contributed to the weakening of competition between provinces by the increasing role played by the federal government in this policy area. Whereas social welfare is constitutionally a provincial responsibility, the federal government has now stepped in to become a major player in childcare policy.

General regulations and budget balancing laws

Finally we examine the case of general regulations and budget balancing laws.

General regulations

In order to measure the effect of interjurisdictional competition on regulation, we used the data compiled by the Fraser Institute on the number of regulations and number of pages of regulations adopted by provincial legislatures for the period 1975 to 1999 already presented in Table 3.4. This broad indicator of regulation is commonly used to measure regulation intensity. Following the approaches of Feld and Heinemann (in this volume), we analysed the impact of interjurisdictional competition on regulation intensity with four panel regressions for the ten Canadian provinces. Our dependent variable is either the number of regulations or the number of pages for each province. We use two indicators of interjurisdictional competition *NEIGHREG* and *NEIGHPAGES*, the neighbouring provinces' average number of regulations and average number of pages adopted. We also incorporated a measure of intraprovincial government competition *LOCREV*, the ratio of local government revenue to local and provincial consolidated government revenue. We finally added several control variables in order to capture the causality between competition and regulation intensity. These control variables were: *TXRT* a broad measure of the tax burden on the economy measured by total government revenue on provincial GDP, *GDP* real per capita provincial GDP, *POP* provincial population growth rate, *INV* the ratio of private investment on GDP, *OPEN* a proxy for the economy's openness to international and inter-provincial trade measured by the ratio of the province's GDP to national GDP. The assumption we made in regards to this measure was that the smaller the province, *ceteris paribus*, the higher the share of goods and services exports in GDP because of a smaller internal market. We also used a political variable *LEFT* indicating if the government in power was left leaning. Historically two parties in Canada can be regarded in this way, the New Democratic Party (NDP) and the Parti Québécois. We include a dichotomous variable for Quebec to examine if the civil law province has a different

Table 3.8 Variable definitions

Variable	Definition
Regulations	Logarithm of number of regulations adopted by provincial legislature
Pages	Logarithm of number of pages of regulations adopted by provincial legislature
NEIGHREG	Logarithm of average number of regulations adopted by neighbouring provinces
NEIGHPAG	Logarithm of average number of pages of regulation adopted by neighbouring provinces
LOCREV	Ratio of total local government revenue to local and provincial government revenue
TXRT	Ratio of total consolidated government revenues to GDP
GDP	Logarithm of real per capita output
POP	Logarithm of total provincial population
INV	Ratio of total private investment to GDP
OPEN	Share of the provincial GDP to national GDP
LEFT	Dummy variable indicating the presence of a left-leaning government
QC	Dummy variable for the province of Quebec
1989+	Dummy variable for the years 1989–99
Time trend	Starts at one in 1976

Source: Compilation by the author from the Fraser Institute and Statistics Canada CANSIM tables 3840002, 3840015, 3840023, 3840024 and 510005.

behaviour from the common law ones. Finally, we include a dichotomous variable to account for the free trade agreement with the USA after 1989 and a lagged value of the dependent variable to examine the robustness of our result. We also examined using a time trend and fixed effects, but found the use of such a variable did not improve our results. Definitions for all variables used are given in Table 3.8. It is to be noted that all independent variables (except for the dummy variables) are included with a one-year lag. This reflects the lag in policy choices. The ordinary least squares technique was used: results for our regressions are given in Table 3.9.

Our results show:

- The number of regulations or number of pages in the neighbouring provinces has a positive impact on the number in a given province, significant three out of four times. This indicates that intergovernmental competition in this case has not led to a race to the bottom, but rather to a race to the top. Of course, as we are not able to ascertain the content of such regulations, we do not know if this is a correct picture of their economic burden.
- Greater intra-provincial financial decentralization, as captured by our local revenue indicator, has a positive, when significant, impact on the regulation intensity of Canadian provinces. Are regulations used as a counterweight to local financial autonomy?

Table 3.9 Regression results for regulatory burden, panel data 1975–99

Independent variables	Dependent variable: number of:			
	Regulations		Pages	
NEIGHREG	0.12	0.04	–	–
	[1.89]*	[0.74]	–	–
NEIGHPAG	–	–	0.30	0.15
	–	–	[5.39]***	[2.96]***
LOCREV	0.83	0.16	−0.38	0.48
	[2.08]**	[2.46]**	[−0.63]	[4.37]***
TXRT	−2.49	−1.32	−1.02	0.16
	[−2.72]***	[−1.77]*	[−0.76]	[0.14]
GDP	−0.15	−0.05	0.70	0.26
	[−1.16]	[−0.53]	[4.01]***	[1.73]*
POP	0.46	0.21	0.50	0.23
	[11.60]***	[5.23]***	[8.21]***	[4.24]***
INV	−0.05	−0.05	−1.85	−0.84
	[−0.13]	[−0.15]	[−3.17]***	[−1.72]*
OPEN	0.14	0.04	−2.57	−1.45
	[0.43]	[0.15]	[−4.74]***	[−3.05]
LEFT	−0.01	0.00	−0.08	−0.05
	[−0.12]	[0.01]	[−1.19]	[−0.89]
1989+	−0.15	−0.10	−0.18	−0.13
	[−2.82]***	[−2.25]**	[−2.28]**	[−1.88]*
QC	−0.36	−0.16	1.10	0.51
	[−4.42]***	[−2.36]**	[9.15]***	[4.17]***
REG(−1)	–	0.58	–	–
	–	[10.74]***	–	–
PAGES(−1)	–	–	–	0.54
	–	–	–	[9.77]***
CONSTANT	0.86	0.31	−7.88	−3.43
	[0.91]	[0.42]	[−5.19]***	[−2.63]***
Adj. *R*-square	0.80	0.87	0.73	0.80
Observations	240	240	240	240

Source: Calculations by the author.

Notes
The *t*-statistics are given in brackets. Asterisks indicate variables whose coefficients are significant at the 10(*), 5(**), and 1% (***) levels.

- A greater share of government (federal–provincial–local) in the economy reduces significantly the number of regulations, but has no impact on the number of pages. Perhaps there is some substitution going on between one type of government activity and another.
- Higher GDP per capita has a significant positive impact on the number of pages.
- Larger provincial population increases significantly regulatory intensity. This may reflect the need to deal with more complex environments such as urban areas, high-tech industries.

- Higher private investments decrease significantly the number of pages of regulations. This may well be a relationship where the reverse causation is taking place.
- A more open economy decreases significantly the number of pages. Perhaps provincial governments have less power in more open economies.
- The political leaning of the provincial government has no impact on regulatory intensity.
- Regulatory intensity has declined significantly after the ratification of CUFTA/NAFTA. This is probably a result of the need to adjust to more competition.[65]
- The province of Quebec has less regulation but more pages. Perhaps this is linked to the Civil code used in that province.
- Lagged values of the dependent variables have a positive and significant effect. Their presence reduces the absolute values of the coefficients of the other variables, but does not change our overall findings.

The overall fit of our model is acceptable. Our results are similar to those of Feld in terms of the positive impact of regulations in the neighbouring jurisdictions.

Budget balancing requirements

From 1993 to 1999, nine of the ten Canadian provincial governments successively adopted laws enforcing balanced budgets (anti-deficit) in an attempt to reduce the accumulated debt. British Columbia and Ontario are the latest provinces to enact balanced budget legislation in 1999, following in the footsteps of Quebec (1996), Alberta (1995), Manitoba (1995), Saskatchewan (1995), New Brunswick (1993) and Nova Scotia (1993). They are summarized in Table 3.10.

Anti-deficit laws share the common objective of preventing government from running a deficit in a given fiscal year, but province-specific provisions clearly demonstrate the heterogeneity of anti-deficit legislation. Manitoba's legislation is the only one containing a taxpayer protection clause stating that any increase in sales, income, payroll, property or corporation tax would have to be approved first by the population through a referendum.[66] In the case of Ontario, the balanced budget legislation included the provision permitting the government not to balance the books when the fiscal year coincides with an election year. For that matter, Victor Vrsnik from the Canadian Taxpayers Federation expressed during the oral question period of Manitoba's Legislative Assembly, on 29 May 1995, the desirability to follow Ontario's actions.[67]

> There is no statute of limitation on government responsibility for the province's finances. The authors of Ontario's new balanced budget law did not find it necessary to include such a loophole. Manitoba should likewise erase section 4(2) . . .

Table 3.10 Budget balancing requirements

Characteristics of provincial anti-deficit Legislation (Y = Yes present; N = Not present)

	Anti-deficit law	Apply to realized deficits	Concrete debt elimination	Single-year budget period	Penalties for not achieving	Referendum for tax	Total index of stringency
Manitoba	Y	Y	Y	Y	Y	Y	6
Alberta	Y	Y	Y	Y	N	N	4
Quebec	Y	Y	N	Y	N	N	3
Nova Scotia	Y	N	N	Y	N	N	2
New Brunswick	Y	Y	N	N	N	N	2
Saskatchewan	N	N	N	N	N	N	1
British Columbia	N	N	N	N	N	N	0
Newfoundland	N	N	N	N	N	N	0
Ontario	N	N	N	N	N	N	0
Prince Edward Island	N	N	N	N	N	N	0

Source: Geneviève Tellier and Louis M. Imbeau, 'Budget deficits and surpluses in the Canadian provinces: a pooled analysis', Centre d'Analyse des Politiques Publiques, April 2004.

The adoption by the Alberta government of the Deficit Elimination Act coincided with a balanced budget in 1995;[68] one suspects that the law would not have been put forward if the achievement of this goal was not fairly certain before hand. The budget was balanced without introducing new taxes or raising tax rates.[69] This accomplishment of the Klein government inspired certain politicians to call Alberta a model for the rest of Canada. However, this conception of government fiscal responsibility is not unanimous. Ms Stanger (NDP – Lloydminster) shared her concerns toward the 'Alberta Model' in her speech at the Legislative Assembly of Saskatchewan on 17 May 2005:[70]

> The Liberals and Tories say that they haven't increased taxes, but what has Mr Klein done? Let me give you some examples. Social Services cut by 18 per cent. . . . Municipal government has been cut by 30 per cent. No increased taxes, but who is going to pay for these services?

Mr Sawicki expressed similar concerns in his speech at the British Columbia Legislative Assembly on the 31 March 1999:[71]

> We just hear endless comparisons with Alberta. It's not my idea of Canada. . . . Yes Alberta has balanced the budget, and they've also closed hospitals. Yes they have balanced the budget, and you have to pay to send your child to kindergarten.

Hence in this case, it is not inspiration but rejection that emerges from interprovincial comparisons.

The Quebec debates do not make comparisons with other provinces. Mr Christopherson (NDP – Hamilton Center) from Ontario made reference to Manitoba's balanced budget legislation in order to point out that anti-deficit laws do not necessarily imply a decrease of government spending:[72]

> Once again, the reality of what happened in Manitoba is not unlike the experience in many of the states of the United States of America where they passed balanced budget legislation . . . what we passed in Ontario, in terms of the other provinces in Canada that have it, Manitoba was the one that we have paralleled the most. Gary Filmon's Conservatives . . . had balanced-budget legislation and ran on an election platform that said their fiscal plan would give the people of Manitoba a $21.4 million surplus . . . they hired an agency at arm's length from any of the political parties . . . and they found a deficit of between $262 million and $417 million.

But are budgets actually balanced? The worst possible way of answering this question is to examine the official provincial Public Accounts as they are subject to the use of time-varying creative accounting. Hence, we use Statistics Canada data that are produced using uniform definitions of public sector, revenues and expenditures. The answer, as shown in Figures 3.5–3.7, is in general no and is

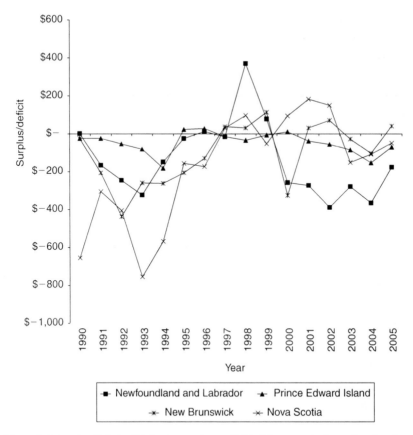

Figure 3.5 Surplus/deficit of Atlantic provinces, 2004–5 (source: Author using data from Statistics Canada).

not linked to the existence or not of an anti-deficit law. The actual picture of the revenues and expenses of provinces from the Maritimes is that New Brunswick is the only province to run a surplus for the fiscal year 2005.[73] Nova Scotia, which enacted balanced budget legislation, was in deficit for the same fiscal year.[74] Quebec and Ontario have not balanced their books since 2002.[75] The four Western provinces,[76] in which balance budget legislation is effective, all had balanced budgets for the fiscal year 2005.

Conclusion

Table 3.11 summarizes our findings. One notes that:

- Quebec is often the initiator of new provincial policies in Canada. This may reflect its need for *national* policies distinct from the rest of Canada given

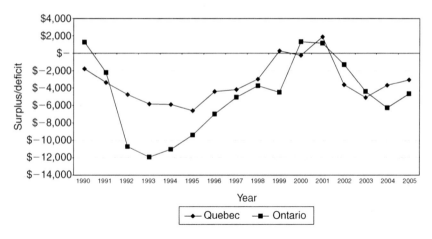

Figure 3.6 Surplus/deficit of Quebec and Ontario, 2004–5 (source: Author using data from Statistics Canada).

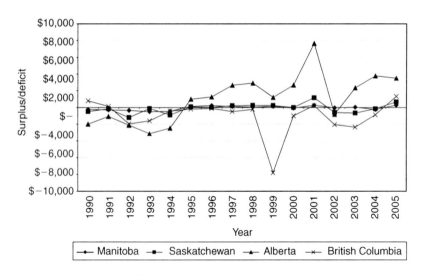

Figure 3.7 Surplus/deficit for Western provinces, 1990–2005 (source: Author using data from Statistics Canada).

its role as a French-speaking jurisdiction. It may also reflect the quality of its provincial civil service.

• Yardstick competition does not necessarily yield good economic policies as the adoption of LSVCFs by almost all provinces shows.

• The federal government through its spending power tends to harmonize social policies in Canada at the highest level of intervention observed.

Table 3.11 Summary of findings

Policy	Initiator	Text evidence of yardstick competition	Impact on economic efficiency	Comment
LSVCF	Quebec	Yes in most cases	Negative; reduces intra-Canada capital mobility	Harmonization is desired by provinces
Incorporation	Federal then provinces	Not available	Not Available	Econometric evidence on impact on amount of sales is mixed
Sunday shopping	Supreme court judgement followed by provincial laws	Yes in some cases	Positive; increases choices of consumers	No econometric evidence of impact on wages
Anti-strike-breaker legislation	Quebec	No	Constrains capital but seem not to affect choices much	A race to the middle is ongoing
Minimum wages	All provinces	Yes: comparability with peer groups which vary from province to province is important	Reduces employment opportunities for unskilled labour	
Mandatory retirement	Quebec	Very little	Increases freedom of choice of labour	Some change in behaviour of older workers is observed
University fees	All provinces	Not much. Electoral promises and the strength of student associations play a larger role in policy setting	Low fees set wrong prices and cross-subsidies from poor to rich result from them	International comparisons with the USA or Europe are often made

continued

Table 3.11 continued

Policy	Initiator	Text evidence of yardstick competition	Impact on economic efficiency	Comment
Medicare	Saskatchewan	None. Federally funded national policies lead to uniformity across provinces	Use of cost-sharing subsidies created wrong incentives in some periods	
Tobacco control	Federal government	Very little. Reference is made to health effects of tobacco	Reduction of health cost and externalities	
Childcare	Quebec	None. Federal initiative in progress	Head start benefits of universal early childhood education should result from this policy	
Budget-balancing	Atlantic provinces	Some but often in a negative fashion, i.e. province x should not emulate province Y	Not obvious as observed more in the breach than in practice. Not logical to prevent borrowing for capital purposes	Adoption of such a law is often seen as an ideological choice

Source: Author.

Overall, there is little evidence of interjurisdictional yardstick competition in Canada in the regulatory domain. What is observed is tax and spending competition to attract jobs; Quebec is the main actor in this field, but the federal government often makes decisions favouring one province or another. What can also be important is the role of US regulations in setting the Canadian framework – the case of electricity is the most obvious one – and of the federal government ensuring through national standards that the best policies, interpreted in the Canadian context as more government intervention – health and childcare policies being the most obvious ones – are adopted throughout the country. One interesting possibility in the future is that Alberta, with a surfeit of oil and gas royalties, could, in the later part of this decade, challenge federal norms and regulations in health and childcare, setting its own course and accepting the reduced transfers that would ensue.

Appendix A: Impact of Sunday shopping regulations on retail sales[77]

This appendix examines if the various – own and neighbourly – provincial Sunday shopping regulations had an impact on retail sales in a given province.

The regression analysis uses retail sales as the dependent variable, six economic control variables, a set of provincial dummy variables (Nova Scotia is the omitted province) and two sets of interactive dummy variables × policy variables. The first set is provincial dummies × the provincial store opening policy (Province* Pol). The provincial store opening policy is a province-specific spline variable that varies from 0 – no store opening on Sunday, to 1 – full store opening on Sunday. The indicator used to calculate in-between values is: (retail employment in areas allowing Sunday shopping/total retail employment in the province).

The second set is provincial dummies × neighbouring provinces provincial store opening policy (details available from the author). Variables are used to examine the impact of policies in other relevant provinces, defined in Table 3.A1, on retails sales in a given province. The period analysed is January 1981 to March 2004.

Table 3.A1 Provinces and their neighbour(s)

Province studied	Neighbours impacting on it
British Columbia	Alberta
Alberta	British Columbia
Saskatchewan	Alberta
Manitoba	Saskatchewan, Ontario
Ontario	Manitoba, Quebec
Quebec	Ontario, New Brunswick
New Brunswick	Quebec, Prince Edward Island, Nova Scotia
Nova Scotia	New Brunswick
Prince Edward Island	New Brunswick
Newfoundland	–

Table 3.A2 Determinants of retail sales, Canadian provinces, monthly data, 1981–2004

Dependent variable: Log (Sales) $_{it}$

Independent variables	Coefficient
Constant	8.3808**
	(176.55)
Unemployment rate, provincial	−0.003814**
	(−4.47)
Consumer loan rate, Canadian	0.002274**
	(2.72)
Female employment rate, provincial	−0.005216**
	(−6.17)
Canada–US exchange rate, in Can$	0.0477**
	(2.91)
TSE300$_t$	0.000018**
(Stock index, Canadian)	(12.27)
Salaries	0.002477**
IV estimation provincial	(46.96)
British Columbia (BC)	−0.2055*
	(−2.43)
Alberta (Alb)	0.0276
	(0.32)
Saskatchewan (Sas)	−0.1606*
	(−15.36)
Manitoba (Man)	−0.1576**
	(−15.50)
Ontario (Ont)	−0.1846**
	(−16.33)
Quebec (Que)	−0.1489**
	(−15.46)
New Brunswick (NB)	−0.0628**
	(−7.59)
Prince Edward Island (PEI)	−0.0291**
	(−3.60)
Newfoundland (New)	−0.1648**
	(−15.40)
$BC_i * Pol_{it}$	−0.0510
	(−0.59)
$Alb_i * Pol_{it}$	0.0708**
	(9.24)
$Sas_i * Pol_{it}$	0.0033
	(0.40)
$Man_i * Pol_{it}$	0.0676**
	(6.72)
$Ont_i * Pol_{it}$	−0.1383**
	(−7.17)
$Que_i * Pol_{it}$	0.0087
	(0.59)
$NB_i * Pol_{it}$	−0.0195*
	(−2.19)

Table 3.A2 continued

Dependent variable: Log (Sales) $_{it}$

Independent variables	Coefficient
$NS_i * Pol_{it}$	−0.00060
	(−0.07)
$PEI_i * Pol_{it}$	0.0354
	(1.36)
$New_i * Pol_{it}$	0.1003**
	(10.34)
$BC_i * NeighPol_{it}$	0.0420**
	(5.05)
$Alb_i * NeighPol_{it}$	−0.2254*
	(−2.59)
$San_i * NeighPol_{it}$	−0.0040
	(−0.44)
$Man_i * NeighPol_{it}$	−0.0653**
	(−5.66)
$Ont_i * NeighPol_{it}$	−0.0768**
	(−4.45)
$Que_i * NeighPol_{it}$	−0.0874**
	(−5.27)
$NB_i * NeighPol_{it}$	0.0042
	(0.45)
$NS_i * NeighPol_{it}$	−0.0070
	(−0.94)
$PEI_i * NeighPol_{it}$	0.0082
	(0.63)
$New_i * NeighPol_{it}$	−

Notes
Number of observations = 2,790
R-squared = 0.9305
Degrees of freedom = 33

The regression results presented in Table 3.A2 show that except for the interest rate variables, the six economic control variables have the expected effects on retail sales. The policy variables do not always have the expected impacts. Own policy impacts should be at least positive if not significant. They are positive in 6/10 cases. Neighbouring provinces policy variables are not always of the right sign but at least in the case of Alberta, Manitoba, Ontario and Quebec, they show that liberalization of store opening policies in their neighbouring provinces reduced sales in their own province. This provided an impetus to liberalize in turn; this is particularly true of the Ontario–Quebec group with a small six-month delay in Quebec following Ontario in liberalizing Sunday shopping.

Appendix B: The impact of banning strike replacement labour on wages[78]

One possible impact of legislation banning strike replacement labour (scabs) is on strike behaviour, which is measured by the incidence and length of strikes. But the ultimate output of union activity should be higher wages for its members compared with similar workers (demographic characteristics, type of work and so on). This is what is examined with the following multivariate analysis. Individual worker data, drawn from the Labour Force Survey administered by Statistics Canada to a representative sample of Canadian Households, are used for 1997 and 2002: 1997 is the first year for which the survey asked questions about union coverage and wages while 2002 is the last year that was available at the time the empirical work was carried out (early 2005). The log of wages, corrected and uncorrected for purchasing power parity (PPP) differences between provinces, is regressed on a series of variables. Results in Table 3.B1 show:

- A high R-square for a cross-sectional wage equation.
- The usual impacts of age (positive, increasing then decreasing with the number of years), education (positive, increasing with the number of years), sex (men earn more than women), tenure in the job (positive).
- No obvious impact of having more restrictive replacement worker laws; it is neither Quebec nor British Columbia that has the greatest coefficient for the interactive dichotomous variable Province × Union Covered.

Thus this difference in the power of unions does not seem to impact on individual wages in either of the two years examined. As a methodological point, note that using PPP-corrected wages matters to the results; we report results with uncorrected wages as the dependent variable in Table 3.B2.

Notes

1 We do not examine the case of the three Northern territories or of aboriginal governments.
2 The disallowance power was last used in the depression years with respect to some financial laws introduced by Alberta's Social Credit government.
3 See 'Key Dates in Morgentaler's battle', *Globe and Mail*, 16 June 2005, p. A9.
4 See Beck *et al.* (2002) for an overview.
5 La Porta *et al.* (1998: 1151).
6 La Porta *et al.* (1999: 262).
7 Harvey (1971: 119).
8 The Senators are formally appointed by the Governor-General, which means they are really appointed by the Prime Minister. Since members serve until age 75, it is quite possible that at any time the majority of Senators were appointed by a different party than that currently in power. However, although in constitutional terms the Senate has almost the same powers as the House of Commons, it has not vetoed a bill from the Commons since 1939.
9 In both cases, it resulted in more federal government intervention in the economy. The current support negotiated in April 2005 requires additional (with respect to ori-

Table 3.B1 OLS regression of log of current (PPP corrected) wages, Canada, 1997 and 2002

	1997		2002	
	Coefficients	t-statistics	Coefficients	t-statistics
Constant	0.0239	85.78	2.0790	55.50
Union coverage	0.0113	6.96	0.0581	3.20
Provinces (Ontario omitted)				
Newfoundland	−0.1560	−5.16	−0.0410	−1.00
PEI	0.0073	0.32	0.0695	2.10
New Brunswick	−0.1123	−6.98	−0.0596	−2.45
Nova Scotia	0.0792	4.58	0.1344	5.84
Quebec	0.1731	12.33	0.2280	11.39
Manitoba	0.2153	13.01	0.3095	12.41
Saskatchewan	0.1601	8.78	0.2791	11.52
Alberta	0.2719	17.71	0.2827	12.90
British Columbia	0.0475	3.54	0.0706	3.43
Age (15–19 omitted)				
20–24	0.0783	6.01	0.1319	6.89
25–29	0.2606	19.01	0.3419	15.11
30–34	0.3622	25.86	0.3874	16.71
35–39	0.3932	28.25	0.3865	16.74
40–44	0.3701	25.17	0.4039	15.91
45–49	0.3558	23.23	0.3793	15.43
50–54	0.3746	21.45	0.3924	15.10
55–59	0.3258	14.29	0.3136	10.62
60–64	0.3527	11.70	0.2783	6.82
65 plus	0.1903	2.68	0.0849	0.92
Men	0.1722	22.63	0.1804	16.11
Unmarried	0.0014	0.11	−0.0510	−4.07
Schooling (primary omitted)				
High school	0.0926	9.19	0.1248	8.31
Post-secondary	0.1935	21.12	0.2392	16.35
BA/BSc	0.4160	28.41	0.4411	19.91
MA/MSc, PhD	0.4791	19.66	0.5734	19.04
Tenure in job	0.0015	25.81	0.0013	15.97
Province X Union (Ontario omitted)				
Newfoundland	0.0390	2.75	0.1278	2.17
PEI	0.0357	1.69	0.2076	4.11
New Brunswick	0.0273	2.71	0.1210	3.23
Nova Scotia	0.0273	2.46	0.0756	2.01
Quebec	0.0198	2.14	0.0339	1.20
Manitoba	0.0245	4.03	0.0427	1.12
Saskatchewan	0.0279	4.27	0.0169	0.44
Alberta	0.0243	0.99	0.0707	1.85
British Columbia	0.0198	0.49	0.0452	1.51
R-square/N	0.5376	163.83	0.5585	77.48

Note
We do not report results for 15 sectoral dummies included in the regressions.

Table 3.B2 OLS regression of log of current wages, Canada, 1997 and 2002

	1997		2002	
	Coefficients	t-statistics	Coefficients	t-statistics
Constants	2.1655	94.61	2.2485	61.36
Union coverage	0.0958	8.14	0.0762	3.97
Provinces (Ontario omitted)				
Newfoundland	−0.2663	−8.68	−0.3041	−7.61
PEI	−0.2256	−10.19	−0.2681	−8.37
New Brunswick	−0.2109	−12.83	−0.2107	−9.51
Nova Scotia	−0.2591	−16.10	−0.2480	−10.05
Quebec	−0.0972	−7.13	−0.0979	−5.00
Manitoba	−0.1368	−8.85	−0.1266	−5.40
Saskatchewan	−0.1878	−11.04	−0.1295	−5.65
Alberta	−0.0566	−3.89	−0.0420	−1.97
British Columbia	0.0786	5.30	0.0110	0.51
Age (15–19 omitted)				
20–24	0.0786	6.08	0.1368	7.21
25–29	0.2610	19.24	0.3484	15.43
30–34	0.3620	26.19	0.3943	16.88
35–39	0.3927	28.48	0.3945	16.99
40–44	0.3692	25.40	0.4102	16.29
45–49	0.3562	23.37	0.3850	15.75
50–54	0.3750	21.65	0.3987	15.40
55–59	0.3249	14.17	0.3229	10.84
60–64	0.3560	11.67	0.2868	6.81
65 plus	0.1903	2.70	0.0920	1.01
Men	0.1715	22.56	0.1813	15.96
Unmarried	0.0023	0.18	−0.0510	−4.01
Schooling (primary omitted)				
High school	0.0913	9.08	0.1255	8.26
Post-secondary	0.1934	21.14	0.2413	16.42
BA/BSc	0.4144	28.53	0.4462	19.99
Ma/MSc, PhD	0.4812	19.87	0.5831	18.97
Tenure in job	0.0015	25.79	0.0013	16.02
Province X Union (Ontario omitted)				
Newfoundland	0.0939	2.38	0.0942	1.64
PEI	0.0225	0.65	0.1476	3.01
New Brunswick	0.0534	1.96	0.0294	0.81
Nova Scotia	0.0273	2.46	0.1009	2.66
Quebec	0.0066	0.34	0.0001	0.00
Manitoba	0.0449	1.95	−0.0101	−0.28
Saskatchewan	0.0589	2.25	−0.0280	−0.77
Alberta	−0.0205	−0.89	0.0298	1.28
British Columbia	0.0141	0.68	0.0405	1.28
R-square/N	0.5259	163.83	0.5411	77.48

Note
We do not report results for 15 sectoral dummies included in the regressions.

ginal February 2005 budget plans) spending of 4.6 billion over two years or about a 1 per cent increase in annual spending.

10 Boyne (1996: 718–9).

11 Something which the English language majority can be reluctant to do. For example, when the Bank of Canada was created in 1933, fears were voiced that putting French on banknotes would debase the currency, while the adoption of the Official Languages Act in 1969 by the federal government is still resented by some Anglophones in 2005.

12 Hence the introduction in 2004 of the Ontario Automotive Investment Strategy (OAIS). See: www.premier.gov.on.ca/english/news/AutoInvestment041404.asp.

13 See: www.reviewcta-examenltc.gc.ca/english/pages/final/ch15e.htm and www. reviewcta-examenltc.gc.ca/Submissions-Soumissions/Dec4/Canadian%20Trucking% 20Alliance.pdf.

14 Implicitly Canadian trucking firms are assumed to offer a level of services (safety of rigs, pollution, etc.) similar to those of American firms, while this is not the case for Mexican firms; see: www.freetrade.org/pubs/FTBs/FTB-013.html. This puts pressure on Canadian regulators to have standards similar to those of the USA.

15 See for example www.ccmta.ca/english/pdf/hos_consultation_report.pdf, pp. 29–30.

16 In 2001 see www.canelect.ca/english/electricity_in_canada_snapshot_Demand_2. html.

17 Alberta is served by three large producers see www.cienergy.org/Presentations/ Doucet-Sept01.pdf.

18 Information for this paragraph is drawn from: *Canadian Electricity: Exports and Imports, An Energy Market Assessment, January 2003* National Energy Board at: www.neb-one.gc.ca/energy/EnergyReports/EMAElectricityExportsIm-portsCanada2003_e.pdf.

19 Block *et al.* (2003: 124).

20 Ibid. pp. 86, 124.

21 ACIR (1991: 20).

22 Ibid.

23 'Official Report', House of Commons Debates, 2nd session, 33rd parliament, Volume X, 1987, p. 12863.

24 'Official Report', House of Commons Debates, 2nd session, 33rd parliament, Volume X, 1987, p. 12893.

25 'Debates and Proceedings', Legislative Assembly of Manitoba, 4th session, 35th parliament, 1993, p. 947.

26 'Debates of Legislative Assembly', Province of British Columbia, 1st session, 35th parliament, 1992, volume 4, n. 10, p. 2403.

27 'Journal of Debates', Legislative Assembly of Ontario, 3rd session, 35th parliament, 1993–4, pp. 4130–1.

28 Cumming and MacIntosh (2000: 165).

29 Ibid. p. 179.

30 Alberta Hansard, Alberta Legislative Assembly, 20th legislature, 3rd session, 1985.

31 'Debates and Proceedings', Legislative Assembly of Saskatchewan, 2nd session, 21st legislature, 1989.

32 'Debates and Proceedings', Legislative Assembly of Manitoba, 4th session, 35th legislature, 1992–3.

33 'Journal des débats', Québec, Assemblée Nationale, 2iem session, 34ièm Législature, 1992.

34 Human Resources and Skills Development Canada, International and Intergovernmental Labour Affairs, 1 January 2005.

35 Prince Edward Island Hansard, Legislative Assembly, 2nd session, 62nd general assembly, 23 November 2004.

36 House of Commons Debates, 1st session, 33rd parliament, 26 June 1986.

37 House of Commons Debates, 1st session, 33rd parliament, 26 June 1986.
38 Source: Statistics Canada, CANSIM II, Table 282–0001.
39 In the case of Quebec, language might reduce both inward and outward mobility of students.
40 Since 1997, Canadian students who are not residents of Quebec must pay an additional amount such that their fee is equal to the average of the other nine provincial fees; that has been taken into account in the calculation of tuition fees. This explains the increase of tuition fees in Quebec after 1997 despite the freeze of tuition fees for Quebec residents.
41 Manitoba Hansard, Legislative Assembly, 36th legislature, 2nd session, Vol. 67, 21 October 1996.
42 Ibid.
43 Quebec Hansard, National Assembly. Commission permanente de l'éducation, 36th legislature, 2nd session, 9 April 2002.
44 Nova Scotia Hansard, Nova Scotia Assembly Committee on Human Resources, 30 November 2004.
45 Ontario Hansard, Legislative Assembly, 38th legislature, 1st session, 16 May 2005.
46 Manitoba Hansard, Legislative Assembly of Manitoba, 36th legislature, 4th session, Vol. 30, 14 April 1998.
47 British Columbia Hansard, Legislative Assembly, 37th legislature, 2nd session, 9 August 2001.
48 Donahue (1998: 390).
49 Collishaw (1980: 156).
50 Donahue (1998: 390).
51 In November 2004, the father of Medicare was voted the greatest Canadian: see www.cbc.ca/greatest/.
52 MacTaggart (1972b: 1237).
53 MacTaggart (1972a: 1234).
54 Ibid. p. 1236.
55 Collishaw (1980: 159).
56 Quebec Hansard, National Assembly, Commission permanente des affaires sociales, 10 June 1998.
57 Alberta Hansard, Legislative Assembly, 17 November 1998.
58 Ontario Hansard, Legislative Assembly, 14 December 1993.
59 Nova Scotia Hansard, Legislative Assembly, Standing Committee on Community Services, 29 November 2001.
60 Lefebvre (2004: 53).
61 OECD (2004: 55).
62 Ibid.
63 See www.sdc.gc.ca/en/cs/comm/sd/news/2005/index05.shtml for a list of signed agreements and their content.
64 Friendly (2004: 47).
65 One suspects that in new members of the EU, one would probably find the reverse impact of joining a larger economic zone.
66 Geneviève Tellier and Louis M. Imbeau, 'Budget Deficits and Surpluses in the Canadian Provinces: A Pooled Analysis', Centre d'Analyse des Politiques Publiques, p. 4, April 2004.
67 Manitoba Hansard, Legislative Assembly, 36th legislature, 1st session, 29 May 1995.
68 Statistics Canada, CANSIM II, Table 385 0001.
69 Saskatchewan Hansard, Legislative Assembly, 22nd legislature, 5th session, 17 May 1995.
70 Saskatchewan Hansard, Legislative Assembly, 22nd legislature, 5th session, 17 May 1995.
71 British Columbia Hansard, Legislative Assembly, 36th legislature, 3rd session, 31 March 1999.

72 Ontario Hansard, Legislative Assembly, 36th legislature, 1st session, 16 December 1999.
73 Statistics Canada, CANSIM II, Table 385 0001.
74 Ibid.
75 Ibid.
76 Ibid.
77 The empirical results in this appendix are drawn from: 'The impact of Sunday shopping deregulation concerning the retail industry for the provinces of Canada' by Jean-François Bélisle, mimeo, 2005.
78 The empirical results of this appendix are drawn from: 'Analyse de l'intensité du syndicalisme sur le salaire réel au niveau de la compétition inter juridictionnelle au Canada', by M. Desrosiers-Drolet, mimeo, 2005.

References

Advisory Commission on Intergovernmental Relations (ACIR) (1991) *Interjurisdictional Tax and Policy Competition: Good or Bad for the Federal System?* M-177, Washington DC.

Beck, Thorsten, Demirgüç-Kunt, Asly and Ross, Levine (2002) 'Law and Finance: Why Does Legal Origin Matter?' Washington DC: The World Bank.

Bélanger, Hardy Louise and Grenon, Aline (1997) *Éléments de Common Law et aperçu comparatif du droit civil québécois*, Scarborough: Carswell.

Block, Richard N., Roberts, Karen and Clarke, R. Oliver (2003) *Labor Standards in the United States and Canada*, Kalamazoo, Michigan: W.E. Upjohn Institute for Employment Research.

Boyne, George A. (1996) 'Competition and local government: a public choice perspective', *Urban Studies*, 33(4–5), 703–21.

Collishaw, Neil E. (1980) 'Histoire de l'évolution des modes de financement des services de santé au Canada', *L'Actualité Économique*, no. 2, 154–63.

Cumming, Douglas J. and MacIntosh, Jeffrey G. (2000) 'the role of interjurisdictional competition in shaping Canadian corporate law', *International Review of Law and Economics*, 20, 141–86.

Donahue, Paul J. (1998) 'Federalism and the financing of health care in Canada and Switzerland: lessons for health care reform in the United States,' *Boston College International and Comparative Law Review*, 21(1), 385–435.

Friendly, Martha (2004) 'Strengthening Canada's social and economic foundations: next steps for early childhood education and child care', *Policy Options*, March: 46–51.

Green, David A. and Harrison, Kathryn (2005) 'Racing to the middle: minimum wage setting and standards of fairness', UBC, mimeo.

Harvey, Pierre (1971) 'Pourquoi le Québec et les Canadiens Français occupent-ils une place inférieure sur le plan économique?' in René Durocher and Paul-André Linteau (eds) *Le 'Retard' du Québec et l'infériorité économique des Canadiens Français*, les éditions Boréal Express, pp. 113–27.

Kugler, Stuart and Kugler, Robert (2004) 'Quebec: the Class Action Haven', *The Canadian Class Action Review*, 1(1).

La Porta, R., Lopez-de-Silanes, F., Shleifer, A. and Vishny, R.W. (1998) 'Law and finance', *Journal of Political Economy*, 106, 1113–55.

—— (1999) 'The quality of government', *Journal of Law, Economics, and Organization*, 15, 222–79.

Lefebvre, Pierre (2004) 'Quebec's innovative early childhood education and care policy and its weaknesses', *Policy Options*, March, 52–7.

MacTaggart, Ken. (1972) 'The first decade: The story of the birth of Canadian Medicare in Saskatchewan and its development during the following ten years', *Canadian Medical Association Journal*, June, 106, 1234–43.

OECD (2004) *Early Childhood Education and Care Policy: Canada Country Note*, October, Paris.

Saunders, O.J (2003) Canada–US energy issues: electricity and regulatory sovereignty, at: www.globalcentres.org/can-us/energy_saunders.pdf.

Singh, Parbudyal and Jain, Harish C. (2001) 'Striker replacement in the United States, Canada and Mexico: a review of the law and empirical research', *Industrial relations*, 40(1), 22–53.

Vaillancourt, François (1997) 'Labour sponsored venture capital funds in Canada: institutional aspects, tax expenditures and employment creation', in P. Halpern (ed.) *Financing Growth in Canada*, Calgary: University of Calgary Press (Industry Canada), pp. 571–92.

Vaillancourt, François and Turgeon, Mathieu (2002) 'The provision of highways in Canada and the federal government', *Publius*, 32(1), 161–80.

Vaubel, Roland (2004) 'Federation with majority decisions: economic lessons from the history of the United States, Germany and the European Union', *Economic Affairs*, 24, 53–9.

COMMENT: HOW CAN A COUNTRY LIKE CANADA BE INHOSPITABLE TO AN INFLUENCE OF YARDSTICK COMPETITION ON REGULATION?

Pierre Salmon

The economic literature on competition among governments tends to hinge on their response to the actual or potential mobility of firms, capital, households and consumers. It concentrates on competition over fiscal variables, mostly taxation. François Vaillancourt's contribution (2005) is a remarkable and pioneering exception to these generalizations. It is concerned with competition over regulation rather than with competition over fiscal variables. It considers the two main forms of intergovernmental competition, not only the one based on mobility but also the one known as yardstick competition. It has to do with intergovernmental competition in Canada, a country not very much studied empirically under that perspective. It does not shy away from using a variety of methods, including some of them uncommon in economics, and it provides interesting cases and evidence.

Vaillancourt infers from his investigations that competition among Canadian provinces is mainly over fiscal or financial variables. He finds only limited empirical evidence of regulatory competition or of yardstick competition affecting regulation.[1] This somewhat negative result concerning a highly decentralized democratic country such as Canada is puzzling. If there is little yardstick competition affecting regulation in that country, is it likely that there will be much of it elsewhere? In other words, might not scepticism about the mechanism in Canada justify scepticism about its relevance overall? But what could also be the case is that, for some reason, the Canadian set-up is less favourable, in some respects at least, to yardstick competition than are other national contexts. The difficulties or uncertainties involved in trying to identify yardstick competition, in particular of the kind that may affect regulation, are especially burdensome for economists, as I will try to show. I will also discuss whether the Canadian context is likely to be particularly favourable or unfavourable to the working of the mechanism. Before addressing these two questions, however, a few precisions about the interpretation of yardstick competition concerned here are timely.

Political yardstick competition and its brethren

Less formally but with more generality than in Besley and Case (1995), the mechanism can be summarized as follows (Salmon 1987). In a changing and uncertain world, it is difficult for voters to assess whether the performance of their government is good or bad. The observation of what obtains in other jurisdictions may help voters to form an opinion on this matter. If, in domains of interest to them, some voters find that services provided, or policies followed, by governments are better in other jurisdictions than in their own, this may decrease the probability that they will vote for the incumbents on the next occasion. The probability may be increased if what they find is the other way around. Awareness of that behaviour may induce incumbents to decide policies with due consideration to what is done elsewhere. This, in turn, may improve performance, in a way shaped or influenced by the way voters themselves perceive their interests. The mechanism may also not work or it may have perverse effects.

It should be distinguished from three mechanisms that also involve interjurisdictional comparisons and also are not based on the mobility of firms, capital or households:

- emulation among office-holders aiming at gaining the approval or admiration of their peers, a mechanism pointed out by Hume,[2] and relied upon with little success by the so-called Lisbon strategy in the context of the European Union;
- laboratory federalism, in which the government of one jurisdiction observes innovations in other jurisdictions and, whether because of their intrinsic value or for electoral reasons, copies those that succeed (Rose-Ackerman 1980; Strumpf 2002);
- competition across jurisdictions among office-holders for the purpose not of re-election but of promotion to some position at a higher governmental tier (see Bodenstein and Ursprung 2005).

The two necessary characteristics of political yardstick competition as understood here are, first, that the agents who make the interjurisdictional comparisons are the voters or, more generally, the providers of political support and, second, that office-holders are influenced by the comparisons because they seek electoral or political support to improve their chance of remaining in power. At least one of the two characteristics is missing in each of the three mechanisms above. However, from the laboratory federalism idea, we will retain that an essential component of competition among governments – of yardstick competition in particular – is policy innovation and experimentation.

Difficulties involved in establishing empirically whether yardstick competition is effective and affects regulation

There are several difficulties. First, with regard to the assertion of non-existence, it is well known that a statement asserting the existence of something in an infinite or very large universe cannot be refuted. If you do not find that thing, supporters of the statement that it exists can always encourage you to go on searching. As a consequence, it is generally argued that existential propositions are not legitimate scientific hypotheses. This, however, does not make them meaningless, which is enough for our purpose. There is a clear case here for advising additional search.

Even though the selection of policies discussed by Vaillancourt is already substantial, possible manifestations of yardstick regulatory competition other than those whose presence or absence he investigates do come to mind. Some policy domains such as the environment seem particularly promising. Vaillancourt's contribution is explicitly (and understandably) limited to the provincial level. In further work, however, yardstick competition among municipalities, including competition between large cities such as Montreal and Toronto, would be particularly worth exploring. It is true that, in Canada as elsewhere, municipal governments do not have as much regulatory power as have provincial governments. But they have some, draw considerable attention from citizens, and can strongly influence compliance with existing regulation in various ways, in particular through financial and in-kind support. In any case, as we will see, yardstick competition does not have to take place directly over regulation to have an effect on it. One might also want to seek evidence about transnational yardstick competition, at all subcentral levels of government (that is, between American states and Canadian provinces, or between American and Canadian municipalities). The geography of the country and the ensuing spatial distribution of its population are particularly favourable to it. Finally, in a decentralized federal country such as Canada, vertical yardstick competition – between the central government and the provincial ones, and between the latter and municipalities (see Breton 1996; Salmon 2000; Breton and Fraschini 2003) – cannot but have a significant influence on policy-making in some areas.

Let me refer to an episode in the environmental domain that involves the three levels of government and reflects these horizontal and vertical relationships. In Canada, regulatory competencies regarding pesticides are normally shared between the federal government and the provinces. In 1991, citizens of Hudson in Quebec, dissatisfied with the existing regulation and the way it was implemented or enforced, obtained from their municipal government a by-law banning the use of pesticides for non-essential purposes. Citizens of other towns in Quebec made their municipalities follow suit. In 2001, the Supreme Court of Canada decided that these municipal by-laws were valid (Valiante 2001). Since then, similar by-laws have been enacted by municipalities outside Quebec, including those of cities such as Halifax, Ottawa and Toronto. This has led the federal government and some provincial governments to amend substantially their legislation and to review their administrative arrangements. A case in point is Quebec's amendments, in 2003, to its *Code de Gestion des Pesticides*.[3]

The case is particularly interesting because, whereas horizontal yardstick competition among municipalities started the process, at the same time it was a manifestation of vertical competition, with local government 'invading', so to speak, a regulatory domain previously shared exclusively by the federal and the provincial governments.[4] At a later stage, both horizontal and vertical competition went on manifesting themselves: the former in the way the enactment of municipal by-laws on pesticides spread within and outside Quebec, the latter in the way the federal and some provincial governments eventually responded to the municipal challenge by changing their legislation and administrative arrangements regarding pesticides.[5]

A second reason why it is difficult to decide whether or not, in a given context, yardstick competition mechanisms operate is that they are difficult to disentangle from other mechanisms leading to the same observable outcomes. Economists are particularly likely to encounter this difficulty. When observing some convergence of governmental decisions or policies across jurisdictions, they face the problem of deciding whether this convergence is due to yardstick competition, to a similar way of responding to an exogenous change affecting all jurisdictions, or to mobility-based competition (not to speak of the 'brethren' of yardstick competition mentioned earlier). The causality has to be inferred from the observation of data basically pertaining to outcomes – either completely static ones or outcomes defined in terms of change.[6] By contrast, the pesticide story summarized above is based directly on the observation and interpretation of causal processes, and it provides therefore direct evidence on the working of yardstick competition and its impact on regulation. Of course, no generality can be claimed on the basis of a single story. Strictly speaking, and assuming that it corresponds to reality, the story is able to refute the assertion that there is no effect of yardstick competition on regulation in Canada, not the more moderate assertion that the mechanism is generally unimportant or insignificant.

An additional difficulty is that the effect of yardstick competition may be virtual or potential in terms of conventionally observable data, while being in reality substantial in terms of variables, usually considered as non-observable, such as the calculations made by office-holders. Knowledge that voters make comparisons across jurisdictions and that this can affect the way they vote may by itself affect incumbents' decisions in such a way that voters' actual comparisons need not have an impact on voting. Then, yardstick competition, though important, manifests itself only in the mind of incumbents. Again, a more frequent recourse to direct methods of investigation, as exemplified by the work of John Ashworth and Bruno Heyndels (1997 for example), seems opportune here.

These remarks are addressed to the work of economists in general. A strength of Vaillancourt's contribution (especially in its revised form) is that it includes a search for direct evidence about the motivations underlying policy reforms at the provincial level. In particular, it looks into the minutes of parliamentary debates of provinces for evidence of inspiration from, or concern with, what obtains in other provincial jurisdictions. The findings that it reports are somewhat disappointing from a perspective stressing the relevance of yardstick competition. But recourse to this type of investigation in a paper written by an economist, even if it needs to be refined, is (at least in the domain concerned) pioneering and, given the methodological problems mentioned above, particularly praiseworthy.

A third obstacle to identifying the effects of yardstick competition on regulation is that they are often indirect. In the pesticide case, yardstick competition, whether horizontal or vertical, develops directly in terms of the regulation it affects. This is possible because the question of regulatory constraints over the use of pesticides attracts, spontaneously or not, the attention of a sufficient number of voters. The expression 'yardstick regulatory competition' is appropriate in that case. The situation is quite similar to the one studied with regard to taxation in several empirical studies, starting from Besley and Case (1995): the value taken by policy variable X in each jurisdiction is affected by the fact that voters compare values of X across jurisdictions. However, many regulations, because they are too technical, or for some other reason, cannot, under normal circumstances, benefit from the attention of a sufficient number of voters (this is also true of some taxes). It is yardstick competition over a much more visible set of variables, typically of a macroeconomic kind, that may induce governments to reconsider the inconspicuous regulations. For example, the fact that voters may feel that their city, region or country underperforms in terms of development or growth, and the possibility that these voters become less prone as a consequence to re-elect incumbents, may induce the latter to reform legislation or policies in technical areas that escape the attention of voters (Salmon 2006). In that case, the expression 'regulatory competition' is somewhat misleading and one should definitely prefer speaking of 'the effects of yardstick competition on regulation', as we have done so far. More importantly, detecting the effect of yardstick competition on regulation by the methods typically used in empirical economics is probably more difficult.

Currently in the European Union, this roundabout influence of yardstick competition on regulation is a major phenomenon, affecting in particular Germany and France. Is it or has it also been important in Canada? I shall not attempt to answer this question directly. The following consideration of the features of that country, which may be favourable or unfavourable to yardstick competition and to its influence on regulation, could be considered a preliminary step towards an answer.

Factors affecting the effectiveness of yardstick competition and its influence on regulation

For intergovernmental yardstick competition to be a very effective mechanism, at least five characteristics of the overall set-up may be important:

1   governments should have some freedom of action;
2   relevant information on what obtains in other jurisdictions should be available at little cost;
3   many voters should be ready or willing to use that information;
4   political competition within each jurisdiction should be strong; and
5   the intergovernmental relationship itself should remain competitive.

It must be stressed, however, that these characteristics are not necessary conditions for yardstick competition to be a powerful mechanism, as the fall of the collectivist regimes in Eastern Europe and elsewhere illustrates. Even in undemocratic societies, entailing in particular strong obstacles to information flows, at a certain level of the gap between their performance and that of other countries, information will trickle in on what obtains abroad, and discontent will develop, eventually translating into pressure on incumbents to change policies or face dismissal. The said features are important in the sense that they make the mechanism of yardstick competition intervene quicker, at an earlier stage of a growing comparative performance gap. It is in this sense that they may be considered as necessary conditions for yardstick competition to be 'a very effective mechanism'.

Are these conditions met in the Canadian case? Independently of them, are there features of the Canadian political, institutional and possibly cultural set-up which favour or hinder yardstick competition and/or its influence on regulation? I shall not consider separately the five conditions above but note the following features. First, it is clear that provinces have a considerable degree of autonomy or freedom, especially regarding regulation or legislation. Canada, like Switzerland, is a highly decentralized federation. But local government is a different matter. Contrary to Swiss cantons, Canadian provinces are standard unitary states. The powers of the municipalities are not constitutionally entrenched in a compelling way. In itself, this does not necessarily prevent municipalities or other junior governments from engaging in intergovernmental competition (Salmon 2000, Feld *et al.* 2003), and the pesticide story above shows that, in Canada, they do engage in such competition at least occasionally. I suspect that further investigation would show that, in most provinces, competition among municipalities and between municipalities and provincial governments constitutes a significant phenomenon.

The autonomy and freedom of action of provincial governments is reinforced by the way the implications of economic union or market integration at the national level are understood and dealt with in Canada. Regulations by subcentral governments typically fragment the overall market and generate, as side-effects and at least temporarily, non-border barriers or impediments to trade and competition, especially in the area of services. When the objective of perfect market integration and elimination of all distortions of competition is given high priority, this tends to justify disallowance of the regulations themselves and thus tends to limit very much the capacity of policy experimentation and innovation at the subcentral level of government (Breton and Salmon 2002). In decentralized federations such as Canada and Switzerland, a generalized concern with safeguarding this capacity has led to the tolerance of non-tariff and non-border internal barriers to trade of a kind that would be ruled as illegal under the Commerce Clause of the United States – or even, often, under the Treaty of Rome or the Single Act in the case of the European Union. This may be the cause (or perhaps the result) of the somewhat surprising fact that, in the case of Canada, the policy of dismantling at least some of the said impediments to trade and competition is pursued, as if in an international context, by a procedure of intergovernmental negotiation (see Doern and MacDonald 1999).

Second, in most Canadian provinces, the conjunction of the electoral system – plurality in single member districts, typically favouring the emergence of two political parties – and of the parliamentary nature of the relation between the legislative and executive branches of government should make their political system quite competitive, and the incumbents in each of them quite responsive to relatively small variations in voters' assessments. Does this lead to a situation in which, each vote counting, the views of each voter will be taken into account by incumbents? A positive answer to that question would increase substantially the plausibility of the yardstick competition mechanism working, as just discussed, 'effectively' – that is, intervening at an early stage of any developing performance gap. Even a relatively small number of voters making comparisons with what obtains outside the jurisdiction and using these comparisons to gauge the performance of incumbents would have some influence on the latter's decisions. Widespread adherence to the median voter hypothesis is an obstacle to the intellectual acceptance of that possibility. Only large discrepancies with what obtains outside the jurisdiction are likely to be noticed by the median voter and to have an effect on his or her electoral behaviour. Fortunately perhaps, the median voter hypothesis on elections is not a good one when there are many issues and none of them has such salience that it tends to pre-empt all others. In such a multidimensional setting, the probabilistic model suggests hypotheses that are much more plausible, and it does yield the proposition that all views are taken into account by candidates.

The question thus is whether some issue dominates voting in all or some Canadian provinces and local jurisdictions to the point of making electorally irrelevant the concerns shared by minorities of voters when they are unrelated to that issue. It might be argued that the separation issue does have such very high salience in Quebec. This issue is completely independent or immune, in the case of Quebec, from any effect of interjurisdictional comparisons.[7] If elections were fought exclusively on it, this would imply that comparisons with other provinces – and, together with them, the mechanism of horizontal yardstick competition – could not have any impact on decision-making by incumbents. Whether this has sometimes happened is difficult to say because, in most policy domains, no significant gap, positive or negative, developed between the performance of Quebec and that of other provinces. Thus it remains possible that the potential effect of comparisons remained in the mind of office-holders and influenced their decisions even when political campaigns focused on the separation question. In some other provinces, there are also idiosyncratic obstacles to the working of the mechanism at an early stage of developing gaps – for instance, obstacles related to unequal endowment in natural resources or to the tendency for the same party to remain in power over long periods of time. As a consequence, it must be conceded that in many cases yardstick competition might not be a 'very effective mechanism' in the sense specified above. This does not imply that it has no significant effects.

Third, a feature of the Canadian federation is that it comprises a small number of second-level jurisdictions – the provinces. This calls for two remarks. The first one is that yardstick competition is a versatile or robust mechanism which, in principle, can work well both when the number of jurisdictions is small and when it is large. That a small number does not constitute an obstacle is obvious from the literature, which, when theoretical, discusses the mechanism as an instance of strategic interaction between two jurisdictions and, when empirical, assumes the mechanism to work only between contiguous jurisdictions. In the latter case, one might say that large numbers are dealt with indirectly. There is a reluctance in public economics and public choice to apply yardstick competition directly to large numbers, despite the fact that this is done systematically in other domains of applied economics such as the economics of labour, health and education. In my view, this reluctance should give way to the recognition that voters, increasingly provided for free, or even *nolens volens*, by the media and other sources with all kinds of comparative data, often evaluate the performance of office-holders on the basis of their jurisdiction's rank and its evolution in time in a large-number ranking or on the basis of a comparison of the statistics for their own jurisdiction with the average for all jurisdictions within a relatively large data set. Voters are often better informed about this kind of comparative data than about what obtains in neighbouring jurisdictions.

The second remark is that small numbers facilitate coordination and coopera-tion. As stressed in Breton (1996), and contrary to a long tradition in political economy, this does not preclude vigorous competition. Observation of the world of business shows that coordination or even cooperation among large firms typ-ically proves fully compatible with aggressive or intensive competition among the same firms. At the same time, small numbers do increase the risk of collu-sion whose purpose is indeed to reduce competition. In Canada, coordination and negotiation activities are particularly important, as noted above with regard to the particular issue of internal trade. I do not see much evidence of collusion although this also would require further investigation.

Notes

1 For convenience, I refer sometimes to regulatory competition (yardstick regulatory competition in particular) even though, as explained below in the text itself, what is really at stake is the effect of intergovernmental competition (of the yardstick type in particular) on regulation.
2 See Bernholz *et al.* (1998: 5). On the same page, yardstick competition proper is clearly identified: '... the increased scope for interjurisdictional comparisons facilitates the control of governments by democratic majorities'.
3 I am extremely grateful to Marcia Valiante for having suggested this illustration and provided the relevant information.
4 The question of whether municipal governments always had the competencies to act in that way or conquered them by an act of creative interpretation (validated by the Supreme Court) of existing constitutional arrangements may have some bearing on the form vertical competition takes, not on its existence.
5 Another interesting case is the regulation by the federal government and the provinces of the exportation of water. Timothy Heinmiller (2003) sees in the case an example of emulation leading to harmonization. But the facts he reports can be interpreted instead, or also, as reflecting the combined effect of horizontal and vertical yardstick competi-tion in a way similar to that underlying the pesticide story. I am again indebted to Marcia Valiante for the reference.
6 A case in point is the interpretation of one of the most telling cases of mimicking behaviour presented by Vaillancourt. Starting in British Columbia, the deregulation of retail hours progressively spread eastward to the other provinces, each province dereg-ulating retail hours with few exceptions only after the province contiguous to it had done so. The question is whether the motivation of the provincial governments was a

concern with the mobility of consumers or with possible electoral effects of comparisons made by voters. Because, as argued in the text towards its end, I do not believe that comparisons with what happens in other jurisdictions always focus on the contiguous ones, I do not see why office-holders, say in Quebec, would wait until a reform started in British Columbia had reached Ontario before deciding that voters would appreciate if they adopted it. By contrast, I suspect that office-holders in a province may fear that some households living not too far from the border with another province would decide, for the purpose of shopping, to benefit from deregulation in that contiguous province (this seems to be confirmed by the evidence Vaillancourt provides). Thus I tend to interpret the fascinating data as reflecting mobility-based rather than yardstick competition. However, direct examination of the way the deregulation decisions were actually made in each province is most valuable for choosing among the two mechanisms or to weigh their relative influence if both played a role.

7 In other contexts, secession could be influenced, as an issue, by voters' perception of the outcomes of secession in other jurisdictions. But this possibility can be excluded in the case of Quebec.

References

Ashworth, John and Heyndels, Bruno (1997) 'Politicians' preferences on local tax rates: an empirical analysis', *European Journal of Political Economy*, 13, 479–502.

Bernholz, Peter, Streit, Manfred E. and Vaubel, Roland (1998) 'Introduction and overview', in Peter Bernholz and Roland Vaubel (eds) *Political Competition, Innovation and Growth: A Historical Analysis*, Berlin: Springer, pp. 3–11.

Besley, Timothy and Case, Anne (1995) 'Incumbent behavior: vote-seeking, tax-setting, and yardstick competition', *American Economic Review*, 85(1), 25–45.

Bodenstein, Martin and Ursprung, Heinrich W. (2005) 'Political yardstick competition, economic integration, and constitutional choice in a federation: a numerical analysis of a contest success function model', *Public Choice*, 124(3–4), 329–52.

Breton, Albert (1996) *Competitive Governments: An Economic Theory of Politics and Public Finance*, Cambridge: Cambridge University Press.

Breton, Albert and Fraschini, Angela (2003) 'Vertical competition in unitary states: the case of Italy', *Public Choice*, 114(1–2), 57–77.

Breton, Albert and Salmon, Pierre (2002) 'External effects of domestic regulations: comparing internal and international barriers to trade', *International Review of Law and Economics*, 21(2), 135–55.

Doern, G. Bruce and MacDonald, Mark (1999) *Free-Trade Federalism: Negotiating the Canadian Agreement on Internal Trade*, Toronto: University of Toronto Press.

Feld, Lars P., Josselin, Jean-Michel and Rocaboy, Yvon (2003) 'Tax mimicking among regional jurisdictions', in A. Marciano and J.-M. Josselin (eds) *From Economic to Legal Competition: New Perspectives on Law and Institutions in Europe*, Cheltenham: Edward Elgar, pp. 105–19.

Heinmiller, B. Timothy (2003) 'Harmonization through emulation: Canadian federalism and water export policy', *Canadian Public Administration/Administration Publique du Canada*, 46(4), 495–513.

Rose-Ackerman, Susan (1980) 'Risk-taking and reelection: does federalism promote innovation?' *Journal of Legal Studies*, 9(3), 593–616.

Salmon, Pierre (1987) 'Decentralisation as an incentive scheme', *Oxford Review of Economic Policy*, 3(2), 24–43.

—— (2000) 'Vertical competition in a unitary state', in G. Galeotti, P. Salmon and

R. Wintrobe (eds) *Competition and Structure: The Political Economy of Collective Decisions: Essays in Honor of Albert Breton*, Cambridge: Cambridge University Press, pp. 239–56.

—— (2006) 'Political yardstick competition and corporate governance in the European Union', in G. Ferrarini and E. Wymeersch (eds) *Investor Protection in Europe: Corporate Law Making, the MiFID and Beyond*, Oxford: Oxford University Press, pp. 31–58.

Strumpf, Koleman S. (2002) 'Does government decentralization increase policy innovation?', *Journal of Public Economic Theory*, 4(2), 207–41.

Vaillancourt, François (2005) 'Inter-jurisdictional competition in regulation: evidence for Canada at the provincial level', revised version of a paper presented at the conference on *The effects of interjurisdictional competition on regulation*, Heidelberg (Germany), June 2005.

Valiante, Marcia (2001) 'Turf war: municipal powers, the regulation of pesticides and the Hudson decision', *Journal of Environmental Law and Practice*, 11, 327–58.

4 Labour market regulation in the EU-15

Causes and consequences

W. Stanley Siebert

Introduction

Labour market regulation sets floors under wages and working conditions. This chapter discusses possible rationales for these floors: whether they are the outcome of efficiency considerations, or whether they are simply politically expedient (Saint-Paul 2000). A third alternative is that labour market regulation is the outcome of a sort of *path dependence*, with French legal origin countries predisposed to regulate more strictly than English common law countries (Botero *et al.* 2004). Within Europe, the UK's 'belief structure' (North 1998: 28) has since the seventeenth century led to the evolution of freedoms. Most of the large literature on labour market regulation considers its consequences, notably for unemployment, rather than its causes. However, if regulation increases unemployment, its efficiency is automatically called into question. Hence, our enquiry into causes will be assisted by a knowledge of effects.

The plan of the chapter is as follows. In the next section we will set out the various dimensions of labour market regulation, how it varies among EU-15 countries, and over time. (In order to give a context to our EU analysis, we use the OECD group as comparators.) These are the phenomena for which we aim to find causes. Then, in succeeding sections, we will discuss the efficiency and public choice theories in turn. We will draw conclusions in the final section.

Dimensions of labour market regulation

To start with a broad view, we will find that, while labour regulation is many dimensioned, countries that are strict on one dimension tend to be strict on others. There are the policy 'complementarities', which support the common idea of country or regional 'models'[1]. Furthermore, while EU countries (apart from the UK, currently, at least) have strict regulation, the group of OECD countries as a whole vary widely in the extent of regulation, despite having similar levels of development. Hence there is something to explain. Finally, a country's regulatory stance does not change quickly. For example, the French law on extension of collective agreements dates from 1936 (Jefferys 2003: 95). Changes in regulation often amount only to tweaking, as in the current round of

Table 4.1 Developments in EU law on the social rights of workers

	1989 Charter of Fundamental Worker Rights (see Addison and Siebert, 1991 1994a, 1999)	Subsequent legislation
(a) Freedom of movement	Workers posted to another EU member state must receive host country wages and conditions.	Freedom of worker movement is part of Title III of the Treaty. 'Posted workers' directive passed as OJ L216 of 21.1.1997. The focus now is on portability of social security benefits, and occupational pensions (EIRR 2005).
(b) Employment and remuneration	'Fair remuneration' and a 'decent standard of living' required, and atypical (part-time and temporary) contracts to be regulated to ensure pro-rata wages and conditions.	A framework agreement on part-time work eventually passed, OJ L14 of 20.1.98 and L131 of 5.5.98. A proposed directive (COM(02)701) on agency workers is still under discussion (DTI 2003). Note: No directives on minimum wages or extension of collective agreements
(c) Improvement of living and working conditions	Minimum working conditions including working hours, to be set. Also, procedures developed to protect workers in the event of collective dismissals and bankruptcies.	(1) Working hours limited by directive OJ L307 of 13.12.1993, though UK appealed to ECJ and only implemented on 23.11.1996. UK's opt-out now under discussion (EU 2004). (2) Collective dismissals/redundancies legislation requiring information disclosure to worker representatives goes back to 1975 (OJ L48 of 22.2.1975). It was modified in 1992 (OJ L245 of 26.8.1992) and 1998 (OJ L225 of 12.8.98). Currently there is a consultation on 'socially intelligent' restructuring, linked to further development of EWCs (EIRR 2005).
(d) Social protection	Every worker to have the right to adequate social security benefits. Note: the unqualified right to collective action (industrial disputes) is not put forward, but is to remain subject to national laws.	No directives.
(e) Freedom of association and collective bargaining		The idea of 'social dialogue' between management and labour at Community level has steadily developed, and the EU Treaty (articles 138 and 139) provides for the Commission to initiate social policy legislation via consultation with management and labour. Note: No directives promoting collective bargaining as such.
(f) Vocational training	Every worker is to have access to vocational training, and to receive it throughout working life.	The EU Structural Funds are used to co-finance training initiatives, though whether they add much to already extensive member state efforts is doubtful (Addison and Siebert 1994b).
(g) Equal treatment for men and women (and others)	Note: the rights to 'equal treatment' required here were linked only to gender.	The right to equal treatment has been extended far beyond gender, and now covers race, ethnic origin, religion, sexual orientation, disability and age (Article 13). Race and origin are covered by

(h) Information, consultation and participation of workers	Information, consultation and participation for workers must be developed, especially regarding technical change, mergers and collective redundancies.	directive OJ L180 of 19.7.2000, and the remainder by OJ L303 of 2.12.2000, with a long period, until December 2006 allowed for implementation of the controversial disability and age regulations. (1) European Works Councils established in large transnationals by directive OJ L254 of 30.9.1994 – excluding the UK until December 1997. This area is being reconsidered by the Commission to advance 'best practice' in industrial restructuring (EIRR 2005). (2) Works councils required in all undertakings employing >50 workers by directive of OJ L80 of 23.3.2002. UK regulations published 2004 (DTI 2004), to cover undertakings employing >150 by April 2005, >100 by April 2007, and >50 by April 2008.
(i) Health protection and safety at the workplace	All workers to enjoy satisfactory health and safety conditions at the workplace.	This area predates the 1989 Charter, and there have been many directives. The latest proposal covers optical radiation (EIRR 2005), including 'solar radiation' which has raised opposition among UK building workers.
(j) Protection of children and adolescents	All child labour below minimum school leaving age is banned, except for non-arduous activities, and night work is completely banned.	The directive OJ 1216 of 20.8.1994 secured these objectives.
(k) Elderly persons	Elderly persons' incomes are to offer a 'decent standard of living'.	Several recommendations mention elderly people, but no directives beyond discrimination above.
(l) Disabled persons	Disabled persons are to have the right to concrete measures (e.g. training) to improve their social and professional integration. Article 137d of the EU Treaty requires Community support for protection of workers where their employment contract is terminated.	No directives as such, but Article 137g of the Treaty requires integration of people excluded from the labour market, and 137j requires that social exclusion be combated.
(m) NEW		Protection of individual workers against dismissal was not covered in the 1989 Charter. However this aim is part of the thinking behind both the agency workers proposed directive (b above), and the new information and consultation directive (h2 above).

Historical note
In 1989 the Charter was supported in a declaration by all EU members except the UK, which eventually signed up in 1998. The Charter now appears in the consolidated Treaty Establishing the European Community as Title XI 'Social policy, education, vocational training and youth'.

reducing restrictions on employing temporary workers. Therefore, our theories of causation will need to explain why what is efficient (or politically expedient) in one country, is not so in others, and why the underlying causes – or responses – change so slowly.

The EU's stance on labour market regulation is grounded in the denial of the benefits of interjurisdictional competition. The many regulatory areas are shown in Table 4.1, which takes the 1989 Community Charter of Fundamental Social Rights of Workers as its starting point. This Charter marks a watershed (see Addison and Siebert 1991 and 1994a). On 15 March 1989, the European Parliament adopted a resolution on this Charter, calling for:

> the adoption at Community level of the fundamental social rights which should not be jeopardised because of the pressure of competition or the search for increased competitiveness, and could be taken as the basis for the dialogue between management and labour
>
> (EU 2005)

Thus, the expansion of EU labour regulation was born out of a concern that the increased competition resulting from completion of the single market in 1992 would lead to a race to the bottom in labour standards.

Moreover, the Treaty of Maastricht (ratified in 1993) contained a Social Agreement introducing majority decisions in several areas of labour regulation contested by the UK, which initially opted out and had most to change. The Chapter has been incorporated into the Treaty of Amsterdam (1997). Table 4.1 gives the situation. The main contested areas are 'atypical work' (part-timers and temporary workers, row b), limitation of working hours (row c), discrimination – which has even been extended to 'age' – and company works councils. The UK position is not simply due to Thatcherism, since the Blair government has also been active (see *The Times* 2005), for example in preserving the UK's opt-out from the 48-hour maximum working week (row c1). The Blair government (*Financial Times* 2005a) has also been trying to preserve the UK's agency work companies from the restrictive agency workers directive (row b). Further, it is thought (*Financial Times* 2005b) that the directive on company works councils (row h2) has been 'aimed squarely at Britain and Ireland', as the only members of the EU-15 without such councils playing a role in employment protection. The UK really is different, and has more in common with other Anglophone countries, as we will see. So far, interjurisdictional competition has mainly been between the UK and the rest.

The body of labour legislation in Table 4.1, wide though it may be, is as interesting for what it does *not* contain, as for what it does. It contains nothing on wage floors. The Commission has confined itself to anodyne opinions on 'equitable wages'. Wage floors can be set by minimum wages, or by extension of collective agreements (row b). Such extension is common in the EU (Siebert 1997: 230). In principle, social security benefits (row d) can also set a floor, but little has been done here either. Perhaps the UK falling into line by establishing a minimum wage in 1999 has pre-empted moves towards a directive. Perhaps, as well, the UK, having had a disastrous flirtation with extension of collective agreements under Old Labour in the 1970s, is not yet thought ready to be brought into the fold.

Still, the fact that wages are not set by national sectoral agreements will leave the UK's wages more flexible, and paradoxically should reduce opposition to further EU legislation raising working conditions. Nickell and Quintini (2003) have found that the proportion of job stayers taking hourly *nominal* wage cuts is as high as 15–20 per cent every year. The implication is that hikes in job conditions have less effect, since wages simply fall to reflect the better conditions, leaving profitability unaffected.

While more research remains to be done on wage flexibility in other EU countries, it certainly seems that wage *compression* is considerable here, and this compression is related to extended collective agreements. Some evidence is given in Figure 4.1, which measures wage compression by the ratio of the 90th to the 10th earning decile, and extension of collective agreements by collective bargaining coverage. The low coverage countries such as the UK, the US, Ireland and Canada have higher inequality than the high coverage (EU) countries making up the mass of the points at the lower right. Still, the compression of wage differentials in most continental European states – a compression that has malign effects on unemployment, as we will see – cannot be blamed on the EU, which has not legislated in this area. However, it can be said that the EU stance such as the 'right to fair and just working conditions' in the ill-fated

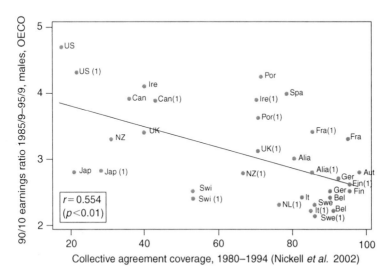

Figure 4.1 Wage differentials and collective agreement coverage.

Note

Each country except Austria (Aut) and Spain (Sp) has two observations, for the 1980s and 1990s, with the first signified by (1).

Constitutional draft (article 11–91) is certainly in the direction of wage compression and inflexibility.

Finally, on the subject of wage compression, it is worth considering Koeniger *et al.*'s (2004) panel study of the 90/10 wage differential of 11 OECD countries over 1973–99. They use the fixed effect approach, and control for employment protection, union density, bargaining coordination, minimum wage laws, taxation, welfare benefits, the relative unemployment rate of unskilled versus skilled, and trade and technology shocks. One thing they find is that trade *widens* the 90/10 differential, *ceteris paribus*. This finding goes against the popular argument that trade openness increases people's demand for labour regulation, which is therefore an efficient response to the risks of trade.

The most important variable by far in Koeniger *et al.*'s (2004) analysis is employment protection, which strongly compresses wage differentials. High welfare benefits, union density and minimum wage indicators also compress differentials, as may be expected. We will consider employment protection in more detail below. Suffice it to say here that strict employment protection is likely to be most costly for the unskilled, and in a competitive market thus to widen wage differentials. The fact that the reverse effect is found implies that trade union power is using employment protection as a hold-up threat to increase unskilled wages at the expense of unskilled unemployment. Therefore, there is evidence here against efficiency explanations of regulation, though we will need to consider the research on unemployment effects of labour market regulation (see below).

To analyse working conditions regulation, summary measures have needed to be developed. Lazear (1990) famously developed an index based on the number of months of severance pay or notice a blue collar worker with ten years of service would receive for termination without 'cause'. Such an index has the advantage of being cardinal, and time-varying (from 1956 to 1984). However, it is narrow, and Grubb and Wells (1993) developed a wider index including not only employment protection, but also restrictions on working hours and restrictions on temporary workers. They assigned ordinal levels of strictness to the various laws, and then averaged the results together to build up an index of 'restrictions on overall employee work'. The resulting index has the disadvantage of not being really cardinal, but at least is broad-based.

The approach of 'scoring' various laws according to their strictness, then averaging the results together has been followed in subsequent OECD work (OECD 1999 and 2004) – including work on product market regulation (Nicoletti *et al.* 2001). Blanchard and Wolfers (2000) have even linked together the Lazear and OECD employment protection indices to make a time series which is regularly used in empirical work (see Koeniger *et al.* 2004, and Daniel and Siebert 2005). Moreover Botero *et al.* (2004) have recently expanded the countries covered, and the types of regulation. They have developed indices not only of restrictions on overall employee work (including employment protection, hours restrictions, and temporary work restrictions), but also collective bargaining protection, and generosity of social security benefits for unemployment, sickness and old age. These indices are available for 86 countries, but are not time-varying.

Figures 4.2 to 4.4 illustrate aspects of this work. Figure 4.2 contrasts the OECD employment protection law (EPL) measure with Lazear's. We see an association, but it is far from perfect. The two indices agree that Italy, Norway and Spain are most regulated, with the UK and the US least. However, the OECD index puts Portugal and Sweden as much more strictly regulated than does Lazear. Thus we see that the force of employment protection legislation cannot be measured with precision. In empirical work, therefore, we would expect the coefficient on the employment protection indicator to be biased towards zero because of measurement error.

Figure 4.3 compares employment protection laws with collective bargaining laws. On the vertical axis, the Botero *et al.* (2004) employment protection measure is given, for a change. (This index correlates well, 0.754, with the OECD index of Figure 4.2, though the Netherlands is rated as very strict here, which is difficult for the 'flexicurity' view of that country.) The horizontal axis gives the Botero *et al.* measure of protection for collective bargaining protection. This measure is broader than the collective agreement coverage measure we have already come across (Figure 4.1), though the two are obviously associated $(r=0.409, p<0.07)$. France is rated as most protective on this index,

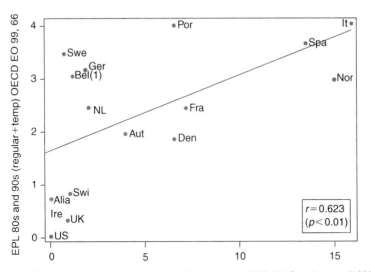

Sum of months severance and notice, average 1956–84, from Lazear (1990)

Figure 4.2 Employment protection measures compared.

Note
The OECD employment protection index is based on indicators of difficulty of worker dismissal, including severance pay costs and procedural restrictions such as requirement for third party approval. It inclues measures relating to both temporary and regular contracts. The Lazear index gives the months of severance pay and/or notice required to compensate a blue collar worker dismissed without cause after ten years' service.

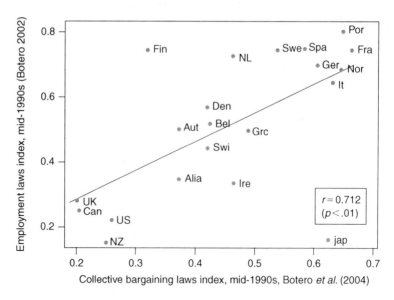

Figure 4.3 Employment protection and union protection measures compared.

Note
The Botero *et al.* employment protection index is made up in a similar way to the OECD's. Their collective bargaining laws index is an average of indicators of protection such as extension of collective agreements, requirements for workers' councils, non-replacement of striking workers, and legality of sympathy strikes.

because employers cannot replace strikers, collective agreements are routinely extended, unofficial strikes are lawful, and workers councils are mandated.[2] The UK is least protective. As can be seen, strict employment protection and strict collective bargaining protection tend to go together, notwithstanding strange outliers like Japan and Finland. There might be a causal connection here, or both aspects of regulation could be the result of a third factor, such as legal origin (Figure 4.5 suggests this, as discussed below).

Figure 4.4 presents a view of the correlation between strictness of employment protection and generosity of unemployment benefits. These two might be thought (see Boeri *et al.* 2004) to be alternative forms of insurance against job loss, though with different distributional outcomes. The unemployed will prefer unemployment benefits to employment protection, which reduces their chances of finding a job. However, the currently employed will tend to have the opposite view (not necessarily very strongly, since unemployment benefits also drive up wages).[3] In fact, the picture presented in Figure 4.4 is one of complementarity, with Portugal, for example, being high on both, and New Zealand low on both. Of course, alternative measures of unemployment benefit generosity can be chosen. Most popular is the OECD's unemployment benefit replacement rate, but this ignores housing subsidies for the unemployed which are important in the

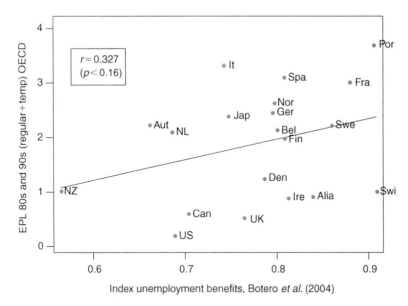

Figure 4.4 Employment protection and unemployment benefits compared.

Note
The unemployment benefits index is an average of indices measuring aspects of the unemployment benefit including percentage of salary deducted, months required to qualify, waiting period for benefits, and the replacement for a one-year unemployment spell.

UK. In any case, use of the OECD replacement rate measure in place of the Botero *et al.* index still gives a positive correlation with employment protection. We are left, therefore, with the fact that employment protection and collective bargaining protection tend to march quite tightly together, with unemployment benefit generosity in a somewhat looser formation, but still part of the pack.

Efficiency

The question of whether the types of labour market regulation reviewed above are a response to market failure, and are therefore efficient, is most simply answered by looking for effects on employment. If employment increases, we have efficiency in the sense that the gains of the gainers will be greater than the losses of the losers, if any – that is, a (potential) Pareto improvement. If it decreases, however, the gains of the gainers will be less than the losses of the losers. For the efficiency argument to hold, it would then be necessary to argue that the gainers are more deserving in some sense than the losers, which economists are understandably reluctant to do. Positive, or at least, not negative, employment effects are thus central to the efficiency case. Accordingly, researchers have from the first searched for these effects.

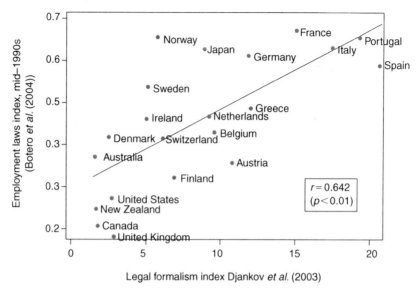

Figure 4.5 Employment protection and legal formalism.

Note
The legal formalism index is the average of indexes measuring statutory intervention in lower-level civil cases for non-payment of rent, or for a bounced cheque, and the number of different procedures required legally to begin a business, the days required, and the costs – source is the Botero *et al.*, 2004, website dataset.

However, to get to the bottom of things, it is necessary to disaggregate employment and unemployment. It is possible for the overall unemployment rate to remain constant, even as its long-term component increases. Hence we need to consider the long-term unemployment rate as well as the overall unemployment rate. Equally, we need to disaggregate employment, and consider what happens to young and old workers, as well as the majority 'prime age' group. But it has taken research some time to get to this point, in fact, since for simplicity the early models (for example Nickell 1986) began with a homogeneous labour assumption. (It was also assumed that unions, as a sort of 'social partner', represented all workers.) Much was then made of the fact that the theoretical predictions for employment protection were ambiguous, and that this ambiguity was borne out in empirical work.

Yet a different picture appears if one disaggregates, because wage and working conditions floors have most impact on the least productive. Simply put, employers become more 'choosy' when selecting workers if there is an increase in firing costs, provided that the increase is coupled with inflexible wages. The inflexible wages proviso ensures that wages cannot fall to reflect the value of the extra job security to the workers, that is, it prevents workers and firms 'contracting around' the employment protection constraint. On this reasoning, strict employment protection accompanied by tight wage differentials due to state support for collective bargaining (the two go together, as we have seen) can be expected to cause a rise in hiring standards. There will be less hiring and less quitting, and long-term unemployment should increase (for models, see Boeri 1998; Guelfi 2004). Employers should spend more on recruiting, and emphasize education. They should also avoid the workers at the two ends of the age distribution, thereby pushing up unemployment for the young and early retirement for the old. The French have an expression for this phenomenon: 'une seule generation travaille à la fois'. Note how union power and employment protection work together.

It would be difficult to argue that these kinds of displacement effects are efficient (as Jean-Michel Josselin, this volume, agrees), but do they occur? Table 4.2 provides some recent OECD evidence, and Table 4.3 considers evidence from a company hiring standards study within the EU.

Table 4.2 summarizes three studies which tell broadly the same story, namely, that employment protection laws displace outsider groups (the young and old), and lengthen the duration of unemployment. First, the study in Panel A by Bertola *et al.* (2004) uses a long panel of OECD countries to analyse employment/population ratios by age and gender. Admittedly, we see here that employment protection is generally insignificant (only for males 55+ does it adversely shift the ratio). However, the three union variables (density, agreement coverage, and bargaining coordination) push down the ratio of young and old worker groups relative to the prime age. The next rows take unemployment as the dependent variable, and here employment protection plays a more important role, increasing unemployment for three of the groups – and reducing it for none. However, the three union variables are not as adverse for unemployment as might be expected.

Next, Panel B takes the 2004 OECD studies, one of which considers long-term unemployment. Here we see that employment protection is significantly positively related to long-term unemployment, *ceteris paribus*. However, in this case the union variables are insignificant. The second study analyses union effects on employment/population ratios. We see that union effects are adverse for both young and old men, relative to prime-age men. However unions are positive for prime-age women, which may indicate that unions are no longer so male dominated.

Panel C summarizes Botero *et al.*'s (2004) results. Here the dataset is quite different, being a cross-section of 85 countries throughout the world. These are much simpler regressions than the ones we have been considering, due to data limitations. Still, this broader population of countries gives a nice contrast to the OECD group. We see that the employment laws index (the same as that graphed in Figure 4.3) again indicates adverse effects of employment protection, reducing labour-force participation and employment–population rates of both men and women, and raising the unemployment rate. The bargaining laws index (again in Figure 4.3) also indicates adverse effects of union power.

The final Panel D give an interesting glimpse of the trade-off between wage compression and job opportunities. As can be seen, the simple correlation

Table 4.2 Labour regulation and jobs – further analysis

(A) Bertola et al. (2004): 17 OECD countries, 1960–95

Controls: country and time effects, total unemployment rate, replacement rate, tax rate, retirement ages for specific groups

Dep. var.: Employment/Population

Independent variable:	15–24		Prime age		55+	
	M	F	M	F	M	F
EPL	insig.	insig.	insig.	insig.	–	insig.
Union density/coverage/coord.	–	–	+	+	–	–

Dep. var.: Unemployment

Independent variable:	15–24		Prime age		55+	
	M	F	M	F	M	F
EPL	+	+	insig.	+	insig.	insig.
Union density/coverage/coord.	–	–	–	+	–	+

(B) OECD (2004, 77 161): 19 OECD countries, 1985–02

Controls: country and time effects replacement rate, tax rate, active labour policies, output gap, plus specific controls such as retirement age for specific groups

Dep. var.: Long-term unemployment

EPL	+
Union density/coverage/coord.	insig.

Dep. var.: Employment/population ratio relative to prime-age men

	Young men	Old men 55+	Prime-age women
Effect of 1 SD increase in union density/coverage/ coord. taken together	−4.3%	−5.5%	+11.8%

(C) Botero et al. (2004): 85 countries

Controls: average years schooling

Dep. vars.:

	Labour-force participation		Unemp.rate	Emp/pop.	
	M	F		M	F
Employment laws index	–	insig.	+	–	–
Collective bargaining laws index	–	insig.	insig.	–	insig.

(D) OECD (2004, 135): 15 OECD countries, 5-year averages 1970/4 to 1990/4

Controls: country and time effects pop.

	Unemp.	Emp./pop.	Employment/ population Young men	Ratio relative to Old men 55+	Prime-age men	Prime-age women
Simple correlations with the 90/10 earnings ratio	−0.44***	0.45***	0.57***	0.44***		0.25*

Sources: Bertola et al. (2004, Tables 2 and 3); OECD (2004: 77, 161), Botero et al. (2004, Table 8).

Table 4.3 Plant-level hiring decisions and employment protection

Variable (mean)	Average starting age (30.1)	Standard deviation of starting age (9.2)	Average education (11.4)	Standard deviation of education (1.6)
	(1)	(2)	(3)	(4)
Blanchard–Wolfers employment protection measure$_{t-1}$	−1.60	−9.12***	2.35***	−1.40
(1.0)	(−0.26)	(−2.94)	(3.13)	(−1.43)
Union density$_{t-1}$	0.09	−0.21**	0.01	0.01
(38.6)	(0.46)	(−1.96)	(0.28)	(0.28)
Tax wedge$_{t-1}$	0.18	−0.11	0.11***	0.03
(33.1)	(0.66)	(−0.85)	(2.80)	(0.65)
Observations	148	153	148	147

Source: Daniel and Siebert (2005).

(allowing for country and time-period fixed effects) between the 90/10 earnings ratio and unemployment is highly significant, and negative, −0.44. Similarly the correlation between the 90/10 ratio and the employment/population ratio is significantly positive, 0.45. The other correlations show that the employment opportunities of both young and old men decline relative to the prime-age group as the 90/10 ratio falls, though opportunities of women apparently increase. Therefore, it seems that earnings equality is bought at the cost of job opportunity inequality.

Finally, let us turn to Table 4.3, which uses a completely different type of data, micro-economic data gathered from the personnel records of 11 firms in the EU and USA. The observations are formed from the characteristics of production worker recruits hired by the firms each year from 1975–95. Specifically, the mean and standard deviation of starting age and education are calculated for each firm and each year. If strict employment protection makes employers more choosy, the standard deviation of starting age should decline with employment protection, as firms avoid both young and old workers, who might be more risky than the prime-age groups. As can be seen, the employment protection variable enters the standard deviation of starting age equation with the predicted negative coefficient, −9.12. A further prediction is that firms should choose more highly educated workers. Again, this prediction is borne out, since the average education equation has a positive coefficient on the employment protection variable, 2.35. The other variables listed, union density and the tax wedge, apparently do not matter so much at the firm level.

In sum, labour market regulation designed to improve working conditions and strengthen collective bargaining obviously does so, but at the expense of reduced job opportunities for outsider groups: the young, the old, the inexperienced. Furthermore, it drives up long-term unemployment, and youth unemployment. Thus, the picture is not one of efficiency and win-win. Rather, semi-skilled workers gain at the expense of others, who are less skilled. The 'cause' of labour market regulation, therefore, seems more likely to be acts of the (employed) median voter, which is the public choice theory, to which we now turn.

Public choice

We now consider labour regulation as the outcome of distributional conflict. These waters are relatively uncharted, because surprisingly few authors have considered distributional conflict *in detail* in this area. (A long time ago, however, Becker 1956 showed that white workers can use discrimination to raise their pay at the expense of capitalists and black workers.) The lack of interest in distribution can perhaps be explained by the popular view that distributive conflict takes place simply between capital and labour, that is, unions are a 'sword of justice'. Redistributive effects of labour regulation are then obviously from the rich to the poor, and can be justified by 'social concerns' (Gray 1995: 314). In other words, the popular, if mistaken, view is that the cause of labour regulation is obvious: to right wrongs.

However, as Saint-Paul says (2000: 5), the conflict which matters is that between different groups of workers, not between capital and labour.[4] The median voter will be drawn from the majority (employed) semi- and unskilled group, which constructs laws to benefit itself. Put simply, this group promotes collective bargaining and employment protection laws to pump up its wages and conditions, and drives unskilled workers into unemployment or temporary work. This redistribution is highly inefficient, since it requires part of the workforce to be idle, and excludes the poorest from the redistribution. The same transfer, but at less cost, could be achieved via the tax system, and we will need to explain why this course is not pursued. But first, it is worth considering the various interest groups and their possible motivations in more detail.

Table 4.4 synthesizes Saint-Paul's various models of the interest groups whose conflict drives labour market regulation. In the version shown, there are five groups, and three types of labour regulation: minimum wage laws (in which we can include minima imposed by collective agreements), employment protection laws and welfare benefits. To this list we should add a fourth area: laws strengthening trade unions and collective agreements. For simplicity, we can simply think of strong trade unions as an aspect of high minimum wages. However, strong trade unions may not be all that important to the semi- and unskilled worker groups (whom they mainly represent) if these groups wield political power and can change the regulatory system appropriately.

In the first row, we consider the skilled worker group, which comprises managers and professionals at the top of the wage distribution. Their interest is simply to oppose a minimum wage (including any minima imposed by collective agreements). A minimum wage cannot raise their pay, which is far above any minimum, and moreover it reduces the employment of complementary unskilled workers.

Table 4.4 Public choice analysis of labour regulation – Saint-Paul

Interest group (illustrative per cent of electorate)	Policies High minimum wages (plus strong trade unions)	Strict employment protection	High unemployment benefits
Skilled workers (30%)	*No* (well above the floor; not in unions; also want more jobs for unskilled who are complements)	*Perhaps* (buys the unskilled off more cheaply than redistribution via high taxes)	*Perhaps* (not directly affected except via required taxes)
Semi- and unskilled (60%)	*Yes* (raises semi- and unskilled wages; also reduces competition from unemployed; unions protect rents)	*Yes* (maintains current job; also reduces competition from unemployed)	*Yes* (raises the outside option, and so the group wage)
Short-term unemployed and temp workers (5%)	*Perhaps* (may benefit if job is landed)	*Perhaps* (may is benefit if job landed)	*Yes* (but not too high since job openings may fall)
Long-term unemployed (3%)	*No* (reduces job openings)	*No* (reduces job openings)	*Yes* (but not too high since job openings may fall)
Capitalists (2%)	*No*	*No*	*No*

Sources: Saint-Paul (1996: 275ff.), Saint-Paul (1997: 293), Saint-Paul (2000: 70, 128, 155, 219).

However, as regards employment protection, the attitude of the skilled group may be ambivalent. On the one hand, the market for their type of work is quite competitive, with flexible wages (Saint-Paul 2000: 5).[5] Hence, they do not benefit directly from employment protection which, after all, is designed to protect rents. On the other hand, permitting employment protection for the (employed) semi- and unskilled groups might reduce calls for more wholesale redistribution via heavier taxation of the rich (Saint-Paul 2000: 68ff.). In a sense, the skilled group allows the unskilled groups their job protection, and so reduces their jealousy. (Though, as Figure 4.4 shows, high employment protection generally goes with high unemployment benefits, and thus high taxes, so this strategy does not seem very successful.)

Finishing the top row, skilled workers are against high unemployment benefits because high benefits will disproportionately raise their taxes. Moreover high benefits reduce complementary unskilled employment. This effect occurs most obviously because high benefits will subsidize longer unemployment spells. Also, high benefits will raise the outside option for unions representing semi- and unskilled workers, improve their wages, and further act to reduce unskilled employment.

The second row shows the position for the semi- and unskilled group which makes up the lower end of the wage distribution. This group is vital because it contains the median voter. The workers here are in favour of a high minimum wage because it may be paid to them. The minimum (plus minimums brought through strong unions and extended agreements) will also push some unskilled workers into unemployment. These workers are substitutes, and so their exclusion further raises the pay of the employed remainder.

Assuming they are receiving rents, the semi- and unskilled group will also be in favour of employment protection. Rents are important for distributional conflict models. Everyone wishes to grow and protect their rent. In earlier versions (for example Saint-Paul 1996 and 1997) the source of these rents is union power and other obstacles to competition such as state-run enterprise and tariffs. (One may add takeover obstacles due to non-transparent corporate governance rules such as prevail in French civil code oriented countries – Laporta *et al.* 1998.) In the more recent model (Saint-Paul 2002) rent is identified with match-specific human capital, which grows with tenure. The obstacles to competition identified above are meant to allow workers to appropriate the returns to this specific capital. The new model allows a distinction to be made between short- and long-tenure workers (the youth or prime-age distinction we have already seen), with short-tenure workers being less in favour of protection. Also, the match-specific human capital idea provides a further way for employment protection to create path dependence. Once employment protection is begun, it raises worker tenure, which in turn swells the constituency of workers wanting more protection. Thus, (employed) semi- and unskilled workers use employment protection to protect their rents. Also, by reducing competition from the unemployed, employment protection grows the rent.

The semi- and unskilled group also favour high unemployment benefits. One obvious reason is because they might become unemployed. An additional reason is that high benefits increase workers' outside option, and thereby the wage. Saint-Paul (2000: 154) even notes circumstances in which the employed prefer higher unemployment benefits than the unemployed. Since high unemployment benefits push up wages, they reduce hiring rates – which helps the employed and hurts the unemployed. Hence the unemployed and the employed may be on paradoxical opposite sides of the fence as regards high unemployment benefits.

The third and fourth rows of Table 4.4 take in the unemployed, with a distinction made between the short-term and the long-term unemployed. The short-term unemployed are close to finding a job, whereas the long-term unemployed have deep-seated problems. There is no reason for the long-term unemployed to want high minimum wages or strict job protection, both of which reduce their already slim chances of landing a job. The short-term unemployed should take an intermediate position on these policies, from which they could benefit once in a job. Finally, on our previous arguments, neither should want too high an unemployment benefit level, though presumably the more discouraged the long-term unemployed become, the higher the benefits they would vote for.

Finally, consider the capitalists. Worker rent growing and protecting policies obviously reduce profits, if unexpected. Admittedly, in the longer run, projects will only be taken on if they can make a profit given the current labour regulation, so capitalists may tend to be somewhat indifferent. However, the long run might be some time coming. Moreover, regulation breeds regulation. So capitalists would rationally vote against all these policies.

Looking at Table 4.4, the surprising thing is that every country is not strictly regulated. With the sizes of the five interest groups as illustrated, it is plain that the interests of the employed semi- and unskilled group will dominate in any voting. It is true, voting might not be all-important, and lobbying could have a role to play (Becker 1983). Here, the capitalists could punch above their weight, since they are well organized. On the other hand, the employed worker groups also have skilful trade union lobbyists who will act as a countervailing force. The unemployed, while quite numerous, are too heterogeneous to form a coherent lobby, and in any case, the short-term unemployed might well be ambivalent. Therefore, the move towards strict labour regulation would seem unstoppable. But why, then, are some countries further down this road than others?

The type of democracy can make a difference. It has been demonstrated that proportional representation (PR) electoral systems, as are the norm in most EU states (though not in France itself!), lead to more corruption than first-past-the-post systems as in the UK (Persson and Tabellini 2003, Ch. 7). Corruption is likely to encourage rent-seeking, which as we have seen is necessary for the median voter to gain from employment protection regulation. Corruption may arise within PR because of the weaker accountability of politicians in the typical PR list system where voters can only choose among parties (Mueller 2003: 525). Also, the PR system allows corrupting patronage to the party leadership, which controls the list. Even better than first-past-the-post in this respect might be direct representation via referenda. Thus, Feld (this volume) shows that Swiss cantons with more direct democracy have less powerful interest groups (fewer exam requirements). Frey and Stutzer (2000) back up this point by demonstrating that cantons with more direct representation have populations with higher self-reported happiness.

If we are looking for ultimate causes, the legal origin theory put forward by Botero *et al.* (2004) makes sense, and can be mated with Saint-Paul's public choice theory quite well. In the beginning comes the legal origin. The French civil law and the English common law are the main origins. 'Countries have regulatory styles shaped in part by their legal systems, and therefore societies that regulate one activity are also expected to regulate others' (Botero *et al.* 2004: 1371). On the continent, centuries of absolute government gave rise to a tradition of powerful administrative authority (Hayek 1960: 193), culminating in Napoleon's civil code – and manifested, for example, today in France's 2000 page *Code du Travail* (Jefferys 2003: 12). As noted at the outset North (1998) agrees with this view. On the other hand, Jean-Michel Josselin (this volume; also Josselin and Marciano 2002) takes the view that the Napoleonic Code and English common law are not very different, since the Code merely codified common laws and practices. But this view ignores the fact that the judge and jury in the common law system permit the law to develop without central government control. However, central government control is the core of the Code system. Moreover, we see a marked difference between Anglophone and continental European states in the extent of their regulation. If efficiency is not the answer (Jean-Michel Josselin agrees it is not), then what is?

Glaeser and Shleifer (2002) argue that the different legal traditions themselves are the efficient outcome of different environments in the twelfth and thirteenth centuries. England was more peaceful than France, and the king less powerful, so judicial independence was able to grow in England. In France, the judge-inquisitor system developed, both to protect the judges against powerful nobles, and to allow the king to control judges. Thus, in the English common law tradition statute law has come merely to supplement the unwritten law, and the judge's decisions effectively make law, which is contrary to the principles of the civil code system. Indeed, the common law reliance on judicial precedent is a 'key guarantee of freedom' say Glaeser and Shleifer (2002: 1220). The evolution of judicial precedent, together with the jury system, can be seen to put individualistic relations above state 'plans'.[6]

French legal origin states can thus be said to be 'predisposed' to regulate (because central government controls the legal system), and here Saint-Paul's theory can be brought in. What Saint-Paul's theory suggests is that regulatory policies (i) tend to be complementary, and (ii) that they develop path dependence. Thus, collective agreement extension laws give rise to rents which employment protection laws complement, by protecting the rents. Again employment protection laws, once set up, build up a constituency dependent on such protection and further advancing it – path dependence. Above we mentioned impediments to competition, such as strong unions, product market regulation or tariffs. These factors make labour demand inelastic, and raise the payoff from labour market regulation from insider groups. However, these factors are not truly exogenous, but are themselves determined by legal origin. In fact, from the small seed of legal origin, the whole panoply of labour regulation may be said to grow.

To test arguments about the importance of legal origin, Djankov *et al.* (2003) have developed legal formalism indices for 109 countries. At the ideal, informal, end they put the 'neighbour' model, where one neighbour resolves a dispute between two others using common sense and custom – lay judges, broad principles, juries and oral argument. At the other extreme, they put professional judge-inquisitors, legal codes, written records and regular appeals. They (2003: 459ff.) collect data from law firms in each country on these procedural variables in the case of hypothetical default in two simple cases, a bounced cheque and the eviction of a non-paying tenant. The aim of the index is to see how far procedure in a given country diverges from the neighbour model. The authors also collect data on how long these two types of case take to settle (for example 60 days in New Zealand for the bounced cheque, as against 645 in Italy).[7] Put simply, procedural formality means, 'worse contracting institutions' (Acemoglu and Johnson 2003).

Figure 4.5 gives a scatter diagram for a legal formalism index against employment protection (formalism here being the average of four measures developed by Djankov *et al.*). French legal origin countries are most formal, averaging 13.5 on this index, with English legal origin countries averaging only 2.5. German (11.5) and Scandinavian (5.0) come in between. Formalism gives a good explanation of OECD country variation in employment protection. As can be seen, the scatter is tight ($r=0.642$), and is in fact much tighter than for other variables such as trade union density ($r=0.324$), or left-wing orientation of government ($r=0.331$). Correlation of the formalism index with union protection (Figure 4.3) is also good, with $r=0.712$. However, there is a much lower correlation between formalism and generosity of unemployment benefits ($r=0.297$), and essentially no correlation with a wider measure of welfare generosity, including old-age pensions ($r=-0.118$). This pattern is not surprising since, as we have seen, while employment protection and collective bargaining protection go together across countries, welfare benefits do not. Nevertheless, the point remains that formalism is closely associated with employment protection and collective bargaining protection.

The legal origin theory has been criticized (Botero *et al.* 2004: 1365) as standing in for an unmeasured third factor, in particular the electorate's social-democratic 'tastes', wherever these come from. In answer to this criticism, Botero *et al.* show that legal origin also predicts employment and union protection well, even among their sample of non-democratic countries. Path dependence is influential even for dictators it would seem.

Acemoglu and Johnson (2003) have also criticized the legal origin theory, as being secondary to democratic institutions. Looking at a worldwide set of countries, they show that growth and employment are more dependent upon whether democratic institutions have taken root, than on legal formalism. In turn, whether democratic institutions take root is dependent upon their colonial history, and specifically whether colonists settled and brought their home country institutions or merely exploited the colony. Their favourite variable is settler mortality in the 1500s because mortality determined whether colonists settled or not. Democratic rights protect contracting parties against expropriation by the state, whereas, they say, legal formalism merely lowers contracting costs. However, this objection does not apply to the EU or OECD group on which we are focusing here, since all are currently democratic.[8] In fact we cannot even test the argument about the importance of colonists settling in the EU or OECD context, since these are all mother countries. (Jean-Michel Josselin's reference, this volume, to the 'developing world' as a way of explaining away the legal origin theory cannot work either, therefore.) Democracy versus legal origin remains only an intriguing possibility, therefore.

Conclusions

Labour market regulation in the EU is extensive and expanding. It takes two forms. First, there is the setting of floors to working conditions, which is the main area for directives, as shown in Table 4.1. Second, there is the setting of wage floors via minimum wages and, more importantly, extended collective agreements. This form appears currently to be left to the member states. Figure 4.1 demonstrates how broad is the coverage of collective agreement in the core EU countries. High floors under working conditions and under wages tend to go together (Figure 4.3).

The UK has historically been the odd man out in the EU, in the bottom-left corner of Figure 4.3, along with other Anglophone countries. The core of the EU is in the top-right corner, suspicious of the power of competition to drive labour standards down. As we have seen, it is this suspicion which underlies the drawing up of the 1989 Charter of Fundamental Social Rights of Workers and the 1993 Social Chapter of Maastricht. The UK is now being brought into line, with proposals to impose shorter working hours, reduce the temporary work agency industry (REC 2002) and impose formal worker consultation via company works councils. Interjurisdictional competition is being eliminated in favour of strict labour regulation.

We have seen that the efficiency arguments for strict labour regulation are questionable, because of disemployment effects. Careful statistical studies with many controls indicate that such regulation reduces job opportunities for outsider groups: the young, the old and the inexperienced. It also drives up long-term unemployment. Labour regulation thus causes redistribution within worker groups, with the least advantaged being excluded from the redistribution. Wage equality is bought at the expense of job opportunity equality.

We have surveyed Saint-Paul's theories of labour regulation as redistribution in some detail (Table 4.4). These theories quite reasonably put the employed semi- and unskilled worker at the centre, because this group contains the median voter. This group is shown rationally to desire strict labour regulation with which it diverts rent from skilled workers, the unemployed and the capitalists (who, however, being more mobile, are difficult targets). Out of this world come the policy complementarities that we have observed. Also, and most important, comes path dependence.

Path dependence – perhaps coupled with proportional representation – is important. It provides a way of explaining why some countries are so much further down the labour regulation road than others, even though all have broadly the same type of median voter. Here we have put Saint-Paul's model together with Botero *et al.*'s (2004) legal origin model. The legal origin comes first: some countries have fallen under the influence of the interventionist French legal tradition, and have continued that way because of the high transactions costs associated with changing. (Indeed, the interventionist tradition might even produce proportional representation: PR has not evolved, as has the UK's first-past-the-post, but is the product of a kind of rationalism.) Given a predisposition to intervene, these countries begin with some degree of labour market regulation, which then creates its own constituency of rent protectors. Path dependency takes over, and regulation grows.

We have noted that the UK's wage behaviour is still quite flexible, which is fortunate. (The new minimum wage there affects only a minority.) If wages can flex downwards as labour standards are hiked upwards, not much damage will be done. Interjurisdictional competition will continue for the time being. But crocodile tears should not be shed for the unemployed while labour regulation is made ever stronger.

Notes

1 Though the straight right–left characterization, with weak employment protection or low taxes versus the opposite is thought to be too simple by some (Amable and Gatti 2004), who also distinguish a 'flexicurity' model with weak employment protection and high taxes, to which the Netherlands and Denmark (see OECD 2004: 95) are thought to belong.
2 Germany is clearly similar, though with the difference that unofficial strikes are not allowed. On the other hand, workers and/or unions have the right to appoint directors to the board.
3 See Amable and Gatti (2004) for a model. However, deriving conditions under which employment protection and unemployment benefits are substitutes or complements or neither is not simple – see Saint Paul (2000, chapter 9).
4 A clear example of such a conflict between workers is in apartheid-era South Africa. The strongest supporters of the 'colour bar' exclusion of blacks from jobs were unskilled white workers in government, on the railways and in the mines (Siebert 1986). The conflict was between white and black workers, with (white) capitalists siding with the blacks, exactly in line with Becker's model.
5 In Saint-Paul's model, the skilled labour market is competitive; the unskilled is uncompetitive with unresponsive wages, and involuntary unemployment. Interestingly, Teulings and Hartog (1998: 262) believe exactly the opposite: 'High skilled workers in high rent industries [in the USA] are largely safeguarded from the hazards of economic fluctuations, while low skill workers in low rent industries get the full load'.
6 Hayek (1960: 56) speaks of an 'essentially empiricist' view of the world in England ('trial and error procedure'), and a 'rationalist' approach in France ('an enforced solely valid pattern'), and goes on: 'The British philosophers laid the foundation of a profound and essentially valid theory, while the rationalist school was simply and completely wrong'. Smith (1766) praises England's juries (Meek *et al.* 1982: 425).
7 The mean for English legal origin countries is 176 days, for socialist 327 days, for French 272 days, for German 193 days, and for Scandinavian 234 days (Djankov *et al.* 2003, Table V).
8 However, the democracies of Spain, Portugal, France and Germany are new and (with the exception of France) use proportional representation, which suggests less accountability of politicians and more rent for protected worker groups, as already noted.

References

Acemoglu, D. and Johnson, S. (2003) 'Unbundling Institutions', *NBER Working Paper*, 9934, Cambridge, MA: National Bureau of Economic Research.
Addison, J.T. and Siebert, W.S. (1991) 'The Social Charter of the European Community: Evolution and Controversies', *Industrial and Labour Relations Review*, 44, 597–625.
—— (1994a) 'Recent developments in social policy in the new European Union', *Industrial and Labour Relations Review*, 48, 5–27.
—— (1994b) 'Vocational training and the European Community', *Oxford Economic Papers*, 46, 696–724.
—— (1999) 'Regulating European labour markets: more costs than benefits?', *Hobart Paper*, 138, London: Institute of Economic Affairs.

Amable, B. and Gatti, D. (2004) 'the political economy of job protection and income distribution', Discussion Paper, 1404, Institute for Labour Research (IZA): Bonn.

Becker, G. (1956) *The Economics of Discrimination*, Chicago: University of Chicago Press.

—— (1983) 'A theory of competition among pressure groups for political influence', *Quarterly Journal of Economics*, 48, 371–400.

Bertola, G., Blau, F. and Kahn, L. (2004) 'Labor market institutions and demographic employment patterns', IZA Workshop on Wage Inequality, Technology and Institutions, www.iza.org/conference_files/witi_2004/kahn_l398.pdf.

Blanchard, O. and Wolfers J. (2000) 'The role of shocks and institutions in the rise of European unemployment: the aggregate evidence', *Economic Journal*, 110, C1–33.

Boeri, T. (1998) 'Enforcement of employment security regulations, on-the-job search and unemployment duration', *European Economic Review*, 43, 65–89.

Boeri, T., Ignacio, J., Ruiz, C. and Galasso, V. (2004) 'Cross-skill redistribution and the tradeoff between unemployment benefits and employment protection', Discussion Paper, 1371, Institute for Labour Research (IZA): Bonn.

Botero, J., Djankov, S., La Porta, R., Lopez-de-Silanes, F. and Shleifer, A. (2004) 'The regulation of labor', *Quarterly Journal of Economics*, 119(4), 1339–82.

Daniel, K. and Siebert, W.S. (2005) 'Does employment protection reduce the demand for unskilled labour?', *International Economic Journal*, 19, 197–222.

Djankov, S., La Porta, R., Lopez-de-Silanes, F. and Shleifer, A. (2003) 'Courts', *Quarterly Journal of Economics*, 118, 453–517.

DTI (2003) *Explanatory Memorandum on European Community Legislation – Amended Proposal for a Directive of the European Parliament and of the Council on Temporary Work*, London: Department of Trade and Industry.

—— (2004) *Information and Consultation of Employees Regulations 2004*, London: Department of Trade and Industry.

EIRR (2005) 'Social policy state of play', *European Industrial Relations Review*, July, 19–26.

EU (2004) 'Proposal for a Directive of the European Parliament and of the Council Amending Directive 2003/88/EC Concerning Certain Aspects of the Organisation of Working Time', COM(2004) 607 final.

—— (2005) 'Fundamental Rights within the European Union', europa.eu.int/scadplus/leg/en/cha/c10107.htm.

Frey, B. and Stutzer, A. (2000) 'Happiness, economy and institutions', *Economic Journal*, 110, 918–38.

Financial Times (2005a) 'EU to review draft law on temps' rights', George Parker, Sarah Laitner and Jean Eaglesham, September 24.

—— (2005b) 'Employers fear consultation law', Stephen Overell, FT.com site; March 2.

Glaeser, E. and Shleifer, A. (2002) 'Legal origins', *Quarterly Journal of Economics*, 117, 1193–229.

Gray, D. (1995) 'All displaced workers are not created equal: the political economy of worker adjustment assistance in France', *Public Choice*, 82, 313–33.

Grubb, D. and Wells, W. (1993) 'Employment regulation and patterns of work in OECD countries', *OECD Economic Studies*, Winter.

Guelfi, A. (2004) 'Employment protection and the incidence of unemployment: a theoretical framework', *Labour*, 18(1), 29–52.

Hayek, F.A. (1960) *The Constitution of Liberty*, London: Routledge and Kegan Paul.

Jefferys, S. (2003) *Liberté, Égalité and Fraternité at Work*, Basingstoke: Palgrave-Macmillan.

Josselin, J.-M. and Marciano, A. (2002) 'Introduction: the economics of the constitutional moment in Europe', in J.-M. Josselin and A. Marciano (eds) *The Economics of Harmonizing European Law*, Cheltenham: Edward Elgar.

Koeniger, W., Leonardi, M. and Nunziata, L. (2004) 'Labour market institutions and wage inequality', Discussion Paper, 1295, Institute for Labour Research (IZA): Bonn.

Laporta, R., Lopez-de-Silanes, F., Shleifer, A. and Vishny, R. (1998) 'Law and finance', *Journal of Political Economy*, 106, 1113–55.

Lazear, E. (1990), 'Job security provisions and employment', *Quarterly Journal of Economics*, 105, 699–726.

Mueller, D. (2003) *Public Choice III*, Cambridge: Cambridge University Press.

Nickell, S. (1986) 'Dynamic models of labour demand', in O. Ashenfelter and R. Layard (eds) *Handbook of Labor Economics*, Amsterdam: North-Holland.

Nickell, S. and Quintini, G. (2003) 'Nominal wage rigidity and the rate of inflation', *Economic Journal*, 113, 762–81.

Nickell, S., Nunziata, L., Ochel, W. and Quintini, G. (2002) 'The Beveridge curve, unemployment and wages in the OECD from the 1960s to the 1990s', CEP Discussion Paper, 502, London School of Economics.

Nicoletti, G., Haffner, R., Nickell, S., Scarpetta, S. and Zoega, G. (2001) 'European integration, liberalisation and labour market performance', in G. Bertola, T. Boeri and G. Nicoletti (eds) *Welfare and Employment in a United Europe*, Cambridge, MA: MIT Press.

North, D. (1998) 'The rise of the Western world', in P. Bernholz, M.E. Streit and R. Vaubel (eds) *Political Competition, Innovation and Growth*, Berlin: Springer-Verlag.

OECD (1999) *Employment Outlook 1999*, Paris: Organization for Economic Cooperation and Development.

—— (2004) *Employment Outlook 2004*, Paris: Organisation for Economic Cooperation and Development.

Persson, Torsten and Tabellini, Guido (2003) *The Economic Effects of Constitutions*, Cambridge, Mass.: MIT Press.

REC (2002) 'Response of the Recruitment and Employment Confederation to the Department of Trade and Industry's Consultation on the Proposed Agency Workers Directive', www.rec.uk.com/rec/lobbying/AWDresponseOct2002.pdf.

Saint-Paul, G. (1996) 'Labour markets: how reform took place', *Economic Policy*, October, 263–316.

—— (1997) 'The rise and persistence of rigidities', *American Economic Review*, 87, 290–4.

—— (2000) *The Political Economy of Labour Market Institutions*, Oxford: Oxford University Press.

—— (2002) 'The political economy of employment protection', *Journal of Political Economy*, 110, 672–704.

Siebert, W.S. (1986) 'Restrictive practices in South Africa's labour market', *Economic Affairs*, 7, October/November, 26-9.

—— (1997) 'Overview of European Labour Markets', in J.T. Addison and W.S. Siebert (eds) *Labour Markets in Europe*, London: Harcourt Brace/Dryden.

Smith, A. (1766) *Lectures on Jurisprudence*, edited by R. Meek, D. Raphael and P. Stein, Indianapolis: Liberty Fund.

Teulings, Coen and Hartog, Joop (1998) *Corporatism or Competition. Labour Contracts, Institutions and Wage Structures in International Comparison*, Cambridge: Cambridge University Press.

The Times (2005) 'Union anger as Britain retains EU working time opt-out', 2 June.

COMMENT: LABOUR MARKET REGULATION: INTERINDIVIDUAL AND INTERJURISDICTIONAL COMPETITION

Jean-Michel Josselin

Introduction

Making sense of labour market regulation first calls for an inquiry into the nature of the labour contract itself. Interindividual competition among workers and employers takes on different forms, from at-will agreements to strait-jacketed contracts. The fact that labour markets in developed countries are usually highly regulated raises both efficiency and distribution concerns. As is shown by Siebert (this volume), regulation is mostly beneficial to insiders (represented in the political arena by the employed median voter) at the expense of outsiders. In the distributive conflict among labour suppliers, the majority employed group is the winner while the unskilled are driven into unemployment or temporary work. On the whole, I agree with this analysis and will try to extend the arguments put forward by Siebert in order to stress further how interindividual competition is hindered by regulation.

This first step does not bring about much controversy, though the empirical evidence is mixed. As far as efficiency is concerned, employment protection legislation has at best either slightly negative or insignificant effect on economic performance. In distributive terms, the implicit collective search for equality (Agell 2004) combined with the rent-seeking strategic bias of employed workers (Siebert, this volume) evinces the apparently paradoxical result of a significant degree of solidarity among the employed while the unskilled stay or are left out of the distributive game. This is of course aligned with the predictions of Nozick (1974) and we shall discuss it later in more detail.

The second step is that of the political economy perspective. Rents require a fertile soil in order to grow and expand. The frame of labour market institutions is their constitutional and legal environment. Do the institutional culture and history of a country matter so much that they deeply influence the performance of the national labour market (and possibly of other markets as well)? In this matter, attention has been mostly focused on legal issues (Siebert, this volume). The work of La Porta *et al.* (1998) and Glaeser and Shleifer (2002) has triggered a lot of interest (van Hemmen and Stephen 2005, provide a methodological and empirical survey) and has mostly enhanced the common law tradition. In counterpoint, civil law is often reviled as the cause for economic trouble, particularly on financial markets but also on labour markets. This is where controversy may appear. I shall oppose the common view that the legal environment matters so much. I will also insist that the constitutional setting, though somewhat neglected in labour market regulation analyses, all the more matters in that it provides the framework for interjurisdictional competition. Much remains to be said in this respect and I will tentatively suggest how competition among alternative forms of jurisdictions could take place.

The developments are organized as follows. The following section examines interindividual competition in the labour market and raises efficiency and equity considerations. This is followed by a section that addresses the problem of inter-jurisdictional competition among governments: What would be the (second) best institutional ground for deregulation? The final section provides concluding comments.

Interindividual competition: efficiency and equity considerations

In markets, free interindividual exchanges require the ability of agents to move from one situation of transaction to another without facing prohibitive costs. The common view that the labour market would be structurally different implies regulation and control of the way exchanges are organized among firms and workers. Like any intrusions into markets, employment protection raises concerns about both efficiency and distribution.

Efficiency considerations

The usual sequence when studying the labour market begins with a market failure that requires a regulatory treatment. Effects on employment are then assessed in order to select potentially Pareto improving measures. This sequence builds on the underlying hypothesis that there is a per se pre-existing market failure that entails more or less efficient regulation. There are two likely fallacies associated with this line of reasoning. First, why should the labour market be so different that it endogenously needs regulation? This hypothesis of structural deficiency is strong enough to justify any form of regulation. To reject it would not mean denying the specificity of the labour exchange (we will come back to this point later) but would challenge the view that this specificity systematically and structurally denies markets any efficiency. Second, are potential Pareto improvements relevant criteria? For instance, the logical inconsistency of the Hicks–Kaldor criterion is such that one can easily demonstrate that opposed policy measures, one for and the other against protectionism for instance, can be both potentially Pareto improving. The usual sequence 'market failure – regulation – effect on employment' can then be challenged in the following way.

The reverse sequence 'regulation – market failure – effect on employment' is interpreted here in a bargaining framework (Rubinstein 1982; Shaked and Sutton 1984). It complements the usual explanations (implicit contracts, search, adverse selection, menu costs, cooperative games and unionization, standard insider–outsider framework and so on) and allows direct emphasis on the impact of regulation on the market structure. The objective is to illustrate how regulation fundamentally breeds market failures. Let us assume that production involves one firm employing one worker. A given amount of output is produced and it has to be shared between the firm and the worker. On the supply side of the labour market, there are $n \geq 1$ workers available. The firm employs an insider and bargains with him or her. It can switch to an outsider, but under two constraints that I qualify as regulatory constraints. The first switching condition for the firm is that it can make an offer to the insider at any time, but must wait for at least one unit of time before switching. This is a necessary condition for a non-Walrasian outcome (there are no simultaneous offers to various workers). The second switching condition is that if bargaining occurs with a given worker at some point in time, then no switch is possible until a minimum period of $T > 1$ units of time has elapsed. This condition is such that if $T \to 1$ then a Walrasian (free market) solution is reached at the limit. At the opposite, if $T \to \infty$ then the labour exchange takes place within a bilateral monopoly.

Values of T such that $T > 1$ are interpreted here as a given level of regulation. Increases in regulation are equivalent to increases in T as they move the market further away from the Walrasian solution and reinforce the 'unemployment equilibrium' (Shaked and Sutton 1984). Regulation obviously hinders efficiency. At the same time, it raises distributive concerns.

Distributive concerns

The unemployment equilibrium discussed above is such that the equilibrium wage is above the competitive level. In this non-Walrasian setting, jobs are rationed, which amounts to the 'unequal treatment' of workers who would strictly prefer to work (Shaked and Sutton 1984: 1351). When the analysis is extended to non-anonymous workers, then the impact of regulation is all the more significant. The arguments raised by Siebert (this volume) illuminate it. Earnings equality is bought at the cost of job opportunity inequality. The common sense distributive conflict would be between capital and labour only. It actually also takes place between different groups among the labour force. I provide here an illustration of such conflicts, building on the seminal article of Buchanan (1976) which interprets the Rawlsian contract in a Hobbesian way. Buchanan uses a two-player production game which I extend to a third player.

The two-player game begins with Buchanan's interpretation of the Rawlsian original position as Hobbesian anarchy. Robinson and Friday are independent fishermen and the social outcome is the natural distribution. The social contract consists of building a boat that will serve joint production. This contract can take three forms. The egalitarian sharing of the joint production is an effective Pareto improvement over the natural distribution. The incentive inequality contract amounts to an effective Pareto improvement over the egalitarian solution. The third type of covenant is utilitarian inequality which provides potential Pareto improvement over the first two contracts (effective improvement over natural distribution). The first four columns of Table 4C.1 give a numerical illustration (subtracting Sunday's share of the total production). Buchanan shows that the incentive-unequal contract is equivalent to the Rawlsian difference principle.

Interpreted here in a non-cooperative setting, the incentive-unequal sharing is straightforwardly the unique Nash equilibrium when the two players have three available actions: playing independently, in a Rawlsian way or in a utilitarian

Table 4C.1 Output sharing among workers

Social structure	Total production	Share of Robinson	Share of Friday	Share of Sunday
Independent production	5	2	1	2
Joint production, egalitarian sharing	15	5	5	5
Joint production, incentive inequality	22	8	6	8
Joint production, utilitarian inequality	28	12	4	12

Note
Adapts and extends Table 1 in Buchanan (1976: 11).

way. This stable collective outcome is obtained without any recourse to risk aversion, which is consistent with Buchanan's rejection of the utilitarian interpretation of Rawls. Let us now add a third player, Sunday, whose productivity is similar to that of Robinson. The allocation of joint production under egalitarian or incentive-unequal sharing is not altered by the arrival of the additional player. However, in the utilitarian setting, collusion between the most productive workers can contribute to both improve the collective outcome and decrease the share of the less skilled. There is a potential Pareto improvement through a collusion made possible for players with market power or favourable labour regulation. Friday is ruled out of the regulated market to assistance or temporary work. This utilitarian inequality is consistent with the likely fact that one of the employed workers is the median voter since it is easy to trace back an implicit utilitarian social welfare function in a voting model of resource or cost sharing. It is also consistent with the prediction by Nozick (1974) that the Rawlsian contract would soon degenerate into selective cooperation among the more productive or the best organized agents. In a quite different theoretical framework, Guelfi (2004) shows how a matching model with employment protection explains the empirical evidence (at least in Europe) that unemployment is mainly concentrated on groups of workers with low educational attainment rather than being randomly distributed among the various categories of the labour force.

The efficiency-equity approach admittedly provides insights into the functioning of labour markets subject to regulation, particularly as the latter can be captured to the benefit of some of the players. This approach nevertheless begs the question of how institutions matter in this field, if they matter at all. This is precisely the point I will consider now.

Interjurisdictional competition: the institutional ground for deregulation

There are times when the constitutional design of countries or unions of countries is the order of the day. This is the case in many respects for Europe now and possibly in other places as well. Is there an institutional ground that would be structurally able to prevent excessive regulation on the labour market? The next section examines the not so clear properties of federalism and of its various forms. Furthermore, the constitutional framework alone does not comprehend all the dimensions of the institutional landscape. The subsequent section discusses the respective properties of common law and civil law and challenges the now standard opinion according to which the former should without hesitation rule out the latter. But then, if no form of government and no form of law provide a decisive advantage towards deregulation, how can interjurisdictional competition bring about competition and efficiency? The final section on this topic discusses an alternative way of designing the institutions governing the labour market and its ability to fit into existing constitutional and legal frameworks.

The constitutional framework for a competitive labour market

Since Qian and Weingast (1997), federalism is considered as a commitment to preserving market incentives. However, it may take many forms, and one must go into some institutional details to find out how applied types of federalism perform as frameworks for a market economy. For instance, the Supreme Court in the USA as well as the European Court of Justice in the EU have had and still have a centralizing role (Vaubel 1996; Josselin and Marciano 2004a). The jurisdictional competition allowed by the confederate model is obstructed as soon as a federal court of justice takes on the task of assigning prerogatives among the components of government. This is particularly true in the case of the USA (Tullock 1965; Josselin and Marciano 2004b), but Europe does not seem to have been able to escape it until now (Vaubel 1994; Josselin and Marciano 2004c).

Centralized federalism raises at least two concerns, one of which is general, the other one being more related to market regulation. First, the centralizing trend may be inherent to the process of federation. If so, the confederate step would only be historical and the road to centralized power irreversible. An optimistic answer would be that the writing of the early constitutional documents should preclude federal courts from being more than agents of the federation rather than one of its principals. Second, democratic choices in a centralized federation may breed more regulation than a unitary state would, as Rose-Ackerman (1981) demonstrates. Adapting her framework, I propose here a very simple example which can illustrate the point. State A has a unitary structure and has passed a law l on employment regulation which goes against the wishes of an interest group I_A. State B also has a unitary structure and has rejected the regulation so that the legislative situation is $\bar{l}$, which fulfils the wishes of an interest group I_B. The initial situation is thus such that $\bar{l} >_{I_A} l$ and $\bar{l} >_{I_B} l$. If the two countries now form a centralized federation in which state legislative choices can always be pre-empted by the federal government (Josselin and Marciano 2004a), then the voters of interest group I_A may be willing to impose this regulation on their competitors. They may strategically reverse their preferences $\bar{I}''<''_{I_A}I$ in order to raise their rival's cost in the now federate state B. This would be more difficult to attain in a confederate structure where the decision would be submitted to bargaining.

Interjurisdictional competition is thus not necessarily enhanced by a federal structure, particularly when the latter exhibits an upwards trend in the assignment of power. Information-based and mobility-based competition (Salmon 2004) is probably better promoted in a confederate framework, though the implicit mimicking of regulatory practices cannot be ruled out. The downward move from centralized federalism to confederation could even be extended to lower levels of government. Indeed, competition seems to be more present there, as numbers decrease the market power of any given jurisdiction. This corresponds to what Kelsen (1962) describes as a static property of decentralization. Governments of a given level interact (for example compete) in an environment characterized by a given allocation of juridical capacity. In the standard tax competition model for instance, local governments are usually assigned the right of setting local tax rates. Despite possible mimicking behaviours due mainly to spatial proximity, competition *à la* Tiebout does not work so badly. Can the model be extended to a local supply of regulation? It should be likely to offer little room for inefficient local regulatory practices in a competitive environment. The problem is that such a competition would require a dynamic property of decentralization, to use again Kelsenian language, namely the downwards transfer of the juridical capacity of regulation. Now, we face the paradox that whereas competition seems to be increasing as we reach lower levels of government, their juridical capacity is quite systematically decreasing.

If federalism per se is not a guarantee for a competitive framework, then one may wish to check whether the legal framework is more likely to provide safeguards against excessive regulatory trends. Competition here is not among constitutional designs, but between two families of law. Does one of them prove to be more efficient than the other?

The legal framework for a competitive labour market

I would like to develop two points with regard to the common law – civil law controversy. First, the two systems have more in common than it may seem at first glance. Second, the civil law setting is a reasonably competitive one.

Civil law versus common law: why so much noise?

The superiority of common law over civil law is sometimes illustrated by the (unquestionable) success of the British economy over the last two decades. Compared with the relatively poorer macroeconomic performances of countries like France over the same period, the temptation is great to associate this success with a legal system more fitted to a competitive economy. One could suggest that the same regression be conducted for the 1950–80 period. Common law would then be associated with a much weaker economy. In the same vein, France experienced an era of extremely active entrepreneurship during the nineteenth century, especially as industrial development was prompted by a new juridical form, the *société anonyme*, created under the auspices of the *Conseil d'Etat* and in constant dialogue with private entrepreneurs. It is nevertheless true that civil law countries have poorer performances than common law countries in the developing world. An alternative explanation could be the influence of the French tradition of an ingrained search for equality (I borrow here an argument expressed by Pierre Salmon) rather than the influence of the civil code per se. Consequently, I would rather rely on public choice explanations (which I do not develop here), through the creation and subsequent use of market 'failures' by interest groups, to explain the poorer macroeconomic performances of developing civil law countries. This rent-seeking mechanism does not have much to do with the legal system, though it obviously rests on permissive political institutions.

Civil law is also sometimes accused of providing less secure property rights. On the contrary, the customary and non-authoritarian origin of common law would provide security and stability. As far as the Civil Code is concerned, this series of statements is puzzling. The French system of property rights is directly inherited from the Germanic tribal customs used in the regional courts of the northern parts of France, the *commune ley*. The Civil Code takes on this customary tradition while it rests on the Roman codification for contract law (Josselin and Marciano 2002). Thus, civil law may exhibit poor performances with regard to the protection of property rights, but then one should (not) blame its origins. Furthermore, as Ogus (2002: 73) puts it, '... French property owners may not care that their domestic legal system does not have the "trust", if alternative legal concepts can ensure the same degree of management of resources as the Anglo-Saxon concept'. In the same way, 'good faith' is not present in the common law system but is indirectly an argument enforceable in courts.

Finally, if interjurisdictional competition has so far mainly been between the United Kingdom and the rest of Europe (Siebert, this volume), then the legal origin quarrel may be somewhat misled. In effect, 'Professor Richard Posner has recently argued that British common law and European civil law are comparable in terms of formality' (Spector 2004: 537). 'It is American common law, rather than British law, that can be contrasted with civil law in terms of formality' (ibid.). By contrast indeed, the American doctrine provides much more room for explicit policy analysis. American judges 'feel free to systematically employ consequentialist, instrumental reasoning' (ibid.). They are all the more in capacity to use policy-based reasoning to interpret precedent cases and to establish renewed rules.

The competitiveness of civil law

The aim here is to show that legal competition does exist in civil systems of law. The standard view claims that common law ensures competitiveness through numerous courts dispensing and adapting 'open rules' whose plasticity allows an evolutionary match with changing circumstances. Even if common law could have developed without government control, which is historically dubious particularly during the time of Henri II (see Hogue 1985, for a history of law perspective; see Josselin and Marciano 2000, for an economic interpretation), the stare decisis doctrine is by nature rigid and conservative. The standard view also claims that civil law falls under the parliamentary monopoly of statutes, which precludes it from sustaining a competitive legal system. Ideally, the latter provides economic agents with a free choice of the rule they submit themselves to, and a free choice of the judge in case of litigation. Does civil law pass the test of competitiveness? I will follow here the analysis by Danet (2003) on the French case, but one can refer to Spector (2004) to get a wider view and a comparison with other civil codes.

A first fallacy concerns the alleged monopoly held by Parliament in the provision of legal rules. In the fields of civil and commercial law, this is simply not true. The Civil Code balances private and public interest through two fundamental articles. The first is Article 1134 which stipulates that as far as contracts abide by general rules (ability, licit cause and object, and so on) they bind the contractors as strongly as law can do. This is a legal basis for the creation of specific and private rules based on what French law calls *consensualisme*. This right to create private rules is bound by Article 6 of the Civil Code, according to which those private agreements cannot depart from public order or morals. Hence, 'apart from restricted areas where public order is at stake, private rules can compete with parliamentary will' (Danet 2003: 197). Even in those areas where public order matters and entails parliamentary prerogatives, courts can and do mitigate the extent and degree of public interference in private matters. To use an argument often raised in favour of common law, courts in the civil tradition can adapt the boundaries of public order to the evolving social circumstances. Outside the public order sphere, there is competition between rule suppliers such as professional orders, private institutions creating local norms (industrial standards for instance). At the same time, private transactions involve the creation of private rules 'on the spot', without any intrusion by legislative provisions. The first condition (free choice of the rule) for a reasonably competitive legal system is thus decently met by the civil law system.

The second fallacy regarding civil law concerns the alleged overwhelming power of public judges. Article 2059 of the Civil Code stipulates that economic agents can lay requests before a court of arbitration, a method frequently used for the resolution of disputes in commercial, inheritance and real estate property for instance. Furthermore, Article 2060 states that if a private contract breaches a public order provision, it will indeed be judged before a public court. However, if the contract is indeed cancelled, subsequent disputes with regard to the damages can be put before an arbitrator (and often are in practice). The second condition (free choice of the judge) for a reasonably competitive legal system is thus also decently met by the civil law system. Those properties will prove to be a non negligible asset as we now enter into the discussion of new jurisdictional forms for a competitive labour market.

The jurisdictional framework for a competitive labour market

As long as public goods are club goods, they can be provided by local communities à la Tiebout in a spatial setting or by agencies à la Nozick in a functional setting. Labour regulation is most of the time either centralized (on the national scale) or locally provided by states (on the international scale). In both cases, the framework remains quite exclusively spatial, the 'location' of the labour contract determining its content. Most of the benefits of the functional competition put forward by Nozick are thus neglected. Just as well as protective agencies can take the task of providing security, functional competition could be introduced in labour relations. Indeed, even in the absence of 'structural' deficiencies, the specificity of the labour contract requires some 'specific treatment'. One way is the regulation of the labour market itself, the alternative suggested here is the upstream creation of a market that could deal with the particular characteristics of labour.

This market would depart from the decentralized allocation associated with complete freedom of contract. Interindividual competition amounts to the Walrasian setting $T \to 1$ in the Shaked–Sutton model. At the other end of the spectrum, jurisdictional regulation is implemented mostly at the national level and can be even further centralized. Values of T are then very high. Interjurisdictional competition is mostly destructive since it usually consists in attempts at raising rivals' costs. The suggested alternative is an application to labour of Nozick's protective agencies.

An example of it can be drawn from MacLeod (2005): 'A solution to the problem of creating and enforcing long term labour contracts might be addressed by creating a market for standard labour contracts, similar to the one that currently exists for construction contracts in the United States' (p. 3). Agencies would provide standard labour contract forms. Variations from one form to another are public information, thus more easily compared than idiosyncratic at-will contracts which provide private information only. Let us add that such labour contract forms also provide some kind of market testing for evaluating the efficiency of regulations, thus avoiding the methodological bias of merely comparing the relative merit of a regulation with regard to yet another regulation.

The market for labour contract forms is an example of interjurisdictional competition based on a function rather than on a territory. Spatial competition obviously makes sense when economic agents are relatively homogeneous and contracts are reasonably complete. Whenever heterogeneity and incompleteness prevail, functional interjurisdictional competition provides more public information on the pricing and protection of labour. This information also makes the task of courts easier in case of litigation. This kind of interjurisdictional competitive setting is also compatible with a civil law setting. Decentralized functional jurisdictions such as labour form agencies would typically fit Article 1134 of the French Civil Code. They would provide a safe institutional ground for deregulation.

Conclusion

On the labour market, interindividual competition is flawed by regulatory practices which are in practice more the expression of rent seeking by organized pressure groups than an effective way to ensure individual rights. No constitutional or legal settings can demonstrate a definite advantage over the others as long as the decentralization of government prerogatives is not accompanied by a devolved juridical capacity. If interjurisdictional competition is to enhance and secure interindividual competition in the labour market, it may be through a careful organization of the competition between suppliers of labour contracts.

References

Agell, Jonas (2004) 'Efficiency and equality in the labour market', *CESifo Economic Studies*, 50(2), 255–78.

Buchanan, James (1976) 'A Hobbesian interpretation of the Rawlsian difference principle', *Kyklos*, 29(1), 5–25.

Danet, Didier (2003) 'From fiscal competition to juridical competition. Lessons from the French experience', in Alain Marciano and Jean-Michel Josselin (eds) *From Economic to Legal Competition. New Perspectives on Law and Institutions in Europe*, Cheltenham: Edward Elgar, pp. 193–206.

Glaeser, Edward and Shleifer, Andrej (2002) 'Legal origins', *Quarterly Journal of Economics*, 117(4), 1193–229.

Guelfi, Anita (2004) 'Employment protection and the incidence of unemployment: a theoretical framework', *Labour*, 18(1), 29–52.

Hogue, Arthur (1985) *Origins of Common Law*, Indianapolis: Liberty Press (1st edn 1966).

Josselin, Jean-Michel and Marciano, Alain (2000) 'Displacing your principal. Two historical cases of some interest for the constitutional future of Europe', *European Journal of Law and Economics*, 10(3), 217–33.

—— (2002) 'The making of the French Civil Code: an economic interpretation', *European Journal of Law and Economics*, 14(2), 193–203.

—— (2004a) 'Federalism and subsidiarity, in national and international contexts', in Jurgen G. Backhaus and Richard Wagner (eds) *The Handbook of Public Finance*, Dordrecht: Kluwer Academic Publishers, pp. 477–520.

—— (2004b) 'Federalism and conflict over principalship: some insights into the American constitutional history', *Constitutional Political Economy*, 15(4), 281–304.

—— (2004c) 'Europe before the Constitution: the road to centralised federalism', *Annual Meeting of the European Public Choice Society in Berlin*, April.

Kelsen, Hans (1962) *La théorie pure du droit*, Paris: Dalloz (first German editions: 1934, 1960: *Reine Rechtslehre*).

La Porta, Rafael, Lopez-de-Silanes, Florencio and Shleifer, Andrei (1998) 'Law and finance', *Journal of Political Economy*, 106(6), 1113–55.

MacLeod, Bentley (2005), 'Regulation or markets? The case of employment contracts', *CESifo Economic Studies*, 51(1), 1–46.

Nozick, Robert (1974), *Anarchy, State and Utopia*, New York: Basic Books.

Ogus, Anthony (2002) 'Legal culture as (natural?) monopoly', in Alain Marciano and Jean-Michel Josselin (eds) *The Economics of Harmonizing European Law*, Cheltenham: Edward Elgar, pp. 73–86.

Qian, Yingyi and Weingast, Barry (1997) 'Federalism as a commitment to preserving market incentives', *Journal of Economic Perspectives*, 11(4), 83–92.

Rose-Ackerman, Susan (1981) 'Does federalism matter? Political choice in a federal republic', *Journal of Political Economy*, 89(1), 152–65.

Rubinstein, Ariel (1982) 'Perfect equilibrium in a bargaining model' *Econometrica*, 50(1), 97–109.

Salmon, Pierre (2004) 'Information and mobility as two ways of horizontal competition among governments', *Annual Meeting of the Public Choice Society in Berlin*, April.

Shaked, Avner and Sutton, John (1984) 'Involuntary unemployment as a perfect equilibrium in a bargaining model', *Econometrica*, 52(6), 1351–64.

Spector, Horacio (2004) 'Fairness and welfare from a comparative law perspective', *Chicago-Kent Law Review*, 79, 521–39.

Tullock, Gordon (1965) 'Constitutional mythology', *New Individualist Review*, 3, 13–17.

van Hemmen, Stephan and Stephen, Frank (2005) 'Rule of law, finance and economic development: cross-country evidence', in Alain Marciano and Jean-Michel Josselin (eds) *Law and the State: A Political Economy Approach*, Cheltenham: Edward Elgar, pp. 185–241.

Vaubel, Roland (1994) 'The political economy of centralisation and the European Union', *Public Choice*, 81, 151–90.

—— (1996) 'Constitutional safeguards against centralisation in federal states: an international cross-section analysis', *Constitutional Political Economy*, 7, 79–102.

COMMENT: INTERJURISDICTIONAL COLLUSION AND THE STRATEGY OF RAISING RIVALS' COSTS IN EU LABOUR MARKET REGULATION

Roland Vaubel

Economic integration breeds political integration. That was the intention from the start. The causal link is that economic integration puts the national governments under increasing competitive pressure. If a single government raised taxes or introduced new regulations, it would have to be afraid that the others do not follow suit and that the market moves to other countries. If the governments unite, the citizens cannot escape as easily and a higher level of taxation and regulation results. Thus, intergovernmental collusion (harmonization) and policy merger (centralization) expand the power of government over the citizens.

Collusion requires unanimity among the members of the cartel. If the unanimity rule is abandoned, there is the additional possibility that the majority of highly taxed and regulated countries may impose their level of taxation and regulation on the minority to raise the latter's costs and impair its competitiveness.

In the European Community and Union, qualified majority voting on labour market regulation was first introduced by the Single European Act (1986), notably Article 118A (safety and health at the workplace). More than a dozen regulations were adopted on the basis of this article. Siebert's list includes the Working Time Directive (1993) to which I shall return. The 1989 Charter of Fundamental Worker Rights which he mentions was a non-binding declaration. In 1993, however, the Social Chapter (Agreement) of Maastricht, which initially did not apply to the UK, introduced qualified majority voting on directives setting minimum requirements with regard to the

1   improvement in particular of the working environment to protect workers' health and safety;
2   working conditions;
3   information and consultation of workers;
4   equality of men and women with regard to labour market opportunities and treatment at work;
5   integration of persons excluded from the labour market

(Art. 2 (1))

A spate of labour regulations followed. The best known are the directives on European Works Councils, parental leave, worker delegation and part-time work. Formally, most of these were unanimously adopted by the Council but this does not mean that all governments were in favour. If you know that you can be outvoted, there may be no point in provoking the others by formally recording your dissent – the more so as, also in 1993, the Council's Rules of Procedure had been amended to allow for the voting record to be published. Moreover, it is not easy to explain to the voters at home why all, or most, of the other governments are wrong. The opposition in parliament is almost certain to seize this opportunity for criticizing the government.

By imposing its regulations on the minority, the majority can suppress regulatory competition from the more liberal minority. This means that the majority can also afford to raise its own level of regulation and will impose this new level on the minority. For the reasons given, open dissent by the liberal minority is not a necessary condition for the strategy of raising rivals' costs being pursued, but it is a sufficient condition. I shall give some examples of such cases.

The first is the Working Time Directive which the UK challenged at the European Court of Justice. The Commission proposed Article 118A (health) as a legal basis for this directive. But limits on working time relate specifically to 'the rights and interests of employed persons' which were covered by Article 100A, section 2, requiring unanimous consent. The Court sided with the Commission and, in substance, upheld the directive.

Also among the early EU labour market regulations, there were abstentions on the following directives:

- safety and health on fishing vessels (23.11.1993: Britain and France abstaining),
- European Works Councils (20.9.1994: Portugal abstained, the British government did not participate in the vote),
- safety and health of working tools (5.12.1995: Britain and Ireland abstained).

A more recent case is the proposal of a Temporary Workers Directive. The UK has the highest share of temporary workers in the EU-15 (4.7 per cent in 2002). It accounts for two-thirds of the temporary workers in the Union. In the EU-15, the proposal was blocked by a minority coalition including the UK, Ireland, Denmark and Germany. When the Constitutional Treaty, which would have lowered the majority requirement, was rejected in the French and Dutch referenda (2005), the Commission withdrew the proposal for the time being, knowing that Eastern enlargement has made it more difficult to meet the majority requirement for such EU regulations.

The strategy of raising rivals' costs is not confined to labour market regulations. For example, the Financial Services Directive (2003) which forces investment banks to publish the prices of internal transactions was adopted against opposition from the British, the Swedish and some other governments. The City of London accounts for three-quarters of this market. The Droit de Suite Directive (2001) which forces art dealers and auctioneers to pay a certain percentage of their sales proceeds to the artists and their (often distant) heirs was adopted against opposition from the UK, Ireland, the Netherlands and Austria. The droit de suite had existed in a majority of member states including France (since 1921), Germany and Belgium.

Comprehensive analyses of voting in the EU Council since 1995 reveal that 'no'-votes and abstentions mainly come from Germany, Sweden and the UK

(Mattila and Lane 2001; Mattila 2004). In 1994–8, 21 per cent of the 1,381 legislative acts were openly contested in the Council (Mattila and Lane 2001, table 1). The North–South division is the main cleavage (Beyers and Dierickx 1998: 312; Mattila and Lane 2001: 45; Elgström *et al.* 2000: 121; Zimmer *et al.* 2005). As Mattila and Lane show, the share of dissenting votes is largest in decisions about the internal market (30 per cent), transport (27 per cent), public health (23 per cent) and social policy (17 per cent). Finally, a survey of 125 EU experts about 174 issues concludes that

> a clear majority (44 issues or 73 per cent) of the 60 issues where there are significant divisions between Northern and Southern delegations concern choices between free-market and regulatory alternatives. . . . In general, the Northern delegations tend to support more market based solutions than the Southern delegations.
>
> (Thomson *et al.* 2004: 251, 255f.)

According to Art. 139 TEC, the majority of governments in the Council may delegate the drafting of labour market regulations to trade unions and employers' associations at the EU level. European labour is organized in the European Trade Union Congress (ETUC), employers in UNICE. In the last few years, nine such agreements have been concluded by unions and employers: about parental leave (1995), part-time work (1997), the working time of seamen (1998), temporary work (1999), the working time of migrant workers in civil aviation (2000), the working conditions of migrant workers in cross-border services (2004) – all these agreements have been implemented by the EU – as well as about telework (2002), working stress (2004) and the European driver's licence for professional border-crossing drivers (2004) – these EU-wide agreements have been implemented by the member states.

If the Council decides unanimously even though a majority would be sufficient, regulatory collusion and raising rivals' costs cannot be distinguished because the minority may not wish to record their dissent. But in both cases, we would expect that the average level of regulation (or taxation) rises. The available empirical analyses of EU regulation confirm this prediction (Eichener 1995; O'Reilly *et al.* 1996).

As for taxation, the VAT directive of 1992 is an excellent example. It introduced a minimum rate of value added tax of 15 per cent. The unanimously adopted measure enabled three governments to raise their tax rates without requiring the approval of their national or the European parliament. If tax harmonization rather than tax collusion had been the aim, one would have expected both a lower and an upper limit on VAT rates. But the directive did not set a maximum tax rate. Since European tax policy requires unanimity (Art. 93 TEC), we can infer that this was not an instance of raising rivals' costs but collusion.

In a way, the earliest example of raising rivals' costs by EU labour market regulation has been the British decision not to veto the Social Chapter of Maastricht but to opt out (Vaubel 1995). Yet the competitive advantage which the Conservative government of 1991 may have sought at the time did not last for long. In 1997, the Blair government opted in.

References

Beyers, Jan C.M. and Dierickx, Guido (1998) 'The Working Groups of the Council of the European Union: supranational or intergovernmental negotiations?' *Journal of Common Market Studies*, 36, 289–317.

Eichener, Volker (1995) 'European health and safety regulation: no "race to the bottom"', in Brigitte Unger and Frans van Warden (eds) *Convergence or Diversity: Internationalization and Economic Policy Response*, Aldershot: Avebury, pp. 229–51.

Elgström, O., Bjurulf, B., Johansson, J. and Sannerstadt, A. (2001) 'Coalitions in European Union negotiations', *Scandinavian Political Studies*, 24, 111–28.

Mattila, Miko (2004) 'Contested decisions: empirical analysis of voting in the European Union Council of Ministers', *European Journal of Political Research*, 43, 29–50.

Mattila, Miko and Lane, Jan-Erik (2001) 'Why unanimity in the Council? A roll call analysis of Council voting', *European Union Politics*, 2, 31–52.

O'Reilly, Jacqueline, Reissert, Bernd and Eichener, Volker (1996) 'European regulation of social standards: social security, working time, workplace participation, occupational health and safety', in Günter Schmid, Jacqueline O'Reilly and Klaus Schömann (eds) *International Handbook of Labour Market Policy and Evaluation*, Cheltenham: Edward Elgar, pp. 868–98.

Thomson, Robert, Bourefijn, Javanka and Stokman, Frans (2004) 'Actor alignments in European Union decision making', *European Journal of Political Research*, 43, 237–61.

Vaubel, Roland (1995) 'Social regulation and market integration: a critique and public-choice analysis of the Social Chapter', *Aussenwirtschaft* (St. Gall), 50, 111–34.

Zimmer, Christina, Schneider, Gerald and Dobbins, Michael (2005) 'The contested council: the conflict dimensions of an intergovernmental institution', *Political Studies*, 53, 403–22.

5 Political competition and economic regulation in German history

WAS THERE REGULATORY COMPETITION IN EARLY MODERN GERMANY?

Oliver Volckart

Introduction

Ever since globalization began to gather pace after the fall of the Iron Curtain, modern political economy has paid increasing attention to the way competition between states is influencing political decision-making. A whole new theoretical concept – institutional competition – has been developed in order to explain how such processes work and what general outcomes they are likely to have.[1] While recent political and economic changes triggered theoretical developments, it has always been recognized that interstate competition is not a new phenomenon. After all, during the Cold War the great powers competed intensively, albeit in ways very different from those analysed by the theory of institutional competition. There, the focus is not on military rivalries, arms races and so on, but rather on how nation states or members of federations compete for mobile factors of production. However, this type of competition is not new either. In the late nineteenth and early twentieth centuries, for example, capital and labour were highly mobile, and states competed intensively for them. In fact, economic historians and historically minded economists have begun to apply the term 'first age of globalization' to this period of economic history. What is more, at least some economic historians have observed intergovernmental competition for capital and labour at even earlier points in time.[2]

In the present chapter, a specific aspect of this kind of competition is examined: the object is to show how it influenced the decisions made by political authorities with regard to the regulation of products and services.[3] The period of time which is studied here is that between roughly the late fourteenth and the early nineteenth centuries, the area that of the Holy Roman Empire north of the Alps. The period, that is, the early modern age, is of particular interest because it saw the evolution of the institutional underpinnings of modern market economies in Germany. Slowly and not without relapses, but towards the end of the eighteenth century with increasing speed, the traditional society composed of a hierarchy of corporate social orders gave way to a modern market society where agents interacted who enjoyed, if not an equal status, then at least equal rights. As for the area, the Holy Roman Empire is particularly well suited for a study such as this because of its notorious political fragmentation. At the end of the eighteenth century, more than 300 territories which were well advanced on the way to statehood existed within its borders, while there were more than 1,700 other lordships which enjoyed a high degree of political autonomy (Möller 1989: p. 68). The average size of a polity within the Empire was thus barely 385 square kilometres.[4] In view of the fact that few cultural barriers to migration existed within Germany (the religious denominations may have posed such a barrier), one would suppose that the large number and small size of territorial political authorities made for intensive intergovernmental competition. Hence, it should be possible to observe the effects this competition had in the field of regulatory policies with particular clarity.

Is this the case? The following pages show that matters were not quite as clearcut as they seem to have been at first sight. As indicated above, most economists who are involved in developing the concept of institutional competition focus on the modern world. The same holds true for the scholars who began to work out the modern theory of regulation (for example Stigler 1971; Posner 1974). Is it possible to apply their theories to a past as distant as that examined in the present analysis? The author answers this question with a cautious 'yes': in principle, it is possible. However, differences between conditions then and now need to be taken into account. Traditionally, economic historians have located such differences in the field of values or preferences, claiming that medieval and early modern economic agents were no utility maximizers and that homo oeconomicus came into being only with industrialization (for example Sombart 1916/87; Polanyi 1944/97; Bauer and Matis 1988). This approach rules out the application of modern economic theory from the start. Luckily, much of it is based on a methodological fallacy. Scholars like Sombart (1916/87: 29f.) did note that pre-modern people left few documents containing direct information about their economic motives and preferences and that what most sources show is rather how people acted. However, they did not hesitate to use the information about the behaviour – or at least about certain aspects of the behaviour – of the historical actors, which they found in the sources in order to draw inferences about the then current motives, values and preferences and to use their inferences in order to explain the behaviour they observed. That this is a logical circle needs no further exposition. At present, we know hardly anything specific about what most medieval and early modern people thought and felt about their work, which values they shared, and what they aspired to. As long as this is the case, it seems reasonable to keep to some consistent behavioural assumption – utility maximization is as good as any and more plausible than most – and to see what can be made of it.

If not in the field of preferences and values, where then do we need to look for differences between pre-modern and modern conditions which need to be taken into account? As human behaviour is shaped by preferences on the one hand, and by restrictions on the other, it is the restrictions which we must examine, that is, the rules relevant for the activities of individuals involved in institutional competition. These rules did, in fact, fundamentally differ from those which exist today and which both the theory of regulation and that of institutional competition take for granted. It is not just that pre-modern society was stratified more strictly than its modern successor; it is rather that basic institutions which shape the relations between modern private individuals and public authorities began to develop only towards the end of the period of time here examined. Where the regulation of economic activities is concerned, these relations are of central importance. After all, the creation of regulatory rules establishes close contacts between actors in politics and in the economy. The central hypothesis of the present analysis is that for much of the period discussed here the institutional underpinnings of the German society severely impeded any competition for capital or labour among political authorities. Only when modern monopolistic states had emerged, this kind of competition could really begin.

The rest of this chapter proceeds as follows. In the next section, the structure of pre-modern society is analysed in detail, the focus being on the question of which political authorities were able to regulate products and services and what this implies for the applicability of modern theories of regulation and institutional competition. Subsequently it is examined which authorities were interested in attracting mobile factors of production, in how far they were able to do that and what changes occurred in this field during the time studied here. Only then, the effects which such changes had on the regulation of the economy can be analysed. In a final section, it is demonstrated how the institutions which shaped the process of institutional competition in pre-modern Germany can be integrated into a modified concept of this competition. Also, the hypotheses of the chapter are summarized.

Who regulated?

The modern theory of regulation starts out from the basic assumption that the relations between business branches, firms or other economic agents on the one hand and politicians on the other constitute an analogy to the market: there is a demand for regulation which originates with economic agents who aim for example at preventing their competitors from entering some economic market, and there is a supply of regulations which are offered by politicians who discover that such rules can be sold in exchange for material resources, increases in their power or similar assets. Seen from this point of view, the density of regulation of an economy corresponds to an equilibrium in the political market (cf. Stigler 1971).

Obviously, the theory sketched above is based on an essential assumption: it must be possible to make a clear distinction between political actors who have a monopoly of law-making and law enforcement within their jurisdictions, and economic actors who demand legal regulations because on their own they are unable to establish institutions which bind not only themselves, but others – for example their competitors – too. Put differently, society and the state must be separated. Today, there may be a number of developing countries where this condition is not given, where, in other words, economic pressure groups are powerful enough to create and enforce their own rules without having to turn to some ephemeral government (Mummert and Mummert 1999: 160). Apart from that, however, individuals, companies or business branch organizations are nowhere able to establish institutions against the will of the territorial government – institutions, that is, which need to be enforced with the help of coercive means. Closely linked with this condition is another one whose existence is implicitly assumed in the concept of institutional competition: not only state and society must be separated, but jurisdictions must be clearly separated from each other by well-defined political borders, too. Sovereign states or members of federations with legislative competencies need to exist side by side. Again, this mirrors present conditions: though the rightful owner of some territory may occasionally be disputed, there is practically no place in the world which is not claimed by one state or another.

A brief glance at the political and constitutional conditions existing in the early modern Holy Roman Empire shows that they did not match those taken for granted in the modern concept of institutional competition. First of all, territorial legislative monopolies either did not exist or began to develop only towards the end of the period here considered. There were two reasons for this. First, at least originally – that is, when feudal relationships emerged at the end of the early Middle Ages – rulers did not have the competency to introduce new rules or to change existing ones. For explanation, most legal historians point to the then current assumption that the origin of law transcended human influence and that any modification would, therefore, damage the divine world order (Kern 1919/58; Wolf 1973: 517; Willoweit 1983: 76; Grimm 1987: 54; Boldt 1990: 50). However, as most areas of life were regulated by the contracts which linked rulers and ruled – feudal lords and their vassals, landlords and their peasants – there cannot have been a strong demand for universally valid rules, at least not as long as society was predominantly rural. The other reason why legislative monopolies did not exist has more to do with the enforcement of institutions. A basic fact of Central European constitutional history is that the feudal system which emerged within the German parts of the Holy Roman Empire did not contain any territorial monopolies of force. Up to the sixteenth century, every single member of society – at least every single male member – was in principle not only able to employ his own means of coercion in order to enforce institutions or contracts, but regarded it as perfectly legitimate if his neighbour did the same (Brunner 1939/92; Volckart 2004b). It follows that when political organizations began to acquire legislative competencies in the late Middle Ages, they did not have territorial monopolies of coercion either. In fact, by the sixteenth century any given area within the Empire contained numerous political authorities which were all able to create new institutions – that had not necessarily been harmonized – and to employ coercion to enforce them.

At the most basic level the household, called '*familia*', was still a political organization and would continue to be that up to the nineteenth century. Directly subject to the head of the household were his wife (in most cases the head was male), the children, servants and other persons who lived within the household and were more or less strongly integrated into it. Servants, who were usually young and unmarried, and relatives had a status similar to that of the children (Mitterauer 1979: 27; cf. Mitterauer 1975: 130; Sprandel 1988: 38ff.; Münch 1996: 191ff.). Like all organizations, the household was based on institutions which formed a kind of rudimentary constitution. However, due to its usually small size, which allowed the head of the household closely to control the activities of the other members, there was a fluid transition between such rules and commands: the less specific the latter became, the more did they resemble institutions. Still, part of the rules of the household had other origins than just the will of the head of the organization. Some of them had been determined by contracts concluded between him and people who decided to enter the household, while others had been formulated under the influence of concepts propagated by the authors of handbooks that were addressed to the heads of these organizations (Münch 1996: 205; Brunner 1958/80).[5] In all cases, the rules of the household determined the division of labour among its members; if the household did produce any goods or services, they included institutions which regulated many aspects of this work, too. Not only originally, but up to the beginning of the modern age, heads of households were able to coerce their subjects into obedience. Their right to do that was confirmed by the Common Law of the Prussian Territories ('*Allgemeines Landrecht für die Preußischen Staaten*') which was promulgated in 1794: master craftsmen were allowed to use coercion against their apprentices, landlords against their farm hands (and subject peasants), heads of households against their servants, parents against their children, and finally husbands against their wives (Koselleck 1981: 641).

Households existed in all strata of society, and this alone made for a bewildering array of organizations that were able to create institutions and to enforce them with the help of coercion. However, there were even more legislative bodies. Since the thirteenth century at the latest, heads of households with similar economic or other interests began to collude and to form corporations at least some of which regulated products and services. The most famous case in kind is, of course, the craft-guild. Craft-guilds had many functions, some of them religious and social, but in the present context their power to create institutions which regulated the productive activities of their members (and, often enough, prohibited those of non-members) is most important. Product regulations were extensive: many goods, most of all mass goods such as cloth, but metal wares, too, were so minutely standardized that individual members of the corporation had hardly any leeway to make decisions about for example the quality of what they were producing. Moreover, even if the finished product was not standardized the productive processes were, craftsmen being for example obliged to use certain kinds of tools and raw materials while others were prohibited. As at the same time the guilds restricted productive capacities, for example by limiting the hours of work and the number of apprentices and journeymen which each of their members were allowed to employ, individual craftsmen had few chances to determine the quality of their product even if it had not been formally standardized (Ennen 1971: 46, 63ff.). Of course, the influence of craft-guilds differed over time and between places. The government of for example Freiburg im Breisgau had been taken over by them in the fourteenth century, so that here they could impose extremely restrictive regulations (Ehrler 1911, 1912). In most towns, however, they needed at least some support in the enforcement of their rules. In the late Middle Ages, they usually turned to the local urban council which was in most cases composed of merchants or patricians who drew on rural rents, while in the early modern period territorial princes became increasingly involved in enforcing regulations which had been created by craft-guilds (Schultz 1983; Millies 1937: 23f.; Weidner 1931: 81, 103; Jahn, no date, *c.*1909: 112 ff.). In some cities, finally, the most famous example of which is Nuremberg, craft-guilds in the sense of organizations able to shape their own institutions did not exist. Here, production was directly regulated by a superior authority, that is, by the merchant-dominated council (Lentze 1964).

Corporations which regulated production were not restricted to towns, agriculture being affected in a way very similar to industry. From at least the twelfth century, peasants in all parts of Germany began to form organizations which claimed a large number of property rights that had hitherto lain in the hands of the individual peasants (Wunder 1986). Such village communities fulfilled diverse functions. They tended to strengthen the bargaining position of the peasants vis-à-vis their landlord; they restricted the use of the common, thereby preventing its proverbial tragedy; they helped to internalize the external costs of the close neighbourhood of the individual peasant plots under the open field system, and, last but not least, they limited agricultural output by restricting the number of farm hands peasant households were permitted to employ, thereby allowing peasants to appropriate monopoly rents of their own (Volckart 2004a). Many villages did not only determine how much of their land was to be used as pasture and how much as arable; they also regulated exactly when the arable was to be ploughed, what kind of crop was to be sown in which fields, when the harvest, the threshing and so on had to be done, and finally what tools and implements were to be used in all these labours (see for example Boelcke 1964: 258; Schildt 1996: 158). As for the enforcement of such institutions, village communities provided sanctions which reached from the exclusion from communal baths or baking houses over the pillory and various fines to prison sentences for inveterate law-breakers (Nikolay-Panter 1989: 76; van Dülmen 1999: 51). Like craft-guilds, rural corporations came under increasing pressure in the course of the early modern age. In East-Central Europe, many of their functions were taken over by landlords who at the same time expropriated individual peasant plots and increased the labour dues rendered by their serfs so far that peasants ceased to be individual agricultural producers even in the limited sense in which they had been in the old village community. Further west, the rural corporations were integrated into the emerging states, becoming regional authorities subject to the central governments (Wunder 1986).

This takes us to the level of the principalities, which began to extend their legislative competencies at the close of the Middle Ages. Before the advent of absolutism, most new laws originated as clauses of contracts concluded between a territorial ruler and political authorities who were at least formally his inferiors (Wolf 1973: 546; Schulze 1981: 161f.). Thus, the diets and proto-parliaments ('*Landtage*') of late medieval and early modern Germany, where such contracts were negotiated, did not represent the population but rather powers in their own right (Mitterauer 1977: 32).[6] The function of such diets was therefore less legislation in the modern sense of the word than the harmonization of the institutions created by the diverse authorities represented in them. Why did a demand for this kind of harmonization – which affected the regulation of products and services, too – appear towards the end of the Middle Ages? Schmoller (1884–7: 19f.) asserted that economic policies pursued on the level of the individual town tended to impose external costs on the surrounding countryside and that these costs prompted the attempts of territorial rulers to centralize political competencies. Thus, state formation and territorial mercantilist policies went hand in hand in Sombart's view. While for a ruler centralizing and most of all monopolizing power was always an attractive proposition, it is plausible enough that the externalities mentioned by Schmoller became the harder to bear the further economic integration advanced in the course of the late Middle Ages and the early modern period. Hence, incentives to internalize them by harmonizing the rules of the diverse authorities became stronger. And as the costs of achieving such a harmonization fell due to the spread of literacy, the invention of printing and the replacement of expensive vellum by cheaper paper in the fourteenth and fifteenth centuries, territorial economic policies became possible only then.

Conditions approaching those of today – at least with regard to the division of state and society – appeared only with absolutism. Absolutist rulers aimed at obliterating the tangle of rights and privileges enjoyed by their diverse ranks of subjects, thereby creating a levelled and uniform mass of citizens. While the limits to their success have long been recognized (Oestreich 1968/97; Henshall 1992), their power to legislate was still greater than that of their pre-absolutist forerunners. Typically, older political bodies were not dissolved but rather integrated into the new political structure and used as administrative units. Thus, in absolutist Prussia craft-guilds were employed as transmission belts in order to pass down regulations and directives to the individual producers (Meyer 1888: 23; Kaufhold 1994: 52). In Austria under Mary Therese (1740–80), even entrepreneurs who founded manufactories were strictly regulated: decisions concerning the kind, quantity and quality, and in part even of the price of their products were not made by them but rather by the officials of the imperial chancellery (Otruba 1981: 85). However, as indicated above, the influence of absolutism should not be overrated. What was characteristic for most of the period discussed here, and for much of the area even at the very end of the Holy Roman Empire, is the parallel and simultaneous existence of a large number of political authorities within any given area – of authorities that were able to regulate products and services. Hence, the clear-cut distinction between state and society which implicitly underlies the idea of institutional competition cannot be made, or can be made only with regard to limited areas and periods of time.[7] Still, this is not the only point where pre-modern conditions diverged from those of today. Another difference of equal importance is discussed in the next section.

To what extent was competition for mobile factors of production possible?

The separation of state and society is one assumption contained in the concept of institutional competition; another is the identity of interests between the legislative powers and those who hope to gain from the influx of capital and labour. Even under ideal democratic conditions, where judiciary and executive are separated from the legislature, the latter is implicitly assumed to aim not only at maximizing the long-term benefits of its members, but the revenues of the state as a whole. The argument goes that foreign capital and labour, most of all skilled labour, are assets that increase the productivity of the domestic economy, that a higher productivity triggers growth and that a growing economy yields higher revenues which ultimately increase the power or the income or whatever the political actors are maximizing.

There are several reasons why these assumptions do not agree with conditions as they were in fourteenth- to eighteenth-century Central Europe. For one thing, political authorities needed to realize that their income grew when foreign capital and labour moved into their sphere of influence – as explained above, territories with clearly defined borders originally did not exist – and that this might have something to do with the institutions valid there. Identifying these links required rather sophisticated techniques of control and information gathering. Less so, of course, in small territories such as those common in South-West Germany: there, a single immigrant or foreign investor had a much larger impact on the territorial economy and on the princely revenues than in the emerging large territorial states of the North-East of the Holy Roman Empire. In these larger states, the governments needed to develop statistical methods. Statistics, which were kept from the eighteenth century, were primarily designed to provide a basis for taxation (Johnson 1964: 389), but nevertheless made it possible to register the entry or exit of mobile factors of production. Only then, this precondition for institutional competition was given.

However, it was not the only necessary condition. It is a general characteristic of pre-modern fiscal systems that the income of political authorities did not necessarily grow when labour or capital moved into their sphere of influence. Rural authorities, from the peasant household over the manor up to the princely court, were originally supposed to exist exclusively 'off their own', that is, off the proceeds of the work done by the members of the households. To a large measure and for a long time, this was indeed the case, not only peasant households and manors living 'off their own', but territorial princes, too. True enough, the income of the latter was supplemented by the proceeds of their princely prerogatives, that is for example mining, customs and certain parts of the jurisdiction.

However whereas in towns taxes were well established by the thirteenth century, in rural areas the shift from what historians call the 'demesne state' to the 'tax state' gathered pace only in the sixteenth century and had been by no means concluded in about 1800 (Schumpeter 1991: 104). In early eighteenth-century Prussia, for example, the proceeds of the demesnes amounted to about one-third of the royal revenues. By the middle of the century, they had grown to about one-half, only to fall again to about one-third at the end of the century (Ullmann 2005: 19). The less important taxes were for the income of the prince the smaller was his concern for the immigration of mobile factors of production. Only in times of acute labour scarcity, as for example in the century after the Black Death (1347–50), feudal rulers who did not receive any taxes can be assumed to have been interested in attracting peasants to their demesnes. This was the case even when these peasants did not render any dues in money or in kind, but the traditional labour services, the products of which the lord could either consume himself or sell on the nearest market.

However, when labour was plentiful, land was usually scarce, so that manorial lords and princes were unable to grant plots to additional peasants. Arguably they would still benefit from immigrants because a larger labour force would tend to depress wages. Any wage labour which supplemented that rendered by members of the manorial household would then become cheaper. Still, this does not mean that feudal rulers were free to attract labour: in the absence of a state with a territorial monopoly of force, they always had to take the activities of other authorities into account – authorities whose interests might be diametrically opposed to their own. Thus, when land was scarce, peasant communities would restrict immigration (Schildt 1996: 113; Endres 1989: 87). Under such conditions, conflicts between manorial lords who were interested in the influx of labour and villages which tried to keep out immigrants were bound to happen (Friedeburg 1997: 94f.). Depending on the rural institutions, similar problems could recur on higher levels of the social hierarchy. When the 'Great Elector' Frederick William (1640–88) tried to attract peasant immigrants to his territory, which had been severely depopulated during the Thirty Years' War, he learned that settlers were willing to come only under the condition that they were not subjected to the serfdom then common in Brandenburg. However, despite the scarcity of labour, the territory's nobility had not the slightest interest in the arrival of non-servile peasants. They unanimously opposed immigration (cf. Vetter 1985: 148).

As mentioned above, princely revenues had always been supplemented by the income derived from tolls and customs, and these sources of finance constituted an incentive to create conditions favourable to trade. Up to the fourteenth century, many towns owed their foundation to their rulers' interest in attracting commerce (Dirlmeier 1966: 26ff.). However, in order to increase the attraction of towns, rulers usually had to grant them a higher degree of autonomy. And the more autonomous towns became, the better chances did organized special interest groups within them have to influence urban policies. Here conflicts comparable with those between manorial lords and village communities or territorial princes could develop. As far as Freiburg im Breisgau was concerned, the city's Habsburg overlords did not even make an attempt to force the council – which was dominated by the craft-guilds – to accept immigrants. The council itself obviously valued the rents appropriated by its members on the basis of the regulations created by the guilds higher than any increase in the taxes which might have been a consequence of a growth of the city due to immigration. It is likely enough that the fact that Freiburg's population shrank from the fifteenth century was due to the restrictive practices imposed by the craft-guild dominated council (Ehrler 1912: 453).

In fact, attempts to force hitherto autonomous towns to accept immigrants or foreign investors seem to have been made only after rulers had monopolized means of coercion so far that their success was not completely unlikely. They still met some resistance, as an episode from early eighteenth-century Hesse-Kassel shows. There the territorial government was strongly interested in the influx of Huguenot refugees from Catholic France, who were promised favourable conditions in order to persuade them to come. Domestic special interest groups from trade and industry, however, regarded the immigrants as their potential competitors. They addressed a memorial to their government where they pointed out that

> the love between lord and subjects would be weakened if foreigners were attracted by granting them advantages and native citizens treated so hard that they were forced to emigrate, in part leaving their belongings behind. Thus a great and irreconcilable hatred between foreigners and citizens would arise, in particular because the latter would regard the former as people who wanted to drive them out.
>
> (Zumstrull 1983: 167)

With the advent of the modern monopolistic state, presenting such memorials – in the terms of A.O. Hirschman (1970), making use of 'voice' (which was characteristically supported with the threat of 'exit') – became the only option left to the representatives of organized special interest groups. In former centuries, they would have been able to create and enforce their own institutions in order to keep out immigrants and foreign investors; this could now no longer be done.

Thus, pre-modern conditions in Germany differed from conditions tacitly assumed in the concept of institutional competition in two important respects: first, political authorities were not necessarily interested in attracting mobile factors of production because their revenues did not, or only in part, depend on taxes. What is more, even if they were interested in making the territories they claimed to rule attractive for foreign capital or labour, they had to take into account the resistance of well-organized special interest groups. Such groups usually regarded foreign investors and immigrant workers as competitors, were able to shape their own regulations and anti-competitive institutions, and made use of their own means of coercion in order to enforce them. This latter obstacle to institutional competition disappeared only when monopolistic states began to emerge in Germany in the late seventeenth and eighteenth centuries.

On the other hand, the preceding centuries had already seen the development of a number of preconditions of this kind of competition – of preconditions whose importance is usually stressed in the modern concept of institutional competition, too. There much stress is put on several essential types of freedom, the most important ones being the freedom of commerce, of emigration and of capital transfers (Streit and Kiwit 1999: 34f.). To be sure, freedom of commerce was not even achieved within territories, trade being subjected to duties not at the as yet badly defined borders, but rather at points where it could easily be controlled, such as the crossings of rivers or the gates of cities. Still, where the freedom of emigration was concerned, the early modern age witnessed important developments.

Of course, many political authorities tried to prevent their subjects from leaving their sphere of influence. Towns, for example, demanded a fine from emigrating citizens, and landlords, particularly in East Germany, where serfdom dominated, did not give their peasants the slightest chance to leave the manor. However, for one thing the question of how effective such prohibitions were is disputed in historical research, some historians claiming that on the whole, landlords were successful in pressing their claims, others asserting that refusals of the right to emigrate remained a dead letter (Blickle 1983: 253; Abel 1976: 21). What is more, the freedom of emigration – at least of religiously motivated emigration – became a widely acknowledged right from the sixteenth century. Already in 1514 the Württemberg diet attested the duke's subjects' right to leave the territory for good (Näf 1975: 71–7). With the reformation, rulers realized that denominational heterogeneity within their principalities undermined the legitimacy of their rule, thereby increasing the costs of enforcing political measures (cf. Schilling 1981: 200f., 367f.; Hsia 1989: 53f., 177). The consequence was a clause agreed on in 1555 in the Religious Peace of Augsburg: there, all princes were granted the right to determine their subjects' denomination, while the subjects were granted the right to emigrate in order to avoid being forced to convert. At the end of the Thirty Years' War in 1648 a similar clause was included in the peace treaty of Westphalia (Scheuner 1950: 208f.; Gerteis 1981/97: 87). In principle, this was the first time that conflicting claims of inferior political authorities – such as landlords who were unwilling to allow their peasants to leave – were overruled by a universally valid institution of constitutional status (Möhlenbruch 1977: 79).

As for capital transfers, finally, there was no political authority in pre-modern Germany which even conceived the idea that they might be controlled.[8] Apart from the opposition of established special interest groups, who might prevent foreign investors from entering a territory, institutional restrictions to capital movements did not exist. And, as described above, these restrictions became less effective when states began to emerge in the late seventeenth and eighteenth centuries. In fact, only the emergence of these states makes it possible to speak of interjurisdictional competition; jurisdictions in the territorial sense of the word having not existed in the time before.

What were the consequences of interjurisdictional competition?

To recapitulate: in eighteenth-century Germany a large number of political authorities able to regulate production or services existed side by side, many of them within the same territory. Not all of these authorities were interested in attracting mobile factors of production. In fact, a large number of them – craft- and other guilds and village communities – tended to regard investors or immigrant labourers as potential competitors; others – for example landlords – were frequently opposed to immigration for other reasons. As long as states that had monopolized the means of coercion within their territories did not exist, all of these authorities were able to use force in order to keep mobile factors of production out of their spheres of influence. Only with state formation, that is, from the late seventeenth and eighteenth centuries, were territorial governments able to deprive these traditional authorities of much of their power. From then on, institutional competition within the Holy Roman Empire gathered pace. How did it affect regulation?

The important circumstance to realize is that the creation and enforcement of institutions are always costly, but that costs differ according to the type of institution concerned. Here it is essential to draw on Hayek's (1982: 48f.) distinction between concrete and abstract rules. Abstract rules are valid for an unknown number of persons and future instances; they are universally valid laws. By contrast, concrete rules are designed to make it possible to achieve some pre-defined end. They apply to specific people only, whom they assign concrete duties or areas of activity. Typically, concrete institutions are regulations, privileges or rules on which organizations are based. In principle, abstract rules are more costly to shape and above all to enforce than concrete ones. This is due to the fact that in most cases, it is hard to predict which consequences they are going to have for the persons and groups involved in legislation. Frequently it is possible to recognize these consequences only after a considerable period of time, and difficult to ascribe them to the actions of specific people. It is far easier to make out the economic consequences of concrete rules, which usually benefit clearly defined social groups or individuals (for example by allowing them to appropriate rents). For this reason, pre-modern political authorities who created privileges or other concrete rules could always count on the support of the agents favoured by these institutions. By contrast, when they attempted to implement new abstract rules, they usually had to act on their own. Frequently, this involved prohibitive costs.

What is more, traditionally the institutions created by pre-modern political organizations were concrete rules. For example the household – regardless of its social status – was based on such rules, which ascribed specific duties to its various members. The same applies to organizations such as village communities and guilds. The only exceptions are towns whose laws did indeed contain abstract rules; typically these were institutions necessary for urban markets. If a pre-modern political authority tried to integrate such abstract rules into its legal system or attempted to create new abstract rules, this usually implied that some hitherto valid privilege had to be abolished. Therefore the ruler who tried to impose new abstract rules could not only count on no support from the ranks of the organized special interest groups, but had to expect their active resistance.

For all these reasons, there are no instances where a pre-modern government tried to increase the attraction of its territory by abolishing the privileges of the traditional corporations and creating level playing fields. What was the alternative? Two strategies may be distinguished which the governments of the emerging states pursued and which did not exclude one another. Both relied on granting privileges, but though the actors responsible may not have realized this, these privileges were of very different kinds and had different economic consequences.

On the one hand, governments granted subsidies or other privileges either to individual immigrants or investors or to groups of them. This was commonly done when the aim was to establish new technologies or industries that were hitherto unknown in the territory to which the mobile capital was to be attracted. For example, in 1765 the Austrian government concluded a contract with a certain Thomas Welsh, an English metal specialist who was to introduce new technologies to the Habsburg Empire. Welsh committed himself to set up his manufacture in Vienna and to instruct Austrians in his trade. In return, the government reimbursed him for his travel expenses, his monthly rent and his tools, paid him a yearly salary of 200 guldens and subsidized the education of his apprentices. Furthermore, he was guaranteed the right to sell his products on his own account (Otruba 1967/97: 189f.). In many otherwise comparable cases, the foreign investor who introduced a new technology was also granted a monopoly for his product. This was the case for example when emperor Francis II (1792–1806/35) granted the 'exclusive privilege' to use the 'English folding- and creasing-stick' to the leather manufacturers Kollmann and Kelly in 1802 (Dölemeyer 1999).

When the government did not aim at establishing new technologies within its territory but just at attracting skilled labour or capital, another strategy was pursued. In such cases monopolies or subsidies seem to have been granted less often. Frequently, it was sufficient simply to exempt the investor or immigrant from the restrictive regulations of the established guilds. Such exemptions appear relatively early. For example, already emperor Maximilian I (1564–76) granted so-called 'exemptions of court' to certain craftsmen who were then allowed to produce without becoming a member of the cognisant guild (Zwanowetz 1971: 100). In other cases, guilds were forced to accept new members free of charge and even when the maximum number of craftsmen which the guild was otherwise prepared to admit had already been reached. Thus, many of the French Huguenots who settled in Brandenburg were integrated into the existing guilds.

Such measures were bound to raise the opposition of the domestic corporations; the memorial from eighteenth-century Hesse-Kassel cited above shows this clearly enough. The success of the governments therefore depended on how well they were able to assert their will against that of the established organized special interest groups. In Austria and Prussia, the governments' chances were relatively good because the guilds were initially prepared to tolerate a few individual producers who were not members of their organizations or who entered them as supernumeraries. The costs of creating institutions which legalized such singular exceptions were therefore relatively low, much lower at any rate than those which would have been involved in wholesale abolishment of the craftguilds and their rules, and in their replacement by regulations created by the territorial government. However, legalizing outsiders had an unforeseen consequence: as most guild-like corporations generated monopoly rents by restricting competition, the value which they had for their members depended on how many outsiders there were. This value decreased further the more outsiders were permitted to compete with the guilds. When artisans who stayed outside a guild could nevertheless get a licence, a process was set in motion which gained its own momentum: the more producers stayed outsiders the less valuable the guilds were for their members and the less were these members interested in stabilizing their organization or in opposing new exceptions. Thus, institutional change developed an inherent dynamism.

This was by no means the ultimate aim of governments decreeing such measures. Rather, fiscal motives were decisive, so for example in Saxony, requests for subsidies by potential founders of manufactures were only granted when major advantages for the princely revenues seemed certain (Forberger 1958: 237). However, the weakening of the resistance of established political authorities such as guilds led to a fall of the costs which the abolishment of regulations created by these organizations involved. Monopolies granted to investors who introduced new technologies were usually limited in time and were not prolonged because, as Mary Therese remarked, 'with regard to manufactures, the aim of spreading them as far as possible over the whole state needs to be kept in mind' (Otruba 1981: 83). In other words, the government wanted to avoid that newly created monopolies prevented the immigration of other investors. Just because of its inherent dynamism and due to the fiscal interests of the governments, the developments set in motion by the competition of jurisdictions for mobile factors of production triggered a de facto abolishment of the traditional regulations, which had been imposed by guilds and similar organizations. Many of these regulations were not formally repealed; they just dropped out of existence because they ceased to be enforced.

These developments did not imply a complete deregulation of trade and industry. Once the governments of the emerging states had monopolized means of coercion far enough, they often imposed regulations of their own. Still on the whole regulations did become much less restrictive. In eighteenth-century Berlin, for example, it was still officially necessary to be a member of one of the two commercial guilds in order to become a merchant. In about 1730, there were barely 200 registered merchants. It is impossible to tell how many Berliners engaged in commerce without being a member of one of the guilds, but given the more than 72,000 inhabitants whom the city then had, there must have been many more merchants. Some of them, whose names are known and who demonstrably stayed outside the guilds, were more influential than any guild merchant. Conditions in industry were similar (Korporation der Kaufmannschaft 1920: 13).

Agriculture was affected by comparable developments: here, too, the regulations which had been imposed both by manors and by the traditional village communities either ceased to be enforced or were formally abolished. By the second decade of the nineteenth century, an almost complete deregulation had been achieved. However, while interstate competition for mobile factors of production did trigger the at least implicit deregulation of commerce and industry, that of agriculture was due to different motives. What was most important was the discovery of links between the distribution of property rights and incentives for productive activities which governments wanted to strengthen for fiscal reasons (Dipper 1980: 46). Nevertheless, institutional conditions relevant for agriculture were at least influenced by interjurisdictional competition. In Prussia, for example, the electors and later the kings had committed themselves to support landlords in enforcing serfdom. Regarding the relations with their own peasants, however, they had more leeway. When they discovered in 1708 that many peasants emigrated from Prussia to Poland, the government considered an improvement in the peasants' property rights. In the following year, experiments were made in some districts (Knapp 1887b: 3). This came to nothing. It was expected that the peasants would pay for their new rights, but few were able to do that (Knapp 1887a: 83). Still concern about the loss of labour evidently led to rethinking the situation of the peasants and to experiments with institutional innovations – innovations which amounted to a deregulation of agriculture because they were supposed to increase the peasants' autonomy as producers.

When in 1781–2 serfdom was abolished in all Habsburg territories, this was due to the interest in the creation of stronger incentives for productive activities (Otruba 1981: 92). The measure had, however, unforeseen consequences. In south-western Germany, Austrian lands lay scattered among a tangle of numerous other lordships: Württemberg territories, free cities, the lands of the large abbeys, estates of Imperial knights and territories ruled by the margraves of Baden. When serfdom was abolished in Austria, the government of Baden was alarmed. It feared that the measure would create unrest among its own rural population. Therefore in 1783 Margrave Charles Frederick (1738–1811) followed suit and liberated the peasants in Baden, too (Liebel 1965: 52f.).

The regulation of agriculture by village communities, finally, ceased when the open field system was abolished in the early nineteenth century. As is well known, this was due to the governmental interest in improving agricultural productivity which was motivated by the need to bear the costs of the Napoleonic wars (Harnisch 1989). Here, interstate competition for capital and labour does not seem to have played a role at all.

Where is the place of the German pre-modern institutions in the concept of institutional competition?

Much of the present chapter is concerned with pointing out differences between conditions implicitly assumed in the concept of institutional competition and conditions as they were in pre-modern Germany. Indicating differences between the past and the present is of course an essential task for a historian. However, as long as the conditions existing before modern market societies emerged are not systematically integrated into a – necessarily modified – version of the concept of institutional competition, this remains somewhat unsatisfactory. Is it possible to do that at all?

In fact it is, at least in part. The starting point for systematically locating pre-modern institutional conditions in the context of the modern concept of institutional competition is the idea of 'meta-institutions' proposed by Michael Wohlgemuth (1995: 281, 1999: 59). What are these meta-institutions? Neoclassical models of institutional competition do by necessity take institutions into account, restricting themselves, however, to those which are competitive parameters, that is objects of choice of politicians or economic actors. What is rarely perceived is the fact that the competitive process is itself institutionally structured. It is the rules relevant here which are called meta-institutions by Wohlgemuth and which constitute the order of institutional competition.

Such rules affect both sides of the market. Above, a number of them have already been discussed, that is those which apply to the demand side: the freedom of economic agents to leave their jurisdictions, to invest abroad or to consume foreign products depends on rules which are, in Wohlgemuth's terms, meta-institutions. As shown above, they did indeed play an important role in pre-modern Germany. However, what about the supply-side? Institutions relevant here restrict, for example, access to this side of the market. They determine who is allowed to act as a supplier of regulations, in other words, who is able to act as a political authority. Today these meta-rules are extremely restrictive: institutions which are enforced with the help of legitimate means of coercion are exclusively supplied by states (including the member states of federations), each of which has a geographically clearly defined territorial monopoly. As I have shown earlier, conditions in pre-modern Germany were radically different. In each given geographical area, a large number of political organizations existed which were all able not only to create their own institutions – regulations among them – but also coercively to enforce them. As this coercion was regarded as perfectly legitimate, monopolistic states did not exist; consequently, state and society cannot be separated either.

What about the influence which the composition of the income of the manifold political authorities of pre-modern Germany had on their interest in attracting mobile factors of production? At least in so far as taxes were concerned, this composition was institutionally determined, too. Before the rise of absolutism, not a single German ruler was able to tax the population without the consent of political authorities inferior to himself: princes, for example, had to bargain with the landlords, the higher clergy and the more important towns of their territories and usually to grant them political rights; in exchange, these authorities would permit their own subjects to be taxed by the central government. Such agreements, which affected not only the two parties to the contract but the whole population, did have an institutional character. Indirectly they had a strong influence on institutional competition, determining whether political authorities were interested in increasing their territories' attraction for foreign capital and labour or not.

By now it has become evident where exactly the institutions which shaped the relations between those actors who where involved in formulating the regulations of products and services, and those who were affected by such regulations, are to be located in the concept of institutional competition. These rules were meta-institutions and therefore components of the order of competition. It is this order which changed radically with the advent of the modern monopolistic state. State formation therefore plays a central role in the transformation of the German economy in the eighteenth and early nineteenth centuries. Before it had come to a close, products and services were strictly regulated by numerous political authorities who were, in effect, nothing but organized special interest groups able to employ their own means of coercion in the enforcement of the rules they created. State formation implied a centralization of regulatory competencies, and under modern conditions such a centralization would certainly not be expected to lead to an easing of the strictness and density of regulation. In the course of the transformation of the pre-modern German economy, however, this change had radically different consequences. For one thing, it did not lead to the emergence of a centralized all-German state: as indicated above, at the end of the eighteenth century, more than 300 states existed within the borders of the Holy Roman Empire. For the first time in history, governments existed that were able to force former subordinate political authorities, who were now no more than economic pressure groups, to accept the immigration of foreign labour and investors from abroad. Only from now on, regulatory competition could begin within the Empire. What is more, centralization implied a fundamental change in the character of the political authorities able to regulate the economy. The traditional authorities – special interest groups invested with means of coercion – were replaced by authorities who were, at least in principle, economically neutral. After state formation, any special interest group that desired the creation of regulations favourable to its members had to engage in rent seeking of the modern type, instead of being able simply to adopt and enforce its regulations on its own. Hence, the costs of regulation grew with state formation. That an at least implicit deregulation of the economy was the outcome of this process cannot, therefore, come as a surprise.

Notes

1 The concept owes a lot to ideas originally developed by Tiebout (1956) and Hirschman (1970). For more recent developments see for example Siebert and Koop (1990),

Vanberg and Kerber (1994), Wohlgemuth (1995) and Streit and Kiwit (1999). Due to the function of competition as a discovery procedure, the concept of institutional competition does of course not allow detailed predictions of future developments.

2 For the 'first age of globalization' see for example Foreman-Peck (1998). Among the economic historians who observed intergovernmental competition are Rostovtzeff (1957: 3f.) for antiquity, Spruyt (1994) for the Middle Ages, and for example Gerteis (1981/97), Liebel (1965/97) and Otruba (1967/97) for the early modern age. More systematic analyses have been presented by the author (Volckart 1999, 2002).

3 Occasionally, all governmental interventions into the economy are called regulations (cf. Posner 1974: 335). Here the term is restricted to interventions concerning the type, quantity, quality and price of products and services.

4 At the end of the eighteenth century, the area of the Empire was estimated at 12,000 square miles (Grellmann 1801: 12); 1 German mile = 7.4204 kilometres.

5 The so-called 'Hausväterliteratur'. These handbooks stand at the beginning of the German tradition of economic writings; they are the predecessors of the cameralist treatises, which were addressed to rulers in their function as heads of territorial states that were conceived as super-households.

6 Or, as Veit Ludwig von Seckendorff (the author of a widely read, late seventeenth-century handbook on territorial politics) specified, authorities who exercised their own rights of jurisdiction (Seckendorff 1665/1976: 50f.). For the problem of continuity from pre-modern diets to modern parliaments see Bosl (1977) and Press (1980).

7 For the lack of distinction between state and society in pre-modern Germany see for example Böckenförde (1963/92: 188) and Grimm (1991: 37f.).

8 The only pre-modern European government which practised effective controls of capital transfers was the English. Already by the fourteenth century, persons entering the country had to declare their foreign currencies and to exchange them for English money; at the same time, the export of capital was strictly controlled (Ames 1965). Other Western European governments tried similar measures, but with much less success (Munro 1972: 11ff.).

References

Abel, Wilhelm (1976) 'Einige Bemerkungen zum Land-Stadtproblem im Spätmittelalter anläßlich einer Neuauflage meines Buches über die Wüstungen des ausgehenden Mittelalters', *Nachrichten der Akademie der Wissenschaften in Göttingen: I. Philologisch-historische Klasse*, 1, 1–46.

Ames, Edward (1965) 'The sterling crisis of 1337–1339', *Journal of Economic History*, 25(4), 496–522.

Bauer, Leonhard and Matis, Herbert (1988) *Geburt der Neuzeit: Vom Feudalsystem zur Marktgesellschaft*, München: dtv.

Blickle, Peter (1983) 'Grundherrschaft und Agrarverfassungsvertrag', in Hans Patze (ed.) *Die Grundherrschaft im späten Mittelalter*, vol. 1, Sigmaringen: Thorbecke, pp. 241–61.

Böckenförde, Ernst-Wolfgang (1963/92) 'Lorenz von Stein als Theoretiker der Bewegung von Staat und Gesellschaft zum Sozialstaat', in ibid., *Recht, Staat, Freiheit: Studien zur Rechtsphilosophie, Staatstheorie und Verfassungsgeschichte*, 2. impr., Frankfurt: Suhrkamp, pp. 170–208.

Boelcke, Willi Alfred (1964) 'Bäuerlicher Wohlstand in Württemberg Ende des 16. Jahrhunderts', *Jahrbücher für Nationalökonomie und Statistik*, 176, 241–80.

Boldt, Hans (1990) *Deutsche Verfassungsgeschichte, vol. 1: Von den Anfängen bis zum Ende des älteren deutschen Reiches 1806*, 2. impr., München: dtv.

Bosl, Karl (ed.) (1977) *Der moderne Parlamentarismus und seine Grundlagen in der ständischen Repräsentation*, Berlin: Duncker & Humblot.

Brunner, Otto (1939/92) *Land and Lordship: Structures of Governance in Medieval Austria*, Philadelphia: University of Pennsylvania Press.

—— (1958/80) 'Das "Ganze Haus" und die alteuropäische "Ökonomik"', in ibid., *Neue Wege der Verfassungs- und Sozialgeschichte*, Göttingen: Vandenhoeck & Ruprecht, pp. 103–27.

Dipper, Christof (1980) *Die Bauernbefreiung in Deutschland 1790–1850*, Stuttgart: Kohlhammer.

Dirlmeier, Ulf (1966) *Mittelalterliche Hoheitsträger im wirtschaftlichen Wettbewerb*, Wiesbaden: Steiner.

Dölemeyer, Barbara (1999) 'Erfindungsprivileg und Technologietransfer' (Lecture notes, 7 December 1999).

Ehrler, Joseph (1911) 'Stadtverfassung und Zünfte Freiburgs im Breisgau: Ein Beitrag zur oberrheinischen Wirtschaftsgeschichte', *Jahrbücher für Nationalökonomie und Statistik*, III, 41, 729–57.

—— (1912) 'Stadtverfassung und Zünfte Freiburgs im Breisgau: Ein Beitrag zur oberrheinischen Wirtschaftsgeschichte', *Jahrbücher für Nationalökonomie und Statistik*, III, 44; 449–75, 743–68.

Endres, Rudolf (1989) 'Absolutistische Entwicklungen in fränkischen Territorien im Spiegel der Dorfordnungen', *Jahrbuch für Regionalgeschichte*, 16(2), 81–93.

Ennen, Reinald (1971) *Zünfte und Wettbewerb: Möglichkeiten und Grenzen zünftlerischer Wettbewerbsbeschränkungen im städtischen Handel und Gewerbe des Spätmittelalters*, Köln: Böhlau.

Forberger, Rudolf (1958) *Die Manufaktur in Sachsen vom Ende des 16. bis zum Anfang des 19. Jahrhunderts*, Berlin (Ost): Akademie-Verlag.

Foreman-Peck, James (ed.) (1998) *Historical Foundations of Globalization*, Cheltenham: Edward Elgar.

Friedeburg, Robert von (1997) *Ländliche Gesellschaft und Obrigkeit: Gemeindeprotest und politische Mobilisierung im 18. und 19. Jahrhundert*, Göttingen: Vandenhoeck & Ruprecht.

Gerteis, Klaus (1981/97) 'Auswanderungsfreiheit und Freizügigkeit in ihrem Verhältnis zur Agrarverfassung: Deutschland, England, Frankreich im Vergleich', in Oliver Volckart (ed.) *Frühneuzeitliche Obrigkeiten im Wettbewerb: Institutioneller und Wirtschaftlicher Wandel zwischen dem 16. und 18. Jahrhundert*, Baden-Baden: Nomos, pp. 82–98.

Grellmann, H.M.G. (1801) *Historisch-statistisches Handbuch von Teutschland und den vorzüglichsten seiner besonderen Staaten, vol. 1: Allgemeiner Abriss des Teutschen Reichs*, Göttingen: Vandenhoeck & Ruprecht.

Grimm, Dieter (1987) 'Der Staat in der kontinentaleuropäischen Tradition', in ibid., *Recht und Staat der bürgerlichen Gesellschaft*, Frankfurt: Suhrkamp, pp. 53–83.

—— (1991) 'Entstehungs- und Wirkungsbedingungen des modernen Konstitutionalismus', in ibid., *Die Zukunft der Verfassung*, Frankfurt: Suhrkamp, pp. 31–66.

Harnisch, Hartmut (1989) 'Die Agrarreformen in Preußen und ihr Einfluß auf das Wachstum der Wirtschaft', in Toni Pierenkemper (ed.) *Landwirtschaft und industrielle Entwicklung: Zur ökonomischen Bedeutung von Bauernbefreiung, Agrarreform und Agrarrevolution*, Stuttgart: Steiner, pp. 27–40.

Hayek, Friedrich August von (1982) *Law, Legislation and Liberty: A new statement of the liberal principles of justice and political economy, vol. 1: Rules and Order*, London: Routledge.

Henshall, Nicholas (1992) *The Myth of Absolutism: Change and Continuity in Early Modern European Monarchy*, London: Longman.

Hirschman, Albert O. (1970) *Exit, Voice, and Loyalty: Responses to Decline in Firms, Organizations, and States*, Cambridge, MA: Harvard University Press.

Hsia, Ronnie Po-Chia (1989) *Social Discipline in the Reformation: Central Europe 1550–1750*, London: Routledge.

Jahn, Georg (no date, c.1909) *Zur Gewerbepolitik der deutschen Landesfürsten vom 16. bis zum 18. Jahrhundert*, Leipzig: Teichmann & Co.

Johnson, Hubert C. (1964) 'The concept of bureaucracy in cameralism', *Political Science Quarterly*, 79, 378–402.

Kaufhold, Karl Heinrich (1994) 'Preußische Staatswirtschaft – Konzept und Realität – 1640–1806. Zum Gedenken an Wilhelm Treue', *Jahrbuch für Wirtschaftsgeschichte*, 2, 33–70.

Kern, Fritz (1919/58) *Recht und Verfassung im Mittelalter*, Darmstadt: Wissenschaftliche Buchgesellschaft.

Knapp, Georg Friedrich (1887a) *Die Bauern-Befreiung und der Ursprung der Landarbeiter in den älteren Theilen Preußens, vol. 1: Überblick der Entwicklung*, Leipzig: Duncker & Humblot.

—— (1887b) *Die Bauern-Befreiung und der Ursprung der Landarbeiter in den älteren Theilen Preußens, vol. 2: Die Regulierung der gutsherrlich-bäuerlichen Verhältnisse von 1406 bis 1857 nach den Akten*, Leipzig: Duncker & Humblot.

Korporation der Kaufmannschaft (1920) *Die Korporation der Kaufmannschaft von Berlin: Festschrift zum hundertjährigen Jubiläum am 2. März 1920*, Berlin: E.S. Mittler & Sohn.

Koselleck, Reinhart (1981) *Preußen zwischen Reform und Revolution: Allgemeines Landrecht, Verwaltung und soziale Bewegung von 1791 bis 1848*, 3. impr., Stuttgart: Klett-Cotta.

Lentze, Hans (1964) 'Nürnbergs Gewerbeverfassung im Mittelalter', *Jahrbuch für fränkische Landesforschung*, 24, 207–81.

Liebel, Helen P. (1965) 'Enlightened bureaucracy versus enlightened despotism in Baden, 1750–1792', *Transactions of the American Philosophical Society, New Series*, 55(5), 1–132.

—— (1965/97) 'Laissez-faire vs. mercantilism: the rise of Hamburg & the Hamburg Bourgeoisie vs. Frederick the Great in the crisis of 1763', in Oliver Volckart (ed.) *Frühneuzeitliche Obrigkeiten im Wettbewerb: Institutioneller und wirtschaftlicher Wandel zwischen dem 16. und 18. Jahrhundert*, Baden-Baden: Nomos, pp. 139–61.

Meyer, Moritz (1888) *Geschichte der preußischen Handwerkerpolitik: Nach amtlichen Quellen, vol. 2: Die Handwerkerpolitik König Friedrich Wilhelm's I. (1713–1740)*, Minden: J.C.C. Bruns Verlag.

Millies, Charlotte (1937) 'Die Anfänge einer staatlichen Wirtschaftspolitik in Mecklenburg im 15./16. Jahrhundert', *Jahrbuch des Vereins für Mecklenburgische Geschichte*, 101, 1–84.

Mitterauer, Michael (1975) 'Vorindustrielle Familienformen: Zur Funktionsentlastung des "ganzen Hauses" im 17. und 18. Jahrhundert', in Friedrich Engel-Janosi, Grete Klingenstein and Heinrich Lutz (eds) *Fürst, Bürger, Mensch: Untersuchungen zu politischen und soziokulturellen Wandlungsprozessen im vorrevolutionären Europa*, Wien: Verlag für Geschichte und Politik, pp. 123–85.

—— (1977) 'Grundlagen politischer Berechtigung im mittelalterlichen Ständewesen', in Karl Bosl (ed.) *Der moderne Parlamentarismus und seine Grundlagen in der ständischen Repräsentation: Beiträge des Symposiums der Bayerischen Akademie der Wissenschaften und der International Commission for Representative and Parliamentary Institutions auf Schloß Reisenburg vom 20. bis 25. April 1975*, Berlin: Duncker & Humblot, pp. 11–41.

—— (1979) 'Zur Struktur alteuropäischer Gesellschaftssysteme am Beispiel des mittelalterlichen Österreich', in ibid., *Grundtypen alteuropäischer Sozialformen: Haus und Gemeinde in vorindustriellen Gesellschaften*, Stuttgart: Fromann-Holzboog, pp. 13–34.

Möhlenbruch, Rudolf (1977) 'Freier Zug, Ius Emigrandi, Auswanderungsfreiheit: Eine verfassungsgeschichtliche Studie', Diss. jur., Universität Bonn, Bonn.

Möller, Horst (1989) *Fürstenstaat oder Bürgernation: Deutschland 1763–1815*, Berlin: Siedler.

Mummert, Annette and Mummert, Uwe (1999) 'Entwicklungsländer im Systemwettbewerb', in Manfred E. Streit, Michael Wohlgemuth (eds) *Systemwettbewerb als Herausforderung an Politik und Theorie*, Baden-Baden: Nomos, pp. 151–79.

Münch, Paul (1996) *Lebensformen in der Frühen Neuzeit 1500 bis 1800*, Frankfurt: Ullstein.

Munro, John H. (1972) *Wool, Cloth, and Gold: The Struggle for Bullion in Anglo-Burgundian Trade, 1340–1478*, Brussels: University of Toronto Press.

Näf, Werner (ed.) (1975) *Herrschaftsverträge des Spätmittelalters*, 2. impr., Bern: Lang.

Nikolay-Panter, Marlene (1989) 'Die bäuerliche Gemeinde im Moselraum im Spiegel ländlicher Rechtsquellen vornehmlich des Spätmittelalters', *Jahrbuch für westdeutsche Landesgeschichte*, 15, 67–83.

Oestreich, Gerhard (1968/97) 'Strukturprobleme des europäischen Absolutismus', in Oliver Volckart (ed.) *Frühneuzeitliche Obrigkeiten im Wettbewerb: Institutioneller und wirtschaftlicher Wandel zwischen dem 16. und 18. Jahrhundert*, Baden-Baden: Nomos, pp. 31–44.

Otruba, Gustav (1967/97) 'Englische Fabrikanten und Maschinisten zur Zeit Maria Theresias und Josephs II. in Österreich', in Oliver Volckart (ed.) *Frühneuzeitliche Obrigkeiten im Wettbewerb: Institutioneller und wirtschaftlicher Wandel zwischen dem 16. und 18. Jahrhundert*, Baden-Baden: Nomos, pp. 186–96.

—— (1981) 'Die Wirtschaftspolitik Maria Theresias und Josephs II.', in Herbert Matis (ed.) *Von der Glückseligkeit des Staates: Staat, Wirtschaft und Gesellschaft in Österreich im Zeitalter des aufgeklärten Absolutismus*, Berlin: Duncker & Humblot, pp. 77–103.

Polanyi, Karl (1944/97) *The Great Transformation: Politische und ökonomische Ursprünge von Gesellschaften und Wirtschaftssystemen*, 4. impr., Frankfurt: Suhrkamp.

Posner, Richard (1974) 'Theories of economic regulation', *Bell Journal of Economics and Management Science*, 5, 335–58.

Press, Volker (1980) 'Landtage im Alten Reich und im Deutschen Bund: Voraussetzungen ständischer und konstitutioneller Entwicklungen 1750–1830', *Zeitschrift für Württembergische Landesgeschichte*, 39, 100–40.

Rostovtzeff, Michael (1957) *The Social and Economic History of the Roman Empire*, vol. 1, 2. impr., Oxford: Clarendon Press.

Scheuner, Ulrich (1950) 'Die Auswanderungsfreiheit in der Verfassungsgeschichte und im Verfassungsrecht Deutschlands', in *Festschrift für Richard Thoma zum 75. Geburtstag*, Tübingen: Mohr, pp. 199–224.

Schildt, Bernd (1996) *Bauer – Gemeinde – Nachbarschaft: Verfassung und Recht der Landgemeinde Thüringens in der frühen Neuzeit*, Weimar: Verlag Hermann Böhlaus Nachfolger.

Schilling, Heinz (1981) *Konfessionskonflikt und Staatsbildung: Eine Fallstudie über das Verhältnis von religiösem und sozialem Wandel in der Frühneuzeit am Beispiel der Grafschaft Lippe*, Gütersloh: Gütersloher Verlagshaus Gerd Mohn.

Schmoller, Gustav (1884–87) 'Das Merkantilsystem in seiner historischen Bedeutung: städtische, territoriale und staatliche Wirthschaftspolitik', in ibid., *Studien über die wirthschaftliche Politik Friedrich des Großen und Preußens überhaupt von 1680–1786*, Leipzig: Duncker & Humblot, pp. 15–61.

Schultz, Helga (1983) 'Handwerkerrecht und Zünfte auf dem Lande im Spätfeudalismus', *Jahrbuch für die Geschichte des Feudalismus*, 7, 326–50.

Schulze, Reiner (1981) 'Geschichte der neueren vorkonstitutionellen Gesetzgebung', *Zeitschrift der Savigny-Stiftung für Rechtsgeschichte: germanistische Abteilung*, 98, 157–235.

Schumpeter, Joseph A. (1991) 'The crisis of the tax state', in Richard Swedberg (ed.) *Joseph A. Schumpeter: The Economics and Sociology of Capitalism*, Princeton, NJ: Princeton University Press, pp. 99–140.

Seckendorff, Veit Ludwig v. (1665/1976) '*Teutscher Fürsten Stat*', 3. impr., Glashütten: Auvermann (reprint of the Frankfurt edition 1665).

Siebert, Horst and Koop, Michael J. (1990) 'Institutional competition: a concept for Europe?' *Aussenwirtschaft*, 45, 439–62.

Sombart, Werner (1916/87) *Der moderne Kapitalismus: Historisch-systematische Darstellung des gesamteuropäischen Wirtschaftslebens von seinen Anfängen bis zur Gegenwart, vol. 1: Die vorkapitalistische Wirtschaft*, 1. Halbbd., München: dtv.

Sprandel, Rolf (1988) '*Verfassung und Gesellschaft im Mittelalter*', 3. impr., Paderborn: Schöningh.

Spruyt, Hendrik (1994) *The Sovereign State and Its Competitors: An Analysis of Systems Change*, Princeton, NJ: Princeton University Press.

Stigler, George J. (1971) 'The theory of economic regulation', *Bell Journal of Economics and Management Science*, 2, 3–21.

Streit, Manfred E. and Kiwit, Daniel (1999) 'Zur Theorie des Systemwettbewerbs', in Manfred E. Streit and Michael Wohlgemuth (eds) *Systemwettbewerb als Herausforderung an Politik und Theorie*, Baden-Baden: Nomos, pp. 13–48.

Tiebout, C.M. (1956), 'A pure theory of local expenditures', *Journal of Political Economy*, 64, 416–24.

Ullmann, Hans-Peter (2005) *Der deutsche Steuerstaat: Geschichte der öffentlichen Finanzen*, München: Beck.

van Dülmen, Richard (1999) *Kultur und Alltag in der Frühen Neuzeit, vol. 2: Dorf und Stadt 16.-18. Jahrhundert*, 2. impr., München: Beck.

Vanberg, Viktor and Kerber, Wolfgang (1994) 'Institutional competition among jurisdictions: an evolutionary approach', *Constitutional Political Economy*, 5, 193–219.

Vetter, Klaus (1985) 'Die Hugenotten im System der ostelbischen Gutswirtschaft in der Mark Brandenburg', in Heinz Duchhardt (ed.) *Der Exodus der Hugenotten: Die Aufhebung des Edikts von Nantes 1685 als europäisches Ereignis*, Köln: Böhlau, pp. 141–54.

Volckart, Oliver (1999) 'Systemwettbewerb als historisches Phänomen: Das Beispiel Deutschlands vom 10. bis 18. Jahrhundert', in Manfred E. Streit, Michael Wohlgemuth (eds) *Systemwettbewerb als Herausforderung an Politik und Theorie*, Baden-Baden: Nomos, pp. 181–209.

—— (2002) 'Central Europe's way to a market economy, 1000–1800', *European Review of Economic History*, 6, 309–37.

—— (2004a) 'Die Dorfgemeinde als Kartell: Kooperationsprobleme und ihre Lösungen im Mittelalter und in der frühen Neuzeit', *Jahrbuch für Wirtschaftsgeschichte*, 2, 189–203.

—— (2004b),'The economics of feuding in late medieval Germany', *Explorations in Economic History*, 41, 282–99.

Weidner, Karl (1931) *Die Anfänge einer staatlichen Wirtschaftspolitik in Württemberg*, Stuttgart: Kohlhammer.

Willoweit, Dietmar (1983) 'Die Entwicklung und Verwaltung der spätmittelalterlichen Landesherrschaft', in Kurt G.A. Jeserich, Hans Pohl and Georg-Christoph von Unruh (eds) *Deutsche Verwaltungsgeschichte, vol. 1: Vom Spätmittelalter bis zum Ende des Reiches*, Stuttgart: Deutsche Verlags-Anstalt, pp. 66–143.

Wohlgemuth, Michael (1995) 'Institutional competition – notes on an unfinished agenda', *Journal des Economistes et des Etudes Humaines*, 6, 277–99.

—— (1999) 'Systemwettbewerb als Entdeckungsverfahren', in Manfred E. Streit and Michael Wohlgemuth (eds) *Systemwettbewerb als Herausforderung an Politik und Theorie*, Baden-Baden: Nomos, pp. 49–70.

Wolf, Armin (1973) 'Die Gesetzgebung der entstehenden Territorialstaaten', in Helmut Coing (ed.) *Handbuch der Quellen und Literatur der neueren europäischen Privatrechtsgeschichte, vol. 1: Mittelalter (1100–1500): Die gelehrten Rechte und die Gesetzgebung*, München: Beck, pp. 517–799.

Wunder, Heide (1986) *Die bäuerliche Gemeinde in Deutschland*, Göttingen: Vandenhoeck & Ruprecht.

Zumstrull, Margret (1983) 'Die Gründung von "Hugenottenstädten" als wirtschaftspolitische Maßnahme eines merkantilistischen Landesherrn – am Beispiel Kassel und Karlshafen', in Volker Press (ed.) *Städtewesen und Merkantilismus in Mitteleuropa*, Köln: Böhlau, pp. 156–221.

Zwanowetz, Georg (1971) 'Der österreichische Merkantilismus bis 1740', in Institut für Österreichkunde (ed.) *Die Wirtschaftsgeschichte Österreichs*, Wien: Ferdinand Hirt, pp. 87–104.

REGULATORY COMPETITION AND REGULATORY HARMONIZATION IN THE NINETEENTH CENTURY: THE EXAMPLE OF FOOD PROTECTION AND LABOUR PROTECTION

Gerold Ambrosius

Introductory remarks

Assuming a status quo of institutional competition between states, two developments can take place:

1 Institutional competition may continue to prevail. If so, it may lead to convergence or divergence and to regulation or deregulation of domestic standards. In this respect, from an empirical-historical perspective the central question is: What were the reasons for the convergence or divergence and stronger regulation or deregulation of domestic standards?[1]

2 Institutional competition can be brought to an end through harmonization within the framework of political agreements. In this context, the regime of interstate cooperation plays a role. The examination undertaken here will be limited to the intergovernmental regime and the supranational or federal regime, respectively. In the first case, the question to be addressed is: Why did the states conclude such agreements under the conditions dominating intergovernmental relations?

The second case is exemplified by the German Reich of 1871: What were the reasons for the harmonization of the standards of the member states in such a federal structure?

When using the term 'federal', it has to be stressed that the German states – the 'Bundesstaaten' of the German 'Reich' – were more or less independent, with their own jurisdictions, parliaments, governments and administrations. Before 1871, they had been completely independent states maintaining intergovernmental relations and in institutional competition with one another, and no fundamental difference distinguished their interrelations from those with other European states. After 1871, in spite of being united in the German Reich through federal institutions like the 'Reichstag' and the 'Bundesrat', they nonetheless remained relatively independent, considerably more so than, for example, the federal states within the framework of the Federal Republic of Germany. In many respects, during the period between 1871 and 1918 the German Reich was similar to the supranational regime of the European Union today.

With regard to the nature of the standards, a distinction may be drawn between the regulatory and the coordinative. Here the concern is exclusively with those in the regulatory genre – product regulation and process regulation. Foodstuffs have been selected as a typical example of product regulation and labour protection measures as being typical of process regulation. The period to be examined encompasses the nineteenth century, especially the second half, up to the First World War.

Basic model

The following empirical investigation is based on a model of institutional competition that goes back to Ch. B. Tiebout, A.O. Hirschman and has been further developed by Manfred E. Streit, amongst others.[2] It assumes that there is a market for institutional arrangements and that an analogy exists between institutional competition and economic competition. Suppliers of institutions – here the concern is with the institution 'regulation' – are politicians or bureaucrats, parliaments or governments. Those making the demands are the citizens as entrepreneurs and workers, savers and consumers. If they are of the opinion that the economic system of another state has advantages for them, they can either oppose their politicians at home, migrate abroad or vote for the institutions of other states in order to achieve a change in their own economic and social system or in order to make use of the system of the other state. At the international level, the context can be modelled in a similar way to that at the national level: in the economic market, businesses are in competition not only with other businesses at home but also with those abroad. The same goes for consumers. In the political market, states compete as suppliers of institutional arrangements, these being offered by national politicians with an eye to the jurisdictions of other countries. Depending on prevailing preferences, possibilities of exerting influence and options for collective action, states will either act unilaterally, or seek to persuade, or try to force other states to act in a particular way. Cooperation is influenced, amongst other things, by the number of states cooperating, mobility among them, the nature of the collective good that the group wishes to create, the possibilities of free riding, the degree of organization of the international regime and the developmental level of the countries cooperating.

There are a number of preconditions that must be fulfilled if the competition between institutional systems is to function within the framework of this model. Amongst other things, labour and capital, goods and services must be able to move freely between states, and this freedom must not be 'distorted' by trade barriers or subsidies. The origin principle should apply. Economic and political competition requires rules. In this model, institutional competition can only really function under liberal-democratic conditions.

There are also a number of limits that reduce the ability of institutional competition to function. There are cognitive limits arising from people's inadequate constitutional knowledge. Their mobility is limited. There are transaction costs limiting the behaviour of participants. Finally, all the weaknesses of political competition simultaneously represent limits of institutional competition: not all the interests of the participants can be equally well organized and this fact affects their political influence. There are more mobile and less mobile products and production factors; there are large and small countries; there are path dependencies or traditions; and there is a whole series of further limits that impede the flexible modification of institutional arrangements.[3]

The state is, thus, neither a black box, nor does it act rationally, nor are its institutional arrangements completely flexible. The implicit assumption of the model is rather that of political-economic pluralism: policy results are the results of the various participants (producers, consumers, politicians, bureaucrats and so on), by utilizing their economic and political power and their opportunities for collective action.

The course of history

Preconditions

The question arises as to whether, in general, the preconditions for institutional competition between the European states existed in the nineteenth century. As the international side of institutional competition is the main subject of this analysis, the national side will be neglected. This means that it will simply be assumed that institutional competition within the states functioned – certainly a bold assumption in the face of the markedly differing political systems in the European states: voting rights that were in some cases more democratic and in others less so, the asymmetric potential of interest groups to exert influence, the varying mobility of labour and capital, as well as many other differences. Judged by today's standards, no European country fulfilled the conditions of a liberal-democratic system. To this extent, it can only be repeated here that all the deficits of political competition within the states were also deficits of the institutional competition among them.

As regards economic competition, too, only a qualified comparison may be made between the circumstances in the nineteenth century and those of today. As yet, market integration between the European states was not intensive. Nevertheless, fierce competition already prevailed in important branches of the economy at the beginning of the century, and cross-border traffic in products and production factors increased.[4] For example, the export share of the German Empire before the First World War was about 20 per cent; that of the smaller states already amounted to 60 per cent and more. The degree of internationalization displayed by Western Europe – the ratio of export volume to real national product – was approximately as high at the end of the nineteenth century as it was at the end of the 1950s. Mobility of labour and capital rose likewise. In the nineteenth century, not only did millions of people leave Europe, but further millions were also moving between the European states. At the end of the century, there was a European labour market more extensive than that of today. A European capital market also existed, although not of today's dimensions. In the field of labour protection, the initial development was only gradual; however, as shown below, the states observed one another very closely and reacted to the initiatives of the others. To this extent, there were not only institutions that differed from one another, but they were also perceived as such and their advantages and disadvantages discussed.

A further precondition is guaranteed free trade in products and production factors. The 1840s saw the onset of an era of free trade in Europe, and with it developed a network of bilateral commercial treaties assuming a multilateral character through the unrestricted, most-favoured-nation principle anchored in most treaties.[5] Goods from other countries were allowed into the domestic market. Foreign regulations were recognized and the so-called origin principle prevailed. Although from the 1880s onwards the pendulum was gradually swinging back to interventionism – to tariffs and barriers to mobility of labour and capital – as a whole, economic relations between the European states up to the First World War were of a very liberal nature.[6] But at the same time there was a tendency towards the destination principle: more and more products had to comply with domestic regulations, thereby weakening institutional competition. Thus, no formally agreed international order of competition existed either for goods or for institutions. However, the belief in the blessings of liberal economic relations made the governments react with restraint to the demands for more protectionism. As a whole, it may be recorded that the important preconditions for institutional economic competition were met.

With regard to the 'competition between civilizations', there were, likewise, no barriers, but neither was there order.[7] Whether or not the competition between the so-called 'civilized nations' was especially intensive in this respect in the second half of the nineteenth century is an open question. The conviction prevailed that the social progress in one's home country should also be adopted by other countries.

Food protection as product regulation

With regard to foodstuffs, the economic and technical background to the improvement in consumer protection that occurred in the second half of the nineteenth century entailed industrialization, the expansion of the food industry and chemical-technical advances in the manufacturing and use of additives. In the course of urbanization, foodstuff production and the grocery trade took over to an ever-greater extent the provisioning of the population in the towns. To these far-reaching changes in the provision of foodstuffs must be added the fact that since the 1860s and 1870s, there had been an increase in the adulteration of basic foods and of semi-luxury foodstuffs. Food scandals spread, as did public discussion about them.[8] As regards legal requirements for the products and the control of production, legislation lagged behind the progress that had been made in the manufacture and use of additives, and also behind the chemical-technical procedures for analysis and proof.[9] The politicians were obliged to react and this they did, with debates in the parliaments of the various German states and, from the 1870s onwards, also in the Reichstag.[10] In other European states, the situation was similar.[11] Regarding products that crossed borders, such as wine, the origin principle prevailed in most cases until well into the second half of the nineteenth century. Customs duties were levied, however.

Until the days of the 'Kaiserreich', the law relating to food and drugs in the German states was regulated by police laws.[12] With the founding of the German Empire, it was the Reich that gained jurisdiction over the medical and veterinary policies. There ensued a regulation applicable in the entire Reich, the food law of 1879, which created the framework for specific implementing statutes.[13] Parliament passed special laws for milk, butter, wine, beer, spirits, colours, cocoa, coffee, sugar, sweetener, meat and so on. Although authority was thereby transferred to the Reich, the individual states (Bundesstaaten) possessed considerable influence and could have prevented the harmonization of food law by majority in the Bundesrat.

In the 1880s, there were many calls on the central government – from consumers, trade and industry, the Reichstag and even from the governments of several member states – to take the initiative. Consumers demanded regulation for the entire Reich in order to create legal certainty, in the interests of consumer protection. There were no organizations for consumer protection as there are today, but consumer cooperatives and consumer protection increasingly became a topic of political significance. This was apparent from the debates in the Reichstag and in the parliaments of the states. Trade and industry pressed for a solution applicable to the entire Reich because, in their opinion, differences in regulations between the member states led to unfair competition and discrimination of domestic producers in the more highly regulated states.[14] The differing regulations of the member states were bothersome in an economic region that was increasingly integrated. The food industry was opening up ever greater markets.

Action by the Reichstag was primarily triggered by increasing adulteration of foodstuffs in the 1870s, which revealed the inadequacies of the existing penal code.[15] It became a matter of increasing urgency to take preventive measures and control the production of, and trade in, basic foodstuffs and semi-luxury foodstuffs. Almost all the parties in the Reichstag agreed that in this respect the individual states were dragging their feet. The argument was also repeatedly brought forward during negotiations in the Reichstag that the German Reich was lagging behind developments in other civilized states such as France, England or Switzerland.[16] At the same time there was the belief among members of parliament that, in an integrated economic region such as the German Reich, at least the most important laws and subordinate legislation relevant to the economy should be unified so as to prevent differences between individual state regulations from hindering the trade in goods.

Among the member states, it was primarily the small players that were active – those who had not yet created their own legal and regulatory framework, had done so but only in rudimentary fashion, or who hoped to be able to bring influence to bear on the regulation for the entire Reich.[17] Conversely, it was precisely because Prussia was interested in reaching an agreement with the other member states that she did not take the initiative. Prussia did not want to strengthen the

Reichstag as the central state body and, as the most important member state, she placed her hopes on the sheer weight of her economy, territory and population. Thus, in this context, aspects of competitive federalism played a significant role. Prussia's inactivity stemmed also from her relatively low standard of food regulation. Other member states where higher standards prevailed, such as Bavaria, accepted the origin principle with the consequence that their own producers were at a disadvantage while the Prussian food industry enjoyed competitive cost advantages.[18]

At the European and global level, there likewise developed increasingly interconnected markets in agricultural products and processed foods. Here, too, the origin principle applied and had long been accepted by the producers.[19] However, in the last third of the nineteenth century, local quality regulations were accepted only when they promised competitive advantages due to higher product quality. Wines, for example, sold especially well in other countries if the state controlled quality in their country of origin.[20] Bavaria's regulations concerning the purity of beer proved to be a decisive boost to exports. A voluntary private quality seal was not sufficient; the product had to be approved by the state to gain the trust of foreign consumers.[21] Producers tended to reject the origin principle if foreign competitors enjoyed competitive advantages because of lower standards of regulation. Meat that according to the German agricultural lobby had undergone insufficient veterinary checks in the US should not, it was agreed, be sold in the Reich.[22] Unlike the German member states among themselves, the European states went over to the destination principle, at least with regard to perishable products. When Britain introduced the trademark 'made in Germany', the initial intention was to discriminate against German products in the British market. At the end of the nineteenth century, there were increasing attempts to use product regulations as non-tariff barriers to trade and hence gain protection against foreign competition.

Parliaments and governments of the European states kept a close eye on one another in the matter of food regulation. They pursued the same aims using the same means, even if differences existed in specific cases. For many decades there was institutional competition, but it declined in intensity and led towards regulatory convergence. In the end, the destination principle was introduced.[23]

Labour protection as process regulation

The protection of labour encompasses inter alia (statutory) regulations that serve to guarantee the safety of the workplace and protect the health of the worker. Dangers for the worker can arise not only from technical equipment and specific production processes but also from a high workload. The statutory protection of labour can be subdivided, according to its object, into such measures as primarily serve to prevent accidents at work (technical provisions) and those concerned with the general conditions of employment (labour law). There were provisions regarding labour protection in the nineteenth century: (1) in special factory acts, (2) in all-embracing civil law such as the 'Code Civil' in France or the 'Allgemeines Bürgerliches Gesetzbuch' in Germany or specific regulations such as the 'Law of Employer and Workmen' in Britain, (3) in special legal provisions, and (4) in Germany, also in trade law. As personal labour protection, it extended to the employment conditions of young people and women – regarding night work, working on Sundays and holidays and maximum working hours. It took a considerable time for any intervention to occur in the working conditions of adult males. Health protection, orientated towards prevention, ensued. There followed factory and labour regulations covering ever more legal matters and branches of the economy, so that the special factory supervision was gradually transformed into general trade supervision. In the field of labour protection, England, leading the way since the beginning of the century, was followed in the second third of the century by Switzerland and the larger German states, but after 1871 the German Empire was overtaken by Switzerland and Austria. In most other states, labour protection policy started in the last third of the century – in Sweden, Finland, Italy, Greece and Russia, not until the 1880s.[24]

In labour protection, the governments of the European states reacted to different interests and influences. There may have been peculiarities specific to each country but ultimately the arguments for or against labour protection were very similar.[25] The civil movement for social reform that first propagated the idea of labour protection was started by philanthropic individuals, but it increasingly gained broader support. Mass poverty, damage to health, the miserable plight of many children, in addition to the fundamental changes which the gradually increasing extent of industrialization was bound to cause in the economy and society, were so clearly apparent that politics and the state could no longer leave the laying down of labour conditions to free agreements. The paternalistic care of the 'physical, spiritual and moral development' of children and young people, the idea of Christian charity and the humanist ideal of character formation were associated with morality, common decency and education. Gradually, however, labour protection developed into a political demand. Both on the Christian-conservative side and on the liberal-progressive and socialist side, extreme economic liberalism was rejected – at least in this field. Even amongst advocates of classical economics, belief in the social harmony of a liberal, competitive economy was gradually lost. Perhaps it is useful to distinguish between regulations such as child protection, which were accepted even by conservative entrepreneurs at the time, and those such as restrictions of working time which were combatted obstinately by employers because they regarded them as an unacceptable interference in the freedom of contract between entrepreneur and worker. Every intervention into the freedom of contract was interpreted as being a sin against the liberal system. For example, in the second third of the nineteenth century, it was held that no additional regulations and hence additional costs should be imposed on German industry because its productivity was still too low in comparison with that of England. The same argument was then employed in the last third of the century in the southern European countries by comparison with the Western and central European countries. The argument that labour regulation has a thoroughly positive effect on the development of children and young people did not disappear entirely from discussions. But even in the 1880s and 1890s improvements in labour protection were rejected in the German Reichstag on the grounds that this would overturn the economic and social order.

In the discussions, the growing mobility of capital played an increasing role. The critics of regulation pointed out that if the restrictions on capital became too tight, it would be moved to other countries. By comparison, the mobility of the production factor labour was considered relatively low despite extensive migration throughout Europe. It was believed that attention had to be paid primarily to mobile capital.[26] Indeed, in several countries emigration continued to be seen as an outlet by means of which economic, social and, hence, political pressure could be reduced.

Until well into the second half of the nineteenth century, Great Britain was the model for continental European countries – for the Prussian factory law of 1839 just as for the French law of 1841, for the initiatives of Swiss cantons just as for Belgian bills.[27] If labour protection was discussed in the Prussian parliament or in the French national assembly, at some point British conditions would be mentioned – normally as a reference model for development at home.[28] Conversely, the British parliament and the British administration took careful note of which labour protection laws were enacted in other states. The Redgrave Report of 1853 dealt equally thoroughly with Prussian factory legislation as did a report on French social reform in 1855, and British legislation continued to point the way in the years that followed. In the 1880s, the German Reichstag drew on the 1876 British survey on labour protection but also on reports based on the experience of Austrian and Swiss factory inspectors. Switzerland closely followed developments in the German Empire which, together with the legislation in Great Britain, influenced the Swiss factory act of 1887.[29] At the same time, the Italian and Spanish parliaments discussed the German, Swiss and, of course, the British experiences – actually scrutinizing the consequences of individual provisions.[30] In Italy, some elements of technical labour protection were incorporated in the 'Legge di pubblica sicurezza coordinata col codice penale' of 1889. A 'Legge per gl'infortuni degli operai sul lavoro' was passed in 1898. In Spain, labour protection began with the 'ley, reglemento el trabajo de los ninos en las fabricas ó talleres' of 1873, which was placed on a broader footing in 1900. Specific regulations of the leading countries were adopted by other states. In the 1870s, the laws and commentaries of progressive states began to be translated into the respective mother tongues so that these became accessible to a wider public. Even in countries with less advanced labour protection such as Finland, the regulations of other states were well known and used as reference models for their own legislation.[31]

Institutional competition prevailed to the extent that the public, parliaments and governments were well informed about the laws and bills in other states and reacted to them. The opponents and the advocates of labour regulation argued not only from an internal market or domestic policy perspective but also with an eye to the regulative provisions of other states, and this remained the case throughout the nineteenth century. Not even minor points went unnoticed. To cite just two examples: immediately before the First World War, when the more advanced states had already relatively well-developed labour protection, France threatened to tone down its own ban on night work of young workers up to the age of 18, if Germany were to fix this limit at 16.[32] At the same time, there was a fear in Italy that, by restricting child labour, the country would suffer a competitive disadvantage vis-à-vis other states.

Even in fields in which no international agreements were concluded, national labour protection regulations moved in the same direction. 'The international harmonisation in an upward direction of labour conditions – international labour protection may be characterised thus', said Stephan Bauer, head of the International Labour Office, in the 1920s to describe developments in the nineteenth century.[33] The various states were affected by more or less the same factors, faced similar problems with regard to working conditions and naturally reacted with very similar measures. This is why regulatory convergence occurred in the nineteenth century.

There were, of course, also plans for international harmonization of national labour protection.[34] In the first third of the nineteenth century, it was primarily individuals committed to social reform who called for internationally coordinated action. Thus transnational, private activities preceded international state activities. At the beginning of the 1850s, however, a first attempt was made at the diplomatic level to conclude a multilateral agreement on child protection.[35] It failed, because the French government insisted on linking it with the protection of manufacturing trademarks. In the years that followed, the idea of international agreements remained on the agenda of parliaments, parties and national as well as international congresses.[36] Switzerland, after having passed a factory act for all the cantons in 1877, tried to convene an international conference on labour protection in 1881, but without success.[37]

The first serious attempt to reach a multilateral agreement on labour protection was the Berlin Conference of 1890, which was attended by 15 states.[38] The negotiations covered the following subjects: employment in coalmines, Sunday working, child labour, youth employment, female employment and problems concerning the implementation and supervision of international agreements. Naturally, the representatives of those countries that had more advanced labour protection tried to extend their own higher standards to the other countries, while the representatives of the other countries sought to maintain their own lower standards as exceptions. No binding decisions were reached at the conference. The conference voted only on so-called 'desirable regulations' and agreed unanimously only on the banning of night work for children and young workers, the prohibition of female employment in coalmines and the protection of women who had just given birth. Following ratification, the implementation of the agreements was to be supervised by national inspectors. Apart from this, an international labour office was to be set up. The Berlin Conference produced concrete results only to the extent that in some states discussion of labour protection was stimulated and moves were made to initiate legislation. Not until

1901, when the International Association for the Protection of Labour was founded, was an International Labour Office established in Berne.[39] It was a private organization supported by the state and semi-governmental in character. The establishment of an official intergovernmental organization had frequently been demanded but to no avail.

Up to the beginning of the twentieth century, various attempts at multilateral or bilateral harmonization of labour protection failed. It was not until 1904 that a Franco-Italian agreement was reached. It provided for the expansion of national legislation and the equal treatment of citizens regarding labour protection and insurance cover, and it constituted a model for similar agreements in subsequent years – in total, 27 bilateral agreements.[40] Above all, in 1906 the first two multilateral treaties on labour protection measures were concluded in Berne between 15 and seven states, respectively. The first banned night work for women. It applied to all industrial firms with more than ten employees, even though it was left to the participating states to define the term 'industrial firm' and to grant exceptions. Under the second treaty, the use of white (yellow) phosphorus in the manufacturing of matches and the import and sale of matches containing phosphorus were prohibited. In 1912, after a transitional phase, these agreements or 'conventions' became effective. They were concluded for at least 12 years and were open to all states, but were not ratified by all signatory states. In the end, only fairly unimportant regulations were implemented. In Berne, however, negotiations were already taking place concerning the next two conventions on night work for young workers and the working hours of women and young workers. These were adopted in 1913 but not ratified. Further conventions were in preparation before the First World War. The main significance of all these agreements was that they represented a breakthrough towards the multilateral harmonization of national social and labour protection.

What were the motives of those who worked for the international harmonization of national regulations? (1) Throughout the entire period, once more, an important stimulus came from the civil movement for social reform. Its members demanded the highest possible standards for as many states as possible to combat the evils arising from the mode of industrial production. They considered it the moral duty of developed 'civilized states' to take appropriate measures, develop an 'international ethic' of solidarity and sacrifice any competitive advantages from non-regulation. (2) Industry demanded the international harmonization of social standards in those countries in which labour protection had already come quite a long way, notably in Germany, France, Switzerland and, of course, Britain. The 'backward' states were to adapt their standards to those of the more progressive. In this way, the competitive advantages from non-regulation were to be eliminated. Thus, the demand for international harmonization of socio-political standards came from quite different ideological and political directions. The regulatory level was to be raised in the 'backward' countries so that social progress in one's own country would not be endangered.

Likewise, the opponents of internationally harmonized labour protection came from a variety of camps: (1) In the less advanced countries, entrepreneurs argued that their weak competitive position due to lower productivity should not be further weakened by additional social costs. The view that industries or countries at different levels of development should also have different social standards was, however, also put forward by politicians and economists who were not pursuing their own economic interests. (2) More fundamental was the objection that the prevailing differences of preference were expressions of differing social orders, that they had to be respected and that, therefore, harmonization had to be rejected. (3) Apart from this, considerable scepticism regarding the effectiveness of international treaties prevailed, affecting not only national legislation but also the national governments. Who would supervise the observance of the agreed obligations? What authority should be entrusted with deciding about contractual violations?[41]

Synthesis

Since in both food and labour regulation, the final outcome was convergence, the central question posed at the outset can be reiterated: What were the reasons for the convergence of regulations? Convergence can be the result of institutional competition or harmonization by agreement. Each of the following three subsections shall first examine the aims of those who demanded regulation (consumers, workers or producers). Subsequently, the motives of the suppliers of regulation (politicians) will be addressed. Finally, I shall analyse the international constellations that have hampered or facilitated competitive convergence or harmonization by agreement.

Convergence by institutional competition

With regard to the period until 1871, the analysis that follows refers to the relations of the German states one with another; from 1871 onwards, it concerns the relations of the German Reich with the European states:

- Since the middle of the nineteenth century, food protection and labour protection had been demanded by an ever-increasing proportion of the citizens of the German and European states. Herein lies the decisive reason for the increasing standards of regulation within the states and the regulatory convergence among them.
- In Germany before 1871, the producers who purveyed goods from one German state to another were interested in harmonizing the product regulations of the states (for example with regard to food) because this would spare them the cost of adapting their products to the various 'foreign' standards of other German states. They could reap scale economies and save transaction costs. Exceptions to this were industries whose products were attractive precisely due to their high standard of regulation (Bavarian beer) and, thus, enjoyed a competitive advantage. These industries did not merely accept their own 'discrimination' but expressly demanded it.

- In the German Reich after 1871, producers called for higher standards of product regulation (wine, meat, beer) in combination with the transition to the destination principle as a non-tariff trade barrier against the other European states.

- Regarding process regulation (for example labour protection), entrepreneurs were generally in favour of low standards of regulation because they did not wish to be burdened with additional costs. When, however, they had to accept a higher standard of regulation in their own country, they were in favour of raising standards in other states, too.

- Producers located in a single German member state tended to oppose the harmonization of process regulation because they hoped for competitive advantages from a lower standard of regulation. Conversely, businesses whose production was located in several German (or European) states – like chemicals, electrical engineering and mechanical engineering businesses – naturally demanded convergence of labour protection laws at as low a level as possible.

- Politicians were divided with regard to product regulation. Those favouring inexpensive provision for the population were more in favour of institutional competition. They considered the quality of the products to be of secondary importance unless it posed a direct threat to health. By contrast, those concerned about health supported the producers' demand for the destination principle, even where the protectionist interest was obvious and led to higher living costs.

- Regarding process regulations, politicians and parties whose concern was for the workers favoured unilaterally high standards of regulation. In countries with low standards they favoured upward harmonization. Politicians and parties who sided with the employers supported institutional competition because they expected it to lead to deregulation or at least not to rising standards of regulation.

- The greater the number of states that adopted labour protection regulations, the greater the benefits of free riding. However, if one considers the growing moral and economic pressure on the states that undertook little or nothing in this respect, increasingly negative consequences for trade policy did indeed threaten to result, and these were not calculable. Belgium, which maintained child labour for an especially long period, in the end risked trade policy sanctions. It was the large states, in particular, that exerted pressure. For Germany, it was Prussia that was decisive; for Europe, it was Great Britain, the German Reich and France.

Harmonization by agreement among independent states

The following analysis refers to the two multilateral labour protection agreements that were concluded at the beginning of the twentieth century:

- The decisive reason for the conclusion of these agreements was the same as that which led to regulatory convergence in institutional competition. In all

European states there was a broad movement demanding an improvement in labour protection. In countries with a higher standard of regulation, the representatives tried to raise the standards of the 'backward' states. The countries with a lower standard of regulation were called upon to catch up with those countries that had a higher standard. Thus the regulatory tendencies that finally led to harmonization also developed because there was yardstick competition in progressive social development. In this respect, there developed a common 'ethic' that none of the so-called 'civilized nations' could escape.

- The successful conclusion of the agreements was facilitated by the fact that the number of cooperating states was relatively small. In some cases, the agreements provided special benefits to some countries – benefits that were not necessarily economic. France used international social policy both as a lever in foreign policy – in order to remove Italy from the alliance with the Austro-Hungarian and German Empires – and as an instrument for domestic policy. Switzerland used it for the power politics image of a small neutral state. The British government wanted to find out to what extent it was possible in general to reach multilateral agreements with continental states where domestic policies were concerned.
- A process standard may be a club good. Through the transition to the destination principle, exclusion is, in principle, possible, but there is no rivalry among the states agreeing on a common standard. In the case of labour protection (child labour), international exclusion was also finally threatened in the form of 'social tariffs' and accusations of social dumping. Thus, countries which were suspected of aiming to improve their competitive position through low standards were not only subject to moral but also to political or economic pressure. Due to the possibility of exclusion such club goods offer a greater chance of international harmonization than collective goods.
- The level of development of the cooperating states also played a role. The states which harmonized their regulations were usually at comparable levels of development. In the face of similar economic structures and similar production and wage levels, the opponents could hardly argue that this would lead to unilateral disadvantages in competition.

Harmonization in a federal structure

This section refers exclusively to the German Reich after 1871. To recapitulate: the Reich had a structure similar to the European Union, being as it was a loose federal state while the EU is more like a tight confederation. At all events, the independent German states (the EU-Member States), with their own jurisdictions, parliaments, governments and administrations, were brought together and surrendered – albeit reluctantly – their powers to the Reichstag and to the government of the Reich (the European Parliament and Commission). The Bundesrat (the European Council) was the intergovernmental constitutional body, with an odd mixture of legislative and executive powers. The Reich had a liberal economic constitution: freedom of trade, free traffic in goods and services, free movement of capital, freedom of movement and of establishment between and within the individual states – the four freedoms were, thus, comprehensively ensured. There was a common external tariff and for various policies, authority lay with the government of the Reich (European Commission). The political systems in the various German states could, nevertheless, be compared with those of the European Member States in as much as an important precondition for institutional competition was fulfilled: links existed between economic and political competition.

The forces which led to competitive convergence or agreed harmonization in intergovernmental regimes among independent states were, of course, also active here. However, in a federation of semi-independent states, additional forces are at work:

- Consumers and workers called for stronger regulation rather than deregulation because they regarded consumer protection, health protection and labour protection as important collective goods. They demanded harmonization for the entire Reich because they shared similar preferences and believed that they were better able to protect themselves from abuse in a common market.
- It is true that more and more foreign foods were bought. Nevertheless, or maybe for that very reason, German consumers became, once more, increasingly critical of foreign regulations. On the one hand, consumers favoured institutional competition because they hoped that competing regulations would improve the quality of domestic products. Thus, they were, in principle, for the maintenance of the origin principle, that is, for the sovereignty of the consumer. On the other hand, however, they sometimes supported the transition to the destination principle, compelling foreign producers to adapt to German standards, because they increasingly distrusted the regulations of other countries – perhaps due to the propaganda of the industrial and agricultural lobby or increasing nationalism.
- The producers called for harmonization of product regulation (food protection) because, in their opinion, economies of scale weighed particularly heavily in an integrated economic region without borders. They supported a regulatory cartel through the transition to the destination principle in order to discriminate against foreign competition. Regulation as a protectionist measure, as a non-tariff trade barrier, could more easily be demanded in a large internal market because the significance of export for domestic producers decreased.
- Distortions of competition were also the reason why the producers demanded harmonization of process regulations (labour protection). They did, though, demand exemption provisions for individual states in order to take structural differences into account. For example, exemptions were demanded for Saxony regarding female and child labour because of its important textile industry.

- Parties, parliaments and governments agreed on regulatory harmonization of food protection and labour protection because these were salient issues and of relevance to electoral tactics. They were not considered suitable for independent action by individual states.
- Even if the term 'allocative efficiency' was not employed, the belief prevailed in politics that in a 'nation state' with a 'national economy', important regulatory standards should be harmonized in order to guarantee a smooth exchange of products and production factors. The neoclassical argument of the levelling of the institutional 'playing field' was explicitly employed. Differing institutional regulations should not lead to allocative 'distortions' in an economic region that included the entire Reich.
- The harmonization of regulations of the individual states was to contribute to the establishment of cultural identity in the united Germany and vis-à-vis the rest of the world.
- Horizontal competition between the individual states was weak because the small states preferred to strengthen the Reichstag and the central government (the federal bodies) rather than be inferior in competition with the large states, especially Prussia. They believed that this was the only way by which they could take part in decision-making affecting their interests.
- Vertical competition was insufficient because the Reichstag and the central government seized upon the contested powers. The subsidiarity principle, enshrined in the spirit of the constitution, was interpreted one-sidedly by them to mean that the only tasks to be left to the regional authorities were those they themselves did not want to deal with, or those that they were prohibited by constitutional law from handling.
- Since the implementation of the regulatory laws varied – in Prussia, for example, control was quite lax but in Bavaria decidedly tight, an administrative centralization of controls was deemed necessary. This did occur, but only to a limited extent. The fact that it was demanded shows that central state regulation requires also a common executive and, in the end, also judiciary.
- The individual states insisted on their areas of responsibility in applying the controls. Thus, even though the federal element (Reich) was strengthened through ever more refined regulation, the intergovernmental element (Bundesstaaten) continued to play a significant role. All federal measures regarding the implementation of laws were left to the Bundesrat instead of the Reichstag. The Bundesstaaten opposed various practical details of the regulations, with even Prussia fighting against the establishment of an independent central government authority for executing the controls. Vertical competition thus delayed the centralization of regulatory policy.
- All in all, the federal construction led to integrative spillovers. From the political construction emanated tendencies to centralization including the harmonization of regulations. The subsidiarity principle was not clearly stated in constitutional law, and the powers of the member states and the local governments (Länder, Gemeinden) were not effectively protected.

Notes

1 Murphy (1995), Bernauer (2000).
2 Tiebout (1956), Hirschman (1969), Streit (1995), Streit (1996), Windisch (1998), Winkler (1999), Wohlgemuth (1995).
3 Kiwitt and Voigt (1998), Kerber (1998).
4 Bairoch and Kozul-Wright (1996), Tilly (1999), Williamson (1995), Williamson (1996), Bordo (1999).
5 Bairoch (1993).
6 Fischer (1976).
7 On the societal dimension of international relations: Conze (2000).
8 Ellerbrock (1987a and b).
9 Schmauderer (1976).
10 Verhandlungen des Deutschen Reichstages.
11 Burnett (1976).
12 Ellerbrock (1987a: 84ff.).
13 Nahrungsmittelgesetz, Reichs-Gesetzblatt 1879, Nr.14, 145ff.
14 Bundesarchiv R 1501 Reichsministerium des Inneren: Medizinalpolizei.
15 Verhandlungen des Reichstages' in the 1870s, e.g. the debate on the 'Nahrungsmit-telgesetz'. The records of the Reichsministerium des Inneren (Medizinalpolizei) give an informative insight into this subject: Bundesarchiv, R 1501.
16 See the proceedings of the special commissions preparing the drafts of the different food laws and the appendices to these bills. Verhandlungen des Deutschen Reichs-tages und Gesetzesmaterialen.
17 Drucksachen zu den Verhandlungen des Bundesrates des Deutschen Reiches.
18 Schemmel (1968), Reichsministerium des Inneren (Medizinalpolizei), Bundesarchiv, R 1501.
19 Reichsministerium des Inneren (Medizinalpolizei), Bundesarchiv, R 1501.
20 Dippel (1998).
21 Pappe (1975).
22 'Verhandlungen des Reichstages' concerning the negotiations on the meat law in the 1890s.
23 Reichsministerium des Inneren (Medizinalpolizei), Bundesarchiv, R 1501.
24 Bauer (1923), Bauerdick (1994), Bouvier-Ajam (1969), Braun (1890), Bücher (1888), Cohn (1881), Hutchins and Harrison (1966), Lohmann (1878), Lowe (1935), Mayer-Maly (1986).
25 Adler (1888), Bücher (1888), Bauer (1923), Evert (1909).
26 A good example for this argumentation is shown by the negotiations in the German Reichstag.
27 Thomas (1948).
28 Bouvier-Ajam(1969), Herren (1993), Landmann (1904: 371ff.), Renard (1913), Mataja (1896: 505ff.).
29 Weidmann (1971), Grobéty (1979).
30 Buzano (1915), Stringher (1887: 233ff.), Sellin (1973).
31 Rahikainen (2001: 41ff.), Sandin (1997: 17ff.), Hjelt (1890: 643ff.).
32 Verhandlungen des Reichstages.
33 Bauer (1903: 686).
34 Lyons (1963: 135ff.).
35 Rothfels (1922: 70ff.).
36 Herren (1993: 52ff.).
37 Grobéty (1979: 195ff.).
38 Von Berlepsch (1987), Brinkmann (1994: 11ff.), Kern (1991: 323ff.), Sellier (1998).
39 Herren (1993: 83 ff.).

40 Herren (1993: 140ff.).
41 Dochow (1907).

References

Adler, Georg (1888) *Die Frage des internationalen Arbeiterschutzes*, München und Leipzig.

Bairoch, Paul (1993) *Economics and World History. Myths and Paradoxes*, Chicago: University of Chicago Press.

Bairoch, Paul and Kozul-Wright, Richard (1996) 'Globalization Myths: Some Historical Reflections on Integration, Industrialization and Growth in the World Economy', *UNCTAD Discussion Paper*, 113, Geneva.

Bauer, Stephan (1903) 'Die geschichtlichen Motive des internationalen Arbeiterschutzes', *Vierteljahrschrift für Social- und Wirtschaftsgeschichte*, 1, 79–104.

—— (1923) 'Arbeiterschutzgesetzgebung', *Handwörterbuch der Staatswissenschaften*, Bd. 1, Jena, pp. 401–698.

Bauerdick, Johannes (1994) *Arbeitsschutz zwischen staatlicher und verbandlicher Regulierung*, Berlin: edition sigma.

Bernauer, Thomas (2000) *Staaten im Weltmarkt. Zur Handlungsfähigkeit von Staaten trotz wirtschaftlicher Globalisierung*, Opladen: Leske & Budrich.

Bordo, M.D. (1999) 'Is Globalization Today really Different than Globalization Hundred Years Ago?' *NBER working paper series*, 195, Cambridge, Mass.

Bouvier-Ajam, Maurice (1969) *Histoire du Travail en France depuis la Revolution*, Paris: Libr. Générale de Droit et de Jurisprudence.

Braun, Adolf (1890) *Die Arbeiterschutzgesetze der europäischen Staaten*, Tübingen.

Brinkmann, Gisbert (1994) 'Der Anfang des internationalen Arbeitsrechts – Die Berliner Arbeitskonferenz von 1890 als Vorläufer der Internationalen Arbeitsorganisation', in Bundesministerium für Arbeit und Sozialordnung *et al.* (ed.) *Weltfriede durch soziale Gerechtigkeit. 75 Jahre Internationale Arbeitsorganisation*, Baden-Baden: Nomos, pp. 11–23.

Bücher, Karl (1888) *Zur Geschichte der internationalen Fabrikgesetzgebung*, Berlin.

Burnett, John (1976) 'Food adulteration in Britain in the 19th century and the origins of food legislation', in Edith Heischkel-Artelt (ed.) *Ernährung und Ernährungslehre im 19. Jahrhundert*, Göttingen: Vandenhoeck & Ruprecht, pp. 117–30.

Buzano, Ernesto (1915) *La legislazione del Lavoro*, Torino.

Cohn, Gustav (1881) 'Über internationale Fabrikgesetzgebung', *Jahrbücher für Nationalökonomie und Statistik*, 3, 313–426.

Conze, Eckart (2000) 'Zwischen Staatenwelt und Gesellschaftswelt. Die gesellschaftliche Dimension in der internationalen Geschichte', in Wilfried Loth and Jürgen Osterhammel (eds) *Internationale Geschichte. Themen – Ergebnisse – Aussichten*, München: Verlag C.H. Beck, pp. 117–32.

Dippel, Horst (1998) 'Hundert Jahre Weinrecht. Zur Geschichte eines Sonderwegs', *Zeitschrift für Neuere Rechtsgeschichte*, 20, 225–37.

Dochow, Franz (1907) *Vereinheitlichung des Arbeiterschutzrechts durch Staatsverträge. Ein Beitrag zum internationalen Verwaltungsrecht*, Berlin.

Ellerbrock, Karl-Peter (1987a) 'Die Entwicklung der Lebensmittelüberwachung in Dortmund im 19. Jahrhundert', *Beiträge zur Geschichte Dortmunds und der Grafschaft Mark*, 78, 75–124.

—— (1987b) 'Lebensmittelqualität vor dem Ersten Weltkrieg: Industrielle Produktion und staatliche Gesundheitspolitik', in Hans Jürgen Teuteberg (ed.) *Durchbruch zum modernen Massenkonsum. Lebensmittelmärkte und Lebensmittelqualität im Städtewachstum des Industriezeitalters*, Münster: F. Coppenrath Verlag, pp. 127–88.

Evert, Georg (1909) 'Arbeiterschutzgesetzgebung', III. Internationale Bestrebungen, in *Handwörterbuch der Staatswissenschaften*, Bd. 1, Jena, pp. 772–6.

Fischer, Wolfram (1976) 'Die Ordnung der Weltwirtschaft vor dem Ersten Weltkrieg. Die Funktion von europäischem Recht, zwischenstaatlichen Verträgen und Goldstandard beim Ausbau des internationalen Wirtschaftsverkehrs', *Zeitschrift für Wirtschafts- und Sozialwissenschaften*, 96, 289–303.

Grobéty, Dominique (1979) *La Suisse aux origines du droit ouvrier*, Zürich.

Herren, Madeleine (1993) *Internationale Sozialpolitik vor dem Ersten Weltkrieg. Die Anfänge europäischer Kooperation aus der Sicht Frankreichs*, Berlin: Duncker & Humblot.

Hirschman, Albert O. (1969) *Exit, Voice, and Loyalty. Responses to Decline in Firms, Organizations, and States*, Cambridge, MA: Cambridge University Press.

Hjelt, August (1890) 'Das erste Arbeiterschutzgesetz Finnlands vom 15. April 1889', in *Archiv für soziale Gesetzgebung und Statistik*, 3, 643–60.

Hutchins, B.L. and Harrison, B.A. (1966) *The History of Factory Legislation* (1911), reprinted, London: Macmillan.

Kerber, Wolfgang (1998) 'Zum Problem einer Wettbewerbsordnung für den System-wettbewerb', *Jahrbuch für Neue Politische Ökonomie*, 17, 199–230.

Kern, Max R. (1991) 'Zur Wirkungsgeschichte der Arbeitsschutzkonferenz im internationalen Bereich', *Neue Zeitschrift für Arbeitsrecht*, 22, 323–33.

Kiwitt, Daniel and Voigt, Stefan (1998) 'Grenzen des institutionellen Wettbewerbs', *Jahrbuch für Neue Politische Ökonomie*, 17, 313–37.

Landmann, Julius (1904) 'Die Ausdehnung des Arbeitschutzes in Frankreich', *Archiv für Sozialwissenschaft und Sozialpolitik*, 1, 371–91.

Lohmann, Theodor (1878) *Die Fabrikgesetzgebung der Staaten des europäischen Kontinents*, Berlin: Duncker & Humblot.

Lowe, Boutelle E. (1935) *The International Protection of Labor*, New York.

Lyons, F.S.L. (1963) *Internationalism in Europe 1815–1964*, Leyden: A.W Sythoff.

Mataja, Victor (1896) 'Die Anfänge des Arbeiterschutzes in Frankreich', *Zeitschrift für Volkswirtschaft, Sozialpolitik und Verwaltung*, 5, 505–23.

Mayer-Maly, Theo (1986) 'Arbeitsrecht', in Helmut Coing (ed.) *Handbuch der Quellen und Literatur der neueren europäischen Privatrechtsgeschichte*, Bd. 3/3, München: Verlag C.H. Beck, pp. 3635–745.

Murphy, Dale Dennis (1995) 'Open Economies and Regulations: Convergence and Competition among Jurisdictions', dissertation, Boston, Mass., MIT.

Pappe, Otmar (1975) 'Zur Geschichte der Lebensmittelüberwachung im Königreich Bayern (1806–1918)', dissertation, Universität Marburg.

Rahikainen, Marjatta (2001) 'Children and "the right to factory work": child labour legislation in nineteenth century Finland', *Scandinavian Economic History Review*, 49, 41–61.

Renard, Georges (1913) *Le parlement et la législation du travail*, Paris.

Rothfels, Hans (1922) 'Die erste diplomatische Aktion zugunsten des internationalen Arbeiterschutzes', *Vierteljahrschrift für Social- und Wirtschaftsgeschichte*, 16, 70–87.

Sandin, Bengt (1997) 'In the large factory towns: child labour legislation, child labour and school compulsion', in N. de Coninck-Smith *et al.* (eds) *Industrious Children: Work and Childhood in the Nordic Countries, 1850–1990*, Odense: Odense University Press.

Schemmel, Walter (1968) 'Das Reinheitsgebot für Herstellung und Vertrieb von Bier in Bayern', dissertation, Universität Würzburg.

Schmauderer, Eberhard (1976) 'Die Beziehungen zwischen Lebensmittelwissenschaft, Lebensmittelrecht und Lebensmittelversorgung im 19. Jahrhundert problemgeschichtlich betrachtet', in Edith Heischkel-Artelt (ed.) *Ernährung und Ernährungslehre im 19. Jahrhundert*, Göttingen: Vandenhoeck & Ruprecht, pp. 131–53.

Sellier, Ulrich (1998) *Die Arbeiterschutzgesetzgebung im 19. Jahrhundert. Das Ringen zwischen christlich-sozialer Ursprungsidee, politischen Widerständen und kaiserlicher Gesetzgebung*, Paderborn: Schöningh.

Sellin, Volker (1973) *Die soziale Reform im liberalen Italien*, Stuttgart: Klett-Verlag.

Streit, Manfred E. (1995) 'Dimensionen des Wettbewerbs – Systemwandel aus ordnungsökonomischer Sicht', *Zeitschrift für Wirtschaftspolitik*, 44, 113–34.

——— (1996) 'Systemwettbewerb und Harmonisierung im europäischen Integrationsprozeß', in Dieter Cassel (ed.) *Entstehung und Wettbewerb von Systemen*, Berlin: Duncker & Humblot, pp. 223–44.

Stringher, Bonaldo (1887) 'Über italienische Arbeitsgesetzgebung', *Zeitschrift für die gesamte Staatswissenschaft*, 43, 233–54.

Thomas, Maurice Walton (1948) *The Early Factory Legislation*, Leigh-on-Sea: Thames Bank Publishing Company.

Tiebout, Ch.M. (1956) 'A pure theory of local expenditures', *The Journal of Political Economy*, 64, 416–24.

Tilly, Richard (1999) *Globalisierung aus historischer Sicht und das Lernen aus der Geschichte* (Kölner Vorträge zur Sozial- und Wirtschaftsgeschichte 41), Köln.

Von Berlepsch, Hans-Jörg (1987) *'Neuer Kurs' im Kaiserreich? Die Arbeiterpolitik des Freiherrn von Berlepsch 1890 bis 1896*, Bonn: Verlag Neue Gesellschaft.

Weidmann Paul (1971) *Die soziale Entwicklung des züricherischen Arbeitsrechts von 1815–1870 (unter besonderer Berücksichtigung der Fabrikgesetzgebung)*, Zürich: Schulthess.

Williamson, Jeffrey G. (1995) 'The evolution of global labor markets since 1830. Background, evidence and hypotheses', *Explorations in Economic History*, 32, 191–211.

——— (1996) 'Globalization, convergence and history', *Journal of Economic History*, 56, 277–91.

Windisch, Rupert (1998) 'Modellierung von Systemwettbewerb: Grundlagen, Konzepte, Thesen', *Jahrbuch für Neue Politische Ökonomie*, 17, 121–54.

Winkler, Tobias (1999) 'Die gegenseitige Anerkennung – Achillesferse des Regulierungswettbewerbs', in Manfred E. Streit and Michael Wohlgemuth (eds) *Systemwettbewerb als Herausforderung an Politik und Theorie*, Baden-Baden: Nomos, pp. 103–21.

Wohlgemuth, Michael (1995) 'Economic and political competition in neoclassical and evolutionary perspective', *Constitutional Political Economy*, 6, 71–96.

COMMENT: THE STRATEGY OF RAISING RIVALS' COSTS BY FEDERAL REGULATION UNDER BISMARCK

Roland Vaubel

Victors write history. When Prussia united Germany by military force in 1870, it carefully tried to avoid the impression that the other states of the Empire were subordinated to Prussian interests. In the Bundesrath, the second chamber of parliament in which the princes of the other federal states were represented, Prussia had 17 of the 54 votes, it depended on a few coalition partners. The voting record of the Bundesrath was usually not published, from 1880 onwards it could even be declared secret to conceal Prussian dominance (Para. 26 of the Rules of Procedure). Frequently, Otto von Bismarck, the President of the Bundesrath did not even take votes and simply announced that the Bundesrath had adopted the legislation. The Bundesrath was presided over by the Prime Minister of Prussia. Prussia had the casting vote and the right of veto. The history books of the time emphasize Prussian liberalism and tolerance and federal harmony. This image has persisted to the present day as is witnessed by Gerold Ambrosius' account (in this volume).

As a matter of fact, there were sharp dissensions in the Bundesrath. Prussia and its agrarian allies in East Germany followed less liberal policies than the more advanced states in the north-west and south-west. In particular, they favoured tighter government regulations, more powers for the guilds, higher taxes and tariffs and more nationalization. Since the Empire had centralized political power and had raised the cost of exit and political comparisons for the citizens, the state had gained more power over the citizens. The Prussian government began to exploit this power. The heyday of German market liberalization which had begun with the creation of the German Customs Union in 1833 was over. Together with its East German allies, Prussia raised the level of regulation, taxation and tariff protection and imposed it on the more liberal minority of states. It adopted the so-called 'strategy of raising rivals' costs'.[1] There was deep frustration among the minority. After Bismarck's death, some South German authors (von Poschinger, Klopp, Reichert) have cautiously drawn attention to these problems. In preparing this article, we[2] have also consulted the Bundesrath proceedings collected in the archives of two south-western state capitals (Karlsruhe for Baden and Stuttgart for Württemberg). In several instances, the orders of the day contain handwritten notes by the delegates indicating how the various states voted. Of course, the No-votes and abstentions understate the size of the minority. Many of those opposed to the legislation preferred to go along with it because, being a minority, they could not stop it anyway and had to fear retaliation from Prussia.

Prussia had defeated the Habsburgs and their allies in 1866, annexing the Kingdom of Hannover, Schleswig-Holstein, Kurhessen (Northern Hesse), Nassau and the city of Frankfurt. The remaining North German states were forced into the Norddeutscher Bund (North German Federation) which lasted until 1871. It became the model for the Empire.

During this period, there are at least three instances of legislative opposition in the federal chamber (also called Bundesrath): the Notgewerbegesetz (Emergency Trade Law) of 1868, the Gewerbegesetz (Trade Regulation) of 1869 and the Gesetz über Aktiengesellschaften (Law concerning Joint-Stock Companies) of 1870.

The Notgewerbegesetz extended the most important parts of the Prussian trade law to the Norddeutscher Bund. In the Bundesrath of the federation, it was opposed by five states: Hamburg, Hesse and Saxony, which regarded it as too restrictive, and the two states of Mecklenburg for which it was too liberal. Von Poschinger (1897, Vol. I: 148) summarizes the complaints of the liberal minority:

> The draft exclusively followed the Prussian trade regulation and recklessly ignored the fact that other member states had progressed much more towards freedom of trade than Prussia had done … In the discussion of the details the other states tried to fight against the proposed bureaucracy which was formed after the Prussian mould and to maintain the more liberal provisions of the member states.
>
> (my translation)

The Gewerbeordnung of 1869 required state concessions for many trades. 'Hesse and Saxony … were opposed from a liberal standpoint' (von Poschinger 1897, Vol. I: 214, my translation). Hesse tabled an amendment that 'it is left to the legislation of each Member State to be less restrictive than this law'.[3] In von Poschinger's words, 'the amendment proposed by Hesse and rejected by the Bundesrath took the view that the federal legislation was not entitled to force one of the member states to retrocede on the path towards freedom of trade' (Vol. I: 215, my translation).

The Gesetz über Aktiengesellschaften (1870) was opposed by Hamburg, Bremen, Lübeck and Oldenburg. It introduced federal regulations ('Normativbestimmungen') which replaced the concessions required in some states. However, in the above-mentioned more liberal Northern states, concessions had not been required. Hamburg, for example, protested against 'the excess of restrictive legal form' (von Poschinger 1897, Vol. I: 310, my translation). Von Poschinger continues:

> As a substitute for the state concessions which would be eliminated, Prussia sought norm regulations which concerned the establishment and the administration of joint-stock companies … Some operations which had been permissible would be completely prohibited … The federal regulations could only be inconvenient and confusing, disruptive and obnoxious. They would hamper the free flexibility of the large banks and insurance companies … They were more restrictive than the laws in France and England … Since foreign joint-stock companies would be freer, considerable inconveniences would arise, and much capital would be withdrawn from the domestic economy.

But the Bundesrath majority took the view that 'in the large cities where the public is already versatile in economic matters, conditions might be quite different than in the other federal member states' (my translation).

In 1870–1 Prussia defeated France and founded the second 'German Empire' which also included Southern Germany and Alsace-Lorraine. The Prussian King was now the Emperor and appointed the imperial chancellor, Otto von Bismarck. Except for a brief interruption in 1872–3, Bismarck was also Prime Minister of Prussia. In 1878 he also took over the Prussian Board of Trade. All federal bills were drafted by the Prussian government, but they had to be approved and could be amended by the two houses of Parliament, the directly elected Reichstag or the Bundesrath. The regulations of the Norddeutscher Bund were automatically extended to the whole Reich.

Up to the First World War the Bundesrath adopted at least five regulations which were opposed by the more liberal states of the north-west and south-west.

The first was the Seemannsordnung (Sailors' Regulation) of 1872, a regulation of the employment of sailors. It was opposed by the seaport cities Hamburg, Bremen and Lübeck as well as the Duchy of Oldenburg with its North Sea harbour Emden. According to the minutes of the Bundesrath (1872, 42nd session, pp. 330f.), the minority complained that the regulation 'will do serious damage to German shipping ... It will require time and costs which can lead to heavy losses for the shipping lines ... Finally, no sea-faring nation knows a regulation of this kind' (my translation). In von Poschinger's words (Vol. I: 273),

> the delegates of the Hanse cities found the interests of ocean shipping relative to the interests of Baltic Sea shipping inadequately respected. Petitions from Ostfriesland made the same point. 'That Prussia as a state would use its military-political superiority to subordinate the interests of the more distant and more recent interests of North Sea shipping, which are alien to the Prussian bureaucracy, to those of Baltic Sea shipping in such a reckless way is something one would not believe until one has seen it with one's own eyes', remarked the Nationalzeitung.
>
> (my translation)

Even the south-western delegates felt uneasy as the following quotations from Reichert's dissertation (1962: 156, notes 34, 39, my translation) indicate. Elstätter, a delegate of Baden, commented that 'the inland states are in the strange position to tip the balance in a matter which does not concern them ... They vote with Prussia even though they may do grave damage to the seaport states'.

Türckheim, another delegate of Baden, complained:

> The worst thing is not the hurry but the clandestine intention with which many bills that have been discussed in the Prussian ministries for months are suddenly pushed through the Bundesrath – with surprise being considered the most effective means of success.
>
> (Reichert 1962: 156, notes 34, 39)

But this was quite usual (Nipperdey 1992: 90).

Second, the Gewerbeordnung (Trade Regulation) of 1884 which extended the privileges of the guilds was opposed by the liberal states Hamburg, Bremen, Lübeck, Baden, Württemberg, Hesse and Meiningen. Henceforth only guild members were permitted to employ apprentices.

The third example is the Bäckereiverordnung (Bakeries Regulation) of 1896. It restricted working time of apprentices in bakeries. It was rejected by Bremen and Württemberg, which were less restrictive, but also by Bavaria and the two states of Mecklenburg, which were more restrictive. When the Prussian Minister for Trade, von Berlepsch, resigned in the same year, the Bavarian delegate to the Bundesrath, Graf Lerchenfeld, noted that 'no Prussian minister has ever understood so little about conditions in the other federal states and has paid so scant attention to the wishes of other state governments' (Born 1957: 133, my translation).

Fourth, the Innungsgesetz (Guilds Law) of 1897 extended the privileges of the guilds. It empowered the guilds to declare membership compulsory if a majority of their members decided so. The bill was opposed by Baden.

Finally, the Gewerbeordnung (Trade Regulation) of 1908 which restricted the working time of women was rejected by Hamburg and Bremen.

Probably these examples are only the tip of the iceberg. For other very important federal regulations, we simply could not find out whether they were unanimously adopted or not. One is the Arbeiterschutznovelle zur Gewerbeordnung (Worker Protection Amendment to the Trade Regulation) of 1878 which restricted the working time of women and juvenile workers, another the Angestelltenschutzgesetz (Employee Protection Law) of 1900 which prescribed a minimum period of notice and limited shop opening hours. The Stellenvermittlungsgesetz (Labour Exchange Law) of 1910 which required state concessions for private labour exchanges was adopted without opposition but there seem to have been abstentions.

The Prussian majority coalition raised their rivals' cost not only by federal regulation but also by imposing excise and customs duties. In 1879, it adopted the Schutzzollgesetz, a tariff law designed to protect East German agriculture and raise revenue for the Empire which, apart from excise taxes on salt, tobacco and brandy, had no power to tax. The seaport cities Hamburg, Bremen, Lübeck, Oldenburg and Mecklenburg-Schwerin voted against it. The Prussian majority coalition took revenge. As Reichert (1962: 27) explains,

> in a split vote, Oldenburg was expelled from the Bundesrath committee for railways, post offices and telegraphs and Mecklenburg from the committees for customs duties and taxation and for trade and transportation ... The 1880 election of committee members showed ... that the adherents of free trade were no longer tolerated in the technical committees.

In 1881, Hamburg's free harbour in Altona, Wandsbek and Unterelbe was abolished against Hamburg's will (so-called 'Zollanschluss'). Eugen Richter, the leader of the liberal Fortschrittspartei, commented that 'the Bundesrath was taking a decision with the sole purpose of doing violence to a federal member state' (von Poschinger, Vol. IV: 390, my translation). And on 20 May 1881, he tabled the following motion in the Reichstag:

> It would be incompatible with the federal relationship and pertinent consti-tutional law if the Bundesrath amended the Tariff Law with the sole purpose of restricting particular member states in the free use of their constitutional rights.
>
> (Stenographische Berichte über die Verhandlungen des Deutschen Reichstags 4 IV 4:794, App. 148, my translation)

In 1884 the Bundesrath amended the Stempelsteuergesetz (Stamp Duty Law) extending the stamp duty from monetary to commodity transactions. The bill was flatly opposed by Hamburg, Bremen and Lübeck and severely criticized by the governments of Baden, Württemberg and Bavaria. Reichert (1962: 61) men-tions that the delegate from Baden was instructed 'to avoid taking a too isolated stance and voting against the bill as a whole if, apart from the Hanse cities, no other federal state was against it' (my translation).

Thus Baden did not agree with the content of the law but considered it inop-portune to join an opposition consisting only of the Hanse cities. This was Baden's general practice. In 1880, the deputy from Baden had been asked to represent also Waldeck and Pyrmont with the instruction 'always to vote with Prussia' (Reichert 1962: 20, my translation).

Quite generally the ruthlessness with which Prussia imposed its will on the minority of liberal states caused considerable resentment as Klopp (1934: 21) emphasizes:

> Bismarck's habit of not taking votes but always claiming consensus meant that the other states had nothing to say any more in the Bundesrath. This was the continuous complaint of the princes and ministers of the smaller states. Much uneasiness and listlessness was provoked in this way.
>
> (my translation)

This evidence stands in marked contrast with Gerold Ambrosius' account (in this volume) which takes the Prussian view:

1   The 'Bundesstaaten' of the 'German Reich' were more or less independent (p. 175).
2   Governments agreed on regulatory harmonization of labour protection (p. 189).
3   The small states preferred to strengthen the central government (p. 189).
4   The Reich had a liberal economic constitution (pp. 187ff.).

Notes

1 For a survey of the literature and a graphical exposition of the theory see Boockmann and Vaubel (2005).
2 I am grateful to Dr Christian Teubner, an economic historian, for his assistance.
3 Bundesrath, Session of 1869, Protokoll der vierten Sitzung, p. 5, my translation.

References

Boockmann, Bernhard and Vaubel, Roland (2005) 'The Theory of Raising Rivals' Costs and Evidence from the International Labour Organization', University of Mannheim, mimeo.

Born, Karl Erich (1957) *Staat und Sozialpolitik seit Bismarcks Sturz*, Wiesbaden: F. Steiner.

Klopp, Hans Joachim (1934) 'Die Wandlung in der Stellung des Bundesrates in der Zeit 1868–1918', dissertation, Universität Marburg.

Nipperdey, Thomas (1992) *Deutsche Geschichte 1866–1918, Vol. 2: Machtstaat vor Demokratie*, München: Beck.

Reichert, Hans-Klaus (1962) 'Baden am Bundesrat 1871–1890', dissertation, Universität Heidelberg.

von Poschinger, Heinrich (1897) *Fürst Bismarck und der Bundesrath*, Vol. I, Stuttgart: Deutsche Verlagsanstalt.

6 Regulatory competition and federalism in Switzerland

Diffusion by horizontal and vertical interaction

Lars P. Feld

Introduction

On the eve of the creation of a Swiss federation, Napoleon Bonaparte is reported to have said that Switzerland will be a federal state or it will never be. By acknowledging the cantonal diversity with such resignation, he (supposedly) accepted that the strength of political and cultural identity of the Swiss cantons rendered his attempt to impose a centralized constitution on the Swiss unsuccessful (Kölz 1992). Swiss federalism has since been accepted as one of the most decentralized versions of this type of (vertical) state organization (Filippov *et al.* 2004). In recent times the fiscal part of Swiss federalism has gained considerable attention by economists (Feld 2000a; Feld and Kirchgässner 2001, 2003). Strong fiscal competencies of the Swiss cantons and local jurisdictions, in particular their extensive tax autonomy, have led scholars to use Switzerland as a laboratory to analyse the effects of fiscal competition on the efficiency of public good provision (Feld 2005a), decentralized income distribution (Feld 2000b; Feld *et al.* 2003a), government size (Schaltegger 2001; Feld *et al.* 2003c; Kirchgässner and Feld 2004) and economic performance (Feld *et al.* 2004).

The focus on fiscal issues in these empirical studies is owing to a large number of theoretical studies in the economic analysis of federalism that more or less heavily criticize the benefits of interjurisdictional competition (for surveys see Feld 2000a, 2005b). One of the most prominent critiques stems from Sinn (2003) who hypothesizes that interjurisdictional fiscal competition will lead to an inefficient provision of public services and to a collapse of the welfare state. An inefficient provision of public services could particularly result if economies of scale (non-rivalness) in consumption exist, that is when the government provides public goods in the Samuelsonian sense. Fiscal competition enforces the benefit principle of taxation such that mobile production factors can only be charged the marginal costs of their use of public goods. Mobile taxpayers do however not contribute to cover the high inframarginal (fixed) costs of public infrastructure. If this is not to lead to an inefficiently low level of public services, the fixed costs must be covered by immobile taxpayers (Sinn 2003). This can induce an undesired income distribution. Sinn (2003) also argues that a large government sector for distributive purposes can hardly be maintained in a decentralized system with fiscal competition. Not only would it become difficult if not impossible for a single community to levy the necessary redistribution tax upon the rich and mobile, but such a policy, if undertaken in one community, would also attract poor individuals from other jurisdictions and, thus, erode the internal redistribution policy. Therefore no major redistributional activities would be possible in a decentralized, competitive system of jurisdictions.

The recent evidence from Swiss federalism rejects Sinn's hypotheses at least in their strong versions. According to the studies mentioned above, fiscal competition between Swiss cantons and between Swiss local jurisdictions rather lead to a relatively high efficiency of public goods' provision. They do not induce a collapse of the welfare state although they restrict the cantons' ability to redistribute income and reduce the size of the public sector.[1] Overall, fiscal competition in Switzerland leads to sounder public finances. In addition, fiscal competition induces a better economic performance of the cantons as measured by their GDP per employee. The Swiss evidence is thus much more in line with the predictions of Tiebout (1956) and Oates and Schwab (1988) who hypothesize an efficient provision of public services as the result from fiscal competition. On the basis of this Swiss evidence, it is tempting to regard interjurisdictional competition as the most favourable principle of (horizontally and vertically) organizing interjurisdictional relationships.

There is however a dark side of federalism or decentralized policy-making, respectively. As one of the most important advantages of federalism, Tiebout (1956), Stigler (1957) and Oates (1972) emphasized that public good provision and financing is close to citizens' preferences such that information problems are minimized and citizens' preferences for public goods are enforced (see also Weingast 1995). Being close to citizens however also involves closeness to local special interests. Instead of serving the interests of mobile individuals, sub-federal jurisdictions may thus be captured by local interest groups and introduce protectionist measures in order to shelter them from external competition (Rodden and Rose-Ackerman 1997; Brueckner 2000; Bardhan 2002). An argument that starts as an advantage quickly turns into a disadvantage if the imperfections of politics are considered. It thus depends on the institutional restrictions shaping policy outcomes whether decentralized decision-making on the provision and financing of public services actually leads to efficient outcomes.

These advantages and disadvantages of federalism are clearly perceived by policy-makers, again in particular in Switzerland. While the positive role of fiscal competition is widely acknowledged, the tendency of the cantons to collude in certain policy areas as well as the cantonal reluctance to deregulate their economies are evaluated very critically (Rentsch *et al.* 2004; Borner and Bodmer 2004). Many regulations of economic activity exist at the Swiss cantonal level and prevent economic innovation from unfolding. Because these regulations are in the competency of the cantons, the federal government has difficulties in deregulating the Swiss economy. In 1995 the Swiss federal government thus passed a law to complete the Swiss common market by establishing an origin principle in cantonal regulation such that regulations of the other cantons have to be accepted by each canton. As the impact of that Common Market Law on regulatory levels of the Swiss cantons has been rather moderate and free market access between the cantons has remained restricted in several areas of economic activity, an amendment proposal has followed in 2004 (Bundesrat 2004). The main goal of the amended Common Market Law is the enforcement of the origin principle in cantonal regulation and the extension of free market access to all economic sectors and branches. The validity of specific cantonal legal prerequisites in each canton supposedly increases inter-cantonal mobility of labour and services. What is going on in Switzerland is a liberalization along the same lines of thought as the EU Services Directive of 2005 has intended in the first place. The result of this deregulation effort will be regulatory competition.

When it comes to regulatory competition, similar concerns as in the case of fiscal competition can be formulated. Again Sinn (2003) is one of those most heavily questioning the benefits of regulatory competition. With respect to product market regulation, he argues that regulatory competition will induce too lax standards if the reason for regulating product markets in the first place is asymmetric information. Customers who are ill informed about product quality would have at least as strong difficulties to judge competing national quality standards properly. The problems induced by asymmetric information and intended to be reduced by government regulation would re-emerge in regulatory competition. According to Sinn, market failure would be re-introduced by the backdoor. Swiss policy-makers articulate the same fears in the current discussion on a revision of the Common Market Law (Bundesrat 2004: 478): Regulatory competition supposedly induces a race to the bottom in regulatory standards.

The main goal of this chapter is to rationalize these theoretical and political discussions by providing some insights into the functioning of regulatory competition and harmonization in Switzerland. A focus of this chapter is the dynamic interaction that takes place in any kind of competitive processes such that innovations and inventions could occur. Apart from some pioneering studies (Hayek 1939; Rose-Ackerman 1980), the impact of interjurisdictional competition on policy innovations has only recently gained more considerable attention in the economic theory of federalism (Inman and Rubinfeld 1997; Kerber 1998; Oates 1999; Schnellenbach 2004a, 2004b; Feld and Schnellenbach 2004). The theory of regulatory competition in international economics and in law and economics more consistently study the relationship between policy competition and policy innovation (Bernholz and Faber 1986; Siebert and Koop 1990; Hauser and Hösli 1991; Bebchuk 1992; Sun and Pelkmans 1995), meanwhile extending the analysis to historical evidence (Bernholz and Vaubel 2004; Vaubel 2005). This analysis adds to the existing evidence by focusing on Switzerland.

The chapter is organized as follows: in the next section, the brief sketch of arguments mentioned before is extended to provide a theoretical basis of the analysis. The often neglected link between competition and innovation is particularly emphasized in this section. Then, there is a very brief overview on the cases of regulatory competition empirically studied in the literature. This is followed by an analysis of the development of the common market, regulatory competition and harmonization in Switzerland across time. Then, an econometric analysis of the extent of regulation at the Swiss cantonal level is conducted in order to find out the main determinants of Swiss cantonal regulations. Concluding remarks are provided in the final section.

The theoretical basis for the analysis

The theoretical point of departure in studies of regulatory competition is the same as the one from which the economic theory of federalism starts. In a seminal contribution, Tiebout (1956) analyses decentralized provision and financing of public goods by drawing a market analogue. Citizens who demand public services face many jurisdictions providing different levels and quantities of them according to different tax prices. Individuals (and firms) shop around selecting that bundle of public goods (including regulations) and tax prices which comes closest to their preferences. In equilibrium, people have sorted according to their preferences and incomes into different jurisdictions offering different types, levels and qualities of public services (including regulations) to different tax prices. A sustainable variety of public solutions results, (relatively) homogeneous populations live in each jurisdiction, and citizens' preferences are enforced by competition between jurisdictions. Like in private markets, migration provides for a mechanism to induce efficient outcomes.

While Tiebout (1956) has developed his thoughts as a reply to Samuelson's (1954) free-rider problem in the provision of public goods by showing that an efficient mechanism to reveal individual preferences for local public goods exists, the theory of regulatory competition has adapted his model by drawing an analogue between local public goods and legal rules (Gatsios and Holmes 1998; Van den Bergh 2000; Heine and Kerber 2002). In that analogy, regulatory competition appears to comprise any state action from taxes and public spending to legal statutes, constitutional provisions and whole economic or political systems. Sun and Pelkmans (1995: 82) serve best to illustrate that analogy in an EU context:

> Given the four economic freedoms of movement, consumers and firms will be able to arbitrage among the differences in national regulations revealed thereby. With mutual recognition, consumers will be able to choose among the goods and services produced according to various regulations. To the extent that greater variety increases utility, consumer welfare will be enhanced. Further, when mobility rests with factors of production . . ., these factors can locate within the jurisdiction the regulations of which most closely approximate their preferences; allocative efficiency will be improved, and output will expand.

For those familiar with the literature on the economic theory of federalism, the analogy appears complete. In fact, the hypotheses developed in this analysis even seem to provide for a vision, like Ronald Reagan's shining city on a hill (Buchanan 2000): regulatory competition under the principle of origin with mutual recognition of regulations of the jurisdictions involved leads to favourable economic outcomes.

The neoclassical criticisms

It is no surprise that such visionary formulations have raised contradiction. Although some of the main critical arguments as to the functioning of interjurisdictional competition could be found earlier in the economic theory of federalism (Oates 1972) and at the same time in the literature on regulatory competition between the US states (Bebchuk 1992; Bratton and McCahery 1997), the most clearly formulated criticism is provided again by Sinn (1990, 1997, 2003). He argues that government regulation in product markets serves as a solution to the lemons problem that emerges due to asymmetric information. Because potential buyers can less easily verify the quality of a product offered by a seller, sellers offering low quality goods can pretend to their customers that these are of high quality. The customers' lack of ability to verify quality standards also prevents sellers from differentiating prices in terms of product quality. According to this rationale, cheaper low quality products will always beat more expensive high quality products because the quality difference cannot be verified. The difficulties to realize product quality are particularly relevant in the case of experience goods in the mid-price segment. In such a situation of asymmetric information, customers will realize that their probability of buying low quality products is very high such that the markets affected by asymmetric information become very thin. Indeed they may finally collapse, as Akerlof (1970) has argued for the market for used cars. This kind of market failure could be prevented by government regulation which establishes quality standards and quality controls.

Allowing for competition between jurisdictions which have different levels of government regulation induces customers to buy the products offered at the lowest prices possible, again having difficulties in judging product quality properly. These will be the products from countries with the lowest quality standards such that the lowest standards are enforced by the market mechanism in international competition. According to Sinn's arguments, customers will have the same difficulties in judging public quality standards in the different jurisdictions as they have in judging different product qualities. The result of that kind of competition would be a race to the bottom in regulatory standards providing additional incentives for each jurisdiction to reduce regulatory restrictions further in order to attract additional demand from abroad. Regulatory competition would induce market failure by the backdoor.

Apart from regulation of product markets, Sinn (2003) extends this type of analysis to other different fields of regulation. Similarly adverse outcomes are predicted from his analysis of ecological competition if jurisdictions internalize environmental externalities by Pigovian taxes and from competition of bank regulators using again an asymmetric information argument. With respect to the competition in social standards, a more optimistic assessment follows according to which a convergence of social standards to the higher level occurs. This result is driven by the symmetric interests of employers and employees. Differences in social standards only occur because the country with the lowest standards has low income levels and can thus not afford higher social standards. Competition between social standards will thus not induce social dumping. Finally, Sinn analyses competition between competition rules and obtains a similarly adverse impact of interjurisdictional competition. His arguments rest on the presumption that national governments want to create monopolies or 'national champions' in order to gain dominant market positions in international terms. The incentives to follow that strategy are derived from the additional benefits presumably obtained for that country if 'national champions' reap monopolistic rents and distribute them to their fellow countrymen as their shareholders. The 'national champions' then act as Stackelberg leaders. Competition between competition rules would induce a considerable relaxation of antitrust laws. Sinn acknowledges however that this way of modelling interjurisdictional competition is relatively unrealistic. He shows that the usual Cournot–Nash assumption applied in the other analyses of interjurisdictional competition is inducing efficient antitrust policies.

The analysis conducted by Sinn (2003) hinges on several important assumptions. Two of them are criticized below in more detail, but mentioned at the outset. First, he assumes the validity of what he calls the selection principle. According to that principle, the state does what it ought to from the point of view of normative neoclassical economics. Governments do not follow their own private agenda, but actually cope with market failures. Second, Sinn's view is static. Competition is however a very dynamic procedure that Sinn does not consider. In particular, the beneficial impact of competition on innovation and dynamic efficiency of a society is thus neglected. There are however inherent criticisms of his analysis (Vaubel 2004). First, the strong assumptions about asymmetric information could be criticized. Many problems in markets for experience goods can be coped with by imposing much less restrictive regulations than Sinn presumes. In many cases, markets develop their own institutions to cope with imperfections. The market for used cars, for example, has not collapsed as the automobile industry uses its brand names to signal high quality. If you want to escape from buying lemons, you can buy a car from a garage operating for brand-name car producers which offers new and used cars. This quality signal suffices to prevent the particular market failure in the used cars market. In other cases, the provision of state quality signs may suffice.

Second, it is not reasonable to assume that the information problems exist to the same extent when consumers judge the quality of a large number of single products and the quality of a small number of state regulations. The differences between regulatory standards could be much more easily revealed than the quality differences between products. Given state quality signs, a race to the top in regulatory standards could even result. Third, as Vaubel (2004) argues convincingly, governments have low incentives to control quality standards of exported goods while the quality of products domestically consumed is in their interest. This could lead to exports of low quality goods to which importing governments would react by restricting these imports. If this reaction does not lead to protectionist measures, a control of justified and unjustified import restrictions needs to take place as is done in the EU. Fourth, it is not useful to assume that governments support 'national champions' if the shares of these firms are widely distributed and publicly traded in capital markets. A dominant position of such a firm would not necessarily benefit domestic interests if capital markets are internationally integrated, which is a part of international competition. The more intense international competition the less incentives a government has to push national monopolies.

Despite an incomplete discussion of all these shortcomings of the neoclassical view on regulatory competition, it has had a strong influence on economists, in particular in the German-speaking countries (see for example Apolte 1999). Similar arguments can however be found in studies conducted by legal scholars on state competition in corporate law (Bebchuk 1992; Bratton and McCahery 1997). These analyses start from the fact that the US states possess the primary responsibility for regulating corporate affairs. Corporations can freely choose a jurisdiction for incorporation and states have incentives to attract as many corporations as possible in order to generate state revenue. Both characteristics lead to a competition between the states for incorporations. It can be observed that Delaware is the state that has emerged from that process as the market leader for incorporations in the US. A large fraction of corporations are governed by Delaware corporate law. Delaware has however relatively lax standards that supposedly benefit managers instead of shareholders. Bebchuk (1992), among others, thus argues that the state competition in corporate law leads to a race to the bottom of corporate regulation. The arguments brought forward to explain such an adverse outcome are the same as those provided in the traditional economic analyses: asymmetric information of shareholders or externalities serve as the main justifications for the federal regulation of state corporate law. Sun and Pelkmans (1995), Gatsios and Holmes (1998) and Van den Bergh (2000) develop or acknowledge at least the potential validity of such arguments in the European context, but also applied to regulatory competition in general.

Some remarks from a public choice perspective

These neoclassical criticisms start from the dubious presumption called the selection principle. As mentioned above, it states that governments do what they ought to when they decide about regulatory policies: government corrects market failures. More than 50 years of public choice analysis indicate that governments cannot be expected to follow social welfare goals or that it may even be impossible to know what social welfare is. It must be expected that governments follow their own private goals or the incentives provided to them by special interests. If this is the case, there is a danger that regulatory policies are used to generate rents for politicians and interest groups. This could well lead to excessive regulation. Brennan and Buchanan (1980) have made this argument with respect to excessive taxation by modelling governments as leviathans. Interjurisdictional competition is a means to escape excessive regulation by leviathan governments, and forces governments to follow the preferences of mobile production factors. A decentralized provision and financing of policies (including regulations) is thus beneficial whenever governments do not do what they ought to.

In a slightly different fashion, Weingast (1995) points to the advantages of a 'market-preserving federalism'. Starting from a *'fundamental political dilemma'*, according to which *'a government strong enough to protect property rights and enforce contracts is also strong enough to confiscate the wealth of its citizens'* (p. 1), he considers competitive federalism as a chance to reduce the scope of the government and thus to maintain market efficiency. Because of the better migration chances of mobile investors, the governments of sub-central jurisdictions conduct investor-friendly policies and adopt solutions promoting market outcomes. Weingast continues an earlier analysis by Hayek (1939), according to which

> planning in a federation cannot assume the forms which today are pre-eminently known under this term ... In a federation economic policy will have to take the form of providing a rational permanent framework within which individual initiative will have the largest possible scope and will be made to work as beneficently as possible.
>
> (p. 268)

Rodden and Rose-Ackerman (1997) doubt that matters are so simple. They also argue from a public choice perspective, but their conclusions are rather different. As decentralized governments are closer to citizens' preferences they may also be more easily captured by local interest groups and possibly protect these by protectionist measures from external competition instead of serving the general interests of mobile investors. Bardhan and Mookherjee (2000) as well as Bardhan (2002) point out that, when looking at decentralization processes, a trade-off between the possible gains from interjurisdictional competition and the possible losses due to an easier access of locally concentrated interest groups to the political decision-makers is faced. Brueckner (2000) even attributes this rent-seeking of local interest groups to corruption. Decentralization in developing countries, he argues, increases corruption because additional decision-makers have to be bribed in that case. Treisman (2001) points at the susceptibility also of central governments to corruption. It means that decentralization of a corrupt regime may result in corrupt officials now expecting bribes also locally, while the government at the central level has to be further 'served'. But decentralization can, through horizontal competition between regions and between local governments, reduce local rents, while corruption at the central level remains. Empirical evidence on the impact of decentralization on corruption is consequently mixed. Fisman and Gatti (2002) provide evidence, for a cross-section of 55 countries, that decentralization leads to less corruption. Treisman (2002) shows contradictory evidence for up to 166 countries.

A dynamic evolutionary perspective

The neoclassical criticisms of the positive Tieboutian evaluation of interjurisdictional competition also lack a dynamic component. Economists perceive competition positively because it is the main force establishing a high variability and quality of product supply and the possibility that individuals can pursue their preferences. Starting from an evolutionary perspective, competition can be interpreted as a process in which competing firms continuously look for products and services that provide better solutions for their customers' problems (Kerber 2000). This should hold *a forteriori* for public services and regulations that continuously adapt to different regulatory needs of private markets because governments lack sufficient knowledge to find the best policies for their electorates' purposes. A decentralized experimentation with different policy options (including regulatory alternatives) however, provides, opportunities to test new policies at lower cost than centralized policy experiments might involve. In this decentralized experimentation of new governmental solutions for economic or social problems, successful solutions are imitated and adapted by competing jurisdictions. Competition between jurisdictions becomes a discovery process which enhances the prospects of political innovation. Thus the positive effects of interjurisdictional competition can be mainly expected in a dynamic economy (Bernholz and Faber 1986; Vihanto 1992).

Already in 1932, Louis Brandeis, judge at the US Supreme Court, summarized this argument in the following way: 'It is one of the happy incidents of the federal system that a single courageous State may, if its citizens choose, serve as a laboratory; and try novel social and economic experiments without risk to the rest of the country' (quoted from Oates 1999: 1132). In this context Oates (1999) speaks of 'laboratory federalism' and points out that the reform of welfare in the USA in 1996 followed exactly these considerations (see also Inman and Rubinfeld 1997). With respect to corporate law, this process is discussed as the race-for-the-top theory (Bebchuk 1992; Romano 2002; Heine and Kerber 2002; Heine 2003) according to which regulatory competition leads to a liberalization in corporate law and to an enforcement of shareholder interests against the management of corporations.

How political innovations diffuse from one jurisdiction to the other is, however, much debated in the literature at least since Walker's (1969) seminal contribution (see Clark 2000 for a survey). Following Nice (1994), three different approaches are distinguished in political science: a regional diffusion model in which it is assumed that the probability of policy innovation rises with the number of neighbouring jurisdictions that have already adopted it (Walker 1969); a national interaction model, which assumes that the probability of policy innovation in a particular year rises with the number of interactions that representatives in a jurisdiction had in that year with representatives of other jurisdictions that have already adopted it (Gray 1973; Eyestone 1977); and an internal determinants model, which describes policy innovations as a process depending solely on socio-economic attributes of a state or region such as per capita income, the degree of urbanization, professionalization of the legislature and the bureaucracy and so on (Walker 1969; Berry 1994; Desveaux *et al.* 1994; Carter and LaPlant 1997; Myers 2001). Often, the role of the judiciary is also considered (Canon and Baum 1981; Glick 1994). This has led to an independent research programme in the field of policy innovation (Rogers 1995). On the one hand, theoretical progress is triggered by the application of new empirical methods used to test the three established models (Berry and Berry 1990, 1991, 1992, Berry 1994). On the other hand, the need for further microfoundation of theory is recognized (Savage 1985: 10).

A convincing theoretical study on policy innovation has been provided by Besley and Case (1995), although the argument has already featured earlier in a paper by Salmon (1987). They analyse the incentives for voters to gather information from the policies conducted in neighbouring jurisdictions in order to use it in their voting decisions. Interjurisdictional competition enables citizens to evaluate comparatively the performances of representatives and hence reduce the information asymmetries in political markets ('yardstick competition'). For example, German voters can compare the performance of the German federal government to that of the French government. If France has a relatively high level and quality of public services under otherwise same conditions, but offers them at lower tax prices than Germany, German voters have incentives to throw the German government out of office at the next election day. Interjurisdictional competition does not only work through the migration mechanism, but also improves citizens' ability to exert voice in the political process (Breton 1996, 2000; Bordignon *et al.* 2003; Salmon 2003, 2005a). The government is forced to provide public services at relatively lower costs and at the level desired by citizens. Moreover, Besley and Case manage to provide evidence for American states that voters tend to punish incumbents for raising taxes if neighbouring jurisdictions do not do the same. Thus, voters appear to use information from other jurisdictions to judge the relative efficiency (or ability) of their own incumbent. This empirical result has important implications in the sense that information crossing the borders between jurisdictions is shown to trigger political change.

The higher innovative capacity of federations compared with unitary states is however also contested in general. If citizens use the performance of the governments of other jurisdictions as yardstick when considering their re-election, a government is re-elected if it provides a bundle of regulation, public services and tax prices that are at least not worse than other jurisdictions. Governments thus have incentives initially to wait to see which policies of other jurisdictions turn out to be relatively successful, and then imitate these. Uncertain about their re-election prospects, governments have an incentive to free ride with respect to the policy innovations of other jurisdictions such that the absolute amount of policy innovations in a federation is reduced (Rose-Ackerman 1980). Strumpf (2002) shows that this is only a serious problem when jurisdictions are very similar. Kollman *et al.* (2000) argue that decentralized experimentation is superior to centralized experimentation if the problems for which solutions are to be found in these experiments are not too complex and if there are no scale economies in experimentation. Kotsogiannis and Schwager (2004) argue that in a federation, policy innovations offer selfish politicians an opportunity to obtain personal advantages while marketing them as the result of the uncertainty of policy innovations. Schnellenbach (2004a) takes the incentives of voters in a decentralized process of political innovations into account. As voters are normally rationally ignorant – due to the low incentives to be politically informed – policy innovations are mainly possible in times of crises. The incentives of citizens to be informed about policy innovations are improved by high mobility and by elements of direct democracy in political decision-making processes. Thus, political rents of governments can be reduced by competition so that politicians have incentives to innovate.

What does this lead us to?

This broad discussion of theoretical arguments as to the impact of and the different procedures shaping regulatory competition highlights that an assessment of decentralized competencies in regulatory issues cannot be made solely on theoretical grounds. Depending on the assumptions of the theoretical models, regulatory competition may have a beneficial or an adverse outcome. Three basic assumptions are crucial. First, the theoretically predicted outcome of regulatory competition depends on *the validity of the selection principle*. If governments do what they ought to, it may be useful to focus on potential failures of regulatory competition. If politics results in political failures, regulatory competition is a means to protect mobile production factors from being exploited by leviathan governments. It is highly improbable that political failure does not occur such that the sole emphasis of potential market failures is very unrealistic. It should however also be realized that decentralized government is not immune to political failures. If the influence of special interests is higher at a sub-central than at the central level, decentralized competencies could lead to adverse economic outcomes. Whether interjurisdictional competition can unfold its huge beneficial potential thus depends on additional factors that shape the process of regulatory competition.

Second, *information assumptions* are important for an adverse outcome of regulatory competition even if the selection principle holds. It is not reasonable to assume, for example, that the information distribution underlying the lemons problems is the same with respect to product quality and to regulatory standards. In addition, institutions originating from market responses to asymmetric information need to be considered. Third, the *dynamic efficiency of regulatory competition* is important for its assessment. Each competitive process has the potential to generate innovations. This also holds for competition in politics or between systems. Whether these innovations actually enhance economic performance of the jurisdictions competing with each other cannot be easily found out. On the one hand, the beneficial impact of innovations is usually recognized ex post often with considerable time lags. On the other hand, arguments of dynamic efficiency, the famous metaphor of competition as a discovery procedure, need not be used to rationalize anything *ex post*. It could, for example, be argued that the abolishment of regulations in regulatory competition must have been efficient because regulatory competition is always dynamically efficient. The pure laissez-faire speaking from such an evaluation is difficult to accept given evidence on market failures. It will be rather difficult to operate in such an uncertain environment in which clear yardsticks to evaluate policies seldom exist. Nevertheless, they are needed to arrive at sound policy conclusions.

The dynamic perspective has its merits from a different point of view. It distracts attention from the outcome-oriented approach and highlights a procedural approach. Aside the question of its impact, it thus helps to focus on how regulatory competition takes place. This shift of emphasis moves us also closer to observations of political innovations. Two mechanisms of regulatory competition have become obvious in the preceding analysis: migration and political action, or: exit and voice (Hirschman 1970; Feld 1997). Tiebout's analysis mainly rests on the migration mechanism, while the studies on political innovation conducted by political scientists, but also the yardstick competition model, rely on voice mechanisms. The political science literature is quite instructive, because it helps to distinguish three procedures that are in place: copycatting or *benchmarking* as regional diffusion of policies; the provision of arenas where political decision-makers can exchange their experiences with political innovations (*national interaction*); and the *internal* political or socio-economic *preconditions* that must be met in order to innovate politically. In the case of the second procedure, the national interaction models, the possibility of collusion between policy-makers needs to be considered. By harmonizing regulations, it is possible for regulators to raise rivals' costs and deteriorate economic performance (Boockmann and Vaubel 2005). These three procedures thus correspond to three classes of variables: internal determinants, external determinants that induce competition and external determinants that enable collusive behaviour.

Studies on regulatory competition

As theoretical arguments on regulatory competition are contradictory, empirical evidence is needed in order to provide evidence on the *outcome* of and the *procedures* underlying regulatory competition. In the literature on regulatory competition, regulations are often widely defined such that tax laws, public goods and services are subsumed under this heading in addition to legal rules. As the literature on fiscal competition is broadly discussing its advantages and disadvantages, the focus in this chapter will be on regulatory competition as competition in legal rules. Still, the empirical evidence mainly exists for taxes and much less for legal rules.

Starting with the *procedures* underlying interjurisdictional competition, it is mainly tax mimicking that has been empirically established (see Brueckner 2003 and Revelli 2005 for surveys). The first studies were conducted for the US states and local jurisdictions (Ladd 1992; Case 1993; Brueckner and Saavedra 2001), but there is meanwhile also evidence on tax mimicking in Canada (Brett and Pinske 2000; Hayashi and Boadway 2000), Belgian communities (Heyndels and Vuchelen 1998), German local jurisdictions (Büttner 1999, 2001), French regions and départements (Feld *et al.* 2003b; Leprince *et al.* 2003; Reulier 2004), Italian cities (Bordignon *et al.* 2003), Spanish local jurisdictions (Solé-Ollé 2003) and Dutch municipalities (Allers and Elhorst 2005). Most of these studies focus on income, business and property taxation. They find that a reduction of the average tax rates of competitors induces a reduction of tax rates of an observed jurisdiction. While these studies establish the existence of strategic tax setting as precondition of tax or yardstick competition, Berry and Berry (1992), Ashworth *et al.* (2003) as well as, in an experimental study, Tyran and Sausgruber (2003) emphasize that tax innovations are induced by regional diffusion, but also, and often more importantly, by the internal political environment.

Much less evidence of strategic interaction has been provided with respect to public spending. Figlio *et al.* (1999) and Saavedra (2000) present evidence on strategic interaction on welfare payments in the US. Again, reductions in welfare payments in competitor jurisdictions induce a reduction of welfare payments in an observed jurisdiction. This is no surprise as the welfare reform of 1996 has been particularly designed to use the states in order to generate innovations in welfare policy (Feld and Schnellenbach 2004). Moreover Fredriksson and Millimet (2002) provide evidence on mimicking behaviour in environmental regulation. With an emphasis on policy innovation, Filer *et al.* (1988) as well as Berry and Berry (1990) find interjurisdictional interaction with respect to state lottery adoption, Carter and LaPlant (1997) with respect to health care policy innovation and Rincke (2005a, 2005b) with respect to innovations in charter school legislation.

All these studies have in common that they cope with classical fields of public economics. Education, health care, environmental issues and welfare are traditionally publicly provided during the last century. Seldom an analysis of the diffusion of legal rules is conducted. There are only a few exceptions. Caldeira (1985) studies the transmission of legal precedent and Canon and Baum (1981) the patterns of adoption of tort law innovations. Most interesting is the diffusion of corporate law across the US states. Romano (1985) and Carney (1997a, 1998) provide extensive analyses of the diffusion pattern of corporate law in the US. They disagree as to the question whether Delaware, as the state with the most liberal regulation of incorporation, has been the inventor or whether it has been a quick follower on successful innovations. However, the authors fully agree as to the fact that Delaware served as a role model for the other states. Carney (1997b) studies the role of interest groups in the adoption of corporate law. He finds that interest groups have a lower impact on corporate law in the US compared with European countries because of regulatory competition between the US states. All in all this evidence supports the hypothesis that regulatory competition induces policy innovation via the regional diffusion and internal determinants channels.

Whether interjurisdictional competition of this sort has a positive impact on economic *outcomes* is widely debated in the literature. This certainly holds with respect to fiscal competition (Feld *et al.* 2004 and Feld 2005a), but also with respect to regulatory competition. While historical studies by Bernholz and Vaubel (2004) and Vaubel (2005) provide evidence on the beneficial impact of regulatory competition, this outcome is much more contested in the case of corporate law. Heine (2003) provides the most extensive survey on this empirical evidence. Although he remains relatively cautious and abstains from drawing too optimistic conclusions, he tentatively supports the hypothesis that regulatory competition in US corporate law leads to beneficial outcomes. In particular, firms incorporated in Delaware have significantly higher firm values and rates of return than firms incorporated in other states. This evidence hints to a compensation of the lower shareholder protection in Delaware by higher rates of return and higher firm values finally benefiting shareholders. As the ECJ has currently paved the way for regulatory competition on corporate law in the EU, the US evidence has important implications (Salmon 2005b).

Regulatory competition and harmonization in Switzerland across time

Given the small amount of evidence on regulatory competition, a closer look at Switzerland is useful. As in international studies, the main Swiss evidence has been provided for tax mimicking (Feld and Reulier 2005). Moreover, there is extensive evidence as to the economic impact of tax competition (Feld 2005a). What is less known is that innovations in tax structure have spilled over from one canton to the other at least since the nineteenth century. In his study on Swiss taxation in the nineteenth century, Georg von Schanz (1890) shows how the idea of comprehensive income taxation, later called Schanz–Haig–Simons (SHS) tax systems, diffused from the canton of Basle to the other cantons. This process took longer than Schanz might have thought because it started at the beginning of the nineteenth century and came to an end only in the 1970s. The diffusion of that political innovation within Switzerland took longer than its adaptation by other countries around the world. Similar processes can be observed in today's Switzerland. For example, the latest corporate tax reform at the federal level, abolishing progressive corporate taxation, reveals vertical copycatting by using cantons as role models.

In addition there is evidence on the existence of mimicking behaviour in the field of administrative law. In the last decade a tremendous amount of reforms in the field of new public management (NPM) have taken place within the cantons. According to a study by Steiner (2000), 24 of the 26 Swiss cantons had collected experience with NPM programmes in 1998. He observes an interesting pattern of adoption of NPM. Cantons in which at least 35 per cent of the communities have implemented NPM concepts could be found only in the German-speaking cantons. As a reason for the introduction of NPM, 57 per cent of the communities pointed to a diffuse preference for change; 31.5 per cent feared that the community's ability to cope with policies would be reached without such reforms; and 30.5 per cent each either mentioned a financial crisis in their community or good experiences in other communities as reasons for the introduction of NPM. The survey study by Steiner thus points to the importance of mimicking behaviour as reasons for political innovation. Widmer and Rieder (2003) provide more formal evidence of such a kind of yardstick competition between the cantons. And according to Ladner and Steiner (2003) only a modest convergence of policy solutions in administrative procedures can be observed as a result from that yardstick competition. The variety of solutions dominates because communities adapt the good examples from other jurisdictions to their own needs and preferences. Neither in taxation nor in administrative law has the competition between the cantons and the local jurisdictions in Switzerland thus led to notable inefficiencies or a 'race to the bottom'. There appears to be a considerable extent of innovation potential that is induced by interjurisdictional competition.

Like in the field of taxation and government administration, the cantons have considerable regulatory competencies in several areas of commercial activities. Since the beginning of the new federal constitution in 1848, the completion of the Swiss internal market by abolishing or reducing trade barriers has been at centre stage of political discussions. The constitution of 1848 abolished the trade borders between the cantons and introduced a common currency (De Chambrier 2003: 16). The abolishment of cantonal tariffs was thus accomplished relatively early. However, the free movement of services has not yet been achieved so that a Common Market Law in 1995 and its recent amendment have become necessary. A closer look at the history of the regulation of commerce and professional activity does, however, give some hints as to the information externalities leading to copycatting procedures.

During the Middle Ages the economy of the area that comprises Switzerland today was organized according to a typical feudal system. In the urban areas the guilds had a strong influence on commerce and trade. The Helvetian constitutions that governed Switzerland during the Napoleonic time between 1797 and 1802 temporarily abolished the coercion exercised by the guilds' rule and regulation of commerce. In 1803 many of these regulations were however reintroduced, despite opposition by influential liberal movements in some cantons. For example, Thomas Bornhauser at that time called the regulation of commerce '*privileges that should be abolished*' (Kölz 1992: 331). In particular, regulations for restaurants and bars as well as butchers and millers persisted in many cantons. The group of restaurant owners was highly influential in politics and lobbied the government by arguing that either regulations should be upheld or the owners should be financially compensated by the cantons. The guilds' rule was equally difficult to abolish. It is remarkable how the ancient arguments to continue regulation resemble arguments brought forward today against deregulation. In the nineteenth century it was the immigration of craftsmen from Southern Germany that most opponents in the cantons feared. In the canton of St. Gallen, freedom of commerce was even discredited as the '*death penalty for craftsmen*' (Kölz 1992: 332). The conflict of interests between consumers and producers was widely recognized. On the one hand, restrictions only originating from security and police order were asked to be allowed, but none that were in the interests of the merchant. On the other hand, the fear of capitalist concentration was also raised.

The cantons newly created during the Napoleonic years, like the cantons of Thurgau or of St. Gallen, secured the freedom of commerce most extensively. In the former all citizens basically enjoyed freedom of commerce, labour and trade, only restricted by policing laws. St. Gallen also explicitly abolished all monopolies. Basel-Country in addition to the abolition of monopolies granted the freedom of commerce also to citizens of other cantons if these cantons did the same in reciprocal terms. Freedom of commerce was also widely protected in the cantons of Solothurn and Ticino. However, the canton of Aargau acknowledged it only basically, but pointed to the difficult trade-off between the liberal proposals of free commerce and the economic interests of local merchants.

More difficulties to realize the freedom of commerce existed in the former centres of the guilds, like the cantons of Zurich and Schaffhausen. In Zurich the regulation of commerce was only modified and adapted to the new time trend (Kölz 1992: 333) keeping the guilds' rule for a large part of commercial activities. Schaffhausen did not manage to abolish the cartels of craftsmen but cautiously liberalized the apprenticeship system. The formerly aristocratic and mostly agrarian canton of Bern introduced the freedom of commerce under the general restriction of social interest. The Catholic cantons of Lucerne and Fribourg did not even mention the freedom of trade and commerce. Industrial activities which developed heavily in the cantons of Zurich, Glarus and St. Gallen were not captured by these regulations. Until 1848, however, many restrictions existed with respect to inter-cantonal trade.

Most cantonal constitutions between the Helvetian period and the foundation of the Swiss federation in 1848 granted the free movement of labour also to citizens of other cantons on a reciprocity basis. The residence concordat of 1819 between the cantons of Zurich, Bern, Luzern, Glarus, Fribourg, Solothurn, Aargau, Thurgau, Ticino, Vaud, Neuchâtel, Geneva and Schaffhausen granted freedom of residence to their citizens under certain administrative conditions including the right of economic activity. The remaining cantons (Uri, Schwyz, Obwalden, Nidwalden, Zug, both Basel, both Appenzell, St. Gallen, Graubünden, Valais) did not join this inter-cantonal agreement in order to protect their Catholic religious identity and unity (Kölz 1992: 334). These cantons finally suffered economic losses since Protestant industrials and craftsmen chose their location in the other more liberal cantons.

While the liberal cantons had continued their policies of freedom of trade until 1848, the freedom of production of goods and services was not fully granted. The situation was even worse in the conservative cantons. As a consequence of the former feudal and guilds' system, commerce was thus still heavily restricted in 1848. The creation of the Swiss federation in 1848 constitutionally established several components of a common market like the abolition of trade borders (and border controls) between the cantons, the introduction of a common currency and of common measures. The federal level obtained the competency to regulate tariffs. But the ways and means of abolishing cantonal tariffs, the design of future federal tariffs and in particular the abolition of cantonal specific consumption taxes on alcoholic beverages were heavily disputed (Kölz 1992: 591). Several opposing interests clashed with each other: agrarian and industrialized cantons on alcohol taxes, or alpine transit cantons and the other cantons on tariffs. The arguments in these discussions were the same as in each programme of economic integration, for example in the EU: the distribution of revenue and the compensation for revenue losses or infant industry arguments to justify tariffs. In the end, however, tariffs became the most important revenue source of the federal level.

The way to establish the free movement of labour between the cantons was expectedly thorny. The fear of competition, potential additional welfare payments for immigrants, and confessional homogeneity were the most frequently heard arguments against the freedom of residence choice, particularly in the conservative cantons (Kölz 1992: 584). The right to restrict immigration of non-Swiss foreigners has remained assigned to the cantonal level. If a canton granted citizen rights to foreigners, they received residential rights in the other cantons only after a period of five years. However, foreign residents could invest in real estate in their place of residence before becoming Swiss citizen. Again, the conservative cantons strongly opposed this regulation because religion supposedly was in danger if citizens from other cantons, in particular Protestants, could reside and purchase real estate (Kölz 1992: 586).

While these were only first steps in the creation of the Swiss common market, the freedom of commerce and trade was explicitly introduced in the Swiss federal constitution in 1874. Art. 31 of the old federal constitution was introduced to abolish cantonal regulations that restricted the transition from a local crafts production to a modern industrialized economy with a Swiss-wide trade of products (De Chambrier 2003: 16). In principle each citizen should be able to start and conduct his own economic activity. Federal constitutional change was preceded by cantonal reforms. The cantonal constitution of Zurich of the year 1869 was dominated by a modern liberal economic doctrine including the free movement of goods, money, labour and organizational forms for economic activity (Kölz 2004: 77). At that time, the introduction of a constitutional article to regulate labour was very fiercely disputed. The final agreement on Art. 23 established the constitutional principle of a welfare state for the first time in Switzerland. It was to become the most important rival principle to the freedom of trade and commerce. The cantonal constitution of Thurgau regulated the freedom of commerce and trade in the same fashion as neighbouring Zurich. On the one hand, these freedoms were fully granted, on the other hand, social considerations were newly introduced (Kölz 2004: 185). In Glarus, St. Gallen, Appenzell, Uri and several other cantons, the liberal movements succeeded to include the full set of individual freedoms in the cantonal constitution only after 1874, even though a gradual liberalization took place before (Kölz 2004: 211).

There were, however, cantons where the guilds' rule persisted to a larger extent despite the regulation of the federal constitution of 1874. One example is the canton of Basel-City, where the abolition of the guilds' rule was proposed in the constitution of 1847 but finally rejected. Kölz (2004: 339) argues that the old established families of Basel-City wanted to assure the support by and loyalty of local craftsmen. The constitution of 1847 thus even forbade the inclusion of the freedom of commerce in cantonal statutes. While several liberal proposals were accepted in the constitutional revision of 1875, the freedom of commerce and trade was again rejected. The next revision of 1889 finally came up with the standard liberal canon of rules, but also established the most extended social policy model of all Swiss cantons.

The federal constitution of 1874 did not grant comprehensive rights to harmonize constitutional laws to the federal level. In the discussions about such an article on legal harmonization, an important argument against a unitary harmonized civil law relied on the well-known arguments from laboratory federalism (Kölz 2004: 612): Johann Jakob Blumer from Glarus argued that, in the absence of legal harmonization, there would be experimentation with these laws at the cantonal level such that the most successful laws could be adopted by the federal level in partial revision of federal law. Giving the cantons considerable competencies in deciding upon their own commercial law, it is no surprise that some cantons, like Basel-City, were more reluctant and introduced the freedom of commerce and trade relatively late in their constitutions, not without restricting free commerce additionally by specific cantonal statutes supposed to protect producer interests.

Although the freedom of commerce and trade was a part of the original concept of the Swiss common market in the nineteenth century, it was realized only with differing regulatory restrictions at the cantonal level. Moreover, the common market programme quickly lost attraction. As early as 1890, cantonal regulations that restricted free trade were allowed by the federal government. On the one hand, basic proposals of the welfare state were introduced and extended. On the other hand, different professions were able to lobby the cantonal governments successfully for protection against outside competition. Health, security and morale were frequently used as arguments for cantonal regulations finally accepted by the federal government. Moreover, labour regulations like maximum working hours and security at the working place provided arguments for restrictions of the freedom of commerce. Construction, traffic, restaurants and bars or the health sector, lawyers, science and other self-employment were subject to cantonal regulations (Kölz 2004: 814). During the First World War, the freedom of commerce and trade was further restricted, however at that time by the federal government.

Like other European countries, Switzerland was under pressure from corporatist models of the state between the First and Second World War. In particular, the constitutional initiative for a total revision of the Swiss constitution of 1935 underlines the importance of these movements. The initiative originated from national-socialist and fascist groups but found support also from other corporatist movements (Kölz 2004: 754). More importantly for our purposes, a discussion about a professional status-oriented constitutional order took place. Economic interest groups continuously gained importance as indicated by the influence of the farmers, commerce and citizen party of the time as well as the introduction of a formal consultation procedure for interest groups in federal legislation. According to some constitutional models discussed during that period, professional groups would have obtained far-ranging legislative competencies as public law corporations. The freedom of commerce and trade would have been abolished and replaced by a monopolistic position of the professional groups. Although the constitutional initiative was finally rejected by a clear margin of 72.3 per cent, it had considerable influence in economic terms (Kölz 2004: 761), finally resulting in a constitutional revision in 1947. On the one hand, labour market regulation at the Swiss federal level was affected leaving the possibility of a general clause of collective labour contracts. On the other hand, the federal level obtained additional instruments to restrict the freedom of commerce and trade, for example in order to preserve a healthy status of farmers, to protect important, endangered sectors of the economy, to regulate cartels, professional education and labour conditions or to declare agreements between professional groups generally binding. Finally, these movements affected Switzerland as a whole, leading to the regulation of professional activities and to protectionist measures also at the Swiss cantonal level. The Swiss cantons could hide in the shelter provided by federal restrictions on the freedom of commerce and trade. They used their new discretion to a considerable but also differing extent (as is usual in Switzerland). It is quite instructive that the conservative-Catholic cantons Fribourg, Valais, Obwalden and Appenzell i. Rh. were the only ones in which a majority of the citizens accepted the proposal for a total revision of the Swiss constitution in 1935, supposedly to obtain stronger competencies at the cantonal level (Kölz 2004: 761). With some probability, these competencies would have mainly been used to restrict commercial freedom.

After 1947 the pendulum only slowly moved back towards liberalization. It took the deregulation movement until the 1980s to gain considerable momentum. Many restrictions, for example on restaurants and bars, have remained in place at least since 1947. Additional restrictions have, however, been created in the course of the emergence of new professions. In 1983 the BIGA (1983) took stock of the regulatory restrictions on professional activity. Its results have recently been updated by De Chambrier (2003). The data for both years are presented in Table 6.1. On the one hand, regulatory activity has been reduced in the commercial and services sectors as well as in the legal profession. On the other hand, newly created professions have been regulated during this time period.

This mainly holds for the health sector. Moreover there are some notable exceptions to the deregulation trend in some professions. For example, notaries and disinfectors have faced additional regulations.

De Chambrier (2003) also provides a detailed account of the number of regulations at the cantonal level. She groups the regulations in two different baskets: examination requirements in the different regulated professions, and additional quality, health or security restrictions. Unfortunately the importance of the regulations for the cantonal economies cannot be assessed since the number of employees covered by these regulations is not provided on a cantonal basis.[2] However, the sheer number of regulations is already interesting (see the Appendix for the data on regulations). Figure 6.1 displays the average number of cantonal regulations for examination requirements obtained from four different sectors: health, commerce, services and the legal profession. In the health sector, as indicated by Table 6.1, such regulations might comprise the requirement to prove ability by examination certificates, for example, in psychology. Cantonal allowances must be obtained before opening a practice as a physician, but also as a chemist, sometimes even as a homeopath. In other cases, a certain profession is only regulated and thus created in some cantons but not in others. For example, emergency medical technicians are required to have a cantonal certificate in the German-speaking part of Switzerland but not in the French-speaking part. In the case of commercial activities, different professional requirements are formulated for architects and engineers. In the services sector, similar divergences across Switzerland can, for example, be found for restaurant owners, taxi drivers, several sports (rafting, canyoning, winter sports) and so on. Finally, the legal professions (lawyers, notaries) are subject to severe restrictions when offering their services across cantons. Thus, an interesting variety of these regulatory provisions results, which becomes obvious from Figure 6.1. With respect to the number of regulations on professional certificates, the canton of Geneva appears to be most heavily regulated. However, the small canton of Appenzell i. Rh. also belongs to that high regulation group. The canton of Zurich and the canton of Appenzell a. Rh. are the least heavily regulated. It is amazing that two cantons which formed a unity in history have such huge differences in the number of regulations.

In addition to the canton-specific professional certificates, there exist additional regulations that are supposed to enhance the quality of the products and services offered. These could, for example, be health provisions, as in the case of restaurant owners, but also take other forms. A common feature of these provisions is that the cantonal concession is only granted if these requirements are met. A look at Figure 6.2 reveals that there is again an interesting amount of variation across the cantons. On average, the cantons of Geneva and of Fribourg have the largest number of regulations in this field. It is again Zurich and the canton of Appenzell a. Rh. that have few regulations.

This brief history and present-day description of regulatory competition in Switzerland reveals the many forces that drive cantonal regulation. In a first step, the freedom of commerce and trade was basically granted by some more

Table 6.1 Development of the cantonal regulations of professions requiring state permissions in 1983 and 2002

Newly regulated professions	1983	2002	Wider distribution of cantonal regulations	1983	2002	Less regulated professions	1983	2002
Health sector								
Acupuncturist	0	7	Chemist	14	26	Medical practice assistant	24	1
Emergency med. technician	0	9	Homeopath	2	11	Dentists' practice assistant	25	2
Hearing device technician	0	4	Psychology	5	7	Veterinarian practice assistant	22	1
Nutrition advisor	0	19	Dental hygienist	6	14	Orthopaedist	10	8
Physiotherapist	0	2	Speech therapist	4	19	Manicurist	4	0
Psychotherapist	0	18	Optician	9	22	Masseur	23	17
Psychomotor specialist	0	3	Dental technician	16	22	Pedicurist	24	22
Optometrist	0	1	Baby care	2	4			
Osteopath	0	6						
Reflexologist	0	2						
Commercial sector								
Game warden	0	3	Disinfector	13	26	Hairdresser	3	1
						Aesthetician	10	4
						Plumber	*Unclear*	
						Chimney sweep	24	13
						Fisherman	20	7
						(Film) Projectionist	9	10
Services sector								
Canyoning guide	0	2	Security service	3	7	Real estate broker	10	3
Rafting guide	0	1				Tax accountant	4	1
Financial intermediaries (TI)	0	1				Trade of alcoholic beverages	15	10
						Private detective agencies	8	3
						Restaurants and hotels	26	20
						Taxi driver	*Unclear*	
						Used car dealer	26	3
Para-state and judicial activities								
			Notary	5	12	Director of private schools	20	3
						Legal avisor	5	1

Source: De Chambrier (2003: 78).

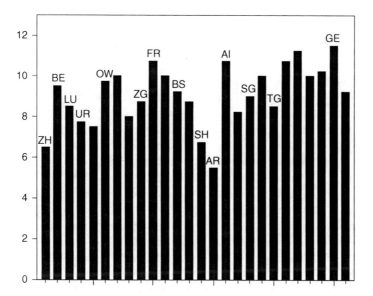

Figure 6.1 Average cantonal regulations for examination requirements in four different sectors in 2002.

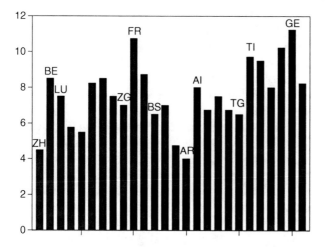

Figure 6.2 Average cantonal regulations for additional quality requirements in four different sectors in 2002.

liberal and progressive cantons, mainly the Protestant ones, before the Swiss federation was founded in 1848 on the basis of mutual recognition. This established a system of *regulatory competition* between the cantons that harmed those cantons which did not follow a liberalization strategy, that is the conservative Catholic cantons. It is interesting to note that the canton of Zurich, certainly one of the more progressive cantons, has a lower regulatory activity than, say, Fribourg. Most striking is the difference between both cantons of Appenzell of which the Protestant Appenzell a.Rh. has a lower number of regulations than the Catholic canton of Appenzell i.Rh. It thus seems as if the conjecture by Boockmann and Vaubel (2005: 6) holds that religion is an important reason for regulation and deregulation of the cantons. There are however also traditionalist cantons, like Schwyz, which have a relatively low number of regulations. It is thus not clear to what extent *internal determinants* played a role. In the early phase before the Swiss common market was created, regulatory competition obviously kept the cantonal ability to regulate in check. The driving force behind regulatory competition was the mobility between the cantons.

Extending the jurisdiction of the freedom of commerce in the two constitutional efforts in 1848 and 1874, only slowly succeeded in liberalizing the regulatory regimes at the cantonal level. Harmonization and centralization efforts appeared to have created the preconditions for a common market. However, providing the arenas and the lobbying incentives at the federal level quickly induced the groups seeking protection to demand exceptions from the freedom of commerce now at the federal level. The federal government subsequently allowed for these exceptions and thus reduced the possibilities for regulatory competition. The restrictions on the freedom of commerce were enhanced in the period between the two World Wars and finally gave special interest groups considerable power to obtain rents from protectionist measures. It is not clear to what extent this could be characterized as a period of raising rivals' costs (Boockmann and Vaubel 2005). It would however be a surprise if that strategy were unimportant in Switzerland. Sommer (1978) provides a history of the Swiss welfare state according to which the strategy of raising rivals' costs was apparently followed during the same time period in the field of social security.

The final phase after the Second World War is characterized by increasingly intensified efforts to deregulate the Swiss economy despite new regulations that emerged when new professions were created. This holds with respect to the 1980s, the discussions of which culminated in the Common Market Law of 1995.[3] Unhappy with the outcome of that reform, a revision of the Common Market Law is now planned. This relatively long period is characterized by a more beneficial impact of the federal government than in the earlier phases. The main goal of the federal government during the last 25 years has been to get rid of superfluous regulations at the cantonal level and to facilitate trade in services across the cantons. The activity of the federal government also teaches the lesson that regulatory competition does not necessarily lead to a race to the bottom. Moreover this phase could well be characterized by an important influence of internal determinants like, for example, religion or conservative values, a tradition of guild and craftsmanship or simply the power of cantonal interest groups. The historical evidence as well as the brief look at the number of regulations prevailing at the end of the 1990s and the beginning of the new century, however, do not provide any evidence as to the mimicking behaviour so prominent in most of the literature.

Explaining Swiss cantonal regulation: an econometric analysis

This section, therefore, tests for mimicking behaviour in regulatory activity in the Swiss cantons. As the dependent variable, the number of regulations in three of the four sectors covered by the study of De Chambrier (2003) is used.[4] Moreover, the average of the four sectors is used as an indicator of the total number of regulations. Following the tax mimicking literature, the respective indicators of the neighbours of a canton are introduced in order to test mimicking behaviour.[5] The idea is simply that the more regulations the neighbouring cantons have in a particular sector of the economy, the higher is the probability that a canton adopts regulations in that sector as well. It is widely discussed whether the spatial correlation between policies needs to be positive such that increases in regulatory activity of the neighbours increase regulatory activity of a canton under consideration. Brueckner (2003) argues that the relationship might well be negative indicating spillovers instead of strategic interactions due to regulatory competition. The regulation of the neighbouring cantons is calculated as an unweighted average of the number of regulations of the neighbours of a canton.

In addition to this relationship which is of most interest to our analysis, further variables are introduced into the model as controls. The index of direct democracy is a proxy for the extent of political competition in a canton. If there are differences between direct and representative democratic cantons, the suspicion is nourished that interest groups influence regulatory outcomes differently. If direct democracy has a negative impact, it is evidence for a stronger impact of interest groups in cantons with representative democracy. The index of direct democracy thus provides an internal determinants variable.[6] The index is obtained from Stutzer and Frey (2000). Because of the argument by Boockmann and Vaubel (2005), the share of the Catholic population of the total population is included in the model in order to measure religious preferences. This variable could be hypothesized to have a positive impact. Finally, income per capita, population and population density are standard controls in political economy models and are also considered.

The information on regulatory activities of the cantons is available for the end of the 1990s and beginning of the new century and obtained from the study by De Chambrier (2003). She is not totally transparent as to the exact date of measurement though. As this is only cross-section data, we use lagged values of the control variables in order to have a certain lead of regulations to the internal political determinants and economic variables. Regulations are notoriously difficult to change, which renders such a procedure sensible. The data on the index of direct democracy, income per capita, population size and population density are thus from the year 1998. The share of the Catholic population is for the year 1990, because it has been the most recent point in time when a comprehensive survey of the Swiss population was conducted. The cross-section model is estimated first by OLS and second by IV. The test strategy is to start with a simple bivariate regression to test for a basic neighbourhood relationship. In the next

Table 6.2 Regressions of the number of total regulations on neighbours' regulations and controls, cross-section of 26 Swiss cantons

Variable	Total number of examination requirements	Total number of examination requirements	Total number of examination requirements	Total number of additional quality requirements	Total number of additional quality requirements	Total number of additional quality requirements
Neighbours' regulations	0.623**	0.345	0.336	0.900***	0.597**	0.613**
	(2.28)	(1.17)	(1.04)	(4.07)	(2.61)	(2.49)
Index of direct democracy	—	-0.441*	-0.476*	—	-0.595**	-0.709**
		(1.85)	(1.73)		(2.48)	(2.65)
Share of Catholic population	—	0.017	0.016	—	0.015	0.008
		(1.53)	(1.10)		(1.40)	(0.61)
Income per capita	—	—	-0.367	—	—	1.840
			(0.09)			(0.46)
Population	—	—	-0.004	—	—	-0.014
			(0.31)			(1.19)
Population density	—	—	0.008	—	—	-0.016
			(0.23)			(0.45)
Constant	3.513	6.910**	7.213	0.822	4.708*	5.462
	(1.43)	(2.08)	(1.65)	(0.49)	(1.93)	(1.56)
R^2	0.179	0.345	0.355	0.409	0.564	0.597
SER	1.388	1.291	1.382	1.453	1.303	1.348
Observations	26	26	26	26	26	26
Jarque-Bera	4.478	0.666	0.598	0.660	1.399	0.866

Note
t-values are given in parentheses. ***, ** and * indicate significance at 1%, 5% and 10% levels, respectively. The Jarque-Bera test statistic is a test on the null hypothesis of normality of the residuals.

step, the internal political determinants are included. The model is finally completed by the inclusion of the economic variables. This is done first for the index of total regulation. Then, regulations of the commercial sector, the services sector and the legal profession are analysed separately. The analyses of the health sector revealed no explanatory power of the model whatsoever, so this was dropped.

The results for the average number of total regulations are provided in Table 6.2. The variation of the number of cantonal regulations of professional degrees is fairly well explained by the models ranging from 18 per cent in the bivariate model to 36 per cent in the complete model. The figures are between 41 and 60 per cent in the case of additional quality requirements. In none of the equations can the hypothesis of normality of the residuals be rejected. While it is possible to establish a statistically significant mimicking behaviour in both types of regulations in the simple bivariate regressions, the impact loses its significance if additional controls are included in the case of the examination requirements. There is, however, still a statistically significant positive impact of the neighbours regulatory activity on the regulations in a particular canton establishing a mimicking behaviour that is fully in line with what is found in most of the tax literature. The estimated coefficients are of reasonable size as their values are always between 0 and 1. In addition to neighbours' regulations, only the index of direct democracy has a statistically significant effect on regulatory activity. In both types of regulations, examination requirements as well as additional quality standards, cantons with more direct democracy have a statistically significant lower number of regulations. The effect is, however, only marginally significant in the case of examination requirements. These results indicate that interest groups are less successful in obtaining additional regulations in direct democracy.

The general story remains more or less like that when the different components of this index of regulation are analysed. With respect to the regulation of commercial activities (Table 6.3), the influence of neighbours is less robust, while direct democracy is very robustly affecting regulatory activity. Regulation of the services sector (Table 6.4) is more heavily and robustly influenced by mimicking behaviour, while direct democracy has a robust negative influence only on the number of quality standards. The unreasonable size of the coefficient of mimicking behaviour in the bivariate regressions is quickly corrected as soon as additional controls are included in the model such that it should not be a matter of concern. In addition income per capita is significant for quality standards in the services sector.

Finally, neighbours' regulations are significantly negatively associated with quality standards in the case of regulation of the legal profession leaving room for speculation of what is actually driving this type of spatial correlation (Table 6.5). Following Brueckner's (2003) arguments this result might simply reflect spillovers of that particular kind of regulation from the neighbours. However, the low variation of the number of regulations of legal professions (Appendix) demands a very cautious interpretation. Direct democracy does not influence the

Table 6.3 Regressions of the number of regulations in commerce on neighbours' regulations and controls, cross-section of 26 Swiss cantons

Variable	Examination requirements in commerce	Examination requirements in commerce	Examination requirements in commerce	Additional quality requirements in commerce	Additional quality requirements in commerce	Additional quality requirements in commerce
Neighbours' regulations	0.664*	0.357	0.405	0.674***	0.310	0.357
	(2.07)	(1.19)	(1.25)	(3.24)	(1.59)	(1.70)
Index of direct democracy	–	−0.659**	−0.682**	–	−0.707***	−0.742**
		(2.80)	(2.57)		(3.80)	(3.58)
Share of Catholic population	–	0.017	0.017	–	0.004	0.005
		(1.44)	(1.18)		(0.46)	(0.45)
Income per capita	–	–	−1.179	–	–	2.178
			(0.28)			(0.71)
Population	–	–	−0.005	–	–	−0.054
			(0.37)			(0.63)
Population density	–	–	0.029	–	–	0.004
			(0.77)			(0.13)
Constant	1.596	4.630**	4.320	0.547	3.997***	3.060
	(1.22)	(2.37)	(1.48)	(1.14)	(3.65)	(1.62)
R^2	0.151	0.416	0.442	0.304	0.580	0.611
SER	1.580	1.369	1.440	1.259	1.022	1.057
Observations	26	26	26	26	26	26
Jarque-Bera	1.509	0.142	0.620	9.247***	0.020	0.217

Note

t-values are given in parentheses. ***, ** and * indicate significance at 1%, 5% and 10% levels, respectively. The Jarque-Bera test statistic is a test on the null hypothesis of normality of the residuals.

Table 6.4 Regressions of the number of regulations in the services sector on neighbours' regulations and controls, cross-section of 26 Swiss cantons

Variable	Examination requirements in services	Examination requirements in services	Examination requirements in services	Additional quality requirements in services	Additional quality requirements in services	Additional quality requirements in services
Neighbours' regulations	1.068*** (4.70)	0.666** (2.20)	0.636* (1.95)	1.247*** (7.13)	0.835*** (4.19)	0.640*** (1.70)
Index of direct democracy	—	-0.646* (1.88)	-0.582 (1.46)	—	-0.982*** (3.16)	-1.295*** (4.17)
Share of Catholic population	—	0.009 (0.70)	0.009 (0.47)	—	0.007 (0.53)	-0.013 (0.45)
Income per capita	—	—	-5.083 (1.08)	—	—	-8.361** (2.16)
Population	—	—	0.008 (0.58)	—	—	-0.017 (1.48)
Population density	—	—	0.013 (0.31)	—	—	0.009 (0.26)
Constant	-1.239 (0.34)	3.020 (1.40)	4.632 (1.29)	-0.992 (1.18)	4.558** (2.20)	11.857*** (3.83)
R^2	0.479	0.556	0.594	0.679	0.780	0.851
SER	1.627	1.569	1.614	1.717	1.484	1.316
Observations	26	26	26	26	26	26
Jarque-Bera	0.583	0.091	0.248	3.629	0.830	1.065

Note
t-values are given in parentheses. ***, ** and * indicate significance at 1%, 5% and 10% levels, respectively. The Jarque-Bera test statistic is a test on the null hypothesis of normality of the residuals.

Table 6.5 Regressions of the number of regulations on legal professions on neighbours' regulations and controls, cross-section of 26 Swiss cantons

Variable	Examination requirements in legal professions	Examination requirements in legal professions	Examination requirements in legal professions	Additional quality requirements in legal professions	Additional quality requirements in legal professions	Additional quality requirements in legal professions
Neighbours' regulations	−0.031	−0.100	−0.257	−0.798*	−0.859*	−0.932**
	(0.05)	(0.17)	(0.40)	(1.79)	(1.84)	(2.17)
Index of direct democracy	—	−0.070	−0.079	—	−0.191	−0.214
		(0.57)	(0.40)		(0.91)	(1.07)
Share of Catholic population	—	0.003	−0.000	—	0.008	0.009
		(0.44)	(0.02)		(0.71)	(0.81)
Income per capita	—	—	−4.463	—	—	9.964***
			(0.19)			(3.03)
Population	—	—	−0.001	—	—	0.001
			(0.17)			(0.05)
Population density	—	—	−0.012	—	—	−0.088***
			(0.55)			(2.93)
Constant	8.407*	9.100*	11.169*	7.854***	8.459***	6.767***
	(1.86)	(1.91)	(1.96)	(4.027)	(3.96)	(2.57)
R^2	0.000	0.023	0.064	0.118	0.169	0.611
SER	0.747	0.771	0.812	1.302	1.321	1.057
Observations	26	26	26	26	26	26
Jarque–Bera	0.656	0.714	1.448	1.506	6.507**	0.217

Note

t-values are given in parentheses. ***, ** and * indicate significance at 1%, 5% and 10% levels, respectively. The Jarque–Bera test statistic is a test on the null hypothesis of normality of the residuals.

regulation of the legal profession while income per capita and population density have significant influences on quality standards. The drawback of the analysis is straightforward. First, only the number of regulations is explained by the average number of neighbours' regulations and controls. There is no information as to the importance of the single regulatory acts. It might simply be that one canton obtains a certain amount of regulatory restriction by a lower number of regulations. This also depends on the coverage of these regulations, which could not be considered for this analysis. Second, data are only available for one cross-section restricting the number of variables that could be used because of low degrees of freedom. Still, the results might be sufficiently interesting such that a flavour of mimicking in the field of regulation of commercial activity comes up.

From an econometric point of view, the most serious shortcoming might be the endogeneity of the average number of neighbours' regulations on the right-hand side and the number of regulations on the left-hand side of the estimated equation. As is often the case in cross-section analyses, convincing instruments are lacking. The traditionally used IV procedure in spatial public finance empirics follows Kelejian and Robinson (1993) and Kelejian and Prucha (1998) using neighbours' exogenous variables as instruments. As the control variables in Tables 6.2 to 6.5 do not have any clear-cut significant impact on the number of regulations, they must be dismissed as potential instruments. Nevertheless, an attempt to use the IV method is made in this chapter. A dummy variable taking on the value of 1 if a canton belongs to the German-speaking part of Switzerland (zero otherwise) is used as the instrument.

The language classification of the Swiss cantons is peculiar because a common prejudice has it that the French- and Italian-speaking cantons are more inclined to search for public rather than private solutions than are the German cantons. The existing studies in cantonal public finance, as surveyed in Feld and Kirchgässner (2006), however, do not lend consistent support to this prejudice. As the inclusion of the dummy variable for German-speaking cantons in the regressions presented in Tables 6.2 to 6.5 reveals, this variable does not have a significant impact on the number of regulations, and the overall pattern is not affected by this procedure. However, the dummy for German-speaking cantons is significantly negatively correlated with the number of neighbours' regulations.[7] The correlation might simply reflect the construction of this variable because German-speaking cantons individually cover a smaller area on average and therefore have more neighbours. It does thus not appear to be a convincing instrument even though the standard tests do not exclude it.

Nevertheless the results as presented in Table 6.6 indicate an interesting pattern.[8] In general mimicking behaviour is not fully robust to the use of this imperfect instrument. In the case of the total number of examination requirements and in particular of additional quality requirements, neighbours' regulations fall short of conventional significance levels. In the second case, it comes close to marginal significance. A similar assessment holds for both indicators of commerce regulation. In the case of services regulation, however, mimicking

Table 6.6 TSLS-regressions of the number of total regulations on neighbours' regulations and controls, cross-section of 26 Swiss cantons

Variable	Total number of examination requirements	Total number of additional quality requirements	Examination requirements in commerce	Additional quality requirements in commerce	Examination requirements in services	Additional quality requirements in services
Neighbours' regulations	0.834	0.709	1.102	0.616	1.255*	0.782**
	(1.36)	(1.60)	(1.56)	(1.54)	(1.90)	(2.83)
Index of direct democracy	−0.275	−0.660*	−0.513	−0.630**	−0.052	−1.140***
	(0.77)	(2.01)	(1.55)	(2.43)	(0.08)	(2.98)
Share of Catholic population	0.016	0.009	0.018	0.003	0.009	−0.012
	(1.10)	(0.62)	(1.09)	(0.30)	(0.51)	(0.85)
Income per capita	0.011	0.022	−0.005	0.020	−0.037	−0.078*
	(0.25)	(0.52)	(0.11)	(0.62)	(0.70)	(1.96)
Population	−0.004	−0.014	−0.009	−0.007	0.015	−0.015
	(0.28)	(1.19)	(0.59)	(0.69)	(0.88)	(1.30)
Population density	0.001	−0.016	0.033	0.011	0.012	0.011
	(0.00)	(0.47)	(0.79)	(0.37)	(0.26)	(0.32)
Constant	1.403	4.391	0.503	2.059	−0.091	10.173**
	(0.19)	(0.81)	(0.11)	(0.88)	(0.02)	(2.59)
R^2	0.274	0.594	0.305	0.580	0.517	0.846
SER	1.466	1.353	1.607	1.099	1.760	1.335
Observations	26	26	26	26	26	26
Jarque–Bera	0.945	0.753	2.894	1.778	0.520	0.594

Note

t-values are given in parentheses. ***, ** and * indicate significance at 1%, 5% and 10% levels, respectively. The Jarque-Bera test statistic is a test on the null hypothesis of normality of the residuals.

behaviour is robust to the use of the IV method. There is only one grain of salt, that is the estimated coefficient of neighbours' examination requirements in services is larger than zero, which is not plausible for reaction functions. The significant negative impact of direct democracy remains robust in all three cases of additional quality requirements. Overall, the results are remarkably robust given that the instrument used is less than perfect to say the least.

Concluding remarks

In this chapter regulatory competition at the Swiss cantonal level is analysed in order to gain some insights as to how decentralized competencies shape regulation. While the dominating theoretical literature in economics as well as the normative literature in law mainly emphasize the dangers of regulatory competition, in particular a potential race to the bottom, political economists point to the beneficial impact of regulatory competition. From the point of view most strongly pursued in this chapter, the dynamic nature of regulatory competition provides its most important advantage. Successful regulations are imitated and adapted by other jurisdictions so that a variety of different policy solutions is found.

The historical study of cantonal regulation in Switzerland reveals a certain ambivalence in at least two different forms. First, some cantons have obviously been reluctant in the past to adopt the Swiss common market and drop the regulations they formerly imposed, mostly in order to protect particular commercial activities. However, the early beginning of regulatory competition between the cantons in the nineteenth century with an imposition of the origin principle undermined the local potential to protect special interests. The singular argument that decentralization favours a benevolent economic outcome is obviously too crude. There is a potential for protectionism in a decentralized polity, but with the origin principle and sufficient mobility it unleashes the positive forces of regulatory competition. Second, the influence of a central authority, in the Swiss case the federal government, need not necessarily be positive. While the first impact in the nineteenth century consisted of an attempt to complete the Swiss common market, the government later provided opportunities for the conservative, more heavily regulated cantons to raise their rivals' costs. This becomes most obvious during the period between the two World Wars. In recent times, the federal government is again a driving force for deregulation of the cantonal economies and thus of total Switzerland.

As the data available are only indicative, cautious conclusions must be drawn with respect to the econometric evidence in this chapter. Mimicking behaviour also appears to be important in cantonal regulation while direct democracy restricts the ability of cantons to introduce additional regulations. The first result points to the potentially important effect that yardstick competition might have on political innovation. Whether this political innovation actually results has not been analysed in this chapter, nor is it possible to draw any conclusions as to the benevolence of mimicking behaviour. But the force of information externalities

Appendix Table 6.A1 Regulation in Swiss cantons 2002

Canton	Total number of examination requirements	Total number of additional quality requirements	Examination requirements in commerce	Additional quality requirements in commerce	Examination requirements in services	Additional quality requirements in services	Examination requirements in legal professions	Additional quality requirements in legal professions
ZH[c]	6.50	4.50	3.00	1.00	1.00	1.00	7.00	4.00
BE	9.50	8.50	4.00	3.00	4.00	6.00	9.00	6.00
LU	8.50	7.50	6.00	4.00	2.00	4.00	8.00	4.00
UR	7.75	5.75	2.00	1.00	2.00	3.00	8.00	3.00
SZ	7.50	5.50	2.00	0.00	0.00	1.00	8.00	3.00
OW	9.75	8.25	4.00	2.00	2.00	4.00	9.00	4.00
NW	10.00	8.50	4.00	1.00	1.00	2.00	8.00	5.00
GL	8.00	7.50	2.00	2.00	0.00	1.00	9.00	8.00
ZG	8.75	7.00	5.00	2.00	0.00	1.00	8.00	7.00
FR	10.75	10.75	6.00	4.00	4.00	8.00	8.00	6.00
SO	10.00	8.75	4.00	1.00	1.00	4.00	8.00	4.00
BS	9.25	6.50	4.00	2.00	4.00	3.00	7.00	3.00
BL	8.75	7.00	3.00	1.00	2.00	4.00	8.00	4.00
SH	6.75	4.75	3.00	1.00	1.00	2.00	7.00	3.00
AR	5.50	4.00	2.00	0.00	1.00	2.00	8.00	3.00
AI	10.75	8.00	6.00	0.00	1.00	3.00	8.00	3.00
SG	8.25	6.75	2.00	0.00	2.00	4.00	9.00	5.00
GR	9.00	7.50	3.00	1.00	4.00	6.00	9.00	5.00
AG	10.00	6.75	6.00	1.00	2.00	3.00	8.00	4.00
TG	8.50	6.50	3.00	1.00	2.00	3.00	9.00	3.00
TI	10.75	9.75	7.00	5.00	8.00	10.00	8.00	4.00
VD	11.25	9.50	5.00	3.00	6.00	7.00	8.00	3.00
VS	10.00	8.00	5.00	2.00	8.00	8.00	8.00	5.00
NE	10.25	10.25	7.00	3.00	3.00	12.00	7.00	4.00
GE	11.50	11.25	7.00	5.00	3.00	8.00	10.00	6.00
JU	9.25	8.25	5.00	3.00	5.00	7.00	8.00	5.00
Mean	9.11	7.59	4.23	1.88	2.65	4.50	8.15	4.38
Median	9.25	7.50	4.00	1.50	2.00	4.00	8.00	4.00
Standard deviation	1.50	1.85	1.68	1.48	2.21	2.97	0.73	1.36
Minimum	5.50	4.00	2.00	0.00	0.00	1.00	7.00	3.00
Maximum	11.50	11.25	7.00	5.00	8.00	12.00	10.00	8.00

Source: Own calculations from A. De Chambrier (2003).

is present in Switzerland. This might either lead to more or to less regulation depending on which canton sets the trend. Thus, internal determinants are crucial for the overall performance of such a highly decentralized system. This is illustrated by the effect of direct democracy, which is in line with former analyses of the impact of direct democracy on public finances.

Finally, there is no discussion of whether cantonal regulatory competition has actually induced a better or worse economic performance of the cantons and of the country as a whole. Of course, there is no clear-cut systematic evidence on that. However, a too strong emphasis of the usefulness of regulatory competition during particular episodes may be beside the point. It is the possibility of dynamically adapting to new challenges, the ability to experiment in a decentralized fashion that is making Swiss federalism so peculiar. It looks as if this conjecture also holds in the case of regulatory activity.

Notes

1 The international evidence on the effects of globalization on welfare states points in the same direction. See for example Rodrik (1998), Vaubel (2000) and the survey by Schulze and Ursprung (1999).
2 Moreover, the data are not differentiated as to whether the regulations are going up or going down. Also, the explanatory variables for a more detailed assessment across industries and professions are not available such that the regulation data could not be differentiated any further.
3 Although I have not found a study supporting this argument directly, it could well be argued that this development was influenced by the creation of a Common Market in the EU.
4 As can be easily inferred from the Appendix, the variation in the number of regulations of the legal professions is so low that the lack of reasonable results should not surprise. The variation of the number of regulations in the health sector is similarly disappointing so that it is left out from the analysis from the start. Regulation of the legal profession is reported only for illustrative purposes.
5 It could be questioned whether the neighbourhood concept is adequate in order to test mimicking behaviour. This question has been discussed in the literature at least since the paper by Case *et al.* (1993), but has not been resolved yet. The current state of the literature appears as opining that each concept chosen is somewhat arbitrary. Given the restricted data set used in this paper, the simplest concept appeared to be the most reasonable one.
6 For an economic analysis of the impact of direct democracy on policy outcomes, providing a more detailed discussion as to the reasons why (economic) policy outcomes in direct and representative democracy might differ, see the recent survey by Feld and Kirchgässner (2006).
7 The latter correlation is almost exclusively on the one per cent significance level. Both sets of estimation results are available from the author upon request.
8 Due to insufficient variation the results for the regulation of the legal profession and of health services are not reported.

References

Akerlof, G.A. (1970) 'The Market for Lemons: Quality, Uncertainty and the Market Mechanism', *Quarterly Journal of Economics*, 84, 488–500.

Allers, M.A. and Elhorst, J.P. (2005) 'Tax Mimicking and Yardstick Competition Among Local Governments in the Netherlands', *International Tax and Public Finance*, 12, 493–513.

Apolte, Th. (1999) *Die ökonomische Konstitution eines föderalen Systems: Dezentrale Wirtschaftspolitik zwischen Kooperation und institutionellem Wettbewerb*, Tübingen: Mohr Siebeck.

Ashworth, J., Geys, B. and Heyndels, B. (2003) 'Political Fragmentation and Tax Innovations: The Case of Environmental Taxes in Flemish Municipalities', Vrije Universiteit Brussel, mimeo.

Bardhan, P. (2002) 'Decentralization of Governance and Development', *Journal of Economic Perspectives*, 16(4), 185–205.

Bardhan, P. and Mookherjee, D. (2000) 'Capture and Governance at Local and National Levels', *American Economic Review, Papers and Proceedings*, 90, 135–9.

Bebchuk, L.A. (1992) 'Federalism and the Corporation: The Desirable Limits on State Competition in Corporate Law', *Harvard Law Review*, 105, 1435–510.

Bernholz, P. and Faber, M. (1986) 'Überlegungen zu einer normativen ökonomischen Theorie der Rechtsvereinheitlichung', *Rabels Zeitschrift für ausländisches und internationales Privatrecht*, 50, 35–60.

Bernholz, P. and Vaubel, R. (eds) (2004) *Political Competition, Innovation and Growth in the History of Asian Civilisations*, Cheltenham: Edward Elgar.

Berry, F.S. (1994) 'Sizing Up State Policy Innovation Research', *Policy Studies Journal*, 22, 442–56.

Berry, F.S. and Berry, W.D. (1990) 'State Lottery Adoptions as Policy Innovations: An Event History Analysis', *American Political Science Review*, 84, 395–415.

—— (1991) 'Specifying a Model of State Policy Innovations', *American Political Science Review*, 85, 573–9.

—— (1992) 'Tax Innovation in the States: Capitalizing on Political Opportunity', *American Journal of Political Science*, 36, 715–42.

Besley, T. and Case, A.C. (1995) 'Incumbent Behaviour, Vote-Seeking, Tax-Setting and Yardstick Competition', *American Economic Review*, 84, 394–414.

BIGA (1983) Übersicht über bewilligungspflichtige Berufe und Gewerbe, Ausgabe Januar 1983, Ref. 2/163.01.

Boockmann, B. and Vaubel, R. (2005) 'The Theory of Raising Rivals' Costs and Evidence from the International Labor Organization', University of Mannheim, mimeo.

Bordignon, M., Cerniglia, F. and Revelli, F. (2003) 'In Search of Yardstick Competition: A Spatial Analysis of Italian Municipality Property Tax Setting', *Journal of Urban Economics*, 54, 199–217.

Borner, S. and Bodmer, F. (2004) *Wohlstand ohne Wachstum: Eine Schweizer Illusion*, Füssli, Zürich: Orell.

Bratton, W.W. and McCahery, J.A. (1997) 'The New Economics of Jurisdictional Competition: Devolutionary Federalism in a Second-Best World', *The Georgetown Law Journal*, 86, 201–78.

Brennan, G. and Buchanan, J.M. (1980) *The Power to Tax: Analytical Foundations of a Fiscal Constitution*, Cambridge: Cambridge University Press.

Breton, A. (1996) *Competitive Governments: An Economic Theory of Politics and Public Finance*, Cambridge: Cambridge University Press.

—— (2000) 'Federalism and Decentralization: Ownership Rights and the Superiority of Federalism', *Publius: The Journal of Federalism*, 30, 1–16.

Brett, C. and Pinske, J. (2000) 'The Determinants of Municipal Tax Rates in British Columbia', *Canadian Journal of Economics*, 33, 695–714.

Brueckner, J.K. (2000) 'Fiscal Decentralization in Developing Countries: The Effects of Local Corruption and Tax Evasion', *Annals of Economics and Finance*, 1, 1–18.

—— (2003), 'Strategic Interaction among Governments: An Overview of Empirical Studies', *International Regional Science Review*, 26, 175–88.

Brueckner, J.K. and Saavedra, L.A. (2001) 'Do Local Governments Engage in Strategic Property Tax Competition?' *National Tax Journal*, 54, 203–29.

Buchanan, J.M. (2000) 'The Soul of Classical Liberalism', *Aussenwirtschaft*, 55, 7–17.

Bundesrat (2004) Botschaft über die Änderung des Binnenmarktes vom 24. November 2004, BBl 2004–2321, 465–504.

Büttner, T. (1999) 'Determinants of Tax Rates in Local Capital Income Taxation: A Theoretical Model and Evidence from Germany', *Finanzarchiv N.F.*, 56, 363–88.

—— (2001) 'Local Business Taxation and Competition for Capital: The Choice of the Tax Rate', *Regional Science and Urban Economics*, 31, 215–45.

Caldeira, G.A. (1985) 'The Transmission of Legal Precedent', *American Political Science Review*, 79, 178–94.

Canon, B.C. and Baum, L. (1981) 'Patterns of Adoption of Tort Law Innovations: An Application of Diffusion Theory to Judicial Doctrines', *American Political Science Review*, 75, 975–87.

Carney, W.J. (1997a) 'Explaining the Shape of Corporate Law: The Role of Competition', *Managerial and Decision Economics*, 18, 611–26.

—— (1997b) 'The Political Economy of Competition for Corporate Charters', *Journal of Legal Studies*, 26, 303–29.

—— (1998) 'The Production of Corporate Law', *Southern California Law Review*, 71, 715–80.

Carter, L.E. and LaPlant, J.T. (1997) 'Diffusion of Health Care Policy Innovation in the United States', *State and Local Government Review*, 29, 17–26.

Case, A.C. (1993) 'Interstate Tax Competition after TRA86', *Journal of Policy Analysis and Management*, 12, 136–48.

Case, A.C., Rosen, H.S. and Hines Jr, J.R. (1993) 'Budget Spillovers and Fiscal Policy Interdependence: Evidence from the States', *Journal of Public Economics*, 52, 285–307.

Clark, J. (2000) 'Policy Attributes and State Policy Innovation', *Southeastern Political Review*, 28, 3–25.

De Chambrier, A. (2003) *Die Verwirklichung des Binnenmarktes bei reglementierten Berufen*, Grundlagenbericht zur Revision des BGBM (Bundesgesetz über den Binnenmarkt), Bern: seco – State Secretariat for Economic Affairs.

Desveaux, J.A., Lindquist, E.A. and Toner, G. (1994) 'Organizing for Policy Innovation in Public Bureaucracy: AIDS, Energy and Environmental Policy in Canada', *Canadian Journal of Political Science*, 27, 493–528.

Eyestone, R. (1977) 'Confusion, Diffusion, and Innovation', *American Political Science Review*, 71, 441–7.

Feld, L.P. (1997) 'Exit, Voice and Income Taxes: The Loyalty of Voters', *European Journal of Political Economy*, 13, 455–78.

—— (2000a) *Steuerwettbewerb und seine Auswirkungen auf Allokation und Distribution: Ein Überblick und eine empirische Analyse für die Schweiz*, Tübingen: Mohr Siebeck.

—— (2000b) 'Tax Competition and Income Redistribution: An Empirical Analysis for Switzerland', *Public Choice*, 105, 125–64.

—— (2005a) 'Fiscal Equivalence and the Increasing Dispersion/Divergence of Public Goods Claims – Do We Need a New Interpretation?', in G. Färber and N. Otter (eds) *Spatial Aspects of Federative Systems*, Speyer: Deutsches Forschungs-institut für öffentliche Verwaltung, pp. 147–80.

—— (2005b) 'On Tax Competition: The (Un-)Expected Advantages of Decentralized Fiscal Autonomy', in Friedrich A. von Hayek Institut (ed.) *Austrian Economics Today II: Reforms for a Competitive Economy*, The International Library of Austrian Economics Vol. 10, Hayek Institut, Wien, pp. 89–126.

Feld, L.P. and Kirchgässner, G. (2001) 'Income Tax Competition at the State and Local Level in Switzerland', *Regional Science and Urban Economics*, 31, 181–213.

—— (2003) 'The Impact of Corporate and Personal Income Taxes on the Location of Firms and on Employment: Some Panel Evidence for the Swiss Cantons', *Journal of Public Economics*, 87, 129–55.

—— (2006) 'Fiscal Policy and Direct Democracy: Institutional Design Determines Outcomes', in A.F. Ott and R.J. Cebula (eds) *The Elgar Companion to Public Economics: Empirical Public Economics*, Cheltenham: Edward Elgar, pp. 215–41.

Feld, L.P. and Reulier, E. (2005) 'Strategic Tax Competition in Switzerland: Evidence from a Panel of the Swiss Cantons', University of Heidelberg, mimeo.

Feld, L.P. and Schnellenbach, J. (2004) 'Begünstigt fiskalischer Wettbewerb die Politikinnovation und -diffusion? Theoretische Anmerkungen und erste Befunde aus Fallstudien', in C.A. Schaltegger and S. Schaltegger (eds) *Perspektiven der Schweizer Wirtschaftspolitik*, vdf, Zürich, pp. 259–77.

Feld, L.P., Fischer, J. and Kirchgässner, G. (2003a) 'The Effect of Direct Democracy on Income Redistribution: Evidence for Switzerland', University of Heidelberg, mimeo.

Feld, L.P., Josselin, J.-M. and Rocaboy, Y. (2003b) 'Tax Mimicking Among Regional Jurisdictions', in A. Marciano and J.-M. Josselin (eds) *From Economic to Legal Competition: New Perspectives on Law and Institutions in Europe*, Cheltenham: Edward Elgar, pp. 105–19.

Feld, L.P., Kirchgässner, G. and Schaltegger, Ch.A. (2003c) 'Decentralized Taxation and the Size of Government: Evidence from Swiss State and Local Governments', CESifo Working Paper, No. 1087.

—— (2004) 'Fiscal Federalism and Economic Performance: Evidence from Swiss Cantons', University of Heidelberg, mimeo.

Figlio, D.N., Kolpin, V.W. and Reid, W.E. (1999) 'Do States Play Welfare Games?' *Journal of Urban Economics*, 46, 437–54.

Filer, J. E., Moak, D.L. and Uze, B. (1988) 'Why Some States Adopt Lotteries and Others Don't', *Public Finance Quarterly*, 16, 259–83.

Filippov, M., Ordeshook, P.C. and Shvetsova, O. (2004) *Designing Federalism: A Theory of Self-Sustainable Federal Institutions*, Cambridge: Cambridge University Press.

Fisman, R. and Gatti, R. (2002) 'Decentralization and Corruption: Evidence across Countries', *Journal of Public Economics*, 83, 325–45.

Fredriksson, P.G. and Millimet, D.L. (2002) 'Strategic Interaction and the Determination of Environmental Policy across U.S. States', *Journal of Urban Economics*, 51, 101–22.

Gatsios, K. and Holmes, P. (1998) 'Regulatory Competition', in P. Newman (ed.) *The New Palgrave Dictionary of Economics and the Law, Vol. 3*, London: Palgrave, pp. 271–5.

Glick, H.R. (1994) 'The Impact of Permissive Judicial Policies: The U.S. Supreme Court and the Right to Die', *Political Research Quarterly*, 47, 207–22.

Gray, V. (1973) 'Innovation in the States: A Diffusion Study', *American Political Science Review*, 67, 1174–85.

Hauser, H. and Hösli, M. (1991) 'Harmonization of Regulatory Competition in the EC (and the EEA)?' *Aussenwirtschaft*, 46, 497–512.

Hayashi, M. and Boadway, R. (2000) 'An Empirical Analysis of Intergovernmental Tax Interaction: The Case of Business Income Taxes in Canada', *Canadian Journal of Economics*, 34, 481–503.

Hayek, F.A. v. (1939) 'The Economic Conditions of Interstate Federalism', reprinted in F.A. v. Hayek, *Individualism and the Economic Order*, Ch. XII., Chicago 1948, pp. 255–72.

Heine, K. (2003) *Regulierungswettbewerb im Gesellschaftsrecht: Zur Funktionsfähigkeit eines Wettbewerbs der Rechtsordnungen im europäischen Gesellschaftsrecht*, Berlin: Duncker & Humblot.

Heine, K. and Kerber, W. (2002) 'European Corporate Laws, Regulatory Competition and Path Dependence', *European Journal of Law and Economics*, 13, 47–71.

Heyndels, B. and Vuchelen, J. (1998) 'Tax Mimicking among Belgian Municipalities', *National Tax Journal*, 51, 89–101.

Hirschman, A.O. (1970) *Exit, Voice and Loyalty: Responses to Decline in Firms, Organisations, and States*, Cambridge: Harvard University Press.

Inman, R.P. and Rubinfeld, D.L. (1997) 'Rethinking Federalism', *Journal of Economic Perspectives*, 11(4), 43–64.

Kelejian, H.H. and Prucha, I.R. (1998) 'A Generalized Spatial Two-Stage Least Squares Procedure for Estimating a Spatial Autoregressive Model with Autoregressive Disturbances', *Journal of Real Estate Finance and Economics*, 17, 99–121.

Kelejian, H.H. and Robinson, D.H. (1993) 'A Suggested Estimation for Spatial Interdependent Models with Autocorrelated Errors, and an Application to a County Expenditure Model', *Papers in Regional Science*, 72, 297–312.

Kerber, W. (1998) 'Zum Problem einer Wettbewerbsordnung für den Systemwettbewerb', *Jahrbuch für Neue Politische Ökonomie*, 17, 199–230.

—— (2000) 'Interjurisdictional Competition within the European Union', *Fordham International Law Journal*, 23, S217–49.

Kirchgässner, G. and Feld, L.P. (2004) 'Föderalismus und Staatsquote', *Jahrbuch für Föderalismus*, 5, 67–87.

Kollman, K., Miller, J.H. and Page, S.E. (2000) 'Decentralization and the Search for Policy Solutions', *Journal of Law, Economics and Organization*, 16, 102–28.

Kölz, A. (1992) *Neuere Schweizerische Verfassungsgeschichte: Ihre Grundlinien vom Ende der alten Eidgenossenschaft bis 1848*, Bern: Stämpfli.

—— (2004) *Neuere Schweizerische Verfassungsgeschichte: Ihre Grundlinien in Bund und Kantonen seit 1848*, Bern: Stämpfli.

Kotsogiannis, C. and Schwager, R. (2004) 'Policy Innovation in Federal Systems', University of Göttingen, mimeo.

Ladd, H.F. (1992) 'Mimicking of Local Tax Burdens among Neighboring Counties', *Public Finance Quarterly*, 20, 450–67.

Ladner, A. and Steiner, R. (2003) 'Die Schweizer Gemeinden im Wandel: Konvergenz oder Divergenz?' *Swiss Political Science Review*, 9, 233–59.

Leprince, M., Madiès, T. and Paty, S. (2003) 'Interactions fiscales horizontales et verticales: Un test sur données départementales', University of Lille, mimeo.

Myers, D.J. (2001) 'Modeling Social Diffusion Processes Using Event History Analysis: Some Conceptual Issues, Practical Considerations, and Empirical Patterns', Working Paper and Technical Report Series No. 2001–07, Dept. of Sociology, University of Notre Dame.

Nice, D.C. (1994) *Policy Innovation in State Government*, Ames: Iowa State University Press.

Oates, W.E. (1972) *Fiscal Federalism*, New York: Harcourt/Brace/Jovanovich.

—— (1999) 'An Essay on Fiscal Federalism', *Journal of Economic Literature*, 37, 1120–49.

Oates, W.E. and Schwab, R.M. (1988) 'Economic Competition among Jurisdictions: Efficiency Enhancing or Distortion Inducing?' *Journal of Public Economics*, 35, 333–54.

Rentsch, H., Flückiger, S., Held, T., Heiniger Y. and Straubhaar, T. (2004) *Ökonomik der Reform. Wege zu mehr Wachstum in der Schweiz*, Füssli, Zürich: Orell.

Reulier, E. (2004) 'Choix fiscaux et interactions stratégique', PhD thesis, Université de Rennes 1, France.

Revelli, F. (2005) 'On Spatial Public Finance Empirics', *International Tax and Public Finance*, 12, 475–92.

Rincke, J. (2005a) 'Policy Innovation in Local Jurisdictions: Testing the Neighborhood Influence Against the Free-Riding Hypothesis', Discussion Paper No. 05–08, Mannheim: Centre for European Economic Research (ZEW).

—— (2005b) 'Neighborhood Influence and Political Chance: Evidence from US School Districts', Discussion Paper No. 05–16, Mannheim: Centre for European Economic Research (ZEW).

Rodden, J. and Rose-Ackerman, S. (1997) 'Does Federalism Preserve Markets?' *Virginia Law Review*, 83, 1521–72.

Rodrik, D. (1998) 'Why Do More Open Economies Have Bigger Governments?' *Journal of Political Economy*, 106, 997–1032.

Rogers, E.M. (1995) *The Diffusion of Innovations*, 4th edn, New York: Simon & Schuster.

Romano, R. (1985) 'Law as a Product: Some Pieces of the Incorporation Puzzle', *Journal of Law, Economics and Organization*, 1, 225–83.

—— (2002) *The Advantage of Competitive Federalism for Securities Regulation*, Washington: AEI Press.

Rose-Ackerman, S. (1980) 'Risk-Taking and Re-Election: Does Federalism Promote Innovation?' *Journal of Legal Studies*, 9, 593–616.

Saavedra, L.A. (2000) 'A Model of Welfare Competition with Evidence from AFDC', *Journal of Urban Economics*, 47, 248–79.

Salmon, P. (1987) 'Decentralization as an Incentive Scheme', *Oxford Review of Economic Policy*, 3, 24–43.

—— (2003) 'Assigning Powers in the European Union in the Light of Yardstick Competition among Governments', *Jahrbuch für Neue Politische Ökonomie*, 22, 197–216.

—— (2005a) 'Horizontal Competition among Governments', Université de Bourgogne, unpublished manuscript.

—— (2005b) 'Political Yardstick Competition and Corporate Governance in the European Union', Université de Bourgogne, mimeo.

Samuelson, P.A. (1954) 'Pure Theory of Public Expenditure', *Review of Economics and Statistics*, 40, 332–8.

Savage, R.L. (1985) 'Diffusion Research Traditions and the Spread of Policy Innovations in a Federal System', *Publius: The Journal of Federalism*, 15, 1–27.

Schaltegger, Ch.A. (2001) 'The Effects of Federalism and Democracy on the Size of Government: Evidence from Swiss Sub-national Jurisdictions', *ifo Studien*, 47, 145–62.

Schanz, G. von (1890) *Die Steuern der Schweiz in ihrer Entwicklung seit Beginn des 19. Jahrhunderts, Vol I to V*, Stuttgart.

Schnellenbach, J. (2004a) *Dezentrale Finanzpolitik und Modellunsicherheit: Eine theoretische Untersuchung zur Rolle des fiskalischen Wettbewerbs als Wissen generierender Prozess*, Tübingen: Mohr Siebeck.

—— (2004b) 'Learning from Decentralised Policy: The Demand Side', paper presented at the Royal Economic Society 2004 annual conference at Swansea (UK).

Schulze, G.G. and Ursprung, H.W. (1999) 'Globalisation of the Economy and the Nation State', *World Economy*, 22, 295–352.

Siebert, H. and Koop, M.J. (1990) 'Institutional Competition. A Concept for Europe?' *Aussenwirtschaft*, 45, 439–62.

Sinn, H.-W. (1990) 'Tax Harmonisation and Tax Competition in Europe', *European Economic Review*, 34, 489–504.

—— (1997) 'The Selection Principle and Market Failure in Systems Competition', *Journal of Public Economics*, 66, 247–74.

—— (2003) *The New Systems Competition*, Oxford: Blackwell.

Solé-Ollé, A. (2003) 'Electoral Accountability and Tax Mimicking: The Effects of Electoral Margins, Coalition Government and Ideology', *European Journal of Political Economy*, 19, 685–713.

Sommer, J.H. (1978) *Das Ringen um soziale Sicherheit in der Schweiz: Eine politisch-ökonomische Analyse der Ursprünge, Entwicklungen und Perspektiven sozialer Sicherung im Widerstreit zwischen Gruppeninteressen und volkswirtschaftlicher Tragbarkeit*, Diessenhofen: Rüegger.

Steiner, R. (2000) 'New Public Management in Swiss Municipalities', *International Public Management Journal*, 3, 169–89.

Stigler, G.J. (1957) 'The Tenable Range of Functions of Local Government', in US Congress, Joint Economic Committee (ed.) *Federal Expenditure Policy for Economic Growth and Stability*, Washington, DC, pp. 213–9.

Strumpf, K. (2002) 'Does Government Centralization Increase Policy Innovation?' *Journal of Public Economic Theory*, 4, 207–41.

Stutzer, A. and Frey, B.S. (2000) 'Stärkere Volksrechte – Zufriedenere Bürger: eine mikroökonometrische Untersuchung für die Schweiz', *Swiss Political Science Review*, 6, 1–30.

Sun, J.-M. and Pelkmans, J.J. (1995) 'Regulatory Competition in the Single Market', *Journal of Common Market Studies*, 33, 67–89.

Tiebout, Ch.M. (1956) 'A Pure Theory of Local Expenditures', *Journal of Political Economy*, 64, 416–24.

Treisman, D. (2001) 'Corruption, Fiscal Incentives, and Output in Federal States: On the Neutrality of Fiscal Decentralization', UCLA, mimeo.

—— (2002) 'Decentralization and the Quality of Government', UCLA, mimeo.

Tyran, J.-R. and Sausgruber, R. (2003) 'The Diffusion of Policy Innovations: An Experimental Investigation', University of St. Gallen, mimeo.

Van den Bergh, R. (2000) 'Towards an Institutional Legal Framework for Regulatory Competition in Europe', *Kyklos*, 53, 435–66.

Vaubel, R. (2000) 'Internationaler Politischer Wettbewerb: Eine europäische Wettbewerbsaufsicht für Regierungen und die empirische Evidenz', *Jahrbuch für Neue Politische Ökonomie*, 19, 280–309.

—— (2004) 'The New Systems Competition: Zu dem gleichnamigen Buch von Hans-Werner Sinn', *ORDO – Jahrbuch für die Ordnung von Wirtschaft und Gesellschaft*, 55, 380–8.

—— (2005) 'The Role of Competition in the Rise of Baroque and Renaissance Music', *Journal of Cultural Economics*, 29, 277–97.

Vihanto, M. (1992) 'Competition between Local Governments as a Discovery Procedure', *Journal of Institutional and Theoretical Economics*, 148, 411–36.

Walker, J.L. (1969) 'The Diffusion of Innovation among the American States', *American Political Science Review*, 63, 880–99.

Weingast, B.R. (1995) 'The Economic Role of Political Institutions: Market-Preserving Federalism and Economic Development', *Journal of Law, Economics and Organisation*, 11, 1–31.

Widmer, T. and Rieder, S. (2003) 'Schweizer Kantone im institutionellen Wandel: Ein Beitrag zur Beschreibung und Erklärung institutioneller Reformen', *Swiss Political Science Review*, 9, 201–32.

COMMENT: YARDSTICK COMPETITION AMONG
CANTONAL FISCAL REGULATIONS

Christoph A. Schaltegger

There are contrasting views of how regulatory competition affects society's welfare. While advocates of regulatory competition stress its innovative capacity and the ability to tame a leviathan government, opponents argue that regulatory competition leads to laxity of standards.

Lars Feld brings more empirical evidence to bear on this controversial issue by studying the effects which Swiss cantonal regulations exert on policy outcomes. I shall complement his investigation by analysing yardstick competition among the Swiss cantons with regard to a fiscal regulation: balanced-budget requirements.

Feld's analysis provides some evidence that the Swiss cantons do not take their regulatory decisions in isolation but consider developments in other cantons when setting their own regulatory policies. An obvious question that arises is whether such mimicking is a 'race to the bottom'. Should we interpret regulatory mimicking as an indication of ruinous competition for laxity? Or does it indicate an adoption of best practices and a taming of a leviathan? Feld leaves the normative evaluation of his results open, commenting that mimicking, 'might either lead to more or less regulation depending on what canton sets the trend'. I shall address this question in the context of balanced-budget regulations.

The impact of formal fiscal restraints on fiscal outcomes has been analysed systematically at the state and local level in the United States. Tax and expenditure limitation laws (TEL) were mainly introduced during the tax revolts associated with the passage of California's Proposition 13. Before 1978, only New Jersey and Colorado had a binding TEL. Afterwards and until 1987, many other states introduced TELs (Shadbegian 1996: 23). The study by Shadbegian (1996)

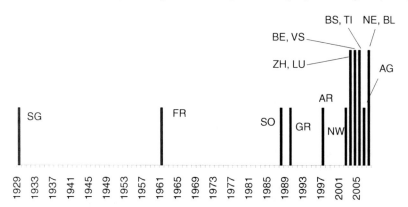

Figure 6C.1 The evolution of balanced-budget requirements in Swiss cantons (for cantonal abbreviations see Appendix).

shows that there is an expenditure cutting effect of TELs on the relative growth of government spending compared with the growth of national income. The same holds for the local level in the US. Shadbegian (1996) provides empirical evidence indicating that TELs also have a restricting effect on the size of the local public sector. The main impact is on the property tax.

Similar to the United States, in Switzerland cantons set their balanced-budget regulations themselves, are not supervised by the confederation and cannot expect a bailout in case of insolvency (Blankart and Klaiber 2004).[1] Most balanced-budget requirements in Swiss cantons evolved only recently. As Figure 6C.1 shows, the canton St. Gallen has the longest experience with such a budget rule. Other cantons followed later, varying in stringency of the requirements from canton to canton. In some cantons the introduced or the enacted budget has to be balanced. In other cantons, policy-makers are required to ensure that expenditures in a fiscal year stay within the predicted revenue available for that fiscal year. Still other cantons may carry unavoidable deficits into the next fiscal year for resolution. In most cases, there are three types of cantonal balanced-budget requirements. First, the government's proposed budget must be balanced. Second, the budget's possible deficit within a range of about 3 per cent of all revenues must be balanced over a business cycle. Third, the level of debt must remain stable.

In practice cantonal balanced-budget requirements refer to operating budgets rather than capital budgets. Operating budgets include annual expenditure – such as salaries and wages, intergovernmental grants, health and welfare spending and other yearly expenditures. Cantonal capital expenditures, mainly for land, highways and buildings, are largely financed by debt. Cantonal requirements for balanced budgets do not impose legal penalties if the rule is violated. There is, however, a very effective enforcement mechanism: the government has to propose a tax increase if the balanced-budget requirement is violated. Normally, such tax increases are also subject to popular referendum (Stalder 2005).

As Figure 6C.1 reveals, balanced-budget requirements are spreading among Swiss cantons.[2] They study the effectiveness of balanced-budget regulations in other cantons when deciding about their own budget rule. A good example is the canton of Ticino. Traditionally Ticino faced relatively unbalanced public finances. Beginning with the mid-1990s, the government managed to balance the budget, but when spending demands soared again, the cantonal minister of finance ordered an expert review concerning an adequate balanced-budget requirement for Ticino. The panel had to review the effectiveness of balanced-budget regulations in other cantons, the federal debt-brake and US experience with budget rules (Frey and Schaltegger 2002). On the basis of this expert review, the government proposed a bill on a balanced-budget regulation, which has yet to be approved by the parliament. Thus the emergence of a balanced-budget regulation in Ticino is a nice example of the innovative power of yardstick competition: cantons do not take their policy decisions in isolation but explicitly consider their neighbours' experience before enacting similar rules.

Figure 6C.2 indicates that balanced-budget requirements tend to make a dif-

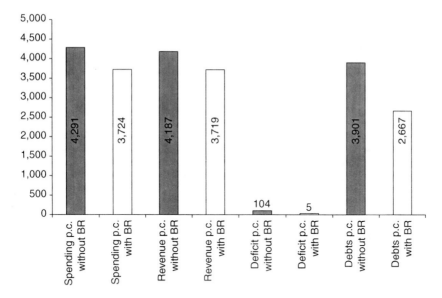

Figure 6C.2 The effects of balanced-budget requirements (BR) in Swiss cantons (Swiss francs per capita).

ference: deficits, debts, spending and revenue per capita tend to be lower in cantons which have enacted balanced-budget requirements. In a panel study for the 26 Swiss cantons from 1980–98, Schaltegger (2002) and Feld and Kirchgässner (2005) show that balanced-budget requirements have a significantly negative effect on deficit spending. In a multivariate analysis, the deficit per capita tends to be 200 CHF lower in cantons with a balanced-budget regulation. Thus, summing up, yardstick competition among fiscal rules seems to favour fiscal discipline.

Appendix: cantonal abbreviations

ZH	Zurich	SH	Schaffhausen
BE	Bern	AR	Appenzell Ausserrhoden
LU	Lucerne	AI	Appenzell Innerrhoden
UR	Uri	SG	St. Gallen
SZ	Schwyz	GR	Grisons
OW	Obwalden	AG	Aargau
NW	Nidwalden	TG	Thurgau
GL	Glarus	TI	Ticino
ZG	Zoug	VD	Vaud
FR	Fribourg	VS	Valais
SO	Solothurn	NE	Neuchatel
BS	Basel-Stadt	GE	Geneva
BL	Basel-Landschaft	JU	Jura

Notes

1   It can be debated whether the no-bailout expectation is reasonable also for big juris-
    dictions that are normally considered as 'too big to fail'.
2   The figure shows dates of first enactment. Some cantons have revised the legal
    requirements afterwards several times. In some cantons at the end of the time span,
    the enactment is decided or at least proposed by the government but not yet effective.

References

Blankart, C.B. and Klaiber, A. (2004) 'Wer soll für die Schulden von Gebietskörper-
    schaften haften?' in C.A. Schaltegger and S. Schaltegger (eds) *Perspektiven der
    Schweizer Wirtschaftspolitik*, vdf, Zürich, pp. 137–50.
Feld, L.P. and Kirchgässner, G. (2005) *On the Effectiveness of Debt Brakes: The Swiss
    Experience*, University of St. Gallen, mimeo.
Frey, R.L. and Schaltegger, C.A. (2002) *Ausgabenbremse – Freno alla spesa pubblica*,
    Expert review for the Ticino government.
Schaltegger, C.A. (2002) 'Budgetregeln und ihre Wirkung auf die öffentlichen Haushalte:
    Empirische Ergebnisse aus den US-Bundesstaaten und den Schweizer Kantonen',
    Schmollers Jahrbuch, 122, 369–413.
Shadbegian, R.J. (1996) 'Do Tax and Expenditure Limitations Affect the Size and
    Growth of State Government?' *Contemporary Economic Policy*, 14, 22–35.
Stalder, K. (2005) 'Fiscal Rules for Cantons and Communes', University of St. Gallen,
    mimeo.

7 The drivers of deregulation in the era of globalization

Friedrich Heinemann

Introduction

The last two decades have not only been an era of increasing international mobility of goods, services and factors, but also one of decreasing regulatory burden in a number of markets. Given these parallel trends the question of the nature of this correlation arises: is it a mere coincidence or does it represent some kind of causal link between globalization and deregulation? Of course, for certain interdependencies the answer is trivial: deregulation of international transactions directly causes or at least amplifies globalization trends. However, the opposite causal link from globalization towards regulatory decisions is less straightforward. It is not clear a priori whether, how and to what extent increasing cross-border factor mobility will impact on regulatory equilibria – be it on the fields of labour, financial market, trade or product regulation.

Thus, the guiding question of this study is to what extent globalization limits the national leeway for country-specific regulatory solutions. This issue is a neglected dimension of the globalization debate. Compared with fiscal policy in general (see Vaubel 2005, for a recent update of references) and tax policy in particular (see the survey of Schulze and Ursprung 1999) the issue of regulatory sovereignty in a globalizing environment has attracted much less attention in the academic literature. This may partly be explicable by data reasons since it is more difficult to quantify regulatory changes compared with changes in government expenditures or revenues. However, conceptually both fields are closely connected: both explicit transfers through government spending and implicit transfers through regulation may serve the same politico-economic purpose of favouring specific interest groups. In this sense, government spending and regulation can be substitutes. Therefore it is equally desirable to study the consequences of increasing factor mobility for government activity both on the fiscal and the regulatory field.

This analysis intends to provide for a better understanding of these issues through a thorough empirical analysis on the basis of an OECD country panel for the period 1975 until 2000. The study is also to contribute to the small but growing empirical literature on the determinants of structural reforms. Regulatory change is a particular sub-type of structural reform which can also target the monetary regime, the tax system or the size and structure of the government sector. This literature has been motivated by a desire to explain why industrial countries show very different speeds of adjusting their structures to new circumstances, which are related to increasing global competition, but also to internal changes resulting from the demographic change.

In the literature on structural reforms, case studies with a focus on developing countries used to dominate (see Rodrik 1996 for a by now somewhat outdated survey of this literature). Examples of more recent and more comprehensive panel analyses are Pitlik and Wirth (2003) and Heinemann (2004) who make use of economic freedom indicators as proxies for structural change and analyse the relevant drivers for large global country panels. In their panel analysis for 35 countries, Abiad and Mody (2003) focus on financial market deregulation and, therefore, are already closer to the regulation focus. The authors find a positive impact of trade openness on the pace of deregulation. Although some robust results originate from these studies – for example, the fact that deep economic crises tend to increase the likelihood of structural reforms – they do not account for the enormous economic and political heterogeneity among countries of very different income classes and constitutional situations and, therefore, are only of limited use to learn much about the drivers of deregulation in industrial and democratic countries.

An analysis more concentrated both on the conditions in industrial countries and deregulation is Helbling *et al.* (2004), whose approach is followed here both with regard to the underlying data set and the basic model. In particular we use the same time series on four regulatory fields: regulation of financial markets, product markets, labour markets and international trade. However, our study addresses the shortcomings of Helbling *et al.* (2004) which – in the light of our guiding question – is the rather simple approximation of the globalization trend by the trade openness variable, which only measures one dimension of increasing internationalization and neglects both capital and labour mobility. Furthermore, among the institutional variables, this study does not take account of a possible impact of internal domestic political competition related to federalism.

The study proceeds in the following way: in the next section, we summarize a number of theoretical arguments relevant for the impact of globalization on regulation. The following section takes a brief descriptive glance at our regulatory indicators and globalization measures. The final section presents our model specification and panel regressions, followed by the conclusions.

Globalization and regulation – an overview of arguments and determinants

Depending on the regulatory context there are very different and often counteracting arguments how globalization should influence regulation.

The diversity of arguments originates from the fact that both globalization and regulation have many facets. In its narrow economic definition, 'globalization' describes the trend that national borders tend to lose their significance as a relevant obstacle to economic transactions or – more technically speaking – the occurrence of 'a reduction in international arbitrage costs' (Schulze and Ursprung 1999: 301). However, there are additional aspects related to the exchange of information and the degree of political competition. The costs of voters becoming informed about the conditions beyond their home countries' borders through the media or physical travelling have come down – a fact which could contribute to an intensification of yardstick competition (Besley and Case 1995), according to which the performance of a government is assessed relative to the performance of some (neighbouring) benchmark.

It is helpful to organize the relevant arguments in the logic of the Stigler–Peltzman model of regulation (see Mueller 1989, for a survey). Politicians with regulatory power face a trade-off: by increasing regulated prices they win political support from the benefiting producers whereas they lose support from consumers. This trade-off between the interests of winners and losers of regulation is a typical feature independent of the specific regulatory context. Consequently, given the hypothesis of vote maximization, a politico-economic equilibrium results where marginal gains in votes are equilibrated with marginal losses. The equilibrium depends on many features of the policy field such as: the existence of well-organized interest groups representing winners and/or losers, their voting and campaign financing power, the extent, distribution and perceptibility of regulation costs and benefits, the level of voters' information or external restrictions.

All these features can be influenced by increasing globalization rendering the closed-country regulation equilibrium unstable. The following arguments suggest a deregulatory effect of globalization.

- The media dimension of globalization, but also people's increasing professional or holiday mobility make it easier for voters to learn from comparisons with other countries about the costs of regulation. This increases the relative power of those who usually pay the price of regulation without being fully aware of it due to the regulation's intransparent character. In this sense, globalization should improve the preconditions for cross-border learning.
- The political benefits of regulation which put the burden on increasingly mobile factors like capital (or high-income individuals) tend to shrink. In the extreme, mobility might simply render certain regulations ineffective – a phenomenon relevant for some types of financial market regulation (for example, interest rate regulation would no longer be effective given the degree of financial capital mobility on current financial markets).
- The beneficiaries of regulation at product markets, which are, on the national level, often homogeneous, limited in number and therefore capable of organizing their interests according to Olson's (1965) theory of interest groups, might not be able to organize internationally. Thus, they would not be able to establish a similar political power on an international level even if on this level political suppliers of regulation exist – as is the case for the

European Union. On the national level, producer groups that used to have significant political influence in a protected market might lose this influence once foreign producers enter the market and start to articulate their differential interests.

However, globalization might not necessarily work exclusively towards deregulation. Under certain conditions it may increase the benefit of specific types of regulation and then even lead to new regulative initiatives. For example, increasing factor mobility creates new risks for the economy as a whole or at least for an influential interest group. This could be particularly relevant in the context of labour market regulation.

On the one hand, increasing capital mobility puts inefficient solutions under pressure by raising structural unemployment in heavily regulated labour markets as is notoriously the case for labour markets in the larger continental European countries. In this sense, globalization has increased the marginal costs of labour market regulation and leads to deregulation.

On the other hand, the political marginal benefit of labour market regulation might increase if globalization increases business cycle volatility and/or structural change inducing job insiders to demand a larger level of job protection as a compensation for accepting trade liberalization. This reasoning is analogous to the debate on the link between globalization and the size of government and social spending. Rodrik has proposed the so-called compensation hypothesis that increasing social spending is the price that has to be paid to make voters accept internationalization of their economies (Rodrik 1998; see Vaubel 2000, for a survey of the literature and an empirical assessment).

Recently Vaubel (2005) has proposed an alternative to Rodrik's compensation hypothesis with fundamentally different policy conclusions. He argues that the correlation between openness and social spending is not the outcome of an ex ante compensation deal but reflects the following chain of causality. Countries with inflexible labour markets experience an increase in structural unemployment with increasing openness. Subsequently, governments use part of the welfare gains of increasing international trade to raise social spending. From this perspective, compensation of labour is not a necessary precondition for acceptance of globalization, but rather reflects the inability of some countries to increase labour market flexibility.

Implicit regulatory transfers can be a substitute for explicit fiscal transfers. Hence, whatever the true structures behind the link between social spending and augmented cross-border trade, they point to the fact that at least in the case of labour market regulation there can be countervailing forces pressing for even more regulation with globalization.

Any assessment of the impact of globalization on regulation should take account of further mechanisms driving the acceptability of structural reforms (see Heinemann 2004; Helbling et al. 2004). One insight from this literature is that a shock which initially causes only a modest adjustment of the institutional status quo can be a trigger of more fundamental change. The 'status quo bias' is empirically well proven in behavioural economics experiments. It describes a situation where people have a preference for one option among many others only because this option happens to be the status quo (Samuelson and Zeckhauser 1988). If a minor change occurs, this specific option loses attraction immediately. The implication for reform is that a small shock could overcome psychological resistance to more radical changes because it opens the way for a less biased reflection on optimal institutional solutions.

The argument can also be based on learning about the true distributional consequences of deregulation. The identity of winners and losers of institutional change, which may be unknown before the reform, is one of the classical explanations for resistance to welfare-improving reforms (Fernandez and Rodrik 1991). Even small first deregulation steps might help to identify the winners and losers and thus contribute to reduce uncertainty (Abiad and Mody 2003). If this turns out to be empirically relevant, small steps matter and deregulation can be self-accelerating.

The phenomenon of the status quo bias is also closely linked to the observation that crisis often appears to be a precondition for reforms. A general feeling of crisis can open a window of opportunity for change because the status quo is then regarded as non-sustainable. Globalization pressure can contribute to this sense of crisis.

The literature on the causes of structural reform cited above suggest further economic and political determinants which may be relevant for structural changes in general and the speed of deregulation in particular:

- General economic conditions: In line with the crisis hypothesis, the general economic situation measured on the basis of standard variables like growth, budget deficits, inflation or unemployment should matter with bad data increasing the likelihood of deregulation.
- Ideology: Governments of different ideologies typically also have different views on the desirable extent of regulatory involvement. These views should influence outcomes only if globalization leaves any leeway. In this sense, testing the relevance of ideology is also a test with regard to the political leeway that remains under globalization.
- Decentralization of government: Internal competition between autonomous regions could accelerate structural adjustments.
- Strength of governments: A strong and stable government should be better able to carry out reforms.
- Election cycle: Post-election years are often windows of opportunity for institutional change – due to the relatively long time horizon which the newly elected (or re-elected) government faces. Newly elected governments are also in a better position to bring about major changes due to the 'honeymoon effect', an initial bonus of confidence which the fresh government normally experiences in the public opinion.
- External restrictions: EU, IMF or WTO membership offer examples of external restrictions a country may face in defining its regulatory policies. In

an empirical study of OECD countries, only an EU dummy offers sufficient cross-section variability for testing.

Regulation and globalization: the experience since the mid-1970s

Our time series data on the restrictiveness of government regulation in trade as well as product, labour and financial markets originate in World Economic Outlook (WEO) 2004 (see Helbling *et al.* 2004, Appendix 3.1. for details on sources and construction). The 21 OECD countries covered are: Australia, Austria, Belgium, Canada, Denmark, Finland, France, Germany, Ireland, Italy, Japan, the Netherlands, New Zealand, Norway, Portugal, Spain, Sweden, Switzerland, United Kingdom and United States (in the econometric analysis, Japan and Greece drop out due to missing control variables). The time series start in 1975 and, currently, extend to 1998 for labour and product markets, to 2001 for financial markets and to 2002 for trade.

All indicators are normalized to range from 0 to 1 where an increasing value signals a declining degree of restriction. The first three indicators are calculated as an unweighted average of sector-specific indicators depicting different dimensions of regulatory intervention.

The regulation indicator for the financial sector (WEOFINANCIAL) takes account of credit controls, interest rate controls and restrictions on international financial transactions. Thus, this indicator does not include regulatory issues linked to reporting and financial stability oriented monitoring of the financial sector which, certainly, would show very different time trends.

The labour market indicator (WEOLABOR) is constructed on the basis of the Labor Market Institutions Database developed by Nickel and Nunziata (2001) and is the aggregate of sub-indicators on employment protection, benefit replacement rates and benefit duration. It excludes information on wage centralization since, for numerous countries, there is no time variance for related variables.

The product market indicator (WEOPRODUCT) was constructed by Nicoletti and Scarpetta (2003) and combines indicators on barriers to entry, public ownership, market structure, vertical integration of networks and final consumer services, and price controls for the following non-manufacturing sectors: gas, electricity, post, telecommunications, passenger air transport, railways and road freights. It thus covers the sectors which used to be characterized by heavy government involvement and protected monopolies or oligopolies in the past.

Finally, the trade-related indicator (WEOTRADE) is constructed on the basis of effective tariffs relating revenues from customs and import duties to the value of imports. It should be noted that this indicator does not account for non-tariff obstacles to trade.

Figure 7.1 summarizes the cross-section distribution of these indicators over time.[1] The first striking observation is that the labour market regulation trend differs fundamentally from the other markets. Whereas the years between 1975

and the end of the 1990s have brought massive dismantling of regulatory limitations for financial transactions, activities on formerly protected service markets
and obstacles to cross-border trade, the same period is characterized by an initial
increase of regulatory standards on labour markets and stagnation in the later
years.

Clear differences are observable among the deregulation fields, too. Product
market deregulation took off later than financial and trade deregulation. As a
consequence product markets are still distant from being fully liberalized
towards the end of the covered period. Cross-country convergence occurred
most clearly for financial and trade regulatory standards, where industrial countries in the light of the employed indictors have almost completely and jointly
overcome regulatory obstacles.

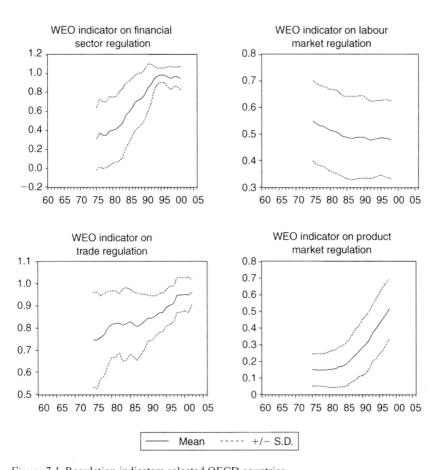

Figure 7.1 Regulation indicators selected OECD countries.

Note
Helbling *et al.* (2004), included are the OECD countries as listed at the beginning of the third
section.

Turning now to the measurement of globalization, we focus on measures for mobility of goods, services, capital and people. Figure 7.2 depicts the time series (the first three in per cent of GDP) for trade openness (sum of exports and imports of goods and services), the gross private capital flows (sum of the absolute values of direct, portfolio, and other investment inflows and outflows), foreign direct investment on its own (which is also included in the former) and finally as a very rough proxy for the mobility of people: the share of foreign population in total population (sources for all globalization measures: the World Bank's World Development Indicators). The share of foreign population variable is not available on a time series basis for a number of non-European countries.

All four time series show that the decades since the 1970s have been an era of more or less constant increase in cross-border transactions and mobility of people. Acceleration took place after the mid-1990s with strongly increasing mobility of real and financial capital.

While a glance at Figures 7.1 and 7.2 justifies the general remark that the

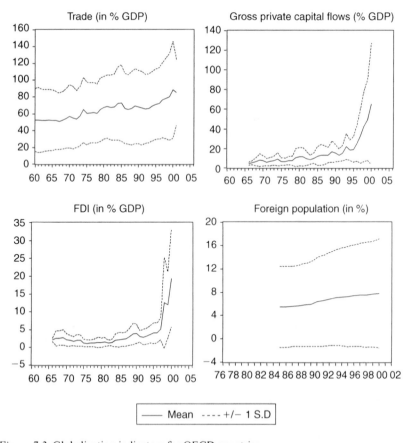

Figure 7.2 Globalization indicators for OECD countries.

period since 1975 has been an era of parallel deregulation and globalization, a more detailed correlation analysis (see Table 7.1) produces more differentiated insights.

The financial regulation indicator has the least ambiguous correlation profile being significantly positively correlated to all globalization indicators. Labour regulation turns out to be the opposite and atypical because it is negatively correlated to all globalization measures with the exception of foreign population – a finding corresponding to the compensation hypothesis or its variants as discussed above. A further remarkable result is the negative correlation between the product market regulation indicator and trade openness.

A look at the correlation among the different fields of regulation reveals that there is only one significant negative correlation which is the one between labour and trade regulation – a finding which hints toward the possibility that more aggressive protection of job insiders and more generous unemployment benefits are the prices that have to be paid in politico-economic bargaining for the impact of trade liberalization on labour markets.

Relevant restrictions for regulatory equilibria need not in every case be of an external nature. The existence of federal structures is an internal restriction which can have an impact on regulatory outcomes as well. Regions with certain fiscal or regulatory competencies might allow for elements of locational competition putting some pressure on inefficient regulations.

In order to test for the relevance of decentralized structures we make use of the data set on revenue decentralization provided by Stegarescu (2004). Compared with simple dummies for the existence of autonomous regions (as provided, for example by the World Bank Database on Political Institutions), these indicators offer the advantage of being continuous and, thus, more differentiated. Stegarescu offers a set of decentralization indicators based on the share of revenues assigned to regions. While Stegarescu's indicator 'degree of revenue decentralization 3' (DRD3) simply measures the share of total government revenue assigned to the regions, the variable 'degree of revenue decentralization 1' (DRD1) only includes revenue sources over which sub-central governments possess significant control in the sense that they control at least the tax base or the tax rate. For countries like Germany with a large importance of shared taxes which cannot be autonomously controlled by the federal countries, DRD1 is considerably smaller than DRD3. It must be conceded that tax autonomy is not identical with regulatory autonomy. However, we simply employ the indicator as a proxy for federal autonomy in a more general sense.

Table 7.2 depicts correlation coefficients among decentralization and regulation indicators. Both (highly correlated) decentralization indicators are positively and significantly correlated with the regulation indicators with the exception of trade regulation. This means that more centralized countries tend to have more regulated product, labour and financial markets.

Table 7.1 Cross-correlations: indicators of regulation and globalization

		WEOFINANCIAL	WEOLABOR	WEOPRODUCT	WEOTRADE	FDI	FOREIGN POP.	TRADE	CAPITAL FLOWS
WEOFINANCIAL	Pearson correlation	1.00							
	two-sided p-value								
	N	540							
WEOLABOR	Pearson correlation	0.05	1.00						
	two-sided p-value	0.24							
	N	477	477						
WEOPRODUCT	Pearson correlation	0.55	0.28	1.00					
	two-sided p-value	0.00	0.00						
	N	480	477	504					
WEO trade	Pearson correlation	0.33	−0.19	−0.05	1.00				
	two-sided p-value	0.00	0.00	0.31					
	N	540	477	480	556				
FDI	Pearson correlation	0.38	−0.13	0.40	0.25	1.00			
	two-sided p-value	0.00	0.01	0.00	0.00				
	N	500	457	482	500	611			
FOREIGN POP.	Pearson correlation	0.36	0.18	0.26	−0.21	0.07	1.00		
	two-sided p-value	0.00	0.00	0.00	0.00	0.26			
	N	276	237	240	276	276	293		
TRADE	Pearson correlation	0.20	−0.42	−0.18	0.46	0.38	0.58	1.00	
	two-sided p-value	0.00	0.00	0.00	0.00	0.00	0.00		
	N	536	477	504	536	611	293	933	
CAPITAL FLOWS	Pearson correlation	0.37	−0.08	0.30	0.35	0.80	0.04	0.52	1.00
	two-sided p-value	0.00	0.08	0.00	0.00	0.00	0.51	0.00	
	N	512	469	494	512	611	276	623	623

Table 7.2 Cross-correlations: indicators of fiscal (revenue) decentralization and regulation

		DRD1	DRD3
DRD1	Pearson correlation	1	
	two-sided p-value		
	N	438	
DRD3	Pearson correlation	0.86	1.00
	two-sided p-value	0.00	
	N	438	438
WEOTRADE	Pearson correlation	−0.04	0.03
	two-sided p-value	0.42	0.54
	N	396	396
WEOPRODUCT	Pearson correlation	0.33	0.25
	two-sided p-value	0.00	0.00
	N	379	379
WEOLABOR	Pearson correlation	0.56	0.39
	two-sided p-value	0.00	0.00
	N	376	376
WEOFINANCIAL	Pearson correlation	0.22	0.27
	two-sided p-value	0.00	0.00
	N	396	396

Specification and results

In the following a dynamic model for the path of deregulation is estimated. The specification follows the model developed by Abiad and Mody (2003) and applied by Helbling *et al.* (2004). It allows for the path of regulation to be driven by a steady convergence of regulation to some 'optimum' level of regulation $REG^*_{i,t}$. On the basis of the Stigler view of regulation, this 'optimum' should not be understood as a welfare-maximizing solution but simply as the stable politico-economic equilibrium level of regulation. In line with the definition of our regulatory indicators, larger levels of *REG* are associated with less restrictive regulatory regimes.

$$\Delta REG_{i,t} = \mu(REG^*_{i,t} - REG_{i,t-1}) + \varepsilon_{i,t} \tag{1}$$

If the status quo bias is relevant the values of *m* should be below 1. This parameter of institutional stickiness is assumed to depend on the strictness of current regulation:

$$\mu = k\, REG_{i,t-1} \tag{2}$$

Thus, this specification allows for learning following the arguments discussed previously: deregulatory steps can be helpful to limit uncertainty about the outcomes of deregulation.

Furthermore, this basic adjustment process is driven by further determinants including some element of yardstick competition where the distance to the regulatory situation of the benchmark group (REG^{BM}) has an impact on the country's deregulation path. This results in the following testable specification:

$$\Delta REG_{i,t} = \alpha_1 REG_{i,t-1} + \alpha_2 REG^2_{i,t-1} + \alpha_3 REG^{BM}_{i,t-1} - REG_{i,t-1}) + \sum_{k=1}^{K} \beta_k x_{k,i,t} + \varepsilon_{i,t} \tag{3}$$

In (3) the coefficient $\alpha 3$ measures the impact of yardstick competition and the b-coefficients the influence of the further control variables including most of the above described globalization and decentralization variables.

By construction, $\alpha_1 = k*REG^*_{i,t-1}$ and is expected to be positive, whereas $\alpha_2 = -k$ would be negative if the status quo bias really loses power due to learning from deregulation. From this reduced form, the implicit 'optimum' level of regulation equals $\alpha_1/(-\alpha_2)$.

For the estimation the following definitions and variables are used (see Appendix for data sources):

For the benchmark level of regulation it is assumed that for European OECD countries the EU average is the relevant yardstick and the US regulation level for other OECD countries. In this sense, our yardstick test is not one of mimicking the neighbours, but rather one of following more general international trends.

As proxies of crisis we make use of growth of real GDP and CPI inflation. We also experimented with unemployment, which turned out to be mostly insignificant.

To control for the impact of the ideological orientation of government a dummy variable is constructed on the basis of the Database of Political Institutions (Beck et al. 2001) variable on the ideological orientation of chief executive's party. From the same database we also tested a number of indicators related to the stability of the government, ideological polarization in the parliament and the electoral cycle (election year dummy, years left in current term, change in government to measure the extent of 'honeymoon effect'). However, these turned out to be largely insignificant and have therefore not been included in the presented final specifications.

Among the globalization indicators depicted in the descriptive analysis above, foreign population has to be dropped from the regressions due to too many missing values. Since the joint inclusion of the correlated indicators on trade and capital mobility would be confronted with multicollinearity problems, a principal component of the three series is calculated and employed as the baseline mobility variable (being negatively correlated to increasing levels of mobility).

With regard to the decentralization indicators, the final specification includes DRD3, which performed better than its alternatives from Stegarescu (2004).

Time and period fixed effects are included in the regressions depending on their joint significance. In order to limit problems of reverse causation (particularly relevant for trade and capital mobility) sensitive explanatory variables are lagged by one year. For the coefficient tests, White covariances are used which are robust to variances differing among cross-sections and periods.

Fixed effects estimations including the lagged dependent variable among the regressors face a problem of biased coefficients. The error term is correlated with the transformed values of the lagged dependent variable where each cross-section's average is subtracted from each observation. Microeconometric regressions where T is normally small deal with this difficulty by applying GMM-techniques along the lines suggested by Arellano and Bond (1991). However, Attanasio *et al.* (2000) have shown that an uncritical application is not always the best solution for country panels with a sufficiently large T. The problem is that instrumental-variable GMM approaches tend to produce imprecise estimates. Thus, there is a trade-off between the lack of precision with GMM estimates and the bias associated with the OLS approach. Attanasio *et al.* (2000) recommend to opt for the OLS approach 'when T is big enough'. The length of our time series dimension (up to 27 years are included for some countries) suggests a bias of only a limited scale and, hence, favours the straight regression option which is applied in the following.

Tables 7.3 to 7.6 summarize the regression results. The estimation period is 1975 up to 2001 with relatively few observations in the years 2000 and 2001. There are substantial differences in dynamics between regulation fields. Deregulation appears to be self-enforcing in the case of financial and product market deregulation. Here learning about deregulation's consequences after first deregulation steps obviously helps to overcome resistance towards further dismantling of restrictions. For both fields, the speed of deregulation follows a reversed U-shape: initially learning effects speed up the process, whereas later the closing gap towards the preferred level reduces the speed until the regulatory level has reached its equilibrium. The pattern for trade deregulation is different: it is characterized by classical steady convergence where an initial situation of high regulation tends to be followed by large deregulation steps. In contrast to that, labour markets do not show a stable dynamic pattern across different specifications.

Following the regulatory politics of the benchmark country (USA for non-Europeans) or country group (EU for Europeans) is a significant and robust feature of deregulation in the case of financial and product markets. Cross-border links of regulatory politics are not significant for labour markets. In the case of trade, the equally significant and robust variable has the wrong sign (dropping the period fixed effects characterizing the trade regressions would leave the yardstick term insignificant).

Turning now to the indicators linked to mobility, some different specifications are presented. Whereas the baseline specification (1) makes use of the summarizing principal component of trade and capital mobility, specifications (2)–(4) look separately at each dimension. For financial markets and product markets there are significant results with the expected sign for FDI (which in the case of financial regulation also results in a significant principal component). The specific impact of FDI supports the argument from the theory of interest

Table 7.3 Panel estimation financial deregulation (dependent variable: change financial regulation indicator)

	(1)	(2)	(3)	(4)	(5)	(6)
	Convergence, learning and yardstick					
Level financial reg. (−1)	0.354***	0.367***	0.349***	0.355***	0.294***	0.360***
Square of lagged level (−1)	−0.405***	−0.402***	−0.403***	−0.396***	−0.318***	−0.406***
Yardstick (−1)	0.082**	0.102***	0.081**	0.096***	0.080**	0.091**
	Trade and capital mobility					
Mobility princip. component (−1)	−0.012*	—	—	—	−0.008	−0.019*
Trade (−1)	—	0.001	—	—	—	—
FDI (−1)	—	—	0.004***	—	—	—
Capital flows (−1)	—	—	—	0.000	—	—
	Decentralization/EU					
DRD3	0.002**	0.002*	0.002**	0.002**	0.001**	0.002**
EU dummy	0.014	0.011	0.014	0.016	0.027*	0.017
	Regulatory interactions					
Level trade reg. (−1)	—	—	—	—	−0.029	—
Level product reg. (−1)	—	—	—	—	0.002	—
Level labour reg. (−1)	—	—	—	—	0.033	—
Mean regulation (−1)	—	—	—	—	—	−0.072
	Crisis proxies					
Growth (−1)	−0.008***	−0.008***	−0.008***	−0.008***	−0.007***	−0.008***
Inflation (−1)	−0.005**	−0.005**	−0.005**	−0.005**	−0.003*	−0.005**
	Ideology dummy (divergence from centre)					
Left (−1)	0.001	−0.001	0.001	0.001	0.026*	−0.001
Right (−1)	0.006	0.000	0.007	0.001	0.029**	0.001
Included fixed effects	cross-section	cross-section	cross-section	cross-section	cross-section	cross-section
N of observations	371	387	371	383	361	361
R-squared	0.24	0.24	0.24	0.24	0.18	0.24

Table 7.4 Panel estimation product market deregulation (dependent variable: change product market regulation indicator)

	(1)	(2)	(3)	(4)	(5)	(6)
Convergence, learning and yardstick						
Level product reg. (−1)	0.145***	0.152***	0.127***	0.145***	0.128**	0.107**
Square of lagged level (−1)	−0.101**	−0.103**	−0.092*	−0.105**	−0.111*	−0.080
Yardstick (−1)	0.148***	0.142***	0.141***	0.131***	0.116***	0.116***
Trade and capital mobility						
Mobility princ. component (−1)	−0.003	–	–	–	−0.004	−0.004
Trade (−1)	–	−0.000	–	–	–	–
FDI (−1)	–	–	0.002*	–	–	–
Capital flows (−1)	–	–	–	0.000	–	–
Decentralization/EU						
DRD3	−0.000	0.000	−0.000	0.000	−0.050	−0.000
EU dummy	0.001	0.003	0.001	0.002	0.001	0.003
Regulatory interactions						
Level financial reg. (−1)	–	–	–	–	0.009	–
Level trade reg. (−1)	–	–	–	–	0.036	–
Level labour reg. (−1)	–	–	–	–	0.079	–
Mean regulation (−1)	–	–	–	–	–	0.038
Crisis proxies						
Growth (−1)	−0.000	0.000	−0.000	−0.000	0.022	0.000
Inflation (−1)	−0.001*	−0.001**	−0.001*	−0.001*	−0.001	−0.000
Ideology dummy (divergence from centre)						
Ideology dummy: left (−1)	−0.007	−0.006	−0.007	−0.007	−0.007	−0.007
Ideology dummy: right (−1)	−0.001	−0.001	−0.001	−0.001	−0.000	−0.001
Included fixed effects	cross-section	cross-section	cross-section	cross-section	cross-section	cross-section
N of observations	354	370	354	366	352	352
R-squared	0.25	0.26	0.26	0.26	0.27	0.26

Table 7.5 Panel estimation trade deregulation (dependent variable: change trade regulation indicator)

	(1)	(2)	(3)	(4)	(5)	(6)
Convergence, learning and yardstick						
Level trade reg. (−1)	−0.895**	−0.880**	−0.902**	−0.886**	−0.941**	−0.916**
Square of lagged level (−1)	−0.040	−0.040	−0.042	−0.039	−0.038	−0.021
Yardstick (−1)	−0.803***	−0.788***	−0.809***	−0.793***	−0.838***	−0.806***
Trade and capital mobility						
Mobility princip. component (−1)	0.002	–	–	–	0.004	0.001
Trade (−1)	–	−0.000	–	–	–	–
FDI (−1)	–	–	−0.001	–	–	–
Capital flows (−1)	–	–	–	0.000	–	–
Decentralization/EU						
DRD3	−0.000	−0.000	−0.000	−0.000	−0.000*	−0.000
EU dummy	0.018*	0.019*	0.019*	0.018*	0.018*	0.020**
Regulatory interactions						
Level financial reg. (−1)	–	–	–	–	0.006	–
Level product reg. (−1)	–	–	–	–	−0.064**	–
Level labour reg. (−1)	–	–	–	–	0.126**	–
Mean regulation (−1)	–	–	–	–	–	0.006
Crisis proxies						
Growth (−1)	−0.000	−0.000	−0.000	−0.000	−0.000	−0.000
Inflation (−1)	−0.001	−0.001	−0.001	−0.001	−0.001*	−0.001
Ideology dummies (divergence from centre)						
Ideology dummy: left (−1)	0.001	0.000	0.001	0.000	−0.001	0.001
Ideology dummy: right (−1)	0.003	0.003	0.003	0.003	0.002	0.004
Included fixed effects	cross-section/period	cross-section/period	cross-section/period	cross-section/period	cross-section/period	cross-section/period
N of observations	371	387	371	383	361	361
R-squared	0.33	0.33	0.33	0.33	0.36	0.34

Table 7.6 Panel estimation labour market deregulation (dependent variable: change labour market regulation indicator)

	(1)	(2)	(3)	(4)	(5)	(6)
	Convergence, learning and yardstick					
Level labour reg. (−1)	−0.100	−0.302***	−0.104	−0.280**	−0.127	−0.099
Square of lagged level (−1)	−0.02	0.118*	−0.069	0.118	−0.081	−0.057
Yardstick (−1)	−0.028	−0.077*	−0.027	−0.060	−0.074	−0.007
	Trade and capital mobility					
Mobility princip. component (−1)	0.001				0.002	0.001
Trade (−1)		−0.000**				
FDI (−1)			0.000			
Capital flows (−1)				−0.000		
	Decentralization/EU					
DRD3	0.000**	0.000***	0.000***	0.000***	0.000***	0.000***
EU dummy	0.004	0.004	0.005	0.003	0.004	0.004
	Regulatory interactions					
Level financial reg. (−1)					0.001	
Level trade reg. (−1)					−0.005	
Level product reg. (−1)					0.003	
Mean other regulation (−1)						−0.012
	Crisis proxies					
Growth (−1)	0.000	0.000*	0.000	0.000	0.000	0.000
Inflation (−1)	0.000**	0.000	0.000*	−0.000	0.000	0.000
	Ideology dummy (divergence from centre)					
Ideology dummy: left (−1)	0.007**	0.005	0.007**	0.005	0.005	0.007**
Ideology dummy: right (−1)	0.011***	0.009**	0.011***	0.009**	0.009**	0.010***
Fixed effects	cross-section / period	cross-section	cross-section / period	cross-section	cross-section	cross-section / period
N of observations	351	367	351	363	351	351
R-squared	0.41	0.33	0.41	0.31	0.33	0.41

groups that national producer lobbies lose political influence by the entry of foreign companies with the consequence that large FDI speeds up deregulation.

Whereas neither trade openness nor capital mobility are significant drivers of trade deregulation, there is an interesting significance of trade openness in the labour market regression: larger trade openness is linked to more regulated labour markets.

Decentralization is a significantly positive driver of deregulation in the case of financial and labour markets, but insignificant in the other cases. Not surprisingly owing to the construction of the internal market in the period under consideration, EU member countries show a significantly larger speed of trade liberalization than other OECD countries.

Further insights from the regressions are the following. There are hardly any signs of mutual reinforcements between the different fields of regulation (with the exception of a positive impact of labour on trade deregulation). Thus learning from deregulation appears to be limited to the same regulatory field.

The crisis hypothesis is supported for financial deregulation and growth crises: low levels of growth increase the likelihood of deregulative action. Interestingly, bad inflation data are not helpful for creating preconditions for structural change: inflation is either insignificant or – as in the case of the financial market regressions – it has a negative sign. This is a result not unimportant for monetary policy: allowing for high inflation rates does not appear to have the positive side-effect of speeding up deregulation. However, it should be added that this experience may be limited to the covered low inflation sample, while cases of high inflation or even hyperinflation clearly contribute to a feeling of crisis and may then act as a deregulation catalyst.

Finally, ideology has a significant impact, mainly in the case of labour market regulation. Here, significant differences exist between, on the one hand, left and right governments and, on the other hand, governments with a centre political orientation. Both left and right governments deregulate labour markets significantly more often than those associated with the political centre.

Conclusions

The central question of this study is the regulatory leeway which governments retain in the age of globalization. Our empirical study shows that, first of all, the era of globalization is a period of continuing (and converging) deregulation trends with regard to trade, financial and product markets of high-income industrial countries. At the same time, the econometric evidence shows that globalization in the narrow sense of trade openness and capital mobility has a rather limited impact as an immediate driver of deregulation. This means that national divergence from the global trends of deregulation is not clearly linked to the extent to which an economy is integrated in global capital, goods and services markets. Hence, in a narrow definition, globalization as such leaves substantial leeway for specific regulatory approaches of the nation state. However in a wider sense globalization definitions also comprise the easier flow of knowledge and information across borders resulting in more effective cross-border learning processes. The evidence suggests that these learning aspects of globalization are empirically relevant – at least in fields like product and financial markets. Yardstick competition is important: governments commanding instruments of regulatory redistribution cannot ignore deregulation processes beyond their national borders.

The notable exception from these insights is labour market regulation. With regard to job protection regulation and the generosity of unemployment benefits, neither deregulation nor convergence can be detected in the covered period. In addition regulatory trends in the labour markets can be explained only poorly by the logic of convergence or cross-border learning. At the same time, government ideologies have a relatively large impact. Furthermore, there is some evidence that labour market regulation increases with more trade openness. These findings do not allow us to discriminate between Rodrik's compensation hypothesis and Vaubel's alternative explanation: voters may demand higher levels of job protection and unemployment benefits because more structural change and job market turnover are the necessary outcome of globalization (Rodrik's view) or because globalization increases structural unemployment in countries with inflexible labour markets (Vaubel's view).

A further remarkable result is the catalyst role domestic decentralization appears to play for deregulation. This is a reminder about the continuing relevance of national constitutional structures for policy outcomes in a globalizing environment.

Some final caveats must be added. The detected deregulation trends may obscure the fact that in fields not covered by available indicators – for example social or environmental policies – regulation may be progressing. David Henderson correctly raises this point in his comment. Furthermore, our empirical evidence is based on the period between 1975 up to the end of the last century. More recent spurs to locational competition, for example, the Eastern enlargement of the European Union, may have changed the situation since then. Recent labour market reforms, for example in Germany, might indicate a new development that, finally, labour market regulation has to adjust to the increasing international competition. However, it remains to be seen whether these isolated cases of deregulation result in a more general trend.

Appendix

Table 7.A1 Data sources

Time series	Description	Source
WEOFINANCIAL	Index financial sector regulation, details see text section 3	Helbling *et al.* (2004)
WEOLABOR	Index labour market regulation, details see text section 3	Helbling *et al.* (2004)
WEOPRODUCT	Index product market regulation, details see text section 3	Helbling *et al.* (2004)
WEOTRADE	Index trade liberalization, details see text section 3	Helbling *et al.* (2004)
DRD1	Share of revenue assigned to regions	Stegarescu (2004)
DRD3	Share of revenue under control of regions	Stegarescu (2004)
Growth	GDP growth	World Bank: World Development Indicators
Inflation	Inflation, consumer prices	World Bank: World Development Indicators
FDI	Gross foreign direct investment in % GDP	World Bank: World Development Indicators
Trade	Sum of exports and imports of goods and services (in % GDP)	World Bank: World Development Indicators
Capital flows	Sum of the absolute values of direct, portfolio, and other investment inflows and outflows recorded in the balance of payments financial account, excluding changes in the assets and liabilities of monetary authorities and general government (in % GDP)	World Bank: World Development Indicators
Foreign population	Foreign population (in %)	World Bank: World Development Indicators
Ideology dummy: Left	Generated from chief executive's party ideology variable	Beck *et al.* (2001)
Ideology dummy: Right	Generated from chief executive's party ideology variable	Beck *et al.* (2001)
EU-member	Dummy for EU membership	

Note

1 Note that, on the basis of the Economic Freedom of the World Indicator, David Henderson in his subsequent comment arrives at a very similar description of deregulation trends.

References

Abiad, Abdul and Mody, Ashoka (2003) 'Financial Reform: What Shakes It? What Shapes It?' *IMF Working Paper*, WP/03/70, Washington.

Arellano, Manuel and Bond, Stephen (1991) 'Some Tests of Specification for Panel Data: Monte Carlo Evidence and an Application to Employment Equations', *Review of Economic Studies*, 58, 277–97.

Attanasio, Orazio P., Lucio, Picci and Scorcu, Antonelle E. (2000) 'Saving, Growth, and Investment: A Macroeconomic Analysis Using a Panel of Countries', *The Review of Economics and Statistics*, 82, 182–211.

Beck, T., Clarke, G., Groff, A., Keefer, P. and Walsh, P. (2001) 'New Tools in Comparative Political Economy: The Database of Political Institutions', *The World Bank Economic Review*, 15, 165–76.

Besley, Timothy and Case, Anne (1995) 'Incumbent Behavior: Vote-Seeking, Tax-Setting, and Yardstick Competition', *The American Economic Review*, 85, 25–45.

Fernandez, Raquel and Rodrik, Dani (1991) 'Resistance to Reform: Status Quo Bias in the Presence of Individual-Specific Uncertainty', *American Economic Review*, 81, 1146–55.

Heinemann, Friedrich (2004) 'Explaining Reform Deadlocks', *Applied Economics Quarterly Supplement*, 55, 9–26.

Helbling, Thomas, Hakura, Dalia and Debrun, Xavier (2004) 'Fostering Structural Reforms in Industrial Countries', in *World Economic Outlook, 2004*, Washington, DC: International Monetary Fund, chapter III, pp. 103–46.

Mueller, Dennis C. (1989) *Public Choice II*, Cambridge: Cambridge University Press.

Nickell, Stephen and Nunziata, Luca (2001) *Labour Market Institutions Database*, September.

Nicoletti, Guiseppe and Scarpetta, Stefano (2003) 'Regulation, Productivity, and Growth: OECD Evidence', *Economic Policy*, April, 11–72.

Olson, Mancur (1965) *The Logic of Collective Action*, Cambridge, Mass.: Harvard University Press.

Pitlik, Hans and Wirth, Steffen (2003) 'Do Crises Promote the Extent of Economic Liberalization? An Empirical Test', *European Journal of Political Economy*, 19, 565–81.

Rodrik, Dani (1996) 'Understanding Economic Policy Reform', *Journal of Economic Literature*, 34, 9–41.

—— (1998) 'Why do More Open Economies have Bigger Governments?' *Journal of Political Economy*, 106, 997–1032.

Samuelson, William and Zeckhauser, Richard (1988) 'Status Quo Bias in Decision Making', *Journal of Risk and Uncertainty*, 1, 7–59.

Schulze, Günther G. and Ursprung, Heinrich W. (1999) 'Globalisation of the Economy and the Nation State', *The World Economy*, 22, 295–352.

Stegarescu, Dan (2004) 'Public Sector Decentralization: Measurement Concepts and Recent International Trends', ZEW Discussion Paper No. 04–74, Centre for European Economic Research (ZEW), Mannheim.

Vaubel, Roland (2000) 'Internationaler Politischer Wettbewerb: Eine europäische Wettbewerbsaufsicht für Regierungen und die empirische Evidenz', in Schenk, Karl-Ernst *et al.* (eds) *Globalisierung und Weltwirtschaft, Jahrbuch für Neue Politische Ökonomie*, 19, 280–309.

—— (2005) 'Sozialpolitische Konsequenzen der Globalisierung: Theorie und Empirie', in Andreas Freytag (ed.) *Weltwirtschaftlicher Strukturwandel, nationale Wirtschafts-politik und politische Rationalität*, Universitätsverlag Köln, pp. 143–58.

COMMENT: THE UNEASY TREND TO GREATER ECONOMIC FREEDOM

David Henderson

Over the past three decades, from the mid-1970s, there has been a general tendency across the world to make economies freer and less regulated: the fortunes of economic liberalism, though chequered as always, have on balance significantly improved. To an extent that was largely unforeseen, a growing number of governments, at different stages and with many individual variations, have taken steps to make national economies less subject to regulation, and international transactions freer. In this chapter I comment briefly, first, on the extent and limits of this trend; second, on the influences which have given rise to it; and third, on the significance of the process as a whole.[1]

In doing so, I start from, and draw on, the analysis presented in Friedrich Heinemann's illuminating chapter, though I refer to trends in developing countries as well as the OECD member countries which he covers and say much less about developments in different areas of policy. Like him, I consider the evolution of policies from the 1970s onwards. As will be seen, my view of the story of economic liberalization differs from his in some respects, though the differences go together with a substantial measure of agreement.

Liberalization from the 1970s

In reviewing the course of liberalization over the past three decades for the world as a whole, a useful point of departure is the latest in the series of reports entitled *Economic Freedom of the World* (hereafter EFW): the most recently published volume brings the story up to 2003, and covers 127 countries.[2] For each country, an overall index of economic freedom is computed, which combines ratings under five main headings with some 38 sub-headings. The five headings are: size of government; legal structure and security of property rights; access to sound money; freedom to exchange with foreigners; and regulation of labour, credit and business. Changes in the overall index for a country thus provide a general indication of the extent to which liberalization and deregulation have been taking place within it, while changes in the various headings and sub-headings reflect developments in specific areas of policy.

Here I focus chiefly on the 50 largest economies among those covered in the Report.[3] They can be classed in four groups: 20 core members of the Organization for Economic Cooperation and Development (OECD); four other economies which the International Monetary Fund (IMF) now categorizes as 'advanced' (Israel, Singapore, South Korea and Taiwan); four former communist European countries, (the Czech Republic, Poland, Russia and Ukraine); and 22 developing countries.[4]

A useful feature of the EFW series is that for each country the overall index is carried back as far as the authors consider the data will permit, with 1970 as the earliest year. A key table shows values for the index at five-yearly intervals over the period 1970–2000, and then for each year from 2000 to 2003. For 42 of the 50 countries, including all the core OECD members, the overall index is taken back to 1970.

Timing

Over the whole period, and focusing on economy-wide changes, the extent of liberalization can be gauged in each case by comparing the value of the overall index for 2003 with the lowest figure shown for an earlier year. Generally speaking, for the countries where the data go back to 1970, that lowest value is for the year 1975: this is true for 30 countries, while for three others the low point falls in 1970. For all these 33 economies, therefore – comprising all but one of the OECD group, three of the four 'other advanced' economies, and 11 of the developing countries – the process of reform can be seen as extending over a period of a quarter of a century or more; and the same is true of the leading case of China where the first crucial moves towards liberalization date from 1978.

In other countries on the list, the lowest value shown for the overall index refers to later years. Thus in three Latin American economies – Brazil, Mexico and Peru – the low point is that for 1985, while in the four European ex-communist countries liberalization got under way only with the collapse of the former planned economy at the end of the 1980s.

While as noted the EFW index is shown only at five-yearly intervals for the period 1970–2000, the above results are consistent with, and can be supplemented by, information relating to intermediate years. My own view is that for the world as a whole, though of course with many exceptions among individual countries, the late 1970s mark a watershed. It was then, and from 1978 in particular, that clear signs emerged of a reversal of what had been a general anti-liberal trend in both the OECD group and many developing countries. As time went on, such reversals occurred in a growing number of countries.

The timing of these shifts in policy has varied from case to case: despite resemblances and common features, there was no uniform cross-country pattern of liberalization. Even within the OECD group, there were instances – such as Canada, France and New Zealand – where the trend of policies remained interventionist into the 1980s. More broadly, and as will be seen below, both the timing and the content of reforms were largely determined by national circumstances and decisions.

Extent

From the EFW series a striking fact emerges. Comparing the 2003 values of the index with its lowest earlier value from 1970 onwards, *49 out of these 50 countries appear as having become less regulated*: the only exception to the general trend, a conspicuous one, is Venezuela.[5] There can be no doubt about the broad direction of change, which was common to all the four groups of countries identified here.

One feature of this process of liberalization is that the gap between the OECD group and the other 'advanced economies', on the one hand, and the developing countries and former communist countries on the other, has narrowed appreciably. This was to be expected for the latter group, since the reforming ex-communist economies were so highly regulated to start with. It is also true, however, of the developing countries viewed as a group. The unweighted average value of the overall EFW index for the 20 OECD core countries in 1975 was 5.8, out of a maximum score of ten, and the counterpart figure for the 22 developing economies was 3.9. For 2003 the corresponding figures are 7.5 for the OECD group and 6.1 for the developing countries. Hence the absolute increase over the period was greater for the latter countries, so that the gap between the two groups was reduced; and the value of the overall figure for the developing countries in 2003 was higher than that for the OECD group in 1975.

Not surprisingly, the extent of deregulation has been far from uniform across different areas of the economy: this emerges clearly from the studies relating to OECD countries that Heinemann draws on, as also from the EFW report. Broadly speaking, the headings under which liberalization has gone ahead most conspicuously have been the decontrol of financial markets; the freeing of international transactions; privatization of state enterprises; the deregulation of particular industries including transport and power generation as well as financial services; and tax reforms. When it comes to labour markets, however, the evidence suggests that in many if not most of the 50 countries, though with some notable exceptions, the overall balance has shifted in an anti-liberal direction. Evidence to this effect is presented by Heinemann for core OECD members, while for a number of developing countries, especially in Latin America, a similar trend shows up in the EFW report.

In interpreting these studies, an aspect to be borne in mind is that the evidence that they draw on does not fully cover the growing extent of regulation under two headings in particular. One of these is environmental regulation, which has certainly become more stringent over the past 30 years or more in ways that may have affected adversely the working of product markets. A second is the growth, again over a long period in many countries, of laws and regulations designed to further the related goals of 'anti-discrimination', 'equal opportunity', 'affirmative action' and 'diversity'. Such measures compel people and enterprises to enter into arrangements that they would prefer to avoid and narrow the range of possibilities open to them. In a wide range of countries they have contributed, in conjunction with regulatory actions designed to restrict working hours or prevent 'unfair dismissals', to a substantial erosion of freedom of contract.

Causes and influences

As always, causation is a complex and debatable topic. In two respects, I would qualify without rejecting lines of argument that Heinemann develops in his chapter. I would also emphasize two aspects that he does not explicitly refer to.

First, however, a word about the aspect of globalization which he focuses on in particular.

Globalization

Heinemann rightly views with reserve the idea that globalization, in the sense of closer international economic integration, has been a strong influence on the extent of deregulation. Two general points are worth making here.

First, and contrary to what is often argued or assumed, closer international economic integration has not been forced on reluctant governments which had little choice but to accept it. It has been the result of national policies, rather than a constraining factor on them (though an element of constraint is there). Over the past 25 years an increasing number of governments have acted, for the most part on their own account, to make international trade and capital flows freer. They have done so chiefly because they considered, with good reason, that such liberalization was in the interest of their peoples.

Second and more broadly, closer international economic integration has not deprived governments of the power to act and decide. Aside from such constraints on external policies as they have freely accepted and wish to maintain, national states today remain almost as free to determine their choice of policies as they were ten, 20 or 30 years ago.[6]

Generally speaking market-oriented reforms across the world have reflected national adaptation to events and situations; and though emulation has played a part, governments have largely retained their freedom to act. Again, 'systems competition' has not been a strong influence, though it may be operative in a few areas of policy such as taxes on corporations.

The impact of crises

My first comment by way of qualification relates to the influence on policy of crises. Heinemann refers to studies which make the point that 'deep economic crises tend to increase the likelihood of structural reforms'. This is true so far as it goes, and fits well a number of episodes – such as France in 1983, New Zealand in 1984, Argentina in the late 1980s, and India in 1991. However, the opposite effect is also to be seen in this period. A leading instance is the OECD core countries during the 1970s. It is no accident that the EFW index shows for almost all these countries a fall between 1970 and 1975, and I would guess that the fall would be greater if 1972 and 1978 were being compared. In response to the acute economic problems that arose in 1972–3, these countries introduced a range of interventionist measures, including price and wage controls, stronger trade restrictions and tighter foreign exchange controls, new state-directed energy programmes, and special assistance to struggling firms and industries. A recent example of a similar policy reaction is Argentina, where the EFW index shows a significant fall between 2000 and 2003. This reversal of policy – for in the 1990s Argentine governments had been among the leading reformers –

largely reflects measures that were adopted as part of the official response to a serious crisis.

Interests, pressures and pre-economic ideas

A second qualification concerns the influence brought to bear by interest groups. Heinemann, in common with other authors, gives too much weight to this. He rightly notes that regulation, like taxes and transfers, can serve to favour such groups; and he views as typical, situations in which governments aiming to max-imize votes weigh the gains in votes to be expected from those who stand to benefit from regulatory changes against the expected losses from those who will be made worse off. There are indeed many issues and decisions which fit this pattern: a topical example is the recently imposed restrictions on imports of Chinese-made clothing into the EU. But most of the liberalization measures of the past 30 years reflected other motives and influences: they were at the same time less opportunist, more driven by events, and more directed towards the general welfare. Typically, governments acted to deal with situations or devel-opments which clearly gave grounds for concern, and where deregulation could be seen as a remedy. They thought that the reforms they put into effect would improve economic performance and thus make people in general better off; and they hoped that after the event they would be backed, or at any rate forgiven, by public opinion. A notable instance was privatization. In the British case, which set the pattern for others, one of the leading ministers concerned has noted that:

> In advance of every significant privatisation, public opinion was invariably hostile to the idea, and there was no way it could be won round except by the government going ahead and doing it.[7]

One form of public pressure on governments today, not mentioned by Heine-mann, arises from the many so-called 'public interest' non-governmental organi-zations (the NGOs). Unlike the more traditional pressure groups, which reflect the well-defined material interests of sectional or professional groups, the NGOs stand for particular causes. They include consumer associations, conservation and environmental groups, societies concerned with economic development in poor countries, human rights groups, movements for social justice, humanitarian societies, organizations representing indigenous peoples, and church groups from all denominations. They are often classed together under the label of 'civil society', though this is a misuse of language. Almost without exception, they are opposed to freedom of cross-border trade and capital flows, suspicious of further moves in that direction (except possibly for unilateral trade concessions by rich to poor countries), and preoccupied with what they see as the damaging effects of globalization. These attitudes typically go with a general hostility to capital-ism, multinational enterprises and the market economy. The influence of the NGOs has grown considerably over the past 20 years or so.

Anti-liberal beliefs, presumptions and attitudes are of course not confined to

NGOs and the groups that benefit economically from regulation. Today as in the past, and in most if not all countries, economic policies are liable to be influenced by firmly held intuitive economic ideas which owe little or nothing to textbooks, treatises or the evidence of economic history. These ideas can justly be termed 'pre-economic': I class them under the heading of 'do-it-yourself economics' (DIYE).[8]

Such notions are not only to be found among ordinary people. To the contrary, they are sincerely held, and voiced with conviction, by political figures, top civil servants, CEOs of business enterprises large and small, prominent trade union officials, well-known journalists and commentators, senior judges, religious leaders and eminent professors. That is why they should be viewed as a serious influence on events. Economists typically ignore or underestimate this factor, for two related reasons. First, they find it hard to believe that 'rational' agents – intelligent, highly educated, well informed, experienced and influential people – think about economic events and relationships in ways that are quite different from theirs. Second, they prefer to model human behaviour in terms of private interests that are well defined and accurately perceived: hence they view the actions of politicians and officials, as also of voters, too exclusively through the prism of public choice theory.

Characteristically, DIYE is collectivist: it combines mistrust of markets, self-interest and the profit motive with an attribution to governments, first, of roles, responsibilities and functions which are not necessarily theirs, and second, of a fully developed capacity to control events and determine outcomes. Generally speaking, therefore, it operates as an anti-liberal influence.

Accounting for liberalization

If the above arguments are correct, the advances made by liberalization over this past 25–30 years present something of a puzzle. Governments were not obliged to take this path by outside factors beyond their control, arising from 'globalization'. Old-style economically motivated interest groups were not a positive influence, since for the most part liberalization did not figure on their agenda or was seen as contrary to their interests. The new-style and increasingly influential NGOs were and are anti-liberal, while the still-prevalent ideas of DIYE retained their collectivist leanings and presumptions. How was it that, in face of these unfavourable or unhelpful factors, deregulation went ahead in virtually all the leading economies of the world?

In a word, the answer is to be found in the impact of events, and perceptions of events, on the general climate of opinion and the thinking of governments in particular. Broadly, four categories, or country groupings, can be distinguished. First, in many cases, as noted already, economic crises provided a strong initial impulse to reform: the crises required a response from governments, and they raised questions about underlying features of the existing policy regime including the role of the state within it. Second, in the former communist countries the existing economic system was abruptly exposed as no longer viable. Third, there were a number of other countries, including the important cases of China, the US and the UK, where the main impulse came, not from crises or collapse, but from chronic and growing concerns about economic performance. In these countries it became more widely held, especially in influential circles, that performance had suffered from excessively strict regulation, the malfunctioning of public enterprises, high levels of public expenditure and tax rates, the failure to curb inflation, and the growth of trade union power. In all the above three groups, both the pattern of events and the shift in attitudes that went with it created opportunities and incentives for governments to take the path of market-oriented reform. Elsewhere, governments that were less subject to these various pressures to act were influenced both by the experience of others and by the shift in the general climate of opinion.

Assessment

Both opponents and supporters of the process of liberalization have overdramatized it. Some of the critics hold that doctrinaire liberalism has been taken to extremes, that it now reigns supreme, and that it represents a threat to community values and social progress: dark references are made to a supposed 'neoliberal hegemony'. On the other side of the ideological fence, some commentators have drawn the conclusion that (to quote one of them) 'the free market has emerged triumphant, accepted once again everywhere as the natural condition of mankind'.[9]

Both of these are overreactions to events. They attribute to the sequence of reforms a coherence, a degree of thoroughness, a breadth of support and a cosmic significance that it does not possess. Everywhere, and predictably, the process of liberalization has been partial, uneven, disputed, and subject to qualifications, reservations and exceptions. In few countries, or areas of policy, can it be taken for granted that the recent trend towards market-oriented reform will be maintained. Collectivist views and anti-market pressures remain influential everywhere, and for many of those who hold such views the collapse of communism might just as well have taken place on another planet. All over the world, hostility to market processes and private business remains widespread; and in no country is there a government, or even a political movement with strong support, which takes as a guiding principle the case for greater economic freedom. Despite its recent gains, therefore, the future scope and status of the competitive market economy are by no means assured.

Today the main growing interventionist challenge – it is not the only one – takes the form of pressures for closer and far-reaching regulation of particular kinds. Underlying these pressures is the widely prevalent belief that progress is to be defined in terms of the adoption and enforcement of ever more stringent and more uniform environmental and 'social' standards. Further moves in this direction may come from governments, through legislation, or from corporations acting in the name of 'corporate social responsibility' (CSR).[10] An especially worrying aspect, already to be seen in some trade agreements, is that attempts will increasingly be made to regulate the world as a whole by imposing common international norms and standards. This would restrict the scope for mutually beneficial trade and investment flows, and hold back the development of poor countries by restricting employment opportunities within them.

However, such trends and possibilities form only part of the picture. Despite the continuing and in some ways growing hold of what I have termed new millennium collectivism, it is possible to present too sombre a view of the situation and prospects of the market economy. For the most part, and in the great majority of countries, the moves that have been made towards greater economic freedom do not at present appear as under threat. Privatization, and alongside it various far-reaching forms of deregulation, have almost certainly come to stay. Much has been done to restore, after a lapse of almost a century, a predominantly liberal system of international trade, payments and investment, and this trend seems unlikely to be reversed. Some progress, albeit limited, has been made in relation to the reform of tax regimes. Above all, the period has brought an end to the huge, prolonged and disastrous experiment of communism, while liberalization has transformed the economy of China. These various changes, largely unforeseen, have given new life to the doctrine and practice of economic liberalism.

Notes

1 At a number of points below I draw on, without specific page references, two publications of mine: *Anti-Liberalism 2000* (2000) and *The Changing Fortunes of Economic Liberalism* (2001).
2 Gwartney and Lawson (2005).
3 The list of 50 is derived from Maddison's estimates for GDP in 2001 (Maddison 2004). Only three of the world's 50 largest economies in that year, as shown by him, are not covered by the EFW series: Saudi Arabia, Vietnam (for which however some estimates are given for 2003), and Kazakhstan. I have also excluded Hong Kong here when referring to changes, since throughout the period since 1970 it has received high ratings for economic freedom which have shown little alteration.
4 By 'core' OECD countries I refer to the 24 countries which were already members of the Organization in the early 1970s. Of these, three economies – Iceland, Luxembourg and New Zealand – are too small to count among the world's top 50, while Turkey is still classed as a developing country and I count it as such here. This brings the figure down to 20. Within the other three country groupings, the Czech Republic, Poland, Mexico and South Korea are now OECD members.
5 Among the smaller economies, another conspicuous exception is Zimbabwe.
6 Arguments and evidence in support of this view are well set out in the final chapter of Sally (1999) and in Chapter 12 of Wolf (2004).
7 Lawson (1992: 201).
8 Evidence as to the character, pervasiveness and influence of DIYE, together with many specific instances of it, can be found in my short book, *Innocence and Design* (1986) as also in pp. 121–7 of the second edition of *The Changing Fortunes of Economic Liberalism* (2001).
9 Letwin (1999). He is now a 'shadow minister', a front-bench spokesman, for the British Conservative Party.
10 I have treated the subject of CSR in *Misguided Virtue* (2001) and in *The Role of Busi-*

ness in the Modern World: Progress, Pressures, and Prospects for the Market Economy (2004).

References

Gwartney, James and Lawson, Robert with Erik Gartzke (2005) *Economic Freedom of the World: 2005 Annual Report*, Vancouver (Canada): Fraser Institute, and Washington, DC: Cato Institute.

Henderson, David (1986*) Innocence and Design: The Influence of Economic Ideas on Policy*, Oxford: Blackwell.

—— (2000) *Anti-Liberalism 2000: The Rise of New Millennium Collectivism*, London: Institute of Economic Affairs.

—— (2001) *The Changing Fortunes of Economic Liberalism*, 2nd edn, London: Institute of Economic Affairs.

—— (2001) *Misguided Virtue: False Notions of Corporate Social Responsibility*, Wellington: New Zealand Business Roundtable, and London: Institute of Economic Affairs.

—— (2004) *The Role of Business in the Modern World: Progress, Pressures, and Prospects for the Market Economy*, Wellington: New Zealand Business Roundtable, London: Institute of Economic Affairs, and Washington, DC: The Competitive Enterprise Institute.

Lawson, Nigel (1992) *The View from No. 11*, London: Bantam Press.

Letwin, Oliver (1999) 'Civilised Conservatism', in *Conservative Debates*, London: Politeia.

Maddison, Angus (2004) *The World Economy: Historical Statistics*, Paris: OECD.

Razeen, Sally (1999) *Classical Liberalism and International Economic Order*, London: Routledge.

Wolf, Martin (2004) *Why Globalization Works*, New Haven: Yale University Press.

Index

References to notes are prefixed by *n*.
Italic page numbers indicate tables not
included in the text page range.

Abiad, Abdul 246
Acemoglu, D. 132
Acton, Lord 2
Adams, Scott 35
affirmative action 269
Ashworth, John 106
Ashworth *et al.* 212
asymmetric information 204, 205
at-will principle 23–6
Autor, David H. 24, 25–6

Baird, Charles W. 28
Bardhan, P. 207
Bartel, Ann P. 19, 21–3
Baum, L. 212
Bebchuk, L.A. 206
Becker, G. 127
Berlin Conference (1890) 183
Bernholz, P. 213
Berry, F.S. 212
Berry, W.D. 212
Besley, Timothy 44, 103, 106–7, 209
Bismarck, Otto von 194
Blanchard, O. 118
Block, Richard N. 19, 24
Blumer, Johann Jakob 217
Bonaparte, Napoleon 200
Boockmann, B. 223
Bornhauser, Thomas 214
Botero *et al.* 118, 119, 130
Brandeis, Louis 208
Brennan, G. 207
Breton, Albert 110
British North America Act – BNA Act
    (1867) (Canadian Constitution) 53–7
Brueckner, J.K. 207, 223

Buchanan, J.M. 139–40, 207
budget balancing requirements 86–9, *92*,
    241–3

Cadieux, Mr 67
Caldeira, G.A. 212
Canada: budget balancing requirements
    86–9, *92*; childcare policies 82–3, *92*;
    economic activity 64–70; education
    74–9; features of provinces *59*; general
    regulations 83–6; interjurisdictional
    competition 53, 58, 64–6; labour
    markets 70–4; legal system 54, 55–6;
    Medicare 79–80, *92*; pesticides
    regulation 105; political setting 57–8;
    strike replacement law *64*, 70–2, *91*, 96;
    Sunday shopping deregulation 69–70,
    71, *91*, 93–5; taxation 54–5; tobacco
    regulation 80–2, *92*; university fees *91*;
    wage rates *97–8*; yardstick competition
    6–8, 79, 90, 93, 103–10
Canada Business Corporations Act
    (CBCA) 68
Canadian Constitution (British North
    America Act – BNA Act – 1867)
    53–7
Canadian federation: framework of
    governance 53–64
Canadian Pension Plan (CPP) 74
Canadian Radio and Television
    Commission (CRTC) 62
Canak, William 27
Canon, B.C. 212
cantonal regulations 12–13, 214–16, 217,
    219–31, 241–3
Carney, W.J. 212–13
cartels 148, 188, 215, 218; *see also* guilds
Carter, L.E. 212
Case, Anne 44, 103, 106–7, 209
Cassidy, Mr 67

CBCA (Canada Business Corporations
Act) *see* Canada Business Corporations
Act
centralization 3–4, 15, 148
Charter of Fundamental Rights 8
Charter of Fundamental Social Rights of
Workers (1989) 8, 114–16, 133, 148
child protection 181
childcare policies: Canada 82–3, *92*
Christopherson, Mr 88
Civil Code 143, 180
civil law: competitiveness 144–5; labour
protection 180; *vs.* common law 142–3
Code du Travail 8
collective bargaining: Canada 64
common law: English 142–3; and labour
regulations 130–1
common law at-will principle 23–6
Common Law of the Prussian Territories
('*Allgemeines Landrecht für die
Preußischen Staaten*') 156
Common Market Law 202, 214, 222
communications: Canada 62
competition: fiscal 200–1; and innovation
205; market 45; political 45; tax 4, 213;
see also institutional competition;
interjurisdictional competition;
regulatory competition; yardstick
competition
competitive federalism 207
construction industry: Canada 61
consumer protection 179
contract law 55
'corporate social responsibility' (CSR) 273
corporatist movements: Switzerland 218
corruption 130, 207–8
CPP (Canadian Pension Plan) *see*
Canadian Pension Plan
craft-guilds 156–7, 164–6
crisis hypothesis 249, 262, 270, 272
CRTC *see* Canadian Radio and Television
Commission
CSR *see* 'corporate social responsibility'
Cumming, Douglas J. 6, 68

Danet, Didier 144
Davis–Bacon Act (1931) 5, 36
De Chambrier, A. 219, 223
decentralization 207–8, 210, 253, 262, 263
Deficit Elimination Act 88
demesne states 160
deregulation: conditions for 4; early
modern Germany 165–6; financial
13–14, *258*; and globalization 13–15,

245–63; and interest groups 15; labour
market 14, 47, *261*; product market 14,
251, *259*; Switzerland 218–19, 231;
trade 14, *260*, 262; and yardstick
competition 14; *see also* liberalization;
Sunday shopping deregulation
Dertouzos, James N. 25
destination principle 180
diffusion: of innovation 208–9; tax
structure 213
Djankov *et al.* 131
'do-it-yourself economics' (DIYE) 15, 272
Douglas, T.C. 80
Doyon, Réjean 70

Early Childhood Education and Care
policy 82
Economic Freedom of the World (EFW)
267
economic liberalization 267–4
EFW *see Economic Freedom of the World*
electricity: Canada 62
Ellwood, David T. 27
Emergency Trade Law (Notgewerbegesetz
– 1868) 195
emigration 162, 182
employment protection 118, 121–7,
127–30
English common law 130–1
Environmental Protection Act (1970) 5
Environmental Protection Agency (EPA)
21–2
environmental regulation 61, 212, 263, 269
environmental standards 61, 273
EPA *see* Environmental Protection Agency
ETUC *see* European Trade Union
Congress
EU *see* European Union
EU-15: dimensions of labour market
regulations 113–21; efficiency of labour
market regulation 121–7; worker's
rights *114–15*
Europe: labour market regulation 46–8
European Trade Union Congress (ETUC)
150
European Union (EU) 2, 8–9, 47, 148–51
'exit' 1, 3, 5, 15, 159, 161, 211

Fair Labor Standards Act 20
Federal Energy Regulatory Commission
(FERC) 62
Federal Fair Labor Standards Act (1938) 5
federal legislation 21–3, 45–6
federal powers: Canada 54–7

federal regulation 4–5, 194–8
federalism 141–2; competitive 207;
    German Reich (1871) 187–9;
    Switzerland 200–2
FERC *see* Federal Energy Regulatory
    Commission
Figlio *et al.* 212
Filer *et al.* 212
financial deregulation 13–14, *258*
financial institutions: Canada 63
Fine, Glenn 27
firm incorporation: Canada 68–9
fiscal competition 200–1
fiscal decentralization 253, *255*
Fishback, Price V. 28–30
fisheries: Canada 58, 60
Fond de solidarité des travailleurs du
    Québec (FSTQ) 66, 68
food regulation 10–11, 178–80
foreign policy: and regulation 49–52
forestry: Canada 60–1
France 130–1, 143
Fredrikson, P.G. 212
Freeman, Richard B. 19, 35, 37
Frey, B.S. 130, 223
FSTQ *see* Fond de solidarité des
    travailleurs du Québec

Gatsios, K. 206
German Reich (1871) 175–6, 186, 187–9
Germany: absolutism 158–9; agriculture
    166; convergence 185–6; craft-guilds
    156–7, 164–6; emigration 162; Holy
    Roman Empire 155–9; households
    (*familia*) 155–7; immigration 160–1;
    meta-institutions 167–8; mobile factors
    of production 159–62; principalities
    158; state formation 162–3, 168; taxes
    167–8; towns 160–1; village
    communities 157, 166
Glaeser, E. 131, 137
globalization: and deregulation 13–15,
    245–63; and economic integration 270
Great Britain: labour protection 182; *see
    also* UK (United Kingdom)
Green, David A. 6, 72
Grubb, D. 118
Guelfi, Anita 140
guilds 214–15, 217

harmonization 148; German Reich (1871)
    175, 187–9; labour protection 183–5;
    regulatory competition 213–22
Harrison, Kathryn 6, 72

Hayek, Friedrich August von 163, 207
Heine, K. 213
Helbling *et al.* 246
Heyndels, Bruno 106
Hirsch, Barry T. 36
Hirschman, Albert O. 1, 2, 161, 176
Holmes, P. 206
Holy Roman Empire: general 155;
    households (*familia*) 155–7; and
    institutional competition 152–3;
    political and constitutional conditions
    155–9; principalities 158
Hospital Insurance and Diagnostic
    Services Act (1957) 79, 80

incorporation regulation 6–7, *91*, 206
institutional competition 152; meta-
    institutions 167–8; model 176–7; in
    nineteenth century 177–8; and
    regulation 163–6; theory 154–5
interest groups: and deregulation 15;
    distributional conflict 127–30; Germany
    10; and globalization 247; influence of
    3–4, 271; rent-seeking 207; Switzerland
    201, 218; USA 46–7
interjurisdictional competition: beneficial
    effects 43–4; Canada 53, 58, 64–6,
    83–9; and federalism 141–2; fiscal
    200–1; functional 145–6; and labour
    market regulation 43–8; models 20–1;
    neoclassical criticisms 204–6; overview
    4–15; theory 1–4; tuition fees 79
International Association for the Protection
    of Labour 184
international harmonization: labour
    protection 182
international trade: regulations 49–52

Jain, Harish C. 72
Johnson, S. 132

Kant, Immanuel 1
Kantor, Shawn Everett 30–2
Karoly, Lynn A. 25
Katz, Lawrence F. 36
Kelejian, H.H. 229
Kelsen, Hans 142
Kessler, Daniel P. 36
Kirchgässner, G. 229, 243
Klopp, Hans Joachim 198
Koeniger *et al.* 8, 118
Kollman *et al.* 210
Kotsogiannis, C. 210
Krueger, Alan B. 23–5

Kwinter, Mr 67

La Porta *et al.* 56, 137
Labor–Management Relations Act (1947) 4, 26, 27
labour laws: Canada 63–4
labour market deregulation 14, *261*
labour protection 180–5; agreements 186–7; harmonization 187–9
labour regulation: Canada 6; common law 21; convergence 185–6; dimensions (EU-15) 113–21; and distributional conflict 127–32, 133, 137, 139–40; drafting 150; efficiency 121–7, 133, 137, 138–9; EU 8–9; Europe 46–8; European nineteenth century 11; federal level 37, 45–46; France 8–9; Germany nineteenth century 10–11; and globalization 248, 253, 263; legal environment 137; living wage laws 32–6; Occupational Safety and Health Administration (OSHA) regulations 21–3; raising rivals' cost 21–3; right-to-work legislation 26–8; UK 47–8; unjust dismissal legislation 23–6; USA 4–5, 20–2; workers' compensation 30–2; workplace safety legislation 28–30
Ladner, A. 214
Lane, Jan-Erik 150
LaPlant, J.T. 212
Lazear, E. 118
Lee, Dwight 20, 37
legal harmonization: Switzerland 217
legal origin theory 130–2
liberalization: economic 267–74; of labour market 47–8; Switzerland 218–19; *see also* deregulation
living wage laws 32–36
LSVCFs (labour-sponsored venture capital funds) *91*; Canada 66–8
Luce, Stephanie 34

Maastricht Treaty *see* Social Chapter (Agreement) of Maastricht
McAleer, Mr 73–4
MacIntosh, Jeffrey G. 6, 68
MacLeod, Bentley 145
Madison, James 3
majority decisions 9, 57, 116, 148–9
Malépart, Mr 74
mandatory retirement 73–4, *91*
Martin, Isaac 34
Mattila, Miko 150
Medical Care Act (1968) 79

Medicare: Canada 79–80, *92*
Miller, Berkeley 27
Millimet, D.L. 212
mimicking behaviour: Switzerland 223–31, 241–3
minimum wages 116–17; Canada 72–3, *91*
mining: Canada 61
Mody, Ashoka 246
Mookherjee, D. 207
Morgentaler, Dr Henry 55

NAFTA 62
Napoleonic Code 130–1
National Children Benefit initiative (NCB) 82
National Labor Relations Act (NLRA) 26
NCB *see* National Children Benefit initiative
negligence liability 30
Neumark, David 32–3, 35
NGOs (non-governmental organizations) 271
Nice, D.C. 208
Nickell, S. 117
NLRA *see* National Labor Relations Act
no-fault insurance cover 30
North, D. 130
Norton, R.D. 4
Nozick, Robert 137, 140
NPM (new public management) 213–14

Oates, Wallace E. 20, 44, 201, 208
Occupational Safety and Health Act (1970) 5
Occupational Safety and Health Administration (OSHA) regulations 21–3
Olson, Mancur 3, 46, 247
origin principle 176, 178, 180
OSHA *see* Occupational Safety and Health Administration regulations

Pelkmans, J.J. 206
Pilik, Hans 246
policy innovation 208–10, 214
political compromise hypothesis 23–6
privatization 271, 274
product market deregulation 14, 251, *259*
provincial powers: Canada 54–7
Prucha, I.R. 229
Prussia 194–8
public choice 127–32, 206–7, 272

Qian, Yingyi 141

Quebec 55–7
Quintini, G. 117

raising rivals' costs: Bismarck 11–12;
    Canada 6; EU labour market regulation
    9, 149–51; federal regulation 5, 194–8;
    replacement for collusion 2; Switzerland
    222; USA labour regulation 20; wage
    legislation 39*n*16; workplace safety
    legislation 28–9
regulation: Canada 6–8; and economic
    competitiveness 1, 2–3; modern theory
    of 154
regulatory collusion 1, 2, 12–13, 150
regulatory competition 2, 202; early
    modern Germany 9–10; EU 8–9;
    nineteenth century Germany 10–11;
    studies 211–13; Switzerland 12–13,
    213–22; theoretical basis 203–11
Reichert, Hans-Klaus 196, 197
rent seeking 6, 9, 33, 51–2, 207
retail business hours regulation: Canada
    69–70, *71*, *91*, 93–5
retail trade: Canada 63
retirement, mandatory 73–4, *91*
revenue decentralization 253, *255*
Rieder, S. 214
right-to-work legislation 26–8
Rincke, J. 212
Robinson, D.H. 229
Rodden, J. 207
Romano, R. 212
Rose-Ackerman, Susan 141, 207

Saavedra, L.A. 212
Saint-Paul, G. 127–9
Salmon, P. 209
Saunders, O.J 62
Sausgruber, R. 212
Sawicki, Mr 88
Schanz, G. von 213
Schanz–Haig–Simons (SHS) tax systems
    213
Schmoller, Gustav 158
Schnellenbach, J. 210
Schwab, Robert M. 20, 44, 201
Schwager, R. 210
services: Canada 63
Shleifer, A. 131, 137
Singh, Parbudyal 72
Sinn, H.-W. 200–1, 202, 204–5
slave labour prohibition 49–50
Social Chapter (Agreement) of Maastricht
    8, 9, 116, 133, 148, 150–1

Sohmen, Egon 15
Sombart, Werner 153
Sommer, J.H. 222
Stanger, Ms 88
Stegarescu, Dan 253
Steiner, R. 213–14
Stieber, Jack 19, 24
Stigler, George 2, 3
Stigler–Peltzman model of regulation 247
strategy of raising rivals' costs *see* raising
    rivals' costs
Streit, Manfred E. 176
strike replacement law: Canada *64*, 70–2,
    91, 96
Strumpf, K. 210
Stutzer, A. 130, 223
subsidiarity principle 11, 189
Sun, J.-M. 206
Sunday shopping deregulation: Canada
    69–70, *71*, *91*, 93–5
Swiss Common Market Law (1995) 13
Switzerland: cantonal regulations 241–3;
    commercial activities 214–18;
    corporatist movements 218; federal
    constitution 216, 217; federalism 200–2;
    legal harmonization 217; liberalization
    218–19; mimicking behaviour 213–14,
    223–31, 241–3; tax competition 213;
    welfare state 216

Taft–Hartly Act (1947) 4, 26, 27
tax and expenditure limitation laws (TELs)
    see TELs
tax competition 4, 213
taxation 15, 54–5, 150, 160, 167–8
TELs (tax and expenditure limitation laws)
    241–2
Temporary Workers Directive 149
Thomas, Lacy Glenn 19, 21–3
THS (temporary help service) 24–5
Tiebout, Ch.M. 1, 20, 44, 176, 201, 203,
    211
tobacco regulation 80–2; Canada *92*
trade deregulation 14, *260*, 262
trade regulation 195, 197, 251, 253
trade unions *see* unions
transportation: Canada 61–2
Treaty of Amsterdam (1997) 8, 116
Treaty of Maastricht *see* Social Chapter
    (Agreement) of Maastricht
Treisman, D. 207
Tyran, J.-R. 212

UK (United Kingdom): common law

142–3; and EU directives 149, 150–1; labour market regulation 47–8; labour regulation 8, 116, 133; Social Agreement of Maastricht 133, 150–1; wages 116–17
unfair dismissals *see* unjust dismissal legislation
unions: Canada 63–4; and distributive conflict 127, *128*; and economic performance 273; living wage laws 32–4, 36; power 3, 46–7, 118; right-to-work laws 26–7; USA 4–5; workers' compensation 31
United Kingdom (UK) *see* UK
unjust dismissal legislation 23–6, 269
utilities: Canada 62–3

Van den Bergh, R. 206
VAT (value added tax) 150
Vaubel, R. 213, 223, 248
'voice' 2, 161, 209, 211; *see also* yardstick competition
von Poschinger, Heinrich 195, 196
Vrsnik, Victor 86

wage compression 117–18
wage floors 116–17
wage laws 32–6
wage offsets 31, 32
wages: minimum 72–3, *91*; rates *97–8*
Walker, J.L. 208
Weber, Max 1

Weingast, B.R. 141, 207
Weiss, Harry 19
Wells, W. 118
wholesale trade: Canada 63
Widmer, T. 214
Wirth, Steffen 246
Wohlgemuth, Michael 167
Wolfers, J. 118
workers' rights 8, 26–8, *114–15*, 133, 148
working conditions regulation 118–21
working hours 149, 269
Working Time Directive 149
Working Venture Canadian Fund (WVCF) 66–7
workplace safety legislation 28–30

yardstick competition: balanced budget requirements 241–3; Canada 6–8, 79, 90, 93, 103–10; and centralization 3; characteristics 2; child welfare policy 83; and deregulation 14; and economic efficiency 47–8; effect of 5; evidence of 15; in fiscal regulation 13; and globalization 263; intensification of 247; labour market regulations 25, 43; Medical Care Act (Canada) 79; redistributive policies 45; wrongful dismissal doctrine 25, 43

Zabin, Carol 34
Zumstrull, Margret 161